25 Hikes
along the
Pacific Crest Trail

25 Hikes along the Pacific Crest Trail

Don & Lolly Skillman

illustrations by
Irene Brady

Published by
STACKPOLE BOOKS
5067 Ritter Road
Mechanicsburg, PA 17055

Printed in the United States of America

First Edition

10 9 8 7 6 5 4 3 2 1

Cover design by Mark Olszewski
Cover photos by Don & Lolly Skillman

Library of Congress Cataloging-in-Publication Data

Skillman, Don.
25 hikes along the Pacific Crest Trail / Don & Lolly Skillman.
p. cm.
Includes bibliographical references and index.
ISBN 0-8117-3093-X
1. Hiking—Pacific Crest Trail—Guidebooks. 2. Pacific Crest Trail—Guidebooks. I. Skillman, Lolly. II. Title. III. Title: Twenty-five hikes along the Pacific Crest Trail.
GV199.42.P3S55 1994 93-36436
796.5'1'09795—dc20 CIP

♦ Contents

♦ Acknowledgments

Much is involved in creating a trail guidebook. You cannot just sit at a desk and dream up valid trail or place descriptions. Before we wrote this book, we hiked every foot of trail it covers, pushing a measuring wheel, taking field notes, and using a tape recorder to keep track of what we saw along each segment. Then we conducted research to confirm our observations and learn local history.

We owe great thanks to those people who helped us: Aubrey M. Hill, M.D., for his suggestions on field management of hypothermia and insect stings; Dr. Ronald D. Lamb, retired Professor of Biology, Southern Oregon State College, and now Executive Director of the Northwest Museum of Natural History, for keeping us on track in the introduction; Dr. Frank Lang, Professor and Chair of Biology, Southern Oregon State College, for his many helpful suggestions regarding plant communities and other botanical advice; Jeff LaLande, Archaeologist, Rogue River National Forest, for his helpful suggestions; the many U.S. Forest Service biologists, archaeologists, historians, geologists, and recreation specialists who responded to our queries and contributed much valuable information; and last, but not measured by that position, our editors at Stackpole Books, who helped us conceive the idea of this book and worked patiently with us through to its realization.

♦ The Pacific Crest Trail Association

The Pacific Crest Trail Association is the citizen-support organization for the Pacific Crest Trail (PCT). Public interest in the PCT is represented by the volunteer, nonprofit service organization of individuals, clubs, and businesses called the Pacific Crest Trail Association.

Some association members have hiked or ridden horseback along the entire PCT, a three- to six-month journey. Many have made shorter trips on the trail, such as those described in this book. Others joined to learn about and support the trail, some knowing that they will never personally experience the trail's challenges and rewards. Every member, however, supports the *idea* of the Pacific Crest Trail—for it to exist, to provide a challenge, to offer the experience of living with nature's pleasures as well as threats, to display a changing landscape of diverse resource management.

The membership of the Pacific Crest Trail Association spans the entire United States and a number of foreign countries, in all age groups. Many members are active in the field, maintaining trail registers, helping put up signs, and most important in this day of agency-citizen cooperation, working on volunteer crews to improve the trail.

For an informational brochure about the PCTA and a complimentary copy of its newsletter, write to the Pacific Crest Trail Association, 1350 Castle Rock Road, Walnut Creek, CA 94598, or call (510) 939-6111.

The mission of the PCTA is to ensure that there is a continuous recreation facility, managed so as to reflect its national significance, to provide enjoyment, education, and adventure for hikers and equestrians on the trail.

♦ Natural Beauty of the Trail

This book presents twenty-five short hikes along the Pacific Crest Trail to inspiring, beautiful, and scenic areas. Hike lengths vary from one to three days or longer. Each hike in this book was selected for inclusion because its destination has strong emotional impact on everyone who visits it.

The narrow, sometimes elusive PCT leads you in a north-south direction across California, Oregon, and Washington. It crosses six of the seven life zones, Sonoran to Arctic, allowing you an opportunity to observe much of the abundant flora and fauna of the Pacific Coast states. Often the route passes through wilderness areas, where animals and birds are less wary of people. Wildflowers are always present during the normal hiking months. Plants run the gamut from cacti in the desert to subalpine firs at the timberline. Above timberline, you are rewarded by exotic wildflowers and colorful lichens in the rarefied world of pikas and yellow-bellied marmots. This is truly a trail of diversity.

Few people have the time or inclination to experience all 2,600 miles of the PCT. The investment in time and effort to do so is considerable. This book guides you on short hikes that, combined, will expose you to the essence of the high country in California, Oregon, and Washington. You can visit the trail's high points, experience high mountain passes and glacial cirque lakes, see impressive headwalls, cataracts, and falls, and do all this without committing large blocks of time.

Many will gain a better understanding of ecology and an environmental awareness through interacting with the wilderness—experiencing the vistas and solitude, the animals, birds, and plants. Thus many will become better stewards of our mountains, waters, and wildlife.

The Pacific Crest Trail is aptly named; it rarely takes the easy way—the sheltered valley, the low ridge, the gentle ascent up watercourses. You sometimes longingly view these features from above, as the PCT embraces the high places—the crests!

There are plenty of crests along the 2,600 trail miles. After climbing the San Jacinto Mountains in southern California, the PCT undulates northward over the San Bernardinos and the San Gabriels, then along the spine of the high Sierras. In Northern California, the trail takes you to the volcanic summits of the Cascades before jogging westward to surmount the Klamath Mountains. An eastward traverse at the Oregon border precedes the northward march along Cascade crests to Washington. High Cascade ridges and peaks host the northbound PCT through Washington to its terminus in Canada.

This book will help you experience the whistle of the marmot, the scolding bark of pine squirrels, the quick scurry of chipmunks, and the inquisitive yet wary observation of deer. You'll be no stranger to the broad, soaring wings of the golden eagle or the vibrating wingbeat of a hummingbird at bright red penstemon at your feet, or even your red bandanna. You will understand the "because it's there" rationale of the climber as you stand on summits with the world spread at your feet. You will experience all

1. *Creosote bush–cactus–sage*
   Shrubs: creosote bush, mesquite, shadescale, bud sagebrush, basin sagebrush, bitter brush, purple sage
   Cacti: desert barrel cactus, silver cholla, beavertail, prickly pear
   Mammals: coyote, kit fox, kangaroo rat, pocket mouse

Beavertail cactus *Desert mariposa*

this and more when you visit these gems along the three-state Pacific Crest Trail!

THE MOUNTAINS

While enjoying the hikes in this book, you'll be walking upon soils and rocks varying in age from a few hundred years to hundreds of millions of

Birds: Gambel's quail, roadrunner, LeConte's thrasher, cactus wren, black-throated sparrow
Reptiles: western diamondback rattlesnake, zebra-tailed lizard, desert horned lizard
Examples: around the Alabama Hills, between Lone Pine and Whitney Portal, Hike 1

Spotted langloisia *Creosote bush*

years old! Their origin affects the plants you'll see as you hike, and those plants largely determine what wildlife you will spot.

The description of each hike includes brief discussions of unusual geological formations and features as a basis for your own observations and to increase your awareness and enjoyment as you hike.

The present-day Sierra range is composed chiefly of granite. This granite was deposited in molten form beneath the older sedimentary and

2. Chaparral
Trees: interior live oak, digger pine
Shrubs: chamise, California scrub oak, hoary leaf ceanothus, bigberry manzanita, whiteleaf manzanita, ocean spray, coyote bush, holly leaf cherry, mountain mahogany

Foothill penstemon *Scrub oak*

volcanic land surface, where it solidified and was gradually raised over the course of 200 million years. The older sediments and volcanic surfaces largely eroded away, and the final uplifting of the granite, continuing to this day, formed 14,000-foot-high mountains. The majestic peaks you see today were sculpted by glaciers during the last ice age, which ended 10,000 years ago.

The Cascade range of Northern California, Oregon, and Washington

Mammals: coyote, brush rabbit, Merriam's chipmunk
Birds: turkey vulture, California quail, rufous-sided towhee, green-tailed towhee, brown towhee, California thrasher
Example: chaparral communities are not found in pure form in the areas described in this book; however, you may encounter some of the species near the juniper level on the Whitney Portal Road, Hike 1

Chamise *California poppy* *Manzanita*

is volcanic in origin. Molten rock, some solidifying beneath the surface and some reaching the surface as lava, provided the building blocks for this range. Underlying granitic plutons have been exposed in only a few places. Classic volcanic cones, such as Mounts Shasta, Hood, Baker, and Rainier, typify the Cascade summits, while Mount St. Helens is a reminder that not all of these volcanos are inactive! Average crest elevations are less than 7,000 feet.

This book does not delve deeply into the geology of the region. You may wish, however, to gain further knowledge of geology in order to

3. Juniper woodland
Trees: California juniper, single-leaved piñon pine, Joshua tree
Shrubs: basin sage, rabbit brush, curl-leaved mahogany, Mojave yucca, California scrub oak, antelope brush, bladder sage, saltbrush

Curl-leaf mountain mahogany *Common phacelia*

enhance your hiking experience, and to that end, additional reading is suggested in the bibliography.

THE PLANTS

Trees, the biggest living things, not only are beautiful but also provide welcome shade while you're hiking. Not every locale has trees, however. Some dry regions of Southern California, where elevations are 2,000 to 3,000 feet, offer only chaparral. As elevation increases, trees begin to appear, until conifers such as pines and firs become dominant above

Mammals: coyote, kit fox, blacktailed jackrabbit, Merriam's chipmunk, California ground squirrel
Birds: sage grouse, California thrasher, sage thrasher, piñon jay, sage sparrow
Example: along road before reaching Baxter Pass trailhead, Hike 2

Western juniper *Desert trumpet* *Pinyon pine*

5,000 or 6,000 feet and upward until the timberline (the maximum elevation where trees can grow) is reached.

All plant life is extremely sensitive to temperature and moisture. As the land surface increases in elevation, the temperature decreases. There is also a temperature decrease as you move farther north. This is why the timberline in Southern California does not occur until above 10,000 feet, while in northern Washington you'll reach the timberline at 6,000 or

4. *Oak–Douglas fir–mixed evergreen forest*
   Trees: Douglas fir, Coulter pine, digger pine, California juniper, Pacific yew, black oak, canyon oak, interior live oak, coast live oak, tanbark oak, madrone, bay, bigcone Douglas fir
   Shrubs: Bigberry manzanita, California coffeeberry, gooseberry, Oregon grape, fremontia, poison oak

Oregon grape *Hound's tongue* *Douglas fir*

7,000 feet. Moisture generally increases as you hike into higher elevations. Mountains cause air to rise, cooling in the process, until moisture is condensed and falls as rain or snow.

As you hike at various elevations along the PCT, you will notice that certain kinds of plants and trees are usually found associated with each other. This is because these particular species thrive under the same conditions of temperature and moisture.

Mammals: coyote, black bear, raccoon, western gray squirrel, porcupine, long-eared chipmunk
Birds: red-shouldered hawk, band-tailed pigeon, California quail, mourning dove, scrub jay, acorn woodpecker
Example: last few miles along Forest Service road 43N45 on the way to trailhead, Marble Mountains, Hike 14

Black oak *Gooseberry* *Trillium*

Humans have introduced exotic species of plants, animals, and insects, often with disastrous results. The starling, an imported bird, now thrives throughout the forty-eight contiguous states and competes with native birds for tree cavities and woodpecker holes to use for nesting sites. The common dandelion and Himalayan blackberry are tenacious exotics; the dandelion has spread to all states, while the latter replaces streamside species and constantly increases its range.

5. Pine forest
Trees: ponderosa pine, sugar pine, Jeffrey pine, Douglas fir, white fir, incense cedar, Pacific dogwood
Shrubs: Scouler's willow, greenleaf manzanita, deer brush, western azalea, spice bush

Jeffrey pine *Scoulers willow*

On a few of the hikes in this book, you will encounter burned-over areas. Fire brings rapid environmental change, and the resultant destruction of range and forest has been viewed as catastrophic. As a result, fires have been vigorously combated in the recent past. But prior to the last century or two, most areas burned over naturally on a periodic basis. Lodgepole forests depend on occasional fires for health and regeneration, and forest managers have gradually become aware of the beneficial

Mammals: black bear, cougar, coyote, mountain beaver, western gray squirrel, golden-mantled ground squirrel, yellow pine chipmunk
Birds: flammulated owl, band-tailed pigeon, Stellar's jay, hairy woodpecker, western bluebird, western tanager
Example: John Muir Wilderness, lower elevations along Fish Creek, Hike 5

Rocky mountain iris *Sierra onion* *Ponderosa pine*

effects of natural fires. Therefore, some plant communities in the West are now allowed to evolve naturally without artificial suppression of fire.

Lightning starts most natural fires, which eliminate ground fuel before it becomes abundant enough to cause catastrophic conflagration. The Yellowstone fire in 1988 was intense because the area had long been protected from natural burning, and fuel accumulation in the forest became nearly explosive.

Plant Communities

The life zones into which Merriam arbitrarily divided this continent in

6. Mountain meadow
Shrubs: Pacific willow, arroyo willow, mountain alder
Mammals: coyote, Belding's ground squirrel

Arroyo willow *Mule's ears*

the late 1800s were based primarily upon temperature and precipitation. These zones are now outdated, and they are too broad to depict the changing scene along the PCT. In this book, these zones are further divided to help you recognize specific communities of plants.

Just as plants have their range, habitat, and niche, so do the animals found in association with these plant communities. Mammals, birds, insects, and reptiles are mobile and may be found in different communities at various times of the year due to annual migration patterns. But during the months of mild weather, when most hikers are in the outdoors, animals

Birds: northern harrier, Brewer's blackbird
Example: Marble Mountain Wilderness, meadows around Sky High Lakes, Hike 13

Corn lily *Bear grass*

will be found in association with the plant communities that best afford them food and habitat.

Sometimes the relationship between plants and animals is symbiotic, as is the case between the Joshua tree and its pollinator, the yucca moth. The Joshua tree is unable to achieve pollination by wind drift and depends on the moth to carry bits of pollen from blossom to blossom. In return, the moth receives a safe incubator in, and later food from, the tree's fruit.

Many birds and animals, such as the mule deer and coyote, are found in several different plant communities. The coyote inhabits every

7. Montane chaparral
Trees: western juniper, sugar pine, Jeffrey pine
Shrubs: slickleaf tobacco brush, greenleaf manzanita, bush chinquapin, huckleberry oak, mountain ash, chokecherry, Oregon white oak (scrub form)

Dwarf monkey flower *Ponderosa snag* *Pussy paws*

life zone along the PCT, as do hummingbirds during seasonal migrations. Birds sighted most often in all zones by PCT hikers are the raven, robin, and Oregon junco.

Other animals, such as the Mount Lyell salamander, which occupies a small region of the high Sierras, depend instead upon habitat within a single community. Just as with the plant communities, overlap occurs; that is, there is a gradual transition between communities. As you hike and become adept at observation, you will learn to anticipate certain animal species in association with particular plant communities, and much of

Mammals: coyote, wood rat
Birds: mountain quail, green-tailed towhee, dusky flycatcher
Example: Desolation Wilderness, along Echo Lake, Hike 11

Greenleaf manzanita *Bush chinquapin*

the time you will see them right where you expect them to be.

Unlike plants, animals and birds can hide at your approach and be difficult to spot. Also, many species that have reason to fear humans have become more wary and hide during daylight hours. Some species, like chipmunks, golden-mantled ground squirrels, and Clark's nutcrackers, quickly become tolerant of humans and, if fed, develop dependency upon this food source. Luckily, most of the areas along the PCT are too infrequently visited for this habituation to occur.

8. Red fir–subalpine forest
Trees: red fir and Shasta red fir in California and southern Oregon, noble fir in Cascades, mountain hemlock, lodgepole pine, western white pine, Jeffrey pine, weeping spruce, aspen, curl-leaf mountain mahogany
Shrubs: bush chinquapin, elderberry, red heather, snow bush, Scouler's willow

Spring beauty *Mountain hemlock* *Broadleaf lupine*

Botanists do not entirely agree as to plant communities. Some categories occur in such limited areas that most hikers seldom if ever encounter them. In other cases, enough species are present in two or more adjoining communities that it is difficult to delineate those communities.

Nine communities are set forth here, arbitrary groupings we found representative of the geographic areas covered by this book. Our purpose is to achieve a workable, simple account of plant communities to aid you in understanding and enjoying the ecosystems you experience along the

Mammals: black bear, coyote, red fox, porcupine, mountain beaver, yellow-bellied marmot, golden-mantled ground squirrel, lodgepole chipmunk
Birds: great gray owl, blue grouse, Williamson's sapsucker, ruby-crowned kinglet
Example: Goat Rocks Wilderness, 5,000 to 6,500 feet around Snowgrass Flat, Hike 23

Bush chinquapin *Blue elderberry*

trail. For each community, several major plant species are identified, along with some mammals, birds, and reptiles you are likely to see. The list is far from complete, but knowing the most prominent and easily identified species will help you easily recognize each community you encounter. Be aware, however, that not all plant species will be present in each community or at each given example site, and the dominant species may vary within a community due to latitude or other factors.

9. Alpine fell-field
Shrubs: some alpine willow and snow willow, but mostly grasses, sedges, and herbs

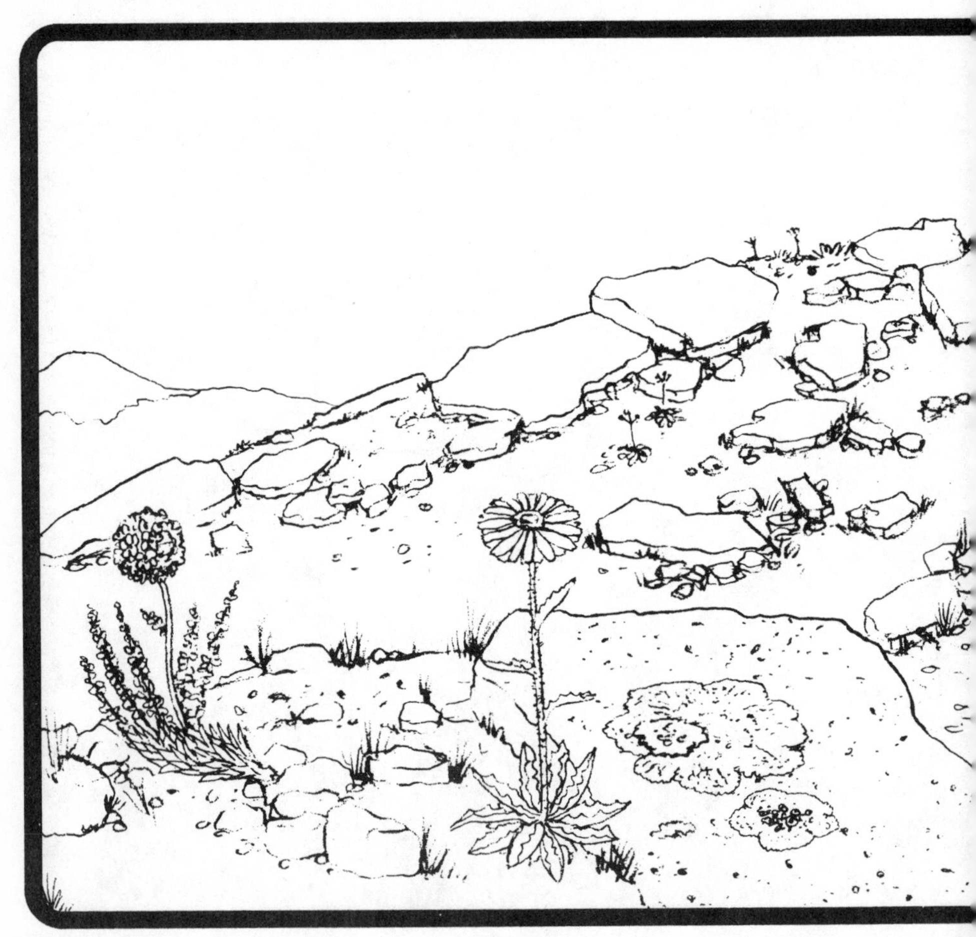

Sky pilot *Alpine gold* *Lichen*

The common names of wildflowers mentioned in the hiking chapters can be found in *The Audubon Society Field Guide to North American Wild Flowers, Western*, by Spellenberg; and *Pacific States Wildflowers*, by Niehaus and Ripper (see Bibliography).

Mammals: coyote, pika, yellow-bellied marmot, alpine chipmunk
Birds: mountain bluebird, gray-crowned rosy finch
Example: Summit of Bishop, Muir Passes, Hike 3

Sierra primrose *Gordon's ivesia* *Alpine paintbrush*

CONDITIONING

Enjoyment is the main reason for hiking, and the best way to enjoy the activity is to be in condition to hike. Conditioning varies greatly from person to person. Unless you hike frequently, however, you will benefit greatly if you do some conditioning hiking before making a trek of any length. Wear the footgear you intend to use on your hike. If you plan to backpack, wearing your pack with some weight in it while training not only will aid in your cardiovascular and muscular conditioning but also will help toughen your shoulders and hips so a full load will be much more comfortable later on.

The distance you travel each day is an important factor in enjoying an outing. Obviously, if you are not hardened to the rigors of hiking and attempt to hike too far, you won't enjoy it much. What is too far for one person may be just right for another, but generally a hike of more than 10 miles in any one day should be viewed with caution unless you are an experienced hiker. Add the tiring factors of pack weight, elevation, and uphill climbing, and 10 miles may be far too ambitious. If you are experienced, you already will know your limits, but if you have yet to measure yourself in real backpacking conditions, assure yourself of more enjoyable trips by planning your daily hikes over very moderate distances.

Elevation of the terrain also must be considered in planning hikes. As altitude increases, you absorb less oxygen from each breath. Good conditioning hastens recovery and the replacement of oxygen in the blood while you take short rests. Some hikers pace themselves to a sustainable output of effort. Regardless, more time is required at higher elevations for a given amount of work than if that work was accomplished at a lower elevation, where oxygen is more plentiful in the atmosphere. As an example, though we were in trail-hardened condition, it took us eight hours to cover 11 trail miles at an elevation of 10,000 feet over rugged terrain that included a pass at more than 13,000 feet.

Whether you are planning a one-day hike or intend to go uninterrupted for several months, conditioning is a major factor and will directly affect the distance you can comfortably cover each day. Even a small amount of conditioning will have positive effects on your hiking enjoyment.

SAFETY

All of the hikes in this book visit high-altitude locales, where hazards exist. The more experienced you are, the safer an outing will be. If the high country is new to you, hike only with someone who has judged weather and trail conditions many times before. Sudden storms, especially electrical ones, are potentially dangerous if you are caught in an exposed location. Snowfields on steep slopes have provided an unintended ride terminating in a fatal crash to more than a few. Some trails thread their way along cliffs from which a fall would be disastrous. Faint trails may lead into remote areas where you could become lost. Enjoy the wilderness for what it is—a wonderful, renewing, and uplifting place but one that can be unforgiving of mistakes.

To a large extent, you can control just how much risk is inherent in any outdoor experience. Those who are at home and comfortable in the outdoors exercise this control naturally. Safety is not much improved by familiarity alone, but rather in understanding where risks lie and how to mitigate those risks.

HYPOTHERMIA

Hypothermia, a lowering of the body temperature, is the greatest risk to human life in the outdoors. When body temperature drops just a few degrees below normal (lower than 95° Fahrenheit = hypothermia), the ability to function decreases, which in turn can inhibit your ability to take steps to prevent further loss of heat or even recognize that the loss is occurring. This can result in death, even under conditions that do not seem particularly dangerous.

The human body is an amazing machine. Its first response to a drop in core temperature is a constricting of blood vessels in the skin. If cooling continues, circulation to the extremities is severely curtailed, which slows heat loss but makes use of hands and feet extremely difficult.

The following are the symptoms of hypothermia:

1. Shivering, especially if violent
2. Speech difficulty, incoherent speech, loss of lip control, slurring, memory lapse
3. Cold, inoperative hands
4. Exhaustion
5. Poor balance, stumbling
6. Drowsiness

Shivering, particularly if violent or continuous, is your body's signal that you are on the edge of hypothermia. This is only one of several signals but the easiest to detect in yourself. Be aware of what your body is telling you, and if you begin shivering or recognize other signs of dropping body temperature, stop immediately and take steps to protect yourself. To continue exposure, especially if you have reached the stage of shivering, is to risk reaching a point where you cannot help yourself. Read Jack London's

To Start a Fire; this account of an unsuccessful cold-weather self-rescue will help you remember to pay attention.

Knowing the treatments for the various stages of hypothermia is important. The goals basically are to stop the loss of heat and warm the victim until normal heat production resumes.

Of greater value is prevention of hypothermia at the outset. Learn to recognize the conditions that are likely to cause insidious heat loss. Cold air movement carries air warmed by your body away and replaces it with more cold air, which draws more body heat, one of the reasons why you feel cold when in a draft. Far more dangerous than just cold temperatures are wet conditions, especially if the potential victim is wearing wet clothing or is subjected to repeated or continuous cold wetting. Water is thirty times more conductive of heat than air.

When in any situation that is robbing you of heat, the important thing is to change the situation to one where your body heat is not in jeopardy. If you are wet, get dry, and if wind is robbing your heat, protect yourself from the wind. Rain gear and a good tent will protect you from such exposures and are essential when hiking in the mountains.

It is of the utmost importance to be able to stay dry in wet conditions. Rain gear is not adequate unless it will protect from wind-driven rain over extended periods. Modern synthetic fabrics, which insulate but do not absorb much water, are extremely valuable in offering good protection. Some of these fabrics wick moisture away from the body, keeping you drier and minimizing evaporative cooling, another way to lose heat. Undergarments of a wicking fabric covered by outer garments of nonabsorbing fabric as an insulator make a warm combination that adds safety. This layering system should be the basis for all outdoor dress. Cotton clothing has little place in the outdoors today, because once it is wet it is extremely difficult to dry out.

Learn to use natural shelters in times of inclement weather. A rock cliff or ledge can protect from both wind and rain. A stump or large boulder will form a partial windbreak. So will dense stands of brush or thick conifers. By using these naturally occurring barriers in an emergency, your other forms of protection will be more effective. Nothing takes the place of a good tent, however, as it provides protection from both wind and water.

Those experienced in the outdoors avoid exposure that causes severe heat loss. If the exposure is not avoidable, they terminate the situation causing exposure. This may mean interrupting a schedule, not reaching a destination, making detours, or taking other actions necessary to stop the loss of heat. Keep aware of potential dangers in any situation where you are having trouble staying comfortably warm.

Do not push yourself to your physical limits, because fatigue greatly increases susceptibility to hypothermia. In some cases your activity may be your only means of generating heat, and you may become very cold the minute you stop walking. Upon recognizing that you are getting cold, stop and make camp. Start your stove or fire first, then put up your tent. This way, in the event you continue to grow colder, you will have a heat source already available. If you wait too long to light the stove or fire, shivering or cold hands may prevent you from performing this task.

If you travel alone, you are at greater risk from hypothermia than if you have companions. Remember that most people who are in the beginning stages of hypothermia still believe that they are all right, so exercise greater self-discipline and awareness if you venture outdoors alone.

Treatment once hypothermia is present involves warming the victim. After exposure has been terminated, warming can be as simple as keeping the victim near a fire or giving him a warm liquid to drink if he is not greatly impaired. Stripping the victim of clothing and placing a heat donor, also stripped, in skin-to-skin contact is another warming method. A sleeping bag will provide protection for both. In parties of three or more people, the third person can also be a heat donor. During rewarming, the victim should be kept prone. Placing a hat on the head also helps.

If the victim is semiconscious or greatly impaired, this is a medical emergency calling for more drastic measures. If the victim is unconscious, make immediate arrangements for emergency evacuation to a hospital.

Don't stop treatment too soon. If heat loss has progressed to the point where unconsciousness has resulted, the patient will die unless warmed to the point where consciousness is regained and heat production is resumed unaided.

Don't try to make an unconscious person drink warm liquid; doing so could cause the victim to drown. Don't give alcohol. Don't attempt to rapidly warm the shell of the victim; attempting to warm the victim with hot-water bottles or other sources of relatively high heat is very dangerous. Warming must begin from the core or the effort can be fatal.

Many manuals recommend carrying fire starter so that a fire is assured under adverse conditions. Most hikers today carry small cooking stoves, and white gas or kerosene fuels make excellent emergency fire starters when poured directly on firewood. You can even use butane or propane stoves to start a wood fire by placing the lighted burner under the wood and kindling until it ignites.

OTHER SAFETY CONSIDERATIONS

While hypothermia is the number-one outdoor risk, drownings and falls are also hazards to unwary hikers. Drowning can occur while enjoying a swim in an inviting lake, or the immersion can be unintentional, like falling into the current while crossing a stream. A swift stream can easily knock you down and keep you in the current until your muscles will no longer respond. The main thing to remember is that water found in the mountains is usually cold—often *very* cold—and even strong swimmers are rendered helpless in a matter of minutes in extremely cold water. Trying to swim across an alpine lake can be very foolhardy.

Most falls do not take place from atop high cliffs. More likely, a rock will kick loose from underfoot as you make a detour off the trail, causing a slip followed by a couple of tumbles. If you land wrong or on more rocks, fractures or head or internal injuries can result. One of the most dangerous activities in mountain hiking is crossing a frozen snowfield, especially one lying on a steep slope. Unless you are skilled in the use of crampons and ice ax, don't cross such barriers. Go around, and if you can't do that, turn back and try the trail again later in the summer when the snow has melted.

Oddly enough, burns are the most common accidental injury in the outdoors, often from boiling water. Be particularly cautious when pouring hot liquids.

Further reading sources for wilderness first-aid procedures are listed in the Bibliography. When hiking in the wilderness, the most important thing is to remain aware of potentially dangerous situations so that you can avoid accidents in the first place.

BEARS AND BEAR-BAGGING

The black bear, *Ursus americanus*, is the only bear species you are likely to encounter along the PCT. These animals are seldom found below the oak–Douglas fir–mixed conifer zones and are usually more numerous in the pine forest, red fir–subalpine forest, and mountain meadow fringe zones. Information about bears is given in the description of each hike in this book.

We do not consider bears a danger if you use common sense. While there is some potential for losing your food supplies, this is not a great danger and would merely be an inconvenience. If you are lucky on your hike, you may get to see a bear, one of nature's more efficient omnivores and the largest you will encounter along the PCT. Enjoy the experience but do not unwisely prolong it.

Most bear confrontations in the mountains are one of two types: Either you surprise the bear, which scurries off as soon as it detects your presence, or the bear comes to your location because of the food you carry. Unfortunately, bears in some highly frequented areas like Yosemite have learned to view the hiker's pack as a food source. And once a bear learns that hikers carry food, it passes this knowledge along to its off-

To effectively bear-bag food, you must first divide it equally into two bags. (A) Using a rock as a weight, toss one end of a strong cord over a tree limb, about eighteen feet high and at least ten feet long. This limb should be stout enough to support the weight of your food, but not that of a bear. (B) Tie one end of the cord to a bag and pull until the bag is tight against the limb. Reaching as high as you can, tie the other end of the cord to the remaining bag. Tie a loop in the cord and stuff the extra cord inside the bag. (C) Use a six-foot-long stick to push the loop up until the two bags are at the same height. Be sure neither bag hangs against any other limbs; they could give rodents easy access to your food. Friction between rope and limb should keep the bags at a safe height of about twelve feet. To retrieve your food, twist the stick through the loop and pull it down.

spring; over the years, this has resulted in some very clever bears. Remember that the bear is not out to harm you; rather, the animal wants your food. Usually, but not always, attempts to obtain it occur at night.

The best way to avoid bear problems is to hang, or bear-bag, all of your food. If you leave a candy bar in your tent or pack, a marauding bear may try to get it, possibly leaving a gaping hole in the nylon.

Some popular campsites in national parks have bear boxes, large metal lockers that the bear cannot breach, in which to store your food. Other sites have an elevated steel cable that bears cannot negotiate from which you can bear-bag food.

SNAKES

The mere mention of rattlesnakes usually elicits a primal reaction of fear and loathing. Most people would rather not encounter one of these creatures. One of the best ways to avoid an encounter, or to make it uneventful, is to know more about these reptiles.

Rattlesnakes are cold-blooded; that is, they are unable to control their body temperature and must therefore depend on the ambient temperature. Cold temperatures make the snake lethargic. Direct sunlight soon becomes too hot for the snake, so it seeks a shady location until late in the day, when it then goes about hunting for rodents. Sun-warmed rocks radiate heat much of the night, enabling active hunting. Brushy areas with dense shade also provide protection from heat; there snakes lie in wait for prey during daylight hours.

While rattlesnakes can be found in any zone at any elevation, they are most common in the arid chaparral communities and in locations with oaks. These reptiles are not aggressive by nature; they are usually as eager to end an encounter as you are. Rattlers find prey by using acute heat-sensitive pits that resemble nostrils. These same sensors, capable of detecting a small mouse at considerable distance, easily tell the snake when you are near. Most rattlesnakes will sound a warning rattle when a human approaches close to their location.

Rattlers may be found anywhere, at any elevation, so avoid placing your hands under logs, brush, or rocks or upon rock ledges where you cannot see. Recommended treatment for bites has changed little over the years; suction at the bite location is helpful. There is a very effective, plunger-operated suction device on the market. A rattlesnake bite requires medical attention as quickly as possible so that antivenin may be administered.

INSECT BITES AND STINGS

Stings from bees and wasps are painful. They can be very serious if the victim becomes sensitized. If you have ever had a systemic (more than localized) reaction from any sting, contact your physician. Desensitization may be recommended, and if you are at high risk, you may need to carry an adrenaline kit.

Some say that mosquitoes are a state of mind. If that is true, one's state of mind can certainly inflict some bothersome bites. Mosquitoes are found at most elevations, requiring only sufficient wet places for breeding. Snow mosquitoes are especially troublesome at higher elevations while the snow is melting. Their numbers gradually diminish until, a few weeks later, only a few of the flying pests survive as adults. Mosquito repellent containing a high percentage of deet is very effective, and a small bottle usually lasts for many days.

HIKING BOOTS

There are hundreds of hiking boots on the market today, many of them excellent products. Everyone has an individual preference, but a few guidelines will aid you in selecting a boot that begins comfortable and stays comfortable.

Heavy load, heavy boot. Light load, lighter boot. This simplistic-sounding advice is proven out on the trail thousands of times each year. Basically, this means that many of the lightweight boots of fabric, leather, and cemented sole construction may be just right if you are making day hikes with very light loads or no load at all. These boots have the advantage of being easy to break in as well as being ounces or pounds lighter than conventionally constructed boots.

Most long-distance hikers, on the trail with heavy loads in excess of 55 pounds, will invariably choose a heavy-soled, all-leather boot with sewn welt. Such footgear is very difficult to break in and is heavy, but it also provides the support and protection required for heavy use. Foot problems are the most common complaint of hikers, and attending to blisters is the most frequently applied first aid.

Many hikers now use polypropylene inner socks in combination with heavy wool outer socks for maximum comfort. This combination wicks away moisture from the feet and evaporates it through the boot and sock top. Dry feet are much less likely to have blister problems.

FOOD

Trail food is very much up to personal preference. The most important consideration are weight, nutrition, and calorie content. A goal of 1.8 pounds of food per day per person is both attainable and desirable. A three-day hike would require 5.4 pounds of food at that rate.

Freeze-dried food, a product of military rations research, is one of the most important items for keeping weight down. Many full meals weigh less than 6 ounces before reconstitution, and some require no cooking. These foods are the basis for lightweight menus.

Breakfasts of grain cereal, some available in instant form, weigh very little and provide filling, nutritious morning meals. Instant beverage powders are light and, if carefully selected, can provide calories and nutrition.

Energy bars, which are heavy, can be supplemented with nuts and dried or dehydrated fruit for lunches, all high-calorie foods with acceptable weight.

To calculate calorie content and nourishment in these foods, consult *Composition of Foods*, U.S. Department of Agriculture Handbook No. 8, available from the Superintendent of Documents, U.S. Government Printing Office, Washington, DC 20402.

WATER

Experienced hikers have two questions about water: Is it available, and how pure is it? While water is abundant along much of the PCT in the higher elevations, in many of the lower-elevation areas and in volcanic regions it can be scarce.

This is why streams, springs, ponds, and lakes are mentioned so frequently in the hike descriptions in this book. Camping near a water source is much more enjoyable than making a dry camp, especially when you consider that water weighs over 8 pounds per gallon. If you've ever carried water for cooking night and morning, plus a one-day supply for drinking, you have already come to appreciate good water sources.

Assume that all water requires treatment, regardless of how remote the source or how cold, clear, or pure it appears. *E. coli* bacteria is present in nearly all water and can cause problems when present in large numbers. *Giardia lamblia*, found in some waters in cystic form, is much talked about today and rightly so. A case of giardiasis can end your hike with severe intestinal distress. These and other unwelcome bugs can be avoided by using any one of the three following methods:

1. Boil it. To be certain of killing all organisms, keep water boiling hard for at least five minutes, and longer at high altitude, where boiling temperature is much lower than at sea level. This method requires time, as well as fuel, which you must carry.
2. Treat it with iodine. We have used this method for years. Available in tablet form or as a saturated solution in a tiny bottle, iodine kills bacteria and, when allowed to act for thirty minutes or so, also kills *Giardia*. Be sure to follow the directions on the product, as treatment time varies with the water temperature.
3. Filtration. Filters are available that not only remove bacteria but also trap *Giardia* cysts. Filters must be carried with you, however, and since they weigh a pound or more, they must be considered carefully.

EQUIPMENT

The less gear you carry, the lighter your load. But do not place yourself in jeopardy by not taking along gear essential for safety. Consider the use of each item. Is it a safety item or is it a convenience? Is it a gadget or do you need it in order to eat or walk or stay warm and dry? Few experienced hikers carry more than the essentials.

In keeping weight manageable, it is as important to have good, lightweight gear as it is to eliminate unnecessary items. There is a lot of excellent, lightweight hiking and backpacking gear on the market today. Good quality gear is reasonable in weight and costs only a little more than shoddy equipment. Even if you own average lightweight equipment, you can still shave pounds from the weight of your gear, but it won't be cheap. Very high quality and extremely lightweight items cost many, many times more than average.

The following is a list of minimum backpack equipment for hikes of more than a few days in length, along with target weights for the larger items.

Item	Weight
Pack, with rain cover	4–6 pounds
Tent, two-person, with fly and ground cloth	6 pounds
Sleeping bag, three-season	4 pounds
Pad and/or air mattress	2 pounds
50-foot nylon parachute cord	0.2 pounds
Portable stove and fuel	2 pounds
Canteen	0.2 pounds
Rain gear	2 pounds
Jacket	2 pounds
First-aid kit	1 pound
Small flashlight with new batteries	0.3 pounds
Insect repellent	
Waterproof matches and propane lighter	
Small folding pocketknife	
Water purification tablets	
Pot for boiling 1.5 quarts water	
Plastic bowl	
Spoon	
Plastic cup	
Sunscreen and lip balm	
Toilet tissue	
Notebook and pencil	
Small compass	
Guide and maps	

All that is lacking in the above kit is food for the trip. Without food, the total weight of the above gear is about 28 pounds.

Some items in this kit serve double duty: If you become cold, you can put on your rain gear, both jacket and pants. The pot and your canteen serve to carry water from nearby sources. The sleeping bag stuff sack and the tent bag serve as bags in which to hang food.

The only contingency items in this list are the pocketknife, first-aid kit, notebook and pencil, flashlight, and small compass. The combined weight of these items is less than 2 pounds. If you were fortunate, you could hike for a long time and not really need any of these items. The remainder of the gear will be used every day.

It is assumed that the hiker will be attired in shorts and other suitable mild-weather clothing, including a hat to protect against the sun. None of this clothing should be cotton.

TRANSPORTATION

Directions to trailheads are given in the description of each hike. In most instances, these hikes are loops that return you to the same trailhead from which you departed, but not always. Sometimes your vehicle will be parked many miles away at a different trailhead. There are several ways to arrange your transportation in these cases. A friend could transport you to the starting point after you leave your vehicle at the exit point. Two or more hikers can take two vehicles and leave one at the exit trailhead. Some people depend on hitchhiking, but this may not be practical at some remote trailheads where there may be little traffic. Remember that some roads leading to trailheads are dead ends, used only for access to the trail.

You may want to consider using a bicycle as a shuttle between trailheads. Mountain bikes are a good choice, because roads often are unsurfaced or steep. You can conceal your bike near the exit trailhead and lock it or securely lock it in a visible location. If you ride a bike back to the first trailhead, cache your pack and return in your vehicle to retrieve it unless you and your bike are capable of handling the extra load.

When calculating departure times from trailheads, remember that many roads leading to these points are gravel surfaced, with lots of turns. Extra time will be required when driving such roads. You may figure driving time at an average of one hour for every 50 miles on the highway, but this will be inaccurate on many mountain roads. On some smaller roadways, it may be difficult to average even 15 miles an hour. Be sure to allow for the extra driving time involved.

REGULATIONS AND PERMITS

Regulatory agencies having jurisdiction over the areas covered in each hike are listed individually in the hike descriptions. Most routes cross lands administered by the Forest Service, the Bureau of Land Management, or the National Park Service. Each of these federal agencies has its own set of regulations, which may be subject to frequent change as they apply to any specific area. For that reason, we will not give all the specific regulations here. Contact the regulating agency for each area you intend to hike to familiarize yourself with their requirements. A few permits are on a reservation basis.

Some regulations are more or less uniform and often are based on common sense.

1. You will need a fire permit when hiking in most areas whether you build a fire or not. Most hikers today do not build wood fires at all but use small stoves. No matter; you will still need a permit.

2. Many wilderness areas have a permit system in place. In many instances, wilderness permits are self-issued or can be obtained by mail beforehand. Some are by reservation.
3. A wilderness permit does not allow you to fish; a person sixteen years of age or older must obtain the proper state fishing license.
4. It is always prohibited to pick flowers, remove plants, damage standing trees, blaze trees, deface signs, or in any way remove or damage natural features. This includes removing materials such as seedlings, plants, or artifacts. Construction is prohibited, so don't build stream crossings, large stone fireplaces, tables, or anything else.
5. Campsites must be well away from the shores of lakes or streams, usually 200 feet. Use existing campsites if they are the legal distance from waters. Keep soap out of lakes and streams. Toilet sites also must be located away from water sources. Campsites must be cleaned, and all litter must be packed out.
6. Pets are prohibited in all national parks.
7. The carrying or discharging of firearms is also prohibited.

"NO TRACE" CAMPING AND TREADING LIGHTLY

"Give a hoot, don't pollute" and "Only you can prevent forest fires" are phrases familiar to most of us. Has the campaign to clean up the act of offenders actually worked? Perhaps partially.

Reverence for wilderness systems and the outdoors builds a conscience that will not tolerate abuse of those areas. The result is the good land ethic that most of us have. But what about those few spoilers?

Some offenders just don't care. No amount of entreaty or threat of punishment will ever achieve sound ecological behavior from them. Fortunately, their numbers are few. Far greater in number, however, are those who do not understand the result of poor practices in the wilderness. Wilderness users in this category seem willing, even eager, to learn good land ethics that minimize impact on the places they love. When the desire to protect the wilderness comes from users' inner motivation, good things happen.

Litter

If you pack it in, pack it out. This admonition is followed by most. Hike the PCT today, and you'll see a different picture than if you had hiked it in the early seventies. Then there was heavy usage, and much of this usage was by those who claimed to love the wilderness. But they didn't love to clean it up or even remove their own garbage. As a result, camping areas took on the appearance of hobo camps, with pieces of plastic, foil, cans, and gear strewn about.

It has taken the efforts of many volunteer groups on cleanup hikes, as well as the Forest Service and in some instances contract packers, to remove the litter. The litter has been removed, however, and today the backcountry generally is in good shape. One reason it remains in good shape is that many users have developed the habit of picking up and packing out debris left by others. This is easy to do, because the load of a backpacker steadily lightens during any trip. It's easy to find room in a plastic bag for a twist tie, a plastic bread-wrapper closure, or a wad of foil out of a fire pit—all items probably not intentionally left but just overlooked.

Much of hikers' refuse is food packaging. If this material is paper, it can be burned if a fire pit is available and if conditions are safe for building a fire. Some plastics, such as transparent film, will also burn, but care must be taken not to just melt it into an indestructible lump. Any packaging material that contains a layer of foil, no matter how thin, will leave foil as litter if burned. Take those wrappers with you.

Leftover food is another problem. If you have been hiking for several days, there shouldn't be any leftover food except for remnants of unlikely cooking accidents. If you must dispose of food, don't try to burn it in the fire pit and don't throw it in or near any water. Instead, take it at least 200 yards from the campsite and trail, and if possible, place it in a crevice between rocks.

Pack out anything else.

Sanitation

Disposal of human waste is difficult in any backcountry area where usage is heavy. This has been addressed in several ways. The Forest Service has installed pit toilets near some heavily used campsites, and composting toilets are working well at others. Composting toilets are being used at camps between Whitney Portal and the summit of that mountain and at High Sierra camps in Yosemite. It is recommended that the user not urinate in such toilets; human urine is nearly sterile, and the urge can be relieved safely in a discreet place well removed from water and devoid of plant life, preferably on rocks or gravel.

Many agree that the best disposal technique for solid waste is in 6-inch-deep "cat holes" dug in the ground. The exact depth is not nearly as important as the location, however. So that you do not contaminate water sources, choose a site that is at least 200 feet from water and not in a surface drainage area. Make sure you are not too close to camp; 600 feet from camp is about right. Select a place that is unlikely to be walked on or dug up by another hiker. This will insure the integrity of disposal should hundreds of others use the same campsite during a single summer.

Toilet paper should be buried, not burned. Burning in any but bare, rocky areas constitutes a fire hazard, and all the paper will not burn anyway. The type of paper designed for RV systems decomposes more quickly.

Selecting Campsites

Many of the campsites referred to in this book are high-impact sites in crucial areas. The beauty of a water feature or alpine meadow begs to be enjoyed by many people. Camp near, but not in, such areas. Hide your camp several hundred feet from the trail if possible, in an area where there is little or no vegetation. Keep a distance from water sources as well. Avoid camping in meadows, which are fragile and easily damaged. If you do camp in a meadow, in the morning you and your tent will be drenched with condensation.

If there is no logical choice but to consider using an existing high-use site, go ahead. Try to keep your camp inside this area; don't enlarge it. Many such areas are already worn down to bare mineral soil and heavily compacted. There's not much further damage you can do; to recover, the site would need to be protected from all use for decades.

Wilderness campsites have minimal impact when placed upon sand, gravel, or rock. Compaction does not take place, and there is no vegetation to damage. Sometimes such sites can be found on old floodplains near watercourses, on moraines, or in rocky soils in the alpine zone.

Campfires

Campfires are nostalgic relics of the past that seduce us with warmth and instinctual stirrings. They are not much good to cook on and usually are built by the novice inside a rock ring on the surface of the ground. From this ring, which seems to attract trash, sooty powder and charcoal invariably spread until the entire site takes on a dirty black color. And so does everything placed upon it—your boots, groundcloth, packs, and so on.

Wood fires also consume fuel, and in many areas that means removal of a very scarce resource. The higher the altitude, the slower the growth of trees and the poorer the soil. There wood is scarce and is needed most to replenish soil nutrients. The quest for fuel all too often leads to broken and axed-off stubs of branches on trees and bushes around campsites.

Campfires have little place in the scheme of ethical wilderness use, outside of emergencies. Use a portable stove for cooking. Though it won't conjure visions of prehistoric eyes gleaming in the darkness around it, a stove is light, quick, and clean.

Backcountry Hiking

The majority of backcountry users concentrate in less then 10 percent of the backcountry; and less than one-fifth of our total trail system sustains four-fifths of the total use. This is why it's important to minimize impact. While you gaze out across hundreds of square miles of territory and realize you have seen only a few hikers that day, it's easy to believe that there is no overuse taking place. The problem is that most of those hikers are going to the same places and getting there by way of the same trail.

The how-tos of good trail usage are simple. First, do not cut switchbacks. Engineers design long switchbacks on modern trails in an effort to keep the gradient reasonable. To a few unthinking users, shortcutting the switchback saves time and distance. But because treading off the trail damages vegetation and moves fragile soils, even one venture of this sort can start a problem. Repeated trampling can kill vegetation, which then cannot hold soils in place, and erosion begins. Shortcutting results in mechanical displacement of soil and soon produces a *de facto* trail. This soon erodes into a broad scar that may take dozens of years to revegetate, if indeed this can be accomplished at all.

Casual-use trails, erosion, and mud are perhaps the greatest threats to a backcountry trail. If some condition such as mud or pools of water makes it easier to walk outside the formal trail, a use trail will eventually result, widening the original track or breaking down the edges. An example of this at its worst is the four or five parallel trails sometimes seen crossing alpine meadows.

Mud, sometimes due to precipitation but often from seeps, can make a trail unpleasant to walk on. Then hikers attempt to get around the bad spot by walking on the vegetation at the edge of the trail. Soon this, too, becomes muddy, and the next informal route will be on the edge of that, and so forth, until the trail becomes quite wide. Unpleasant as it sounds, the correct action is to wade through the mud.

The boots you wear actually are mechanical devices that transmit the compaction force of your weight, in addition to the lateral force of push-off in your stride, to the ground surface. The type of soles you use has a marked effect on how much wear you inflict on trail surfaces and how much you damage vegetation. The original lug soles wore well but had a deep tread pattern. Step on the ground and turn your foot, and you would dig up a lot of real estate. Newer designs are available with modified lugs that have good traction. This type of sole is less damaging to the ground you walk on, and boots with such soles are quite light. While you must have boots stout enough for the load you will carry, select those that will do the least harm to the backcountry.

♦ How to Use This Book

The twenty-five hikes in this book guide you into areas along the PCT in California, Oregon, and Washington, where the scenery is outstanding. The areas themselves are interesting and unique. In many cases the hikes are loops, allowing you to return to your trailhead by a route that minimizes backtracking. In other cases, due mainly to terrain or the desire to avoid building more than one trail to the same spot, no loop trails exist and portions of the route must be retraced. Occasionally, alternatives are given for a longer and a shorter hike. In a few instances the hike ends at a different trailhead than the entry point. In some cases alternatives exist and you can decide on your own route.

Each chapter begins with the hiking distance in miles, followed by the low elevation (the lowest elevation encountered on the trip, often at the trailhead) and the high elevation (the highest elevation actually reached by the trail, not the elevation of the highest peak in the area).

The hike is then ranked as easy, moderate, difficult, or strenuous. Any ranking system of this sort can be misleading, but the following factors have been taken into account: (1) the length of the hike; (2) the elevation at which the hike is made; (3) the elevation gained on the hike; (4) the distance over which that elevation is gained; and (5) the relationship of these statistics to one another. A hike that is short enough for the average hiker to complete in one day, at a moderate elevation of 6,000 feet, with not more than 1,000 feet of elevation gain, would be classed as easy. A two-day hike, which means carrying gear, at 9,000 feet elevation, with a cumulative elevation gain of 5,000 feet necessitated by climbing in and out of canyons, would be classed as difficult or strenuous.

Average hiking time is given, even though this is a great variable. In very difficult terrain, much more time is allowed than for easier going. The hiking time is expressed in hours and is calculated as the time spent hiking only. Time out for lunch breaks and overnights is not included.

Each chapter begins with an introduction to the geographical area involved and its special features. Some climatic data may be given, as well as information about wildflowers and wildlife. Occasionally, helpful caveats are included. The Description section then gives details on the hike, including the best season, bear cautions, and details about mosquitoes. Contacts for the administrative agencies are listed, followed by the name of the USGS quadrangle map or maps used and the compass declination. Next, Directions to Trailhead give driving directions.

The Trail Route Description section sets forth the major features, watercourses, and junctions along the route. Junctions are followed by three numbers in parentheses, for example (1.2 miles; 6690 feet; 7.6 miles). The first number is the distance from the last point in miles, the second is the elevation in feet above sea level, and the third is the cumulative mileage from the start of the hike.

Bracketed descriptions pertain to side or extension trips. This way, if you are not interested in side trips, you can skip these portions.

A vertical profile of each hike, diagramming the total route described, is included. This profile lets you see at a glance exactly where major elevation gains and losses occur.

Margin references to the right or left of the hike narrative tell you which map to use for the segment being described.

1 ♦ HORSESHOE MEADOWS—MOUNT WHITNEY

Distance:	47.9 Miles
Low elevation:	8,365 Feet
High elevation:	14,494 Feet
Class:	Difficult
Hiking time:	36 Hours

There is something magical about a mountain that reaches 14,494 feet above sea level. Mount Whitney is the highest peak in the contiguous United States, yet it is benign enough to allow thousands of hikers upon its slopes each year, and a good number reach the summit.

Mount Whitney's bulk forms just a part of the imposing vertical cliffs forming the western skyline as seen from Lone Pine, California, on U.S. Route 395. As if part of a team effort, this mountain does not stand boldly apart. Even those who have just descended from the Whitney summit sometimes argue about which jutting face belongs to the king. But from the top, the majestic view leaves no doubt about where you are standing.

The Owens Valley lies to the east, some 10,000 feet, or 2 miles, below. The eastern scarp of Whitney is nearly vertical, dropping thousands of feet to talus jumbles and tarns, crowning imposing canyons that in turn drop to the valley floor below. Westward, row after row of peaks beyond the canyon of the Kern River march to the horizon, a seemingly endless expanse of rugged, snow-capped mountains.

To the north and south lie sister peaks, several over 14,000 feet high. In 1864 there was considerable confusion as to just which peak in the southern Sierra was the highest, until Clarence King climbed a nearby mountain from which Whitney was visible. He recognized it as the highest point in the U.S. and named it after J. D. Whitney, state geologist at the time. It was not until 1873 that Mount Whitney was first climbed by several parties, including King. The fifth ascent, on October 21, 1873, was made by naturalist John Muir, who was not content to use the less precipitous routes and went solo straight up the present "mountaineer's route" on the northeast face of Whitney.

Although marine air has been robbed of much moisture by the time it reaches Whitney, amazing amounts of snowfall occur, especially on the western slopes. Strong winds lash the peak during winter storms, often blowing snow away as fast as it falls. This snow drifts into low areas and onto shady north slopes, where persistent icefields occupy niches originally carved by glaciers.

While below-freezing temperatures can occur during any season, summers are usually mild. Afternoon thunderstorms are a hazard to hikers, forming quickly and unpredictably. Lightning is a very real danger on any peak, and Mount Whitney is no exception.

Traveling from Lone Pine, at slightly less than 4,000 feet elevation, to the summit ridge of Mount Whitney takes you through all life zones from the Sonoran, at Lone Pine (with its black-tailed jackrabbits and creosote bushes), through the arctic-alpine zone. Timberline at this latitude hovers around 11,500 feet. Above that, "trees" are represented by the hardy alpine willow, which grows to an impressive 4 inches in height.

Ascending from the Sonoran zone, you will encounter piñon pine, Jeffrey pine, lodgepole, and fir in the Canadian zone, then mountain hemlock, and finally, as the timberline is neared, white-bark pine.

During an early-season trip, before all the wildflowers were in bloom, we saw paintbrush, snowflower, wild rose, shooting stars, meadow goldenrod, corn lilies, elephant head, heather, crimson columbine, Sierra wallflower, pennyroyal, and sky pilot.

We also spotted plenty of wildlife: mule deer, Douglas squirrel, least chipmunk, alpine chipmunk, yellow-bellied marmot, golden-mantled ground squirrel, raven, Stellar's jay, Clark's nutcracker, and rosy finch. We observed this last bird, as well as a marmot, at the Whitney summit. Black bears are also present, especially along the Kern River drainage.

How did this land of contrast come to be? Four hundred million years ago the Sierra lay beneath the sea. About the time mammals developed, some 60 million years ago, uplifting began, followed by erosion of much of the sediment covering granitic rock that had been intruded 140 million years earlier. Accompanying the uplift was much volcanic activity. The Sierra Block, more than 400 miles long and averaging 35 miles in width east to west, began tilting westward about 1 million years ago.

About that same time, during the ice age, glaciation started shaping the surface of the uplifting mountains, carving cirques and their vertical headwalls, and widening V-shaped canyons to characteristically U-shaped valleys. The fault block tilted to a greater extent, uplifted by forces of plate tectonics, while the Owens Valley sunk. The near-vertical face of the fault block is still very much in evidence today, although the Whitney scarp has eroded some 2 miles westward. The ice age lasted

MAP 1A

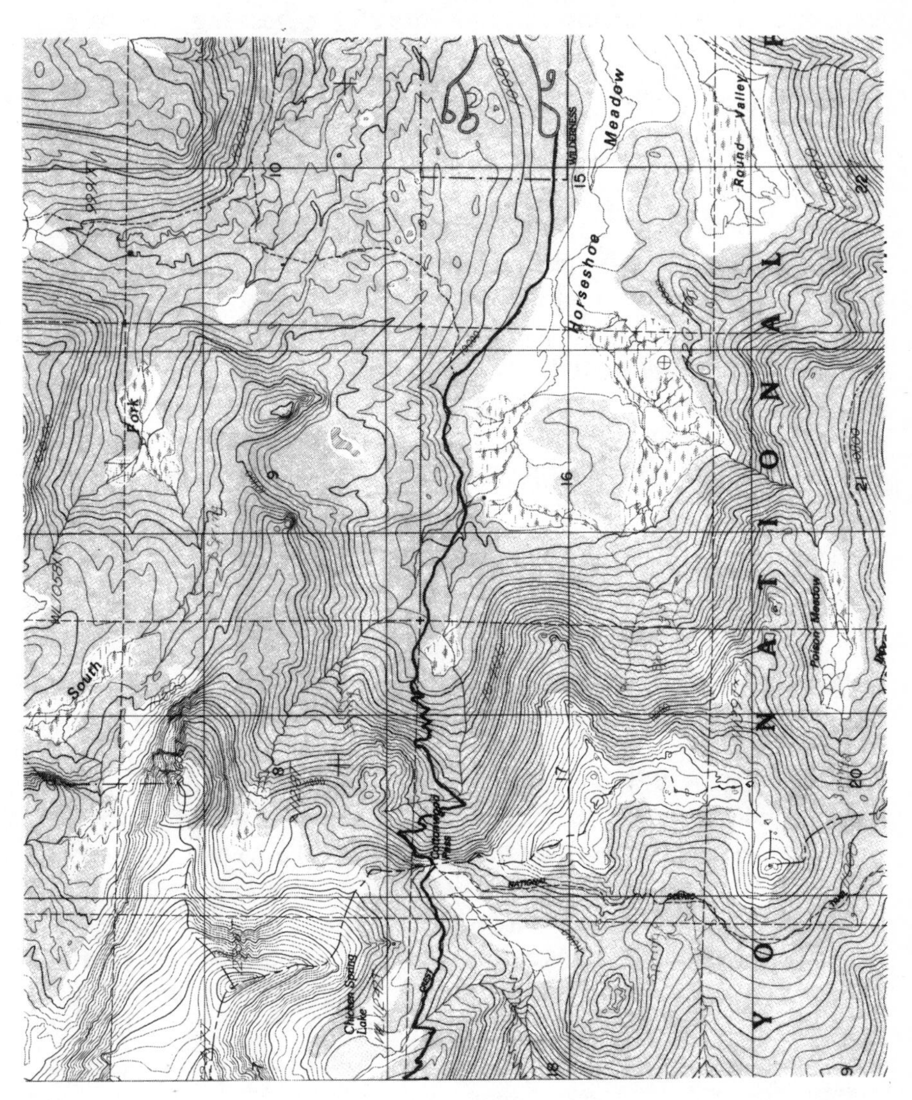

until about 10,000 years ago, and localized glaciation continues to take place in the Sierras at present.

There is evidence that uplifting also continues at the present. In 1872 a violent earthquake in the Owens Valley virtually destroyed the town of Lone Pine. In the aftermath, it was found that near Lone Pine there had been a sudden drop of 20 to 30 feet. Did Mount Whitney uplift at the same time? One can view the relatively new exposed fault surface and speculate.

Today, the crest ridge along the north-south scarp marks the boundary between Sequoia National Park on the west and the John Muir Wilderness along the east slope.

DESCRIPTION

This hike is especially exciting for two reasons: The routing from the Horseshoe Meadows trailhead brings you onto the Pacific Crest Trail in the area where the PCT first enters the true high Sierra subalpine environment; and you accomplish the ascent of Mount Whitney, at 14,494 feet the highest point in the forty-eight contiguous states.

Using the Horseshoe Meadows access has the advantage of allowing some acclimatization to the altitudes in this hike. The trailhead at 9,940 feet, and the day or two of hiking involved before you address the west slope of Whitney and ascend to its summit are a great help in getting you accustomed to the rarefied atmosphere. Failure to acclimatize is responsible for more aborted ascent attempts than any other cause. Also, the ascent is much less rigorous from the west side of the mountain. Trail gradients are very reasonable, something that cannot be said for the Whitney Portal route by its very nature.

A disadvantage to this routing is that the hike is not a loop; transportation must be secured from the Portal back to Horseshoe Meadows or some other arrangements made. Both trailheads have frequent traffic.

You will experience the John Muir Trail from Crabtree Meadows to its beginning at Whitney Portal. The aura of Mount Whitney and the southern Sierra is very much upon you, and it is easy to see why John Muir was so deeply moved by this lofty utopia. Perhaps that is why the wilderness bearing his name is nestled against the east slope of Whitney. Doubtless, had not the west slope already been inside Sequoia National Park, the entire mountain would have been included in the wilderness.

A Smithsonian hut is perched atop the summit. Its history began with the first scientific expedition to the top of Whitney in 1881. As a result of this effort, the U.S. Army declared Mount Whitney a U.S. Army military reservation for use of the Signal Corps, which functioned as the weather bureau at the time. By 1901, the military reservation status was abandoned, and the mountain was returned to the Sierra Forest Reserve.

In 1903 a group of 103 climbers from the Sierra Club visited the summit. A year later, the citizens of Lone Pine funded and constructed a stock trail to the summit. In 1909 the Smithsonian Institute initiated construction of the present stone building on the summit for use during a solar radiation study. At present, half of the shelter building is used for locked storage of mountain rescue equipment, and the other half of the building is open for use by climbers and hikers. There is a climber's register located in a metal box at the front of the Smithsonian building.

In 1990 a group of hikers sheltering in the hut during an afternoon thunderstorm were struck by lightning, resulting in one fatality. A grounding system using heavy copper conductors and copper grounding rods for the metal roof on the shelter was being installed in 1993. The best precaution during lightning storms, however, is to avoid being on the mountain at that time. While electrical storms can come up quickly, you will almost always receive warning in the rapid formation of clouds. If an electrical storm seems imminent, retreat from the exposed slopes and delay continuing until the storm has passed.

Typically, the season for this hike is early July through late September. Since precipitation can vary and alter these general dates a great deal, checking with the Mount Whitney ranger district is wise.

Take care to protect food from bears in Sequoia National Park and the John Muir Wilderness. Bear boxes are provided in some locations, particularly around Crabtree Meadows.

Administrative agency: USFS, USNPS

Inyo National Forest
873 N. Main Street
Bishop, CA 93514
(619) 873-2400

Mount Whitney Ranger District
(619) 876-6200

Sequoia National Park
Backcountry Permits
(209) 565-3761

USGS map: 7.5' series, Cirque Peak, Johnson Peak, Mount Whitney, Mount Langley, California

Declination: 15 degrees

DIRECTIONS TO TRAILHEAD

From Lone Pine, California, on U.S. Route 395, take the Whitney Portal Road, which turns west at a junction near the center of town. (The Whitney Portal Road leads 13 miles east to the Portal trailhead. Campsites and a small store are located there.) Go 2.9 miles on Whitney Portal Road to the junction with the Horseshoe Meadows Road. Turn left (south) on the Horseshoe Meadows Road and proceed 19 miles to the Horseshoe Meadows trailhead. There are toilets at the trailhead, and a campground is nearby.

MAP 1A

TRAIL ROUTE DESCRIPTION

From the trailhead parking lot, elevation 9,940 feet, the sandy trail leads westward through an open forest, descends slightly to the edge of Horseshoe Meadow within one mile, and then begins a very gentle ascent through lodgepole pines. Now in the Golden Trout Wilderness, you reach the north fork of Cottonwood Creek (2.6 miles from last point; 9,960 feet above sea level; 2.6 total miles) and cross near the confluence of a tributary. A short distance on your left is the Horseshoe Meadow Ranger Station.

Very soon you cross the south branch of the north fork and begin a gentle, undulating ascent, again in open forest. In 0.8 miles, you pass near a marshy meadow through which this south branch flows and soon begin a steady climb, with switchbacks, to the west. Crossing the south branch of the north fork of Horseshoe Creek (2.4 miles; 10,660 feet; 5.0 miles) a second time, your route continues ascending sharply via longer switchbacks. You reach Cottonwood Pass, cross its summit, and within yards reach a junction (0.7 miles; 11,140 feet; 5.7 miles) with Pacific Crest Trail.

The delightful meadow in which you now stand is one of the first experiences of a subalpine meadow for northbound long-distance PCT hikers. Turn right (northwest) now onto the PCT, circle around the upper edge of the meadow, and enter scattered forest. Meandering on a gentle ascent, you leave the trees and cross the outlet stream (0.6 miles; 11,220 feet; 6.3 miles) of Chicken Spring Lake. There are legal campsites at this lake, if you take care to stay well back from the water's edge. Chicken Spring Lake is the first true alpine, glacial cirque lake the northbound long-distance hiker encounters.

MAP 1B

A sharp ascent is eased somewhat by switchbacks as you leave the lake and climb to an elevation where your route leads on a lengthy traverse of the southwest slope of Cirque Peak. The now dusty tread stretches over decomposed granite, and foxtail pines grow along the trail. You may encounter pack trains here.

Four miles to the southwest, and 1,800 feet lower, you will see Big Whitney Meadow, one of the headwater areas of Golden Trout Creek. The sandy track continues the traverse over occasional high steps where stock have pounded out the trail, then reaches a small cirque, which it traverses in a half circle, the western end of which leads south. A sign nailed to a tree in this cirque (3.4 miles; 11,340 feet; 9.7 miles) warns against stock grazing, which is not allowed here. Adequate campsites can be found below the trail, and water is usually found here during the hiking season.

In sparse forest, you round the west side of the cirque, turn abruptly north, and climb through 11,040 feet before descending again. You nego-

MAP 1B

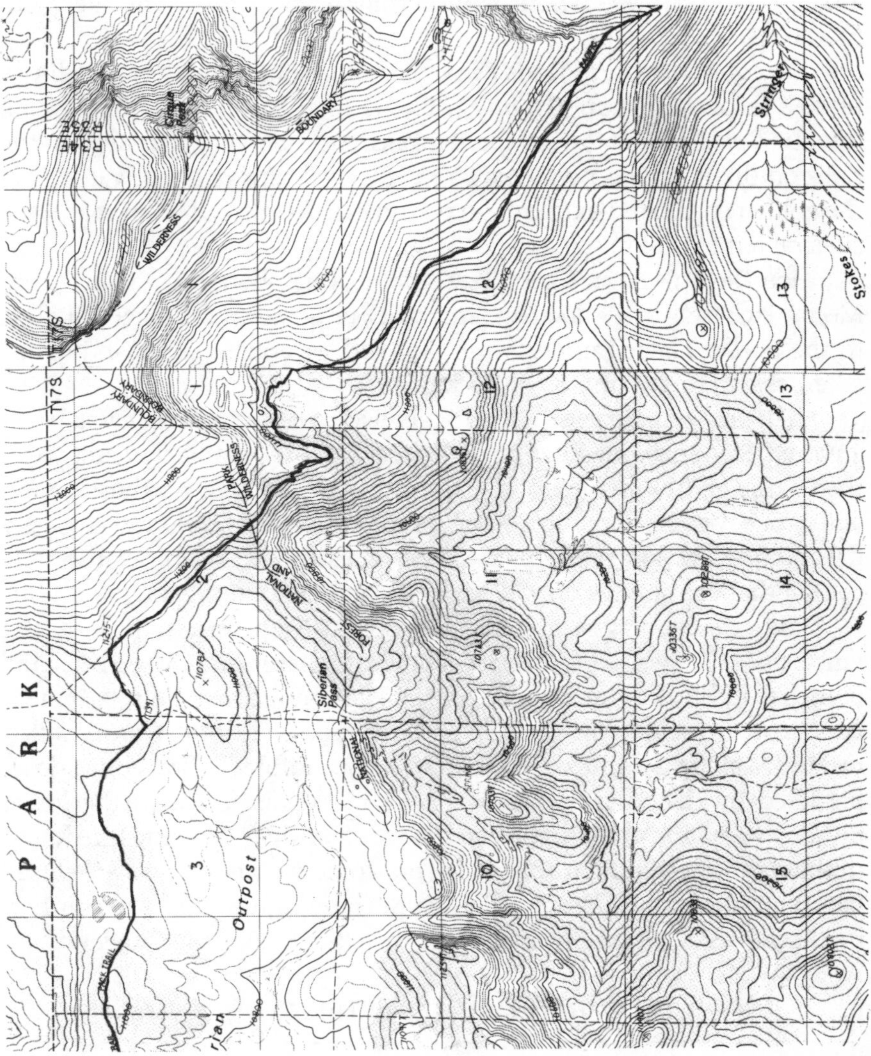

tiate a switchback or two, and then descend in a northwesterly traverse to the boundary (1.1 miles; 11,320 feet; 10.8 miles) of Sequoia National Park. Here you leave the Golden Trout Wilderness and ramble downhill into the park. Note that no firearms or pets are allowed in the park.

Moving briskly along the descending path, you reach a junction (1.1 miles; 11,215 feet; 11.9 miles) where the trail branches left and leads in a southwesterly direction toward Siberian Outpost, actually the huge meadow you have been seeing just below and to your left. One can imagine the weather conditions that prompted the naming of this meadow. Take the left fork (west) here, while a trail to Rock Creek continues right (north).

The gentle descent leads through patches of forest, after which you reach a second junction (0.6 miles; 11,391 feet; 12.5 miles) where a continuation of the Rock Creek/Siberian Pass Trail branches left. Keep to the right on the PCT. You now enjoy a nearly level traverse westward. Note the golden colors and exotic grain patterns of weathered stumps and the skeletal remains of foxtail pines.

Joe Devil Peak at 13,300 feet, Mount Chamberlain at 13,100 feet, Mount Pickering at 13,400 feet, and other peaks form the jagged skyline to the north. These impressive peaks, with attendant tarns and cirque lakes, spawn the beginning of Rock Creek.

MAP 1C

The route undulates gently for about 3 miles, after which you begin a more pronounced descent on switchbacks as the trail leads first west, then turns gently in a half circle until you are heading northeast. Soon you're once again proceeding northwest as the tread levels and crosses a flat. Notice the lodgepole pines here. These trees are often the only conifer that can survive on well-drained sand or pumice flats.

Your descending ramble via switchbacks drops you to the level of a junction (4.9 miles; 9,960 feet; 17.4 miles) where the Rock Creek Trail branches right. Continue ahead on the PCT, and in less than 0.3 miles, you cross a creeklet, an all-season water source. You now are heading westward along a gentle descent, crossing beautiful wildflower meadows bordered by the forest. A snow depth marker is found in the lower meadow, used for snow surveys in the winter. Adequate camps are found to the right of the trail at this point, but some overused areas are closed for restoration. One-quarter mile east of these camps, and just south of the Rock Creek–Perrin Creek confluence, is the Rock Creek ranger cabin.

Vertical Profile of Hike 1

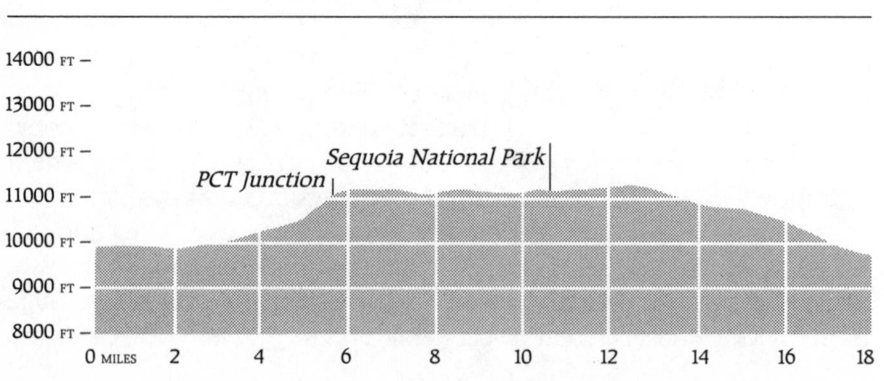

Presence of a ranger at this post should not be relied upon. Spend a moment appreciating the waterfall in this area, and if you're lucky, you may spot large trout in the pool beneath the falls.

Soon you cross a small tributary and reach the Rock Creek crossing (1.2 miles; 9,560 feet; 18.6 miles). You can cross this by either rock hopping or using a large foot log, 5 feet above the water, found just a few yards downstream.

Your route now leaves Rock Creek, leading in a series of northwest-trending switchbacks, and ascends the drier south slope. Here you will notice junipers and bushes from montane chaparral communities. There is welcome shade from foxtail pines, as well as water from the spring-fed streams you cross. Look for seep-spring monkey flowers clustered near the water here.

As you complete the switchbacks and the grade eases, you will notice old trail alignments paralleling our tread. Rock hopping across Guyot Creek (1.5 miles; 10,170 feet; 20.1 miles), you enter an avalanche runout area. Looking to the west, you can see where this destructive slide began, on the east slopes of Mount Guyot. In 1986 a massive 13-foot snowfall occurred over a short time in the Sierras, and many avalanches were triggered. This particular avalanche crossed the bottom of the shallow ravine to your left and finally came to rest around your trail, leaving much timber debris.

As you continue northward, you begin a series of short switchbacks that ascend granite ledges and wind around boulders. An open forest provides shade as the grade finally eases, and you cross a saddle at 10,925 feet elevation, followed by an easier ramble along a nearly level traverse around the east end of Guyot Flat.

The foxtail pines here are larger than most you will have seen thus far. In their shade you continue in a westerly and then northerly direc-

Vertical Profile of Hike 1

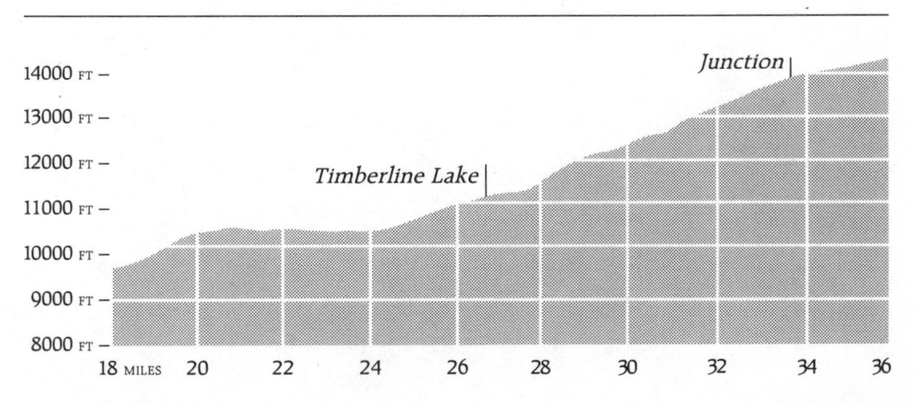

tion, as your sandy track crosses a flat near which are located several wind-carved, eroded tree stumps. Crossing the west end of a broad ridge in a gentle ascent, your trail now leads down a sharp descent through loose granite and talus blocks via a number of switchbacks. There is a wooden gate for stock control in the middle of the granite jumble. Next, you ascend gently to the northeast to contour along the west edge of Crabtree Meadows.

Several use trails branch from your route here, near a number of large campsites with bear boxes. Rock-hop across Whitney Creek (6.0 miles; 10,300 feet; 26.1 miles); almost immediately you reach a junction where the PCT continues northwest. Your route turns right here on a lateral trail that follows on the level around the northwest end of Crabtree Meadows before ascending along the west side of Whitney Creek in its small canyon.

Your trail now leads away from the meadow and soon passes another trail, which forks to the right. [This trail goes east, crosses the meadow below, and leads eventually to upper Crabtree Lake.] Continue ahead on the left fork; you soon cross to the east side of Whitney Creek. In 0.5 miles, you reach a junction (1.2 miles; 10,630 feet; 27.3 miles) with the John Muir Trail. [Turning left would lead to the PCT just 1 mile west.] Keep to the right, and within a few hundred yards you reach a message sign and a spur trail to the Crabtree Ranger Station. This outpost is usually occupied during the normal hiking season, but the ranger is often out on patrol. There are many campsites in the vicinity of the ranger cabin, but other campsites approximately 1 mile up the trail leave you better poised for the ascent of Whitney.

Continue northeast from the ranger cabin, ascending as the route turns east and passes just north of a lake that may be dry in late season. Beyond the lake you cross a low, north-jutting ridge (1.0 miles; 10,850

Vertical Profile of Hike 1

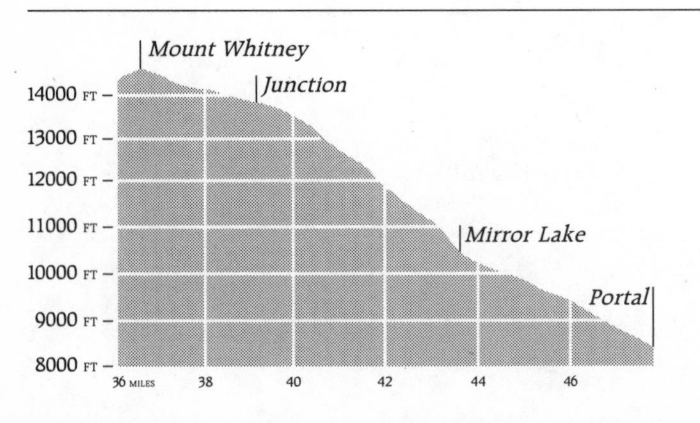

MAP 1C

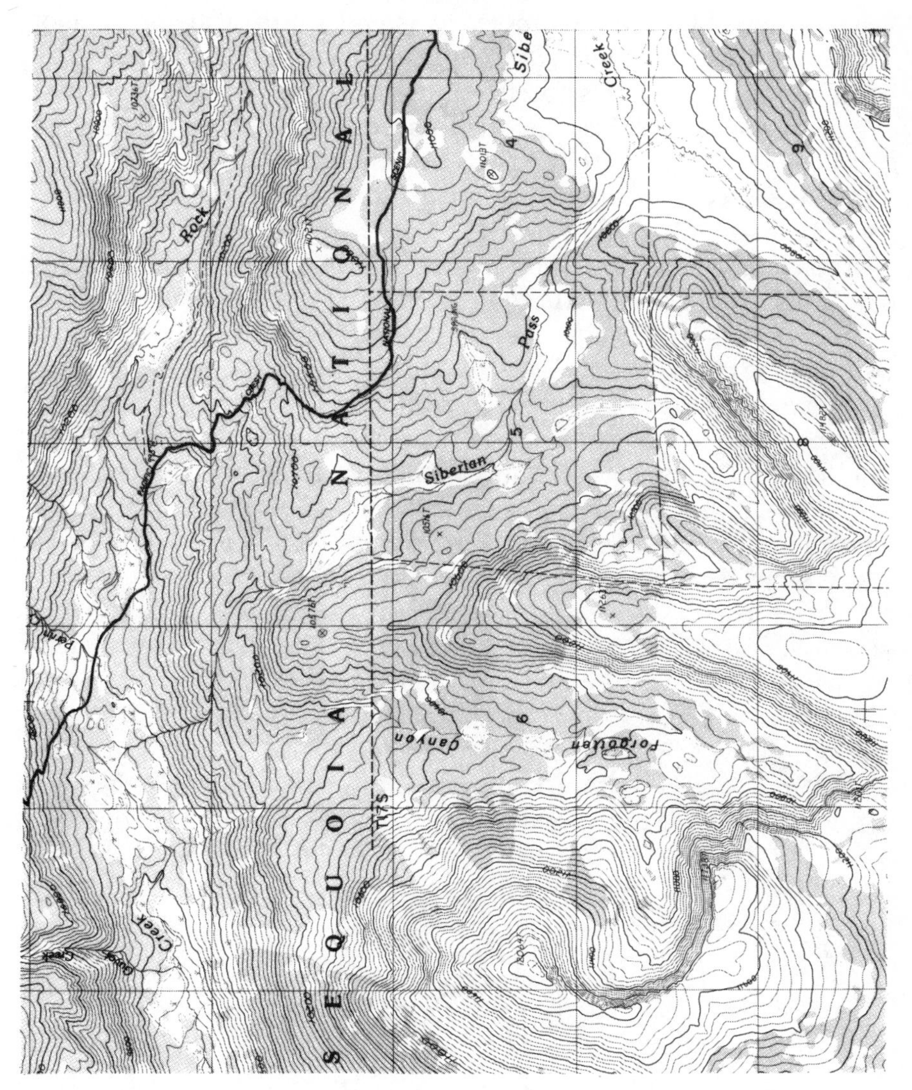

feet; 28.3 miles) with many campsites. Water is available from Whitney Creek. This spot is logistically positioned for the Mount Whitney climb.

Just east of this ridge, you rock hop across diminishing Whitney Creek. You have a moderate climb as you move away from the creek. You then return to it at Timberline Lake, elevation 11,020 feet. Camping and stock grazing is not allowed at Timberline; this area is undergoing rehabilitation to heal damage from overuse in the past, when it was a favored takeoff point for the Whitney climb.

As its name suggests, the timberline is located just beyond this lake. You pass the timberline and proceed to ascend a shallow ravine through which flows a tributary of Whitney Creek. Sandy areas and much exposed granite lie along this glacier-scoured route. The hard, resistant outcroppings you see have been polished smooth by glaciers that eroded the east slopes of Mount Russell and Mount Whitney.

The undulating path climbs briefly, levels along a ridge shoulder, and then descends to approach the shore of Guitar Lake. Crossing two inlet creeks to Guitar Lake, you continue over a sandy flow where sedges have gained a foothold and other wildflowers struggle. Yellow-bellied marmots watch as you pass a small lakelet, the last reliable source of water for the climb ahead.

Ascending to a ridge, you reach a sandy area where trail ducks guide you, then begin on a section of trail that has a completely different feel. This section has been well engineered and well built, with stone steps and, in places, laboriously laid granite-block retaining walls. You move upward into thinner air along a moderate gradient. Rest stops offer views whose scope increases with the altitude gained.

MAP 1E

Hitchcock Lakes become visible, acting as a mirror for the vertical northeast face of Mount Hitchcock, and Guitar Lake below grows smaller and smaller as you continue upward. Long switchbacks allow you views both north and south as you ascend, finally reaching the junction (5.5 miles; 13,600 feet; 33.8 miles) with the Mount Whitney trail. A right turn at this junction, to which you will return on your way back from the summit, would take you to the Whitney Portal trailhead 8.7 miles to the east.

Yellow-bellied marmot

MAP 1D

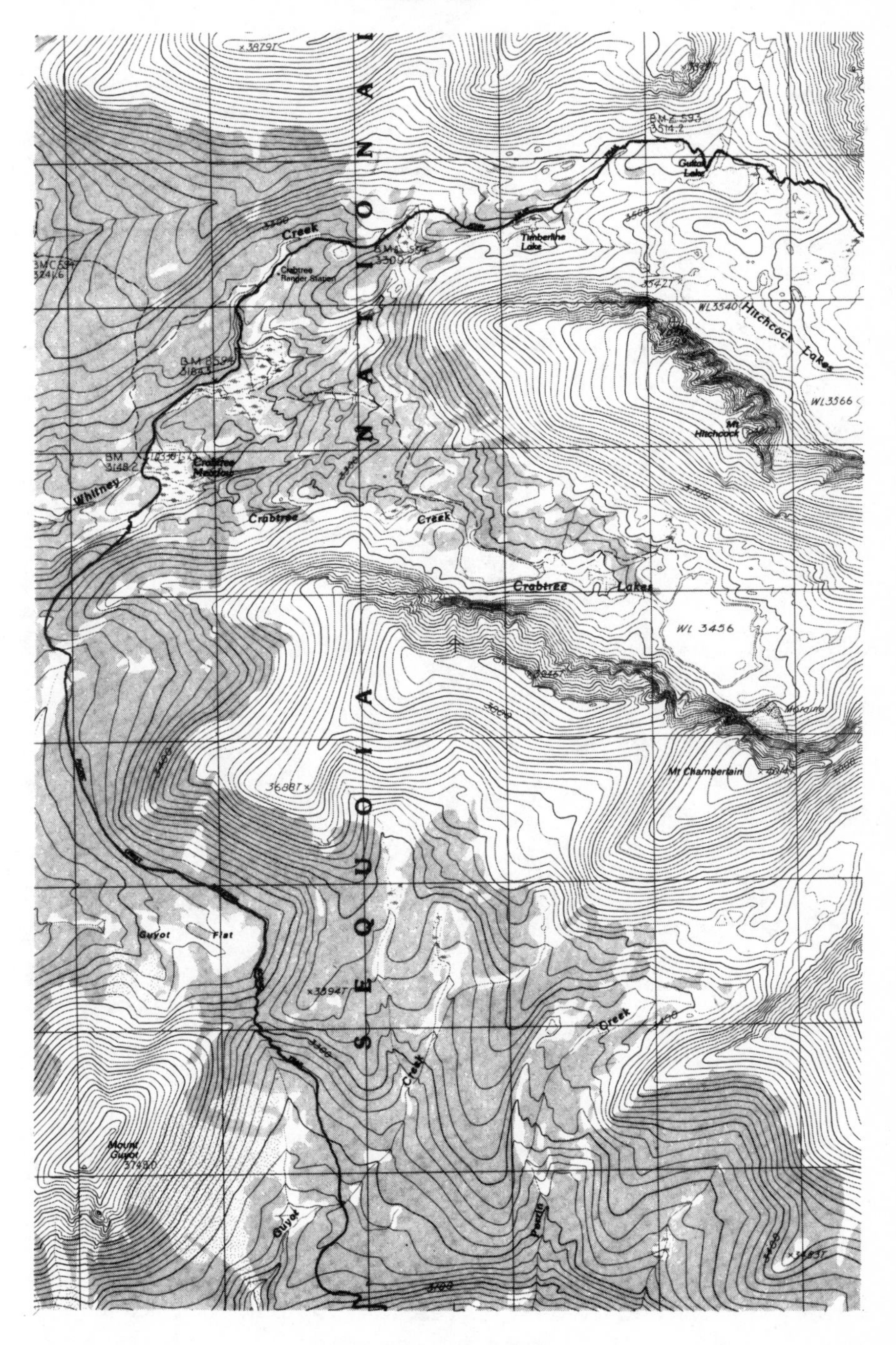
SEQUOIA NATIONAL
Creek
Crabtree Ranger Station
Timberline Lake
Guitar Lake
Hitchcock Lakes
WL3540
WL3566
Mt Hitchcock
Crabtree Meadow
Whitney
Crabtree
Creek
Crabtree Lakes
WL 3456
Moraine
Mt Chamberlain
Guyot Flat
Mount Guyot
3749.0
Guyot
Creek

MAP 1E

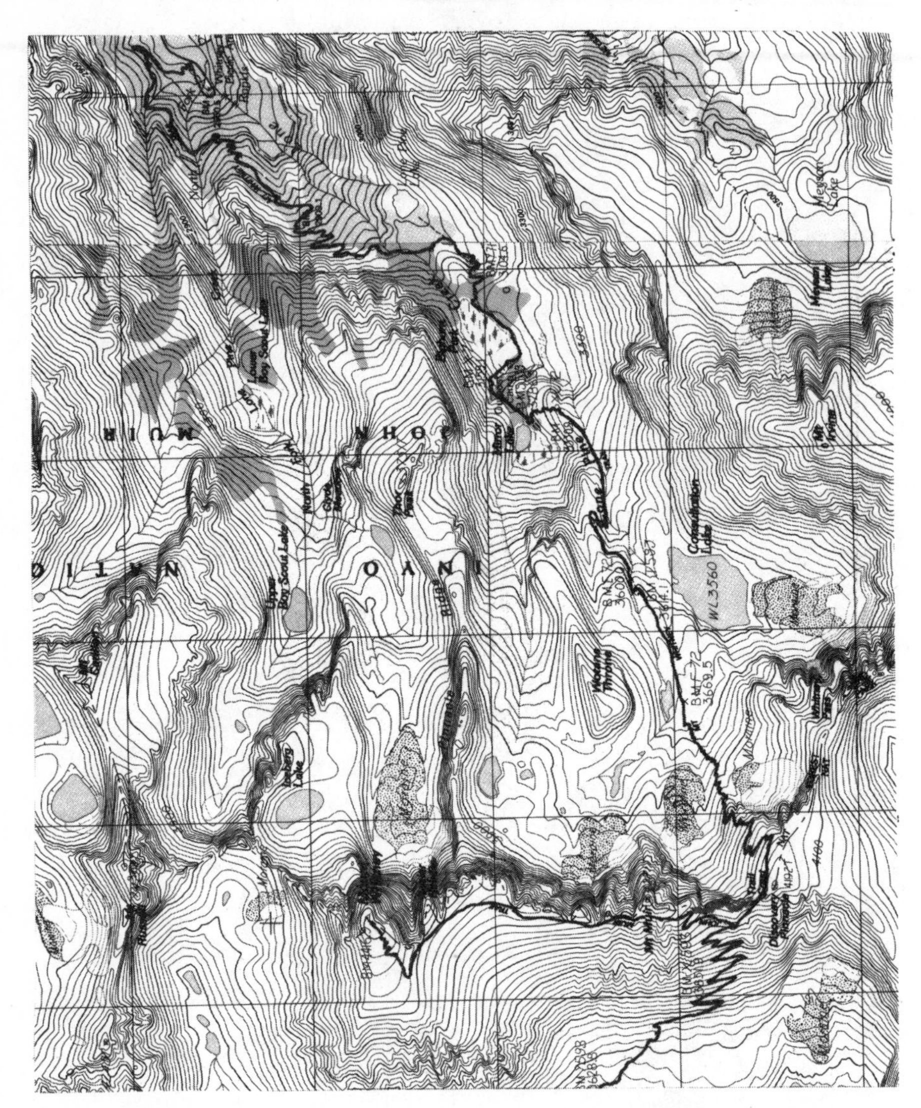

Turn left (north), and begin a traverse along the east flank of 14,015-foot Mount Muir. A long switchback aids you in gaining altitude. The trail provides unbelievable views to the west. Rounding knife-ridges and crossing talus slides, you ascend, finally reaching a series of notches between gendarmes, where the trail balances for a few feet on the crest and gives you a view down the vertical east scarp to alpine lakes nestled thousands of feet below. Use caution at these notches, for wind velocities can be high.

The trail makes a final, long traverse nearly west, then turns and negotiates the flank of Mount Whitney in a series of switchbacks through jutting boulders and slabs. At last you reach the Smithsonian stone hut on the summit (2.7 miles; 14,494 feet; 36.5 miles).

To the east from the summit, you can look down into the Owens Valley. The fault line marking the boundary between upthrusting and subsidence runs along its near side. East of the Owens Valley lie the White Mountains. North of Mount Whitney, and west across the Kern River, lie other peaks in the 14,000-foot class.

A chemical toilet is located on the west flank of Mount Whitney, about 150 yards west of the hut. Numerous rock enclaves testify to overnight tenting on the summit, not a good idea unless you are both hardy and experienced.

Once you are ready to leave the summit, retrace your steps past the gendarmes and Mount Muir to the junction (2.7 miles; 13,600 feet; 39.2 miles) with the Crabtree Meadows trail you passed on your way up. You now keep to the left and ascend a short distance south to the crest, here leaving Sequoia National Park and entering the John Muir Wilderness. Crossing onto the east side of the crest, you traverse along a scree slope, cut through rocky outcroppings, and descend this north-facing slope via medium switchbacks. The switchbacks become shorter and shorter as you continue downward. The imposing east face of Muir/Whitney lies to your left.

Soon the descent eases and you reach Trail Camp (2.6 miles; 12,040 feet; 41.8 miles). Here, hikers ascending from Whitney Portal camp overnight before their climb. The Forest Service has installed a composting toilet at Trail Camp, and many sandy camping sites are found among the granite ledges north of the trail.

Continuing along the trail, you switchback and descend rather steeply, crossing a small creek and passing a trailside meadow in which camping is not allowed. More switchbacks along the creek drop you to Mirror Lake (1.8 miles; 10,460 feet; 43.6 miles), a multicolored, 1-acre

Grey-crowned rosy finch

The slots between Whitney's gendarmes provide fantastic views of Trail Camp and the Owens Valley below. Fierce winds usually whistle through these openings.

tarn. Descending further, you reach Outpost Camp, where there is also a solar composting toilet. Camping here is on sandy alluvium.

Dropping lower, you pass a waterfall and then descend through brushy Bighorn Park, where camping is not allowed. Lower still, you see Lone Pine Lake on your right and soon cross a stream via a log. Just below you, that stream cascades over a rounded ledge. You cross the creek again and descend over broad, slick granite boulders.

Long, gentle switchbacks lead you out of the John Muir Wilderness (3.5 miles; 8,900 feet; 47.1 miles) and within a hundred yards pass the junction where the North Fork Drainage Trail turns left. You cross yet another creek and finally follow the wide, sandy path to the trailhead (0.8 miles; 8,365 feet; 47.9 miles) at Whitney Portal. There is a small store and a campground here, and lots of traffic. If you have not positioned your own transportation here, it should not be too difficult to secure a ride.

2 ♦ KEARSARGE PASS—RAE LAKES—BAXTER PASS

Distance:	27.2 Miles
Low elevation:	6,320 Feet
High elevation:	12,200 Feet
Class:	Strenuous
Hiking time:	24 Hours

Directly west of Independence, California, on U.S. Route 395, lies the eastern scarp of the Sierras, penetrated at this point by the popular Kearsarge Pass. East-side approaches are generally abrupt, steeper than corresponding access trails from the west. This is natural, for the tilted fault block that is the Sierra range was uplifted along the eastern edge to form a nearly vertical scarp, while the western backslope is more gentle.

In several places on this hike, you can see metamorphosed sedimentary and volcanic rock that has not been stripped away by erosion and glacial action, such as on 12,126-foot Painted Lady just south of Rae Lakes, and on the east slope just north of Dollar Lake. Aside from such remnants, the area has much the same appearance and geology as that described for the Horseshoe Meadows—Mount Whitney hike.

In 1863 Yale graduate Clarence King journeyed west and became a volunteer assistant with the California State Geological Survey under state geologist J. D. Whitney. Today, the Kings River drainage, Kings Canyon National Park, and 12,905-foot Mount Clarence King honor the enthusiasm and explorations of this man in the southern Sierra during the 1860s.

Including the trailhead access road from Independence westward, life zones from Sonoran to Arctic are traversed. The trip begins in creosote bush and sage, continues into chaparral, piñon pine, and juniper as elevation increases, reaches the Jeffrey pine forest of the Transition Zone, and then moves upward into the lodgepole-fir forest of the Canadian Zone. Above this is the Hudsonian Zone, where mountain hemlock and red fir blend smoothly into whitebark pine at the timberline. Higher still is the Alpine-Arctic zone, with fewer species of highly adapted plants.

Now protected from camping overuse, Bullfrog Lake is situated in King's Canyon backcountry, considered by many to be one of the most strikingly beautiful areas in the high Sierra.

You can observe the above vegetation from the window of your car on the way to the trailhead, and then as you hike the well-graded ascent of the 11,623-foot Kearsarge Pass.

DESCRIPTION

This hike begins at Onion Valley, the trailhead for Kearsarge Pass, and exits via Baxter Pass. The total route as described is for the experienced only. Eleven miles of the loop, over Baxter Pass, are on trails that are not maintained and may be in bad condition or difficult to follow in some places. Portions are extremely steep and covered with loose scree; other sections have been nearly obliterated. Good orienteering and scrambling skills as well as good physical conditioning are required for this portion of the hike. If you are not an experienced backcountry hiker, you may want to return by retracing your route from Dollar Lake via Kearsarge Pass to Onion Valley.

There are at least two options on this hike. Though described here as a loop, that loop is incomplete and two roadheads are involved, which means that transportation will require two vehicles or other arrangements.

Kearsarge Pass is one of the less difficult access routes into the John Muir Trail section of the high Sierra. The trail is well maintained and popular with hikers, not all of whom continue from the summit down into the basin wonderlands to the west.

From the summit of Kearsarge Pass, the imposing, jagged ramparts of Kearsarge Pinnacles form the southwestern horizon; their northwest terminus points toward nearby, ethereal Bullfrog Lake. It is impossible to gaze westward from the top of Kearsarge Pass and not experience a strong affinity for wilderness and its beauty.

While Kearsarge Pass Trail from Onion Valley winds through the John Muir Wilderness, from the summit westward you are hiking in Kings Canyon National Park. Many visitors to the remote areas of this park carry a lifelong conviction that the canyons of the Kings River rate among the most striking places on earth.

Bullfrog Lake attracted enough visitors in the past that camping and stock usage are currently prohibited there. Whether you want to detour from the hike route to visit this lake or just take in the beauty from the trail above is up to you.

A summer ranger is usually present at Charlotte Lake; the cabin is on the east shore. North of this lake is Glenn Pass. At first glimpse, the headwall appears nearly vertical—an impossible route for a trail. But as you climb higher and higher above the glistening, gemlike tarns, you discover what the route finders discovered before you—a trail can surmount Glenn Pass.

The Rae Lake Basin is a favorite with everyone who experiences it. Almost extreme glaciation has provided the many tarns that introduce the hiker to Rae Lakes. Lightly forested, the shoreline areas have a friendly feeling, while the lakes are often still, placid reflecting ponds for the western ramparts. Brook trout are seen patrolling in the clear water, indications that the fishing is good. To add a measure of confidence and safety to all this, a summer ranger is usually stationed at Rae Lakes. Bear boxes are provided at several of the campsites.

During an early-summer hike, we saw many wildflowers: paintbrush, Sierra wallflower, corn lily, shooting star, crimson columbine, wild onion, wild rose, cliff penstemon, hot rock and other penstemons, heather, pine lupine, dandelion, beavertail cactus, Lewis monkey flower, and blue-headed gilia. Other species bloom later in the year. Wildlife we sighted included alpine chipmunk, pika, golden-mantled ground squirrel, yellow-bellied marmot, blue grouse, Clark's nutcracker, flicker, tree swallow, mountain bluebird, gray-capped rosy finch, American dipper, junco, and robin.

From Dollar Lake, just north of Rae Lakes, this routing uses the unmaintained Baxter Pass Trail. This trail may be in bad condition or difficult to follow. Portions of it are very steep and covered with loose scree while other sections have been nearly wiped away. If you are not experienced at route finding and rough country scrambling, you may want to retrace your steps from Dollar Lake back over Kearsarge Pass to Onion Valley.

For experienced and accomplished backcountry route finders who choose to follow this trail, solitude is almost guaranteed the minute you leave the PCT at Dollar Lake and begin the ascending traverse northeast into Baxter Creek Canyon. A broad, glaciated canyon with modest gradient, Baxter also provides at least two beautiful, emerald green tarns tucked into gouges against the south canyon wall. Upon reaching Baxter Lake, a sizable body created by a moraine dam and circled with a grassy shoreline, you can easily feel isolated and alone, except possibly for a band of bighorn sheep on the ridges forming the eastern horizon.

A steep, two-tiered climb from Baxter Lake deposits you on Baxter Pass, a seldom-visited, 12,290-foot crest whose adjoining ridges show myriad trails made by bighorns that favor the cool, high slopes over the heat of lower elevations in the summer. Descending west from this summit, you traverse the California Bighorn Sheep Zoological Area. During the descent from Baxter Pass to the trailhead, there is a 6,000-foot decrease in elevation. Baxter Pass, Baxter Lake, and Baxter Creek all carry the name of John Baxter, who settled in the Owens Valley in 1871 to raise cattle and peaches near Independence.

Weather is usually mild in the hike area during summer, as it is in the entire Sierra range. The lofty peaks in the Kings River drainage do help formation of afternoon thunderstorms, however, and it is good to keep an eye on the weather when you are on or near the pass summits. Avoid exposure on summits or passes during these thunderstorms.

Administrative agency: USFS, USNPS

Inyo National Forest
873 N. Main Street
Bishop, CA 93514
(619) 873-2400

Kings Canyon National Park
Backcountry Permits
(209) 565-3761

USGS map: 7.5' series, Kearsarge Peak, Mount Clarence King, California

Declination: 15 degrees

MAP 2A

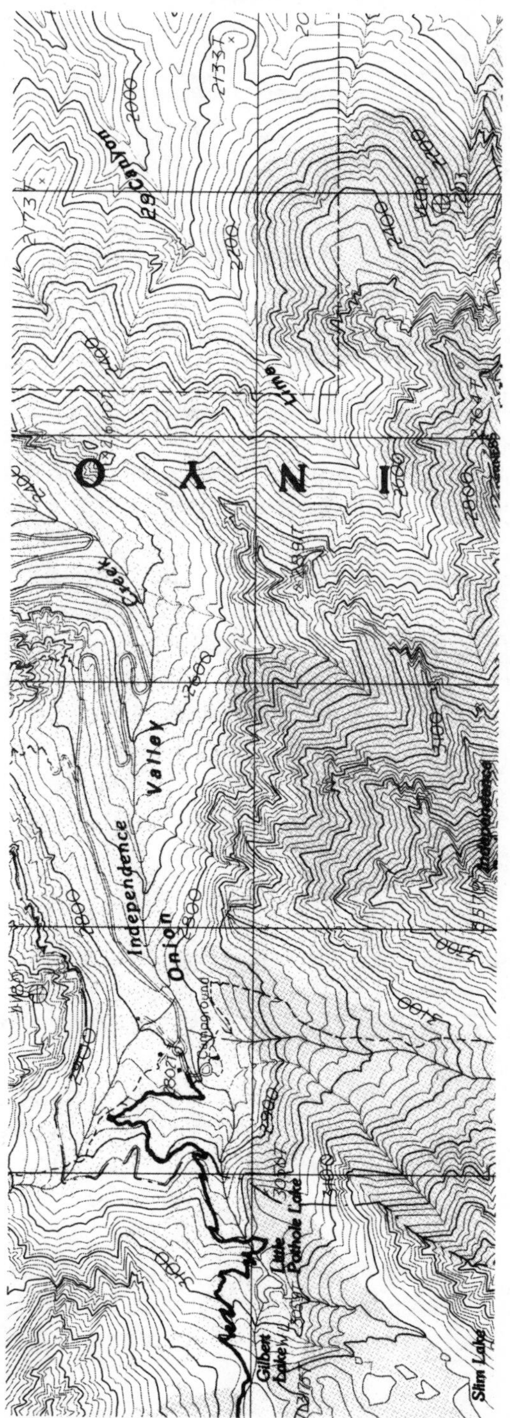

Canyon
Lime
INYO
Creek
Independence
Valley
Onion
Little
Pothole Lake
Gilbert
Lake
Slim Lake

The hiking season can vary, but generally early July to late September is the best time to enjoy Rae Lakes basin. Snow will remain on the high passes much longer than in the basin and arrive on those summits first in the fall.

Black bears are fairly common in most areas visited by this hike, especially in the Rae Lakes Basin. Bear boxes have been provided at Rae Lakes; in other areas take proper precautions.

DIRECTIONS TO TRAILHEAD

Baxter Pass: From U.S. Route 395, 2 miles north of the town of Independence, turn west on the Mount Whitney Fish Hatchery road, also signed "Oak Creek Campground and Baxter Pass." Continue beyond the hatchery at 1.1 miles, and turn right at the junction 0.2 miles beyond. Pass the USFS Oak Creek Campground on Oak Creek at mile 2.6, where the road becomes gravel surfaced. Continue on to the parking area at the end of the road at 5.8 miles. There are toilets here but no water. If you will be camping overnight, it would be better to stay at the Oak Creek Campground. There is plenty of parking at this little-used roadhead.

Kearsarge Pass: Near the center of the town of Independence on U.S. Route 395, turn west on Market Street. Pass Independence Campground, a county facility, 0.6 miles from the highway. At 5.6 miles on excellent, paved two-lane highway, pass the USFS Lower and Upper Grays Meadow Campgrounds, and continue up this spectacular, looping highway to Onion Valley roadhead at 13.5 miles. There is parking for about fifty cars. Toilets and piped water are found here. Onion Valley USFS fee campground has fifteen sites plus fourteen walk-in sites for tent campers. There is also a pack station at popular Onion Valley.

TRAIL ROUTE DESCRIPTION

MAP 2A

Leaving the hikers' parking area in Onion Valley near the toilets, you begin a switchback from 9,200 feet elevation, advancing up a slope where a sparse montane chaparral community exists on the bouldery hill. Mountain mahoganys survive on this east-facing slope, which also displays many varieties of wildflowers. You dip into a draw to the north, traverse up among red firs, and at 0.4 miles pass a sign informing that the Kings Canyon Park boundary is 5 miles ahead. Dogs and firearms are prohibited in the park, and Bullfrog Lake, a very scenic spot, is closed to all camping.

Your ascent levels momentarily on a flat. Look for foxtail pines, a unique tree found in a relatively small area in this portion of the Sierra and in one other region in the Cascade Mountains. You reach the boundary of the John Muir Wilderness (0.8 miles from last point; 9,550 feet above sea level; 0.8 total miles), shortly after which you come level with a snowcourse marker, #538. This marker is designed to be read from a helicopter or from a distance using binoculars.

Four-tenths of a mile farther you are within 30 feet of Kearsarge Creek at a good place to get water. You'll see whitebark pines just before a bench; then half-moon-shaped Little Pothole Lake (0.8 miles; 10,110 feet; 1.6 miles) and a waterfall appear to your left. Cascades tumble down the hill above the lake. Next you traverse a talus field, easily accomplished on this excellent trail, and reach Gilbert Lake (0.7 miles; 10,350 feet; 2.3 miles) on your left. A sign cautions you to camp at least 100 feet from the water. There are minimal campsites on the knob to your left and bearproof steel boxes in which to protect your food. Wood fires are prohibited here.

MAP 2B

Continuing on the trail, you soon come to a junction (0.3 miles; 10,450 feet; 2.6 miles); the Matlock Lake trail branches left to that lake, which lies just 0.5 miles south. There is a camp on the left, close to the creek, that also has bear boxes.

In minutes you begin a serious ascent along the base of a talus slide. Two switchbacks later to your south is beautiful, aquamarine Heart Lake, nestled in a cirque below. Now your trail switchbacks up the spine of a granite ridge. Once atop the ridge, the trail leads up the loose talus and scree slope to your right (north). The darker rock at the top of this slope is not granitic, and you'll soon see metamorphic rocks along the trail. To the south, stark, cold-gray granite spires reach upward, outlined against the deep blue sky characteristic of higher elevations.

To your left now is a 70-foot-high moraine upon which hardy whitebark pines attempt to hold the timberline at this elevation. In a few yards you reach a sign asking hikers not to cut switchbacks; on your right there is evidence of erosion on the loose scree hill from this damaging practice. Gaining more elevation, you can see a beautiful jewel, Big Pothole Lake, behind the moraine on your left. The deeply gouged hole was dug during the dying throes of an east-side glacier.

Your track leads in long switchbacks up the open slope; here there are several very steep, old trail alignments. As you crest Kearsarge Pass (2.1 miles; 11,823 feet; 4.7 miles), you can view the Kearsarge Pinnacles marching in a jagged-topped row a mile to the southwest. In the basin below are the Kearsarge Lakes, and as you step over the summit and down the gravelly trail, you enter Kings Canyon National Park.

In 0.3 miles you reach a junction where the left-hand trail leads down into the Kearsarge-Bullfrog Basin. No stock travel is allowed in this

MAP 2B

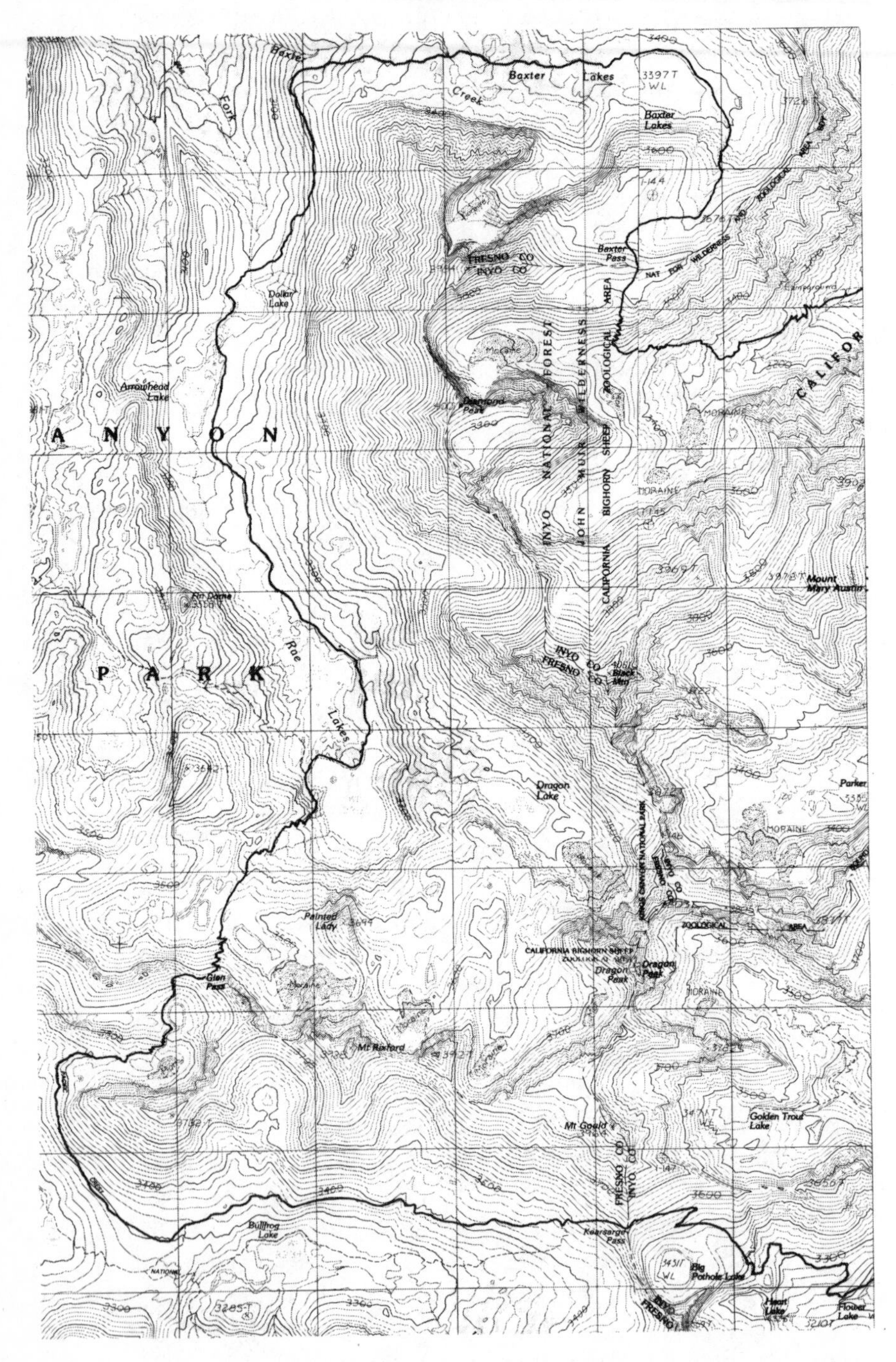

Baxter Lakes
Baxter Creek
Baxter Lakes
Baxter Pass
FRESNO CO
INYO CO
Dollar Lake
Arrowhead Lake
Diamond Peak
INYO NATIONAL FOREST
JOHN MUIR WILDERNESS
CALIFORNIA BIGHORN SHEEP ZOOLOGICAL AREA
Mount Mary Austin
Fin Dome
Rae Lakes
Black Mtn
Dragon Lake
Parker
MORAINE
Painted Lady
Glen Pass
Mt Rixford
Dragon Peak
Golden Trout Lake
Mt Gould
Kearsarge Pass
Bullfrog Lake
Big Pothole Lake
Heart Lake
Flower Lake

basin, and there is a reminder that camping is not allowed at Bullfrog Lake. Take the right-hand trail, and continue toward the Pacific Crest Trail and Charlotte Lake.

It is hard to imagine a more beautiful scene than this gentle traverse above Kearsarge Lakes and Bullfrog Lake. Backed by the sharp, angular pinnacles, these beautiful expanses of azure nestle in the forested granite basin, while to the west Bubbs Creek gains momentum from the southeast, turns west, and escapes from this jungle of peaks through a deep, tortuous canyon that equals any for rugged grandeur. You cross two spring streams and level to an easy route above Bullfrog Lake. Here you can see farther down the Bubbs Creek canyon, which trends west into the Kings River.

The wide trail is well constructed and well maintained. Several sections have laid-up rock walls and required blasting into a granite cliff. It may seem that the view above Bullfrog Lake couldn't possibly get any prettier, but it does as you switchback down the sandy trail among foxtail pines. You reach a junction (2.6 miles; 10,800 feet; 7.3 miles) where the left-hand fork goes to Charlotte Lake and Vidette Meadows. Continue along the right-hand fork toward Glenn Pass and Charlotte Meadows.

The path meanders along a decomposed granite bench among foxtail pines not quite tall enough to provide good shade, and in 0.3 miles you reach a junction with the Pacific Crest Trail, which here is also the John Muir Trail. The left-hand fork leads to Charlotte Lake and Vidette Meadows. You again take the right-hand fork, toward Glenn Pass and Rae Lakes.

You follow the PCT over bouldery hummocks, traversing high above beautiful Charlotte Lake. This long, deep lake is the headwater of Charlotte Creek, which flows out of this basin in a northwesterly direction, then swings west where it passes below the sheer face of a granite monolith before turning southward to become another tributary of Bubbs Creek. The orange-capped peak west of Charlotte Lake is Mount Bago,

Vertical Profile of Hike 2

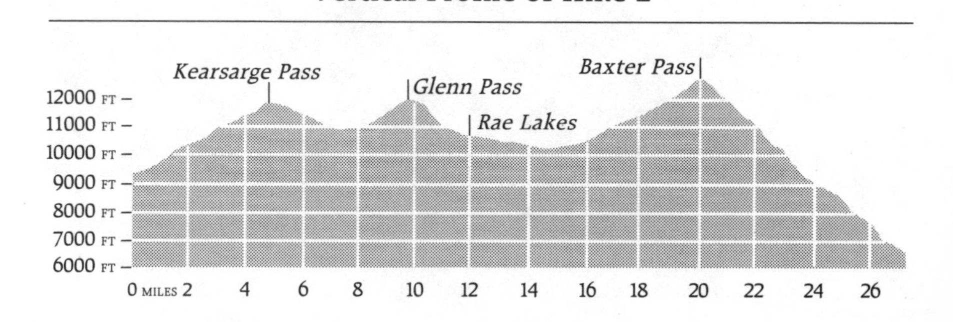

upon whose slopes whitebark pines survive in bush form nearly to the 11,868-foot summit. A summer ranger usually is stationed at Charlotte Lake.

Some steep climbs lead you toward a gap in the slope ahead on the right. You swing abruptly eastward into this canyon and continue upward among several small trailside tarns whose surrounds abound with wildflowers. A terminal moraine lies to your right. Your route ascends to a viewpoint into the 150-foot-diameter, azure-blue tarn imprisoned by the moraine. Nearly vertical headwalls on two sides make this spot no less than impressive.

Contouring around the west side of the tarn, you cross a jumble of talus on the steep trail, crest a rocky spur, and see another, equally impressive tarn on your right at 11,630 feet. The headwalls of this cirque form the nearly vertical headwall of Glenn Pass. Your route curves around to the west and north of this cirque, then climbs in sharp switchbacks up the face of a scree and talus slide to reach Glenn Pass. (2.4 miles; 11,978 feet; 9.7 miles).

Below and to the north is a glaciated, tarn-studded basin with Rae Lakes beyond. To the east is colorful Painted Lady peak, reaching to 12,126 feet. Other peaks march to the horizon. To the south, a jumble of 12,000- and 13,000-foot-high peaks stand guard in the backcountry wilderness of Sequoia National Park. If you were not previously aware of being in wilderness, that feeling will definitely overcome you now. Ac-

Monuments to tenacity, gnarled pines grow from granite, die, and are etched by blowing snow into fantastic shapes and textures.

cess to the trappings of civilization has always been difficult from this area, and you are standing right in the middle of it, about as remote as you can get. This is no place to become ill or injured.

Now you switchback down the talus on the north slope of Glenn Pass toward the shallow tarns in the basin to your left and reach the bottom of the switchbacks in 0.6 miles, more than 600 feet below the summit you have just crossed. Moving up onto a rounded granite ridge, you walk parallel to joints in the pink granite, then descend in switchbacks. You can see Upper Rae Lake below. Your sometimes cobblestoned trail drops steadily, and more of beautiful Rae Lake becomes visible. Just before you reach the lake, the trail ascends abruptly over a spur ridge, then drops down again toward the lake.

A sign advising of the one-day camping limit is posted at the approach to Rae Lake. Another sign identifies this as the John Muir Trail, with Glenn Pass 2 miles south and Twin Lakes 2.5 miles north. Your route continues out along the ridge, past a faint trail branching left that leads northwest across the ridge towered over by spirelike Fin Dome and into the Sixty Lake Basin to the west. Keep to the main trail, and as you make your way out onto this peninsula, you get a close-up view of the clear Rae Lake water and, if you're lucky, of the brook trout swimming in it.

Now you reach the creek (2.0 miles; 10,540 feet; 11.7 miles) that runs the few feet between Upper Rae Lake and Middle Rae Lake. You cross on logs and move to the south side of this new peninsula. Passing a 300-foot-wide isthmus, your tread now leads along the east shore of Middle Rae Lake to a camping area west of the trail, where a bear box has been placed. There is room here for several parties to camp with privacy, a good thing, because the Park Service has made an effort to consolidate camping areas at Rae Lakes. The almost unbelievable beauty of this spot certainly merits efforts to keep human wear and tear to a minimum. To help preserve this area, a summer ranger is usually present at Rae Lakes.

The landscape is more open as you advance along the east side of Middle Rae Lake and Lower Rae Lake. Fin Dome stands like a guard, ever watchful over the clear water, tiny islands, and emerald meadows. On the calm waters are reflections of the peaks. Here, too, you will feel deep in a vast wilderness, but now in the middle of the almost palpable beauty of the Rae Lakes, the feeling is gentle, desirable.

The trail next leads to Arrowhead Lake. At the lake's south end (2.4 miles; 10,435 feet; 14.1 miles) are good campsites and a bear box. Then 0.2 miles farther, you pass within 100 yards of a waterfall in the South Fork of Woods Creek, which drains the Rae Lakes Basin. Shortly after, you cross the creek on a log. Within yards you hear and see the tumbling descent of the creek as it drops toward Dollar Lake, which lies to your right after you switchback down to traverse its west shore. A large scree slide descends into the lake on the east side.

Moving along to the north end of the lake, the obvious campsite is a restoration site, and no camping is allowed. A few yards beyond is a now-familiar sign (0.6 miles; 10,230 feet; 14.7 miles) advising that Rae Lakes Basin has a one-day camping limit.

At this point, you need to decide whether to continue on the described hike or turn back. Do not attempt the remainder of this hike unless you are capable of following faint trails and able to find your own way should you loose the trail. If you are hardened and experienced, you can continue to complete the semiloop hike and exit at the Baxter Pass trailhead described earlier. Be sure you have good maps showing topographic details between this point and the Baxter Pass roadhead. If you or a companion is not experienced, return the way you have come. The distance is the same, the effort required is less, and you will have a good trail.

Should you decide to tackle Baxter Pass, turn right at the one-day camp limit sign and head straight toward the creek. You'll find a creek crossing of piled stones 100 feet downstream of the lake outlet. Cross at that point, just before the creek begins to drop in serious rapids. Beyond the creek, within 75 feet, the route leads up onto an east-trending ridge, and you can see trail tread on patches of soil among the metamorphic rocks. Watch carefully for small trail ducks that have been piled by helpful hikers who also searched for this seldom-used route.

Within 100 yards, you cross a soggy meadow; where sedges and grasses have overgrown the trail. Continuing in the same direction, you soon pick up the tread again as it turns left, to the north. This hillside has many varieties of wildflowers both early and late, and it is a pleasure to traverse in spite of the very poor, rocky trail.

After a steady climb, during which the trail disappears for 50 yards or so, you reach a beautiful, undulating section among very large foxtail pines. Much effort was expended here at some time in the past to construct this trail among these talus slopes. Note the difference between the trail routing and construction of the past and the relatively easy grade, smooth-tread trails you by now have become accustomed to. Were hikers much sturdier just a few decades ago?

The trail now approaches Baxter Creek to within 100 yards, swings to the east (1.4 miles; 10,500 feet; 16.1 miles), and begins ascending. Just 0.2 miles farther, there is a pretty, cascading waterfall on Baxter Creek to your left. Then, 0.4 miles farther, you ascend a meadow area. Keep an eye out for small rock ducks, which may or may not be present. As you move upward from bench to glaciated bench, the mechanics of old-time trail engineering become obvious. The route maker was often on horseback, and the trail evolved through use along the route taken to wind through obstructions. Grade often was not considered, a fact that will become very, very clear to you before you reach the roadhead.

The trail becomes slightly better defined as you climb and cross Baxter Creek (0.8 miles; 10,890 feet; 16.9 miles). Behind you to your right is a 2-acre lake with a campsite among pine trees 100 feet from the outlet creek. Soon, in this virtually unvisited area, you pass a shallow, sedge-rimmed pond to your left, warm enough to provide good swimming. You can experience real solitude here; this area may not see another human for weeks, one reward of hiking on unmaintained trails.

Don't count on making good time through this section; it may take some time to spot trail ducks marking the route. It's just as well though, because to hurry here would be to miss some of the fine minienvironments that exist in this drainage.

Soon, at the base of two large talus slides on your right (south) is another beautiful lake. Very few hikers visit the shoreline of this deep lake. Should this lake be on a modern, maintained trail, it would have visitors almost daily.

The faint trail continues up another series of glaciated benches, and a headwall on your right curves around to become a west-facing cliff. At the bottom of this headwall is another deep, blue lake, 300 yards south of the trail. A moraine lies 100 yards ahead, and you pass a campsite among the pines on your right. Cresting the moraine, you can see beautiful, alpine Baxter Lake, an 80-acre jewel crowning the basin. Note the characteristic pileup of stones rimming the entire lakeshore (1.0 mile; 11,140 feet; 17.9 miles). The action of ice freezing on the surface continually moves rocks from the shallows up against the shore.

Other campsites are located on the moraine at the west end of the lake. As you negotiate the meadowlike shore north of Baxter Lake, note the once heavily used compacted, parallel trail ruts. Almost complete healing has taken place. That so many years have been necessary to repair even slight damage should make you more aware of the importance of good trail maintenance and etiquette.

Leaving the basin bottom, the trail leads southeast and then ascends the steep talus and scree slope in wiggly, little trails that are hardly switchbacks. This taxing climb will make you appreciate modern trails and the ease with which they lead you across difficult country. As you leave the basin in a southerly direction, the ascent eases slightly, and you cross a broad, stone-paved bottom where metamorphic rocks prevail.

The often faint track now leads westward, but soon you reach a sharp turn to the left (south) (1.7 miles; 12,045 feet; 19.6 miles) and the trail again takes an almost direct route up the orange-colored rocks.

Eventually the route abandons all pretext at switchbacks and leads straight upslope. Note the trails along the hogback in the red and black formations to your right. These trails were made by bighorn sheep, which inhabit this ridge and the California Bighorn Zoological Area that lies to the east. On hot days, sheep like to lie in the shade of boulders on the ridges, where the wind cools them and they have a good view of any approaching predators. The crest ridge is the boundary with Kings Canyon National Park.

Looking to the north, you should now be able to distinguish 13,183-foot Acrodectes Peak from Mount Baxter, 13,125 feet. The former lies directly north of Baxter Lake, while the latter is a mile to the east. Small tarns grace many of the lofty cirques on these peaks. The trail leads you to the summit of Baxter Pass (0.2 miles; 12,290 feet; 19.8 miles).

Your view to the southeast is spectacular. The town of Independence in the Owens Valley to the east appears as a miniature green oasis. To the south, guardian peaks stand like watchtowers, imposing, with sheer spires and broken, tumbling faces. Long scree slides spread down from joint lines, and you can see more than one tarn created by east-side glaciation. From here, the hardy would have an easy scramble along the ridge to the southwest, gaining in the process perhaps 300 feet more elevation.

Your descent begins on a loose, gravelly trail. You soon reach the edge, from which you can see the timberline still well below. Once you've picked your way over a precarious talus jumble, you reach a better trail grade and finally pass the uppermost outrider whitebark pines to the right of the trail at 11,385 feet. The trail is rocky and slippery, with gravel lying on slick rock surfaces. The grade is atrocious, but other than that it's great.

In 1.0 mile, you approach North Fork Oak Creek on your right. Notice that the flow has scoured out a soft joint in the rock that crosses the drainage bottom on a diagonal. Shortly thereafter, you cross a small spring stream and pass through a limited meadow, the first time since Baxter Lake some 3 miles back that you can take a few steps without rocks under your feet. Below the meadow in a pine grove is a campsite, and another campsite lies just below.

A short swing beyond, you cross a deep runoff gully that gapes straight down the slope. A few minutes later, you cross another gully and soon switchback into and out of yet a third. Note the view downcanyon. After a short climb, at the base of a long series of switchbacks, you come

MAP 2C

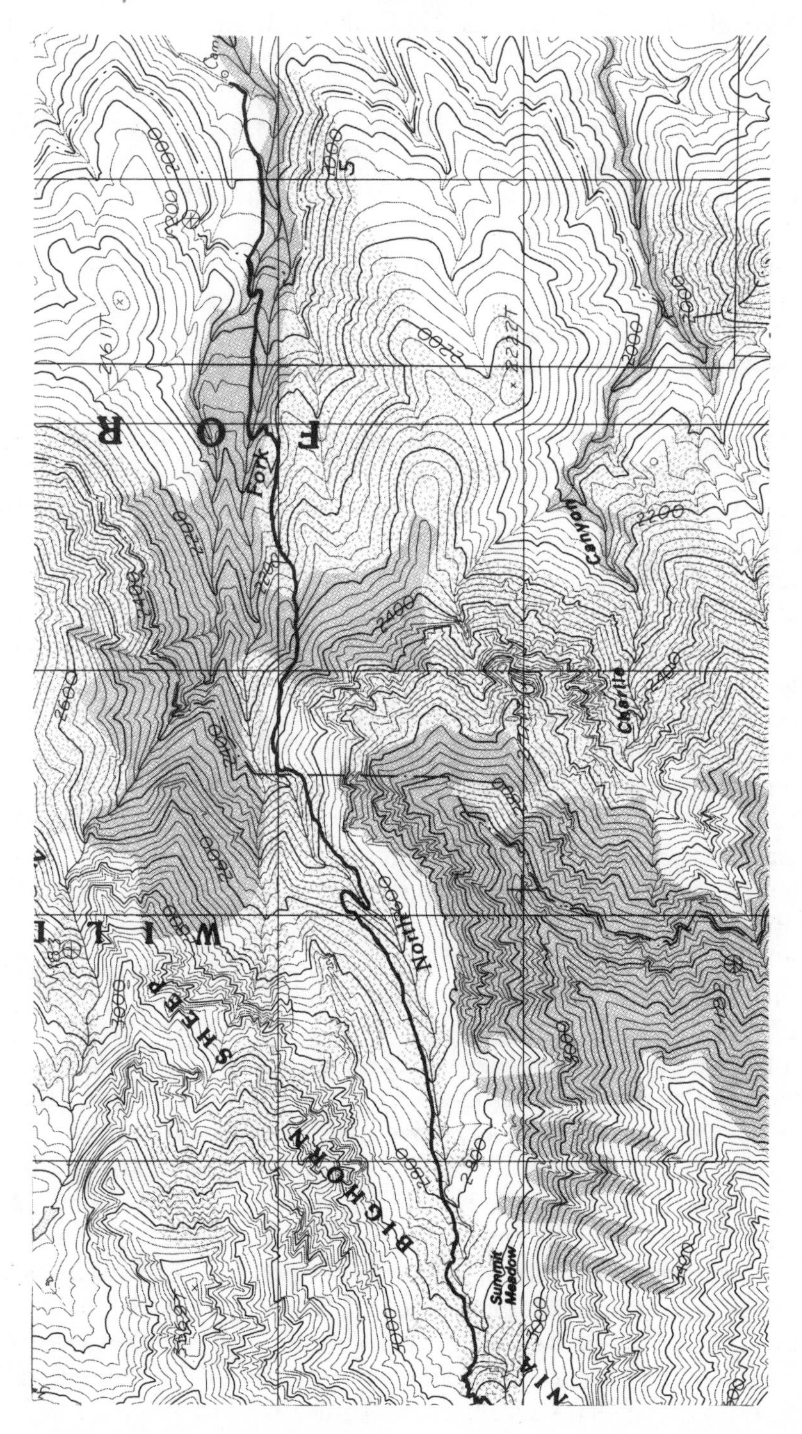
Fork
North
Canyon
Charlie
Summit Meadow
BIGHORN
SHEEP
2200
2400

upon a grove of willows and approach an early-season runoff stream. The trail is badly washed out here and difficult to follow. Watch for rock trail ducks. If you should lose the trail at the willows, you will soon find it paralleling the creek bottom on the north side just 30 feet above the trees.

MAP 2C

By a large boulder on your left is another passable campsite. You can hear Oak Creek roaring from your right on its mad dash down this canyon, so water isn't far away, even though it may be a struggle to reach through the matted willows.

Water from thunderstorms and snowmelt is changing this canyon rapidly in terms of geologic time, and the washed-out tread is hard to follow. You now cross yet another large watercourse chute cut by flash floods, along whose sides the speed and force of the current has piled large boulders.

You come to a colony of cottonwoods (3.3 miles; 9,440 feet; 23.1 miles) and soon approach Oak Creek. Your route does not cross here but remains on the north side of the creek. After you rock hop across a 100-foot-wide talus jumble, you pick up the trail tread again and follow trail ducks into a brushy jungle.

Red and white fir now appear, accompanied by Jeffrey pine (0.8 miles; 8,815 feet; 23.9 miles). Just below, to the right of the trail, is a good campsite. Many wildflowers favor this elevation and slope. You now cross Oak Creek (0.5 miles; 8,500 feet; 24.4 miles) and drop 0.2 miles farther. A use trail switches left to a large camping area visible in the canyon bottom. Farther down, there are occasional beavertail cactus beside the trail and a few Jeffrey pines. In 0.5 miles, you pass a sign on a large white fir snag advising westbound hikers that they are entering the California Bighorn Sheep Zoological Area, where dogs and cross-country travel are prohibited.

Piñon pine, mountain mahogany, and California black oak appear on the hillside. Lava blocks fallen from a cliff above lie by the trail. You soon reach a crossing of the creek. In early season, you need to cross on one of two logs usually in place there. Later in the season, you can make a dry crossing by rock hopping. One way or the other, use caution here, because the south bank is crumbly gravel alluvium and quite abrupt.

After crossing the creek, the route switches up the bank to the left at a sign directing westbound hikers. One switchback up and you are on a wide, sandy trail that traverses away from the creek on a gentle descent. You pass a boundary sign (1.9 miles; 6,885 feet; 26.3 miles) as you leave the John Muir Wilderness, and in 0.7 miles you reach an old road. Follow this sandy roadbed to the left, and in a few hundred yards you pass through an obscured pipe archway beneath a tree. A minute after that, you are at the Baxter trailhead (0.9 miles; 6,320 feet; 27.2 miles).

3 ♦ BISHOP PASS—LE CONTE CREEK—MUIR PASS

Distance:	40.8 Miles
Low elevation:	8,720 Feet
High elevation:	11,972 Feet
Class:	Difficult
Hiking time:	30 Hours

In 1870 Joseph Le Conte first visited the Sierra in company with John Muir and others. Le Conte listened to Muir's theories on glaciation and realized that young Muir had indeed identified the force that shaped the high Sierra. Le Conte returned to the Sierra for pleasure and research many times after that. His explorations contributed in their own right, while his urging young Muir to write was a pivotal force and one of the main reasons we have Muir's recorded thoughts today.

In Kings Canyon National Park, southwest of Bishop, California, both Muir and Le Conte are honored. Le Conte Creek typifies a high Sierra drainage system, with beautiful pools, waterfalls, and rapids. Running first east and then south, Le Conte Creek winds among forested bottoms, loops through green meadows, and drops in tumultuous white falls over granite ledges, all within sight and sound of the paralleling PCT. At the head of its drainage, an 11,956-foot pass bears Muir's name. On that pass is a stone shelter erected in Muir's memory by the Sierra Club and others in 1931.

Just before the summit of Muir Pass, if you are hiking northbound on the PCT, lies clear, cold Helen Lake. Beyond the pass, and visible from the memorial shelter, is Wanda Lake. These lakes were named after Muir's daughters. Helen Lake drains into the Kings River, while Wanda Lake waters flow into the San Joaquin.

Somewhat eased by erosion, the east scarp of the Sierra is here accessed by 11,972-foot Bishop Pass. East-side glaciation is more noticeable than in locations father south in the range. From the chain of tarns at the pass, northward to the bowl holding South Lake at the trailhead, and far

Leave the door ajar, and mice will welcome you at night in this shelter at the summit of Muir Pass. The building was erected by the Sierra Club and others as a memorial to John Muir.

below, glaciation has shaped a long, north-draining canyon that flows into the east-side closed system of Mono Lake.

Because of the high altitude of this locale, vegetation is sparse along much of the route, and the feeling of truly traveling near the top of the world comes unmistakably to hikers of this lofty real estate. Many nearby peaks are over 12,000 feet, and several exceed 13,000. Even the Le Conte Canyon bottom, the low point of this route, where Bishop Pass Trail winds down, is at an elevation of 8,720 feet.

Whenever such huge elevation differentials are adjacent, it can be awesome and educational to consider what isn't there. In other words, imagine a great, flat plain filling all the valleys to the tops of the peaks. Now imagine the erosion force of water and, later, glaciers wearing away the rock and sediment to form the valleys, leaving just the peaks as they are today. What isn't there is an immense volume of material, almost impossible to comprehend. In the case of the Le Conte Canyon, most of that material now underlies the great interior valley of California, between the Sierra and the Coast Ranges.

The area's early-summer wildflowers include shooting stars, narrow goldenrod, paintbrush, Sierra wallflower, golden stars, pussypaws, alpine aster, and crimson columbine. Wildlife includes the golden-mantled ground squirrel, yellow-bellied marmot, junco, robin, hermit thrush, western flycatcher, olive-sided flycatcher, and gray-capped rosy finch. By mid-July, many additional flower species can be found, and wildlife, especially bird species, are more numerous.

DESCRIPTION

This is not a loop hike. The route calls for backtracking along the same trail from Muir Pass over Bishop Pass, because there are no exit routes from the vicinity of Muir Pass. The redundancy is, however, more than offset by the beauty and isolation of this segment. It is easy to understand why this lonely, wild, and yet beautiful pass is the one chosen to memorialize John Muir.

The hike is classified as difficult because of the elevation gains involved. As far as the condition of the trail or ease in finding one's way, the classification would be moderate. But moderate would be misleading in describing a hike that surmounts two major Sierra passes.

Because the South Lake trailhead is near 10,000 feet, you are in the high country from the start. Glacial features are on every hand as you ascend, and lakes and tarns add their beauty. The approach to Bishop Pass itself is reminiscent of the eastern Sierra scarp, as the trail switchbacks several hundred feet up a steep face just before reaching the summit.

Your first glance westward from Bishop Pass summit is likely to take in little more than a part of Dusy Basin. Only once you've completed the descent into and across Dusy Basin can you perceive the true depth of Le Conte Canyon—a huge gash in the landscape, especially in contrast with such Black Divide peaks as The Citadel, Mount Duffle, and Langille Peak, backdrops on the west side of the canyon.

Eventually, possibly with knees knocking, you reach Le Conte Creek, where a summer ranger is usually stationed. It would not be unusual to resent the elevation you just lost, for it is a steady uphill grade all the way to Muir Pass.

Perhaps as your reward for descending into the canyon, these environs, in season, offer a profusion of wildflower species. The west-slope descent from Dusy Basin, especially near Le Conte Creek, is a favored location. Look for additional specimens between this point and the timberline along the ascent of Muir Pass.

By the time you reach Muir Pass summit, you will have seen John Muir's Sierra and experienced the same solitude, beauty, and grandeur that fueled his passion to preserve wild places.

Moisture-laden air, pushed up the deep Kings River canyons and eventually to the crest, guarantees no shortage of precipitation in this

MAP 3A

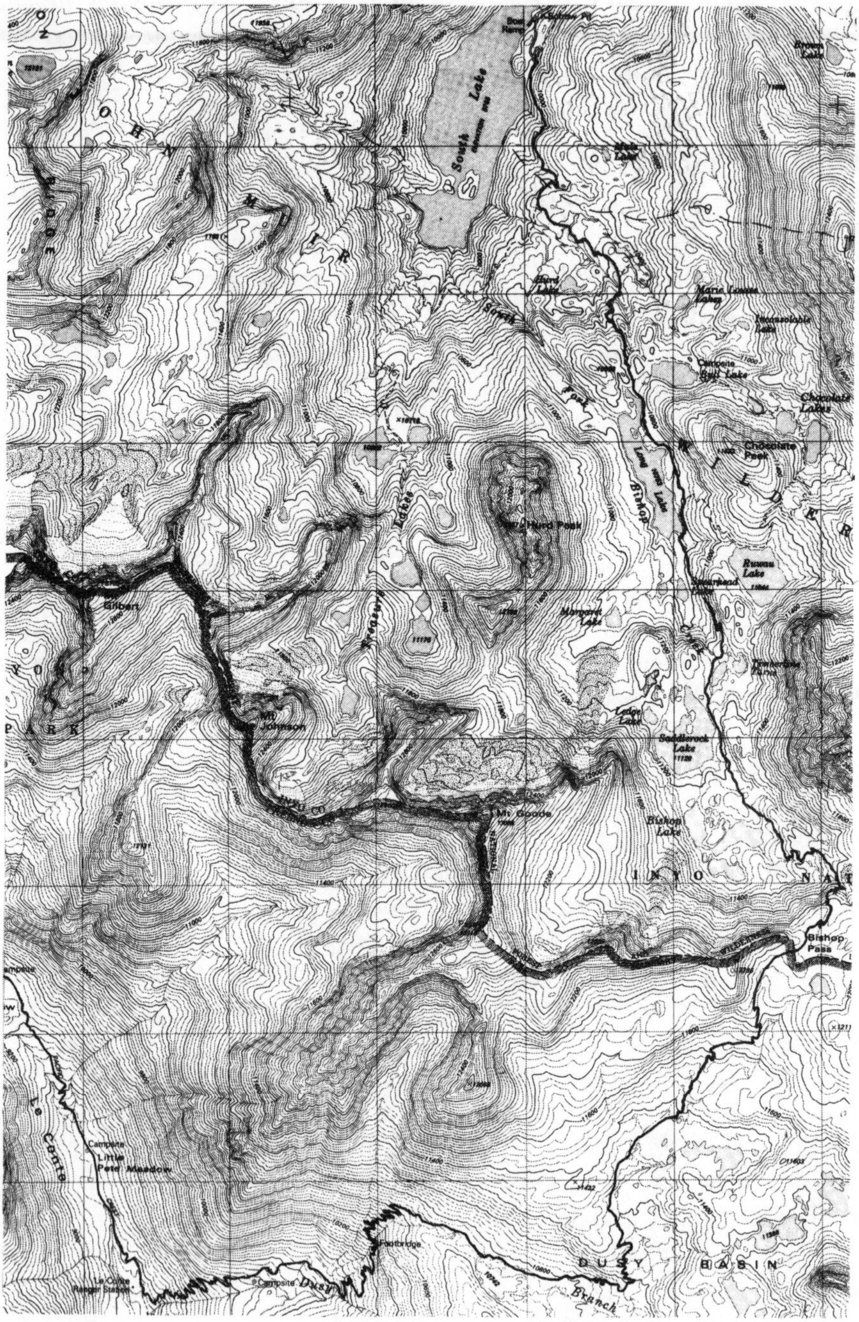
South Lake
Chocolate Peak
Chocolate Lakes
Bull Lake
Inconsolable Lake
Ruwau Lake
Mt. Johnson
Gilbert
Mt. Goode
Bishop Lake
Saddlerock Lake
Bishop Pass
INYO NAT
Le Conte
Little Pete Meadow
Footbridge
DUSY BASIN
Branch

sector. During heavy snowfall years, snow often lies in the upper slopes of Le Conte Canyon all summer. Summer precipitation, while limited as in most of the Sierra, can be more frequent here west of the crest. Avoid being caught in the open on the high passes during the frequent summer thunderstorms.

This hike is best scheduled between mid-July and late September. Check with the administering agencies regarding snowpack, as conditions can vary widely.

Black bears range over all the area covered in this hike, so be sure to bear-bag your food.

Administrative Agency: USFS, USNPS

Inyo National Forest	Kings Canyon National Park
873 N. Main Street	Backcountry Permits
Bishop, CA 93514	(209) 565-3761
(619) 873-2400	

USGS map: 7.5' series, Mount Thompson, North Palisade, Mount Goddard, California

Declination: 15½ degrees

DIRECTIONS TO TRAILHEAD

From Bishop on U.S. Route 395, turn west on Route 168 at the center of town and proceed west 14 miles to a junction with a road leading to Lake Sabrina. Turn left, toward South Lake, and proceed 7.5 miles to the South Lake trailhead, parking at the end of the road. There are toilets here, and parking for about thirty cars. Overflow parking is 1.3 miles back down the road.

TRAIL ROUTE DESCRIPTION

Leaving the roadhead interpretive sign at the south end of the South Lake parking lot at 9,840 feet elevation, you soon cross over a spring stream, intersect with a stock trail, and start climbing immediately along the lake. There is an old steam boiler below the trail. You soon pass signs warning against taking pets, wheeled vehicles, and firearms into Kings Canyon and Sequoia National Parks. Imposing peaks lie ahead as you

Golden-mantled ground squirrel

climb steadily, passing an old stock-control fence and winding around small meadows and clumps of shooting stars.

You soon reach a junction (0.8 miles from last point; 10,255 feet above sea level; 0.8 total miles) with a trail branching right toward Treasure Lakes. Continue straight ahead for 0.2 miles; then the trail levels momentarily and you cross a stream on a wooden bridge. Rising above this meadow, you can see another to your right. A sign advises that no wood fires are allowed from this point on. Past a spring stream that drains a narrow, willow-choked meadow, you ascend a series of short, steep switchbacks along the base of a granite cliff.

You arrive at another junction (1.0 mile; 10,700 feet; 1.8 miles), where a left-branching trail leads to Bull Lake and Chocolate Lakes, two spots popular with youth groups. Continue straight ahead toward Bishop Pass. Passing a small pond on a saddle, you soon come upon a larger meadow. The trail takes you along the level between a tarn and the meadow. Now you pass the shore of Long Lake on your right. The granitic rocks you walked on earlier have been replaced by metamorphic rocks, and Long Lake lies in a gouge in this colorful formation. From a small promontory, you can see a tailings pile from a mine tunnel just to

Vertical Profile of Hike 3

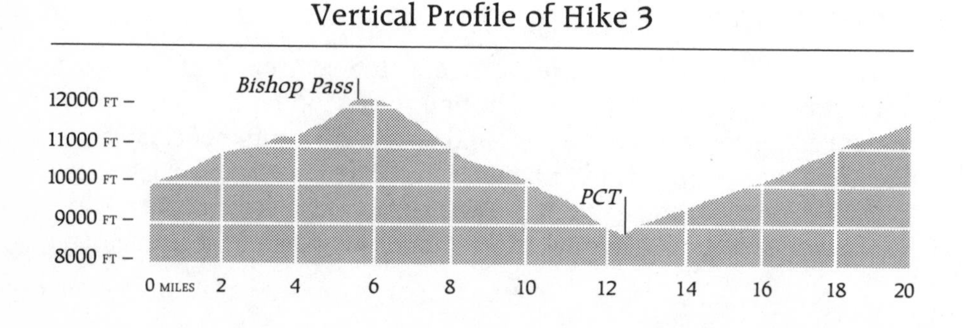

the left. More exploration will reveal the foundation of a structure on a flat area just below. This is all that remains of an early mining operation.

Returning to the shore of Long Lake, continue along the trail above the shore. You come to a junction (0.8 miles; 10,800 feet; 2.6 miles) where a trail branches left to Ruwau Lake. Continue straight ahead, negotiating a jumble of talus at the base of a cliff as you leave the south end of Long Lake. A colony of pika inhabits this talus, and you may be whistled at as you pass. Pika often whistle, sometimes moan softly, and have the ability to make a wide variety of sounds when humans intrude too closely. If you wait and don't move, you may see two beady eyes and the short, rounded ears that immediately identify the "rock rabbit."

Crossing two minor inlet streams, you pass a usable trailside camp and, just after, see narrow Spearhead Lake below on your right. A rushing stream from a cirque above and to the west flows to join with the outlet from Spearhead. You ascend a talus slope, where old trail alignments are visible. Now, 1.0 miles above the Ruwau Lake Trail junction, you are opposite Timberline Tarns on your left at 11,040 feet. Your trail closely approaches, and eventually crosses on a wood bridge, the outlet stream to Ledge Lake. Note the islands in the lake.

Traversing a subalpine meadow, you are treading on soil derived from metamorphic rock. You soon cross over onto granite, however, at a contact zone between the two. In a swale above Ledge Lake, you come across four snow course markers for measuring snow depth. Within 0.3 miles, you can see the Bishop Lakes on your right and below.

You pass a few timberline clumps of whitebark pine as you ascend over jumbled moraines to the base of the headwall to the west; then you ascend via many short, rocky switchbacks. Care should be taken here if the trail is snowbound or icy, for while this alignment allows you to ascend the cliff quite easily, some spots are exposed and a fall could be disastrous. Reaching more gentle slope now, it is an easy sandy and rocky stroll over to the summit proper (3.0 miles; 11,972 feet; 5.6 miles).

Vertical Profile of Hike 3

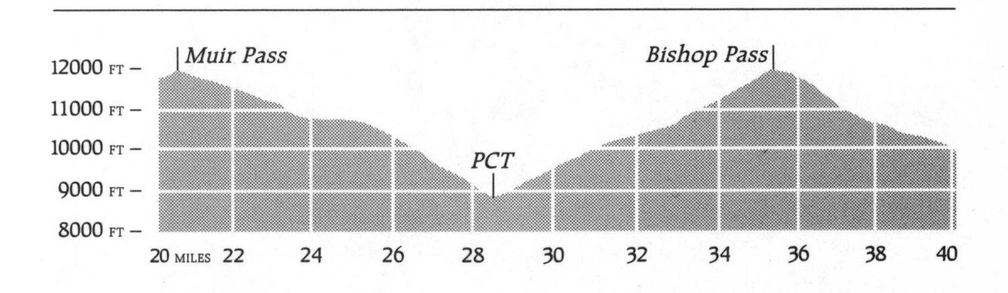

Signs at this point advise that you are entering Kings Canyon National Park. In 200 feet another advises that wood fires are prohibited in Dusy Basin, a good idea for all areas at this rarefied altitude.

An easy, sandy trail leads down off the summit. Note a small lake to your left. Mount Agassiz lies to the east, and Thunderbolt Peak, Isosceles Peak, and Columbine Peak from left to right to the southeast. You pass some small tarns, and reach a solar-powered snow-depth instrument that reports automatically in the winter to the California Department of Natural Resources. Evidently manual snow course sampling is too difficult at this location.

As you approach the bottom of Dusy Basin, you drop down through the timberline, traversing an expanse of slick rock where the trail is lined by stones on each side. You reach a junction (2.3 miles; 10,800 feet; 7.9 miles) with an old trail leading left. A sign indicates that the way you have just come leads to Bishop Pass. This junction could lead uphill hikers astray. Go to the right on the main trail.

You parallel a lakelet on the left as you traverse alpine meadows. A sign warns that gas stoves only are allowed above this elevation in Dusy Basin. There are good, but sometimes too popular, campsites in this area. At 10,690 feet elevation, Dusy Creek breaks over the edge of the basin and begins to descend in earnest in falls and cascades. The trail leaves the creek and traverses to the right, soon switching back and forth along this face.

Across Le Conte Canyon, you now face statuesque Langille Peak, which equals the Bishop Pass elevation within 1 foot. The benched basin before you, dropping in steps down to the canyon floor, is imposing as your route leads to where Dusy Creek drops down a polished granite chute. You switchback farther, pass a few lodgepole pines, then follow

Tiger lily

MAP 3B

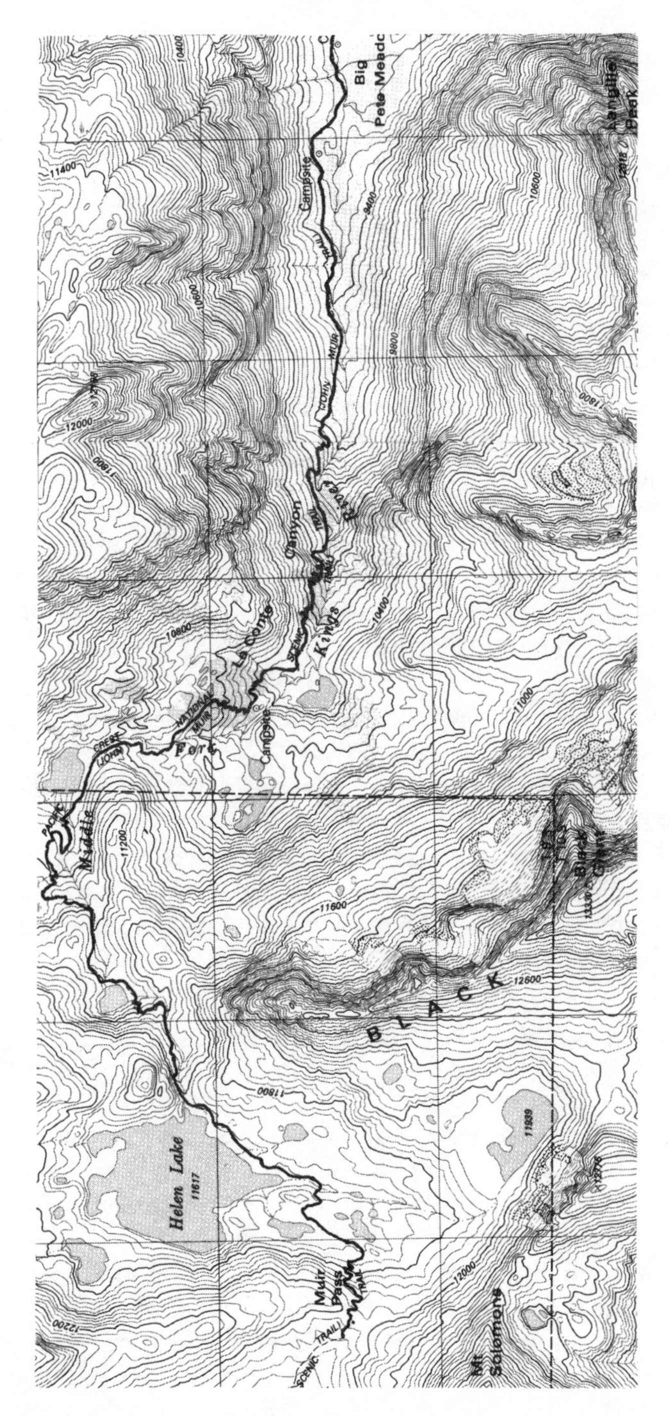
Big
Campsite
JOHN MUIR TRAIL
Le Conte
Canyon
Kings
Middle
Fork
Campsite
BLACK
Helen Lake
11617
Muir
Pass
Mt
Solomons

more fancy trail work to the foot of the cascades, where you cross on a 30-foot-long wooden bridge. Just below the bridge, at the end of a north-trending switchback, you see a waterfall that contains a waterwheel—current sent whirling skyward by an upward-slanting irregularity in the streambed.

Continuing the descent down this rocky track, you come upon a large pile of dead trees below and to your left. The roots point uphill, the trunks parallel in the usual manner of avalanche rubble. You are now standing in the center of the chute; these trees came from slopes above and below when extremely heavy snowfall in 1986 caused hundreds of avalanches in the high Sierras.

The trail takes you across the jumble, drops along a straight stretch through a thicket of quaking aspens, and passes through a forest. Soon you are descending switchbacks down an open face, with only scattered trees among chaparral. You finally reach the bottom, after passing through the remains of an old stock-control gate, and come to the junction (4.6 miles; 8,720 feet; 12.5 miles) with the Pacific Crest Trail.

A left-hand turn here would take you down to Grouse Meadows on the Middle Fork Kings River. Turn right, up the PCT toward Muir Pass. Within 50 feet you pass a trail leading left to a ranger cabin, which is sometimes occupied. There is adequate room at the ranger cabin to camp if you were so inclined, but there are more private camps a short way upstream.

The trail heads northwest up Le Conte Canyon, alternating between idyllic meadows and groves of lodgepoles. You pass a campsite restoration site beside the river, cross the meadow there, and move ever upward. You are never far from the river, which sometimes makes its presence known by the sound of rapids. At times you can see the watercourse winding smoothly through meadows in oxbow bends.

Numerous campsites are distributed along this section, usually in lodgepole groves with plenty of room for one or more tents. Wood fires are allowed here, but don't build one unless you absolutely have to, as there is not a large wood supply.

MAP 3B

You cross around the end of a small, rocky projection (4.0 miles; 10,320 feet; 16.5 miles), where the trail has been realigned, and overlook a beautiful sedge meadow through which the river winds. A gain of a few feet in elevation allows you to spot a beautiful, aquamarine lake nestled in a high-walled depression just yards south of the meadow. After another 0.3 miles, you switch around a small knob, drop a few feet, and rock hop across a creek. Shortly, you reach a lake on your right. Go straight across the outlet stream and pick up the somewhat obscure trail on the other side. The trail begins to switchback left at the base of a talus slope. Alternately ascending by switchbacks and crossing alpine meadows, you eventually climb past a somewhat incongruous sign at 10,970 feet advising "no fires beyond here."

You pass a beautiful, turquoise lake on the right, whose outlet creek (2.2 miles; 11,220 feet; 18.7 miles) runs to your left in a deep, eroded rock chute, dropping 200 feet in 200 yards. From this point, you climb and soon cross the outlet creek of Helen Lake and work your way along a confusing boulder patch for a few yards. The tread continues along the shore of beautiful Helen Lake, named for one of the daughters of John Muir. The namesake lake of his other daughter, Wanda, lies on the far side of the pass at about the same distance and elevation from the summit.

A well-engineered route takes you the rest of the way to the summit. Your first glimpse of the John Muir Memorial hut at the summit is of the unique cap on the stone chimney. A few hundred yards farther, and you are standing beside the hut at the summit of Muir Pass (1.7 miles; 11,955 feet; 20.4 miles), a fitting place for a monument to the far-sighted conservationist. Mount Solomon lies to the south and Mount Fiske to the north. At this point, you are many miles from the outside world. The nearest civilization to the southeast is at Bishop via South Lake, the way you have come.

[To the north, a return to the everyday world can be made via Florence Lake by exiting to the west, or up Piute Creek and back to Bishop via Lake Sabrina. Neither route is easy, and both are longer than the way you've just hiked.]

In mid-season, water can be found only many yards down from the summit in either direction. Campsites at the hut are extremely limited and exposed, and staying inside the hut is not really fitting, so plan to camp near Helen Lake or Wanda Lake. Either location will be austere enough from the protection standpoint but near perfect in aesthetics of the high Sierra.

You return the way you have come. This time, however, you have only one pass to surmount. The following is a brief backtrack itinerary of the trail in reverse.

Leaving Muir Pass, drop down to Helen Lake's outlet (1.3 miles; 11,520 feet; 1.3 miles), then continue the descent to where the trail is blasted into the side of the cliff (3.4 miles; 9,890 feet; 4.7 miles).

Now continue the descent of Le Conte Canyon to the ranger cabin and the junction (3.2 miles; 8,720 feet; 7.9 miles) with the Bishop Pass Trail. Turn left here and proceed up Dusy Creek, through Dusy Basin to the summit of Bishop Pass (6.9 miles; 11,972 feet; 14.8 miles). Swinging down Bishop Pass, in 5.6 miles you reach the South Lake trailhead.

4♦ LAKE EDISON—SILVER PASS—LAKE OF THE LONE INDIAN

Distance:	20.0 Miles
Low elevation:	7,685 Feet
High elevation:	10,960 Feet
Class:	Difficult
Hiking time:	16 Hours

One of the west-side accesses to the coincident Pacific Crest Trail and John Muir Trail deep in the high Sierra is via Edison Lake. This lake or, more properly, reservoir, lies northeast of Fresno, California. An optional, 4-mile-long water taxi ride adds nice variety to this hike.

Lake Thomas A. Edison was created when the Southern California Edison Company built a dam across Mono Creek in 1954 as part of their Big Creek hydroelectric project. The resulting lake is 6 miles long and nearly 2 miles wide, occupying the former Vermillion Valley. The Mono Indians summered in the valley and foraged in the surrounding forests and canyons. Today, the John Muir Wilderness boundary wraps around the lake and an adjoining preexisting road system like a glove, ensuring that little additional development will occur in this wild, remote area.

Vermillion Resort, on the western arm of the lake, is currently run by Toby and Katie Horst. As part of the services provided, the Horsts operate a water taxi that runs the length of the lake on a regular schedule and can be engaged for pickups at specified times. The Horsts can be contacted via telephone to give information on water taxi schedules. Arranging for a water taxi ride will shorten this hike by 6 miles.

Aside from those portions of the lakeshore and campground that are excluded, this hike is entirely within the John Muir Wilderness. Slightly more than a half million acres in extent, the Muir lies in both the Sierra and Inyo National Forests. Elevations run from around 4,000 feet to 14,494 feet at the summit of Mount Whitney. Characterized by deep canyons, most of them glaciated, the overall landscape is that of the typical granitic high Sierra. Beautiful meadows, lakes, tarns, and streams abound in this wilderness, which spawns the headwaters of the South and Middle forks of the San Joaquin River, the North Fork of the Kings

Like all summits, Silver Pass summit exhilarates hikers with a feeling that is much more than mere relief that the uphill climb has ended.

River, and many creeks that drain into the playas and Mono Lake in the closed basin to the east.

Lower western elevations of the wilderness support incense cedar, Jeffrey and lodgepole pines, and red and white fir, while on higher slopes, lodgepole, western white pine, red fir, and mountain hemlock are found. Whitebark pines occupy exposed ridge locations at the timberline. The familiar stratification of species holds true in the John Muir Wilderness, with only slight variations due to latitude and microclimates.

It is rare that a single trip through an area will reveal all or even very many of the flora and fauna species present. Making an early-summer hike, we noticed azure penstemon, paintbrush, larkspur, lupine, skyrocket, yarrow, narrow goldenrod, cliff penstemon, shooting stars, crimson columbine, meadow parsley, seep-spring monkey flower, wild strawberry, hound's tongue, pussypaws, snowflower, and mariposa lily. Wildlife we spotted included coyote, California ground squirrel, golden-mantled ground squirrel, Clark's nutcracker, golden eagle, raven, robin, and junco.

DESCRIPTION

This is a true loop hike that can be done in at least two ways, one making use of the water taxi at Vermillion Resort. Using this taxi service enables you to enjoy some of the beauty of being out on the waters of this reservoir. Hiking begins at the end of the boat ride at a point 6 miles from the roadhead, and hike mileage is calculated accordingly. For current information and reservations on the water taxi, it is best to contact resort owners Toby and Katie Horst at least three weeks in advance. Their year-round message phone is (209) 855-6558. Be sure to leave both your day and night contact phone numbers so they can return your call. There is no phone at the resort.

A second option is to forgo the water taxi and begin the hike at Vermillion campground, using Mono Creek Trail, which traverses along the northwest edge of Lake Edison, joining the described route at the water taxi dock. The dock is located near the northeast end of the lake and is moved as the water level fluctuates. This option adds 6 miles to the hike.

When Lake Edison is at full pool, it is only a short walk from the water taxi disembarking dock to the Pacific Crest Trail. Even during low-water periods, the distance is not much more than a mile. This fact makes the Edison Lake access to the PCT at Mono Creek unique; after only a mile of foot travel, the hiker is deep in the wilderness on the PCT.

From the lake elevation, the low point of this route, elevation steadily increases as you move up North Fork Mono Creek, and finally Silver Pass Creek, to Silver Pass on the Silver Divide. From there, you descend into a high, broad canyon where lakes bear names such as Chief, Papoose, and Warrior. These lakes are favorites with fishermen, but pressure is low because of their remote location.

You can reach this untamed remoteness after only a few miles of uphill hiking. And despite the wildness of the place, the characteristic

---

Administrative agency: USFS

Sierra National Forest	Sierra National Forest
Federal Building	High Sierra Station
1130 "O" Street	(209) 877-3138
Fresno, CA 93721	
(209) 487-5155	

USGS map: 7.5' series, Graveyard Peak, Sharktooth Peak, California

Declination: 15½ degrees

MAP 4A

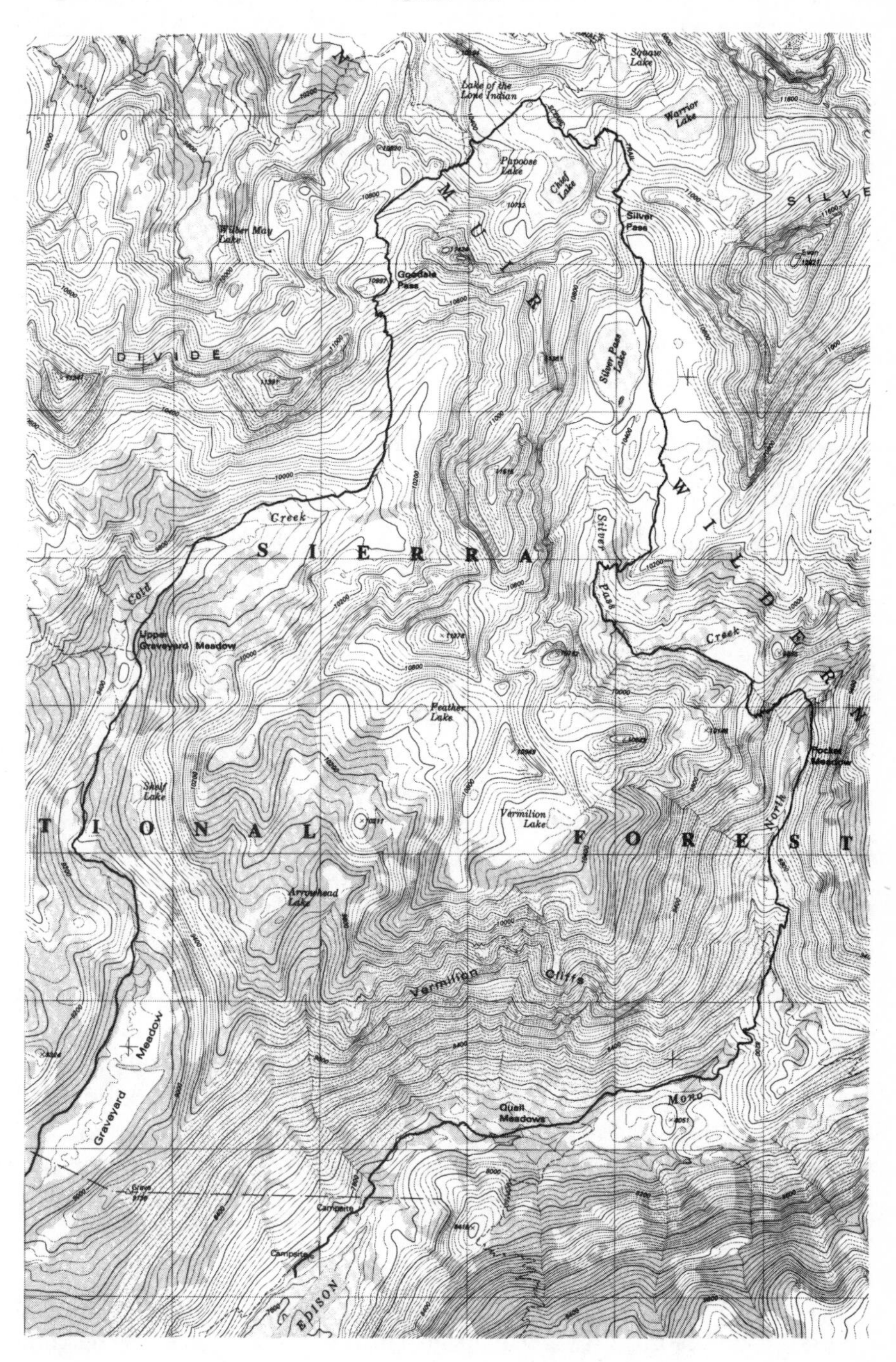

Squaw Lake
Lake of the Lone Indian
Warrior Lake
Papoose Lake
Chief Lake
Silver Pass
Wilbur May Lake
Goodale Pass
Silver Pass Lake
DIVIDE
M U I R
W I L D E R N
S I L V E
Creek
S I E R R A
Silver Pass
Cold
Creek
Upper Graveyard Meadow
Feather Lake
Pocket Meadow
Shelf Lake
Vermilion Lake
North
T I O N A L
F O R E S T
Arrowhead Lake
Vermilion
Cliffs
Meadow
Graveyard
Quail Meadows
Mono
Campsite
Campsite
EDISON

benevolence of Sierra weather enables you to enjoy it with little concern or discomfort.

From this beautiful, wild canyon, the routing leads southwest, ascending the summit of Goodale Pass, also on the Silver Divide, before dropping down into Upper Graveyard and Graveyard meadows. Along this segment you will see many avalanche chutes and runout areas. Finally, the routing returns you to the level of Lake Edison at the beginning point.

Hiking is best here from early July through mid-October in most years. Check local conditions before hikes planned early or late, as climatic variations can shift, or shorten, the good-weather window.

Black bears are common around Lake Edison and the Silver Divide. Be sure to bear-bag your food, and use the normal precaution of keeping your tent, pack, and person food-free at night.

DIRECTIONS TO TRAILHEAD

From Fresno, on U.S. Route 99, turn east on State Route 168 and proceed northeast 71 miles to the end of State Route 168 at Huntington Lake. Just north of the Rancheria Creek bridge at the end of Route 168, turn right on the Kaiser Pass road to Edison Lake. This begins as a two-lane highway that in 3.6 miles turns to a very narrow single lane, paved, with turnouts. Proceed carefully and slowly on this road, for oncoming traffic is not always visible until it is very close. The High Sierra Station of the Sierra National Forest is 12.5 miles farther. Permits are issued here.

One mile beyond the ranger station is a junction. Turn left here toward Edison Lake (straight ahead leads to Florence Lake).

In 1.7 miles, cross the South Fork of the San Joaquin River on a steel bridge, and 0.2 miles farther, pass another junction where the road to Mono Hot Springs turns right. Continue straight ahead here for 4.2 miles to a junction at the east end of Vermillion Dam. Turn left at this junction and proceed across the outboard slope of the dam to another junction at the opposite end where the pavement ends. This is a four-way junction. Make a right-angle turn to the left as directed by a sign that offers food and lodging; then proceed 1.4 miles to Vermillion Resort. A few hundred yards beyond the resort is a Forest Service campground, and another few hundred yards west is the Mono trailhead.

TRAIL ROUTE DESCRIPTION

MAP 4A

From the trailhead, if using the water taxi, it is best to take packs and hikers to the resort in a vehicle and then return the vehicle to the trailhead parking area. It is only a few minutes' walk back to the resort after parking the vehicle.

The water taxi travels from the resort, northeasterly up Lake Edison, depositing passengers as near to the upstream end of the lake as water levels allow. At full pool, this spot is quite close to the Pacific Crest Trail. During dry years, or late in the season, lowered water levels may mean an additional hike of half a mile or more. This trail narrative and mileage will begin at the upper end of the lake, at an average low-water location.

From the boat landing (elevation 7,685 feet at full pool), walk up the west bank; in a few yards you encounter the trail. Turn right on this trail, and in a few more yards you reach a signboard where use regulations are posted. Almost immediately you enter the John Muir Wilderness. There are plenty of camping sites in this area. Continuing, you cross a small stream and enter a forest of red and white firs, sprinkled with quaking aspen. Soon cresting a glaciated granite knob, you drop a few feet in elevation and begin an undulating path through the forest.

In 0.8 miles, you encounter a stock control fence and pass through Quail Meadows on wooden bridges and one long, wooden causeway. After crossing numerous spring streams, you reach a junction (1.2 miles from last point; 7,865 feet above sea level; 1.2 total miles) with the Pacific Crest Trail. If you were a long-distance hiker heading north, you would have just come from the Bear Creek Drainage some 6 miles to the southeast, and that is where the right branch leads. Turn left, toward Silver Pass. There are several good campsites near this junction with the PCT, which has just crossed sizable Mono Creek on a beautiful wooden bridge.

The trail begins to climb more seriously now. Moving northward, you soon reach the North Fork Mono Creek, which you can cross by rock hopping. Good camping possibilities exist in this area also. Across the creek, the trail continues to climb, entering a montane chaparral community generously sprinkled with Sierra junipers, ponderosa pines, and occasional firs.

At a junction (1.0 mile; 8,360 feet; 2.2 miles) with trail 29E01, which leads right to First Recess Lake, continue straight ahead on the PCT-JMT,

Vertical Profile of Hike 4

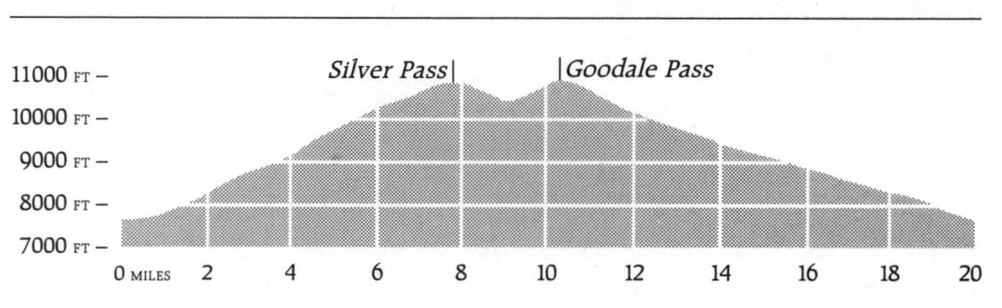

marked along this section with small PCT emblems burned into wooden blocks attached to trees.

After more climbing, you near the banks of Silver Pass Creek. Note that this creek is flowing downward on smooth granite that was planed by glaciers. The creek has done little to incise a channel since the glaciers freed it to tumble downward into Mono Creek.

Just a few minutes later, you cross a series of seeps and spring streams. A campsite lies to your left. The trail levels momentarily as it again nears the banks of Silver Pass Creek, which here takes on an entirely different character—a slow, placid ribbon meandering through a grassy meadow and willow environment.

Soon you reach a junction (1.4 miles; 8,980 feet; 3.6 miles) with a trail that branches right to Mott Lake. Continue straight ahead on the PCT-JMT, which soon crosses Silver Pass Creek. You can usually cross by rock hopping, but in early season or during thundershowers this creek can be difficult to cross. At these times, look for logs just upstream of the trail crossing. This stream rises rapidly because the large expanses of exposed granite quickly shed any precipitation.

Beyond the creek, you climb a series of switchbacks. After 0.5 miles, you cross another creek, whose flow runs out across the trail and drops down in falls to your left. The section of creek immediately below the trail has been described as "a fatally high cascade," and indeed care must be taken in crossing here in times of high water. It is unlikely that you would survive being washed off the trail at this spot. Except during early season and sudden storm periods, however, this crossing is not difficult.

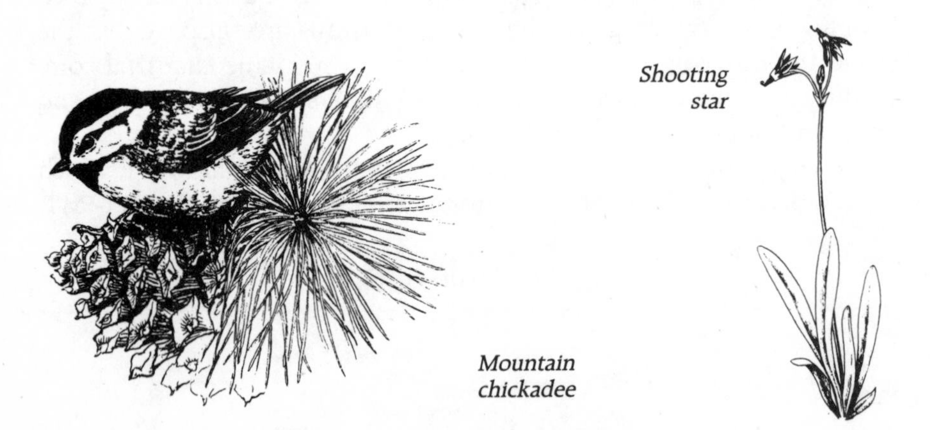

Shooting star

Mountain chickadee

More short, steep switchbacks test you above the crossing. If you look back, you can see falls and playful cascades of the creek as the water slides and drops down the rounded granite outcroppings. You get more than one view as the switchbacks point you toward and then away from the stream course.

At the top of this particular challenge you find yourself at the edge of a beautiful, grassy meadow (0.9 miles; 9,535 feet; 4.5 miles); here the formerly rambunctious stream now peacefully winds beside you. You recross the stream 0.4 miles farther. A lodgepole grove on your left provides a good campsite. Now you begin to switchback up over glaciated granite benches into a wide, U-shaped valley whose walls are nearly vertical. You switchback up these benches for 0.8 miles, then traverse the top of a low, rounded ridge of glacial rubble that undulates down the center of the valley.

You soon leave the trees for open country; a fine meadow parallels you on the right. A few minutes later, you are on top of the low ridge, with Silver Pass Lake a short distance to your left and two tarns in the meadow on your right. The glacier that carved this valley apparently melted first along the west side, depositing this lateral moraine while scouring the bed for Silver Pass Lake.

The beautifully curved north shore of Silver Pass Lake has a gravel and sand beach that invites you to take off your shoes. If the water temperature feels comfortable, this is a good spot to get wet.

Past the north end of the lake, you work upward in the thinning air to a broad saddle divide. A tarn lies immediately below on the north side. Two long, open switchbacks across the sandy hill take you to Silver Pass (3.1 miles; 10,880 feet; 7.6 miles). This pass is on the Sierra crest and marks the boundary between Inyo and Sierra National Forests. For the next mile or so, your trail passes through the Inyo National Forest.

The trail now drops off the north side of Silver Pass in switchbacks, and a beautiful series of lakes and tarns lies to your left. The closer, large lake on your right is Warrior Lake; Squaw Lake lies more to the west. Descending farther, you can see Chief Lake heading up the series on your left, while just below that is Papoose Lake.

Traversing above Chief Lake and some small tarns, you lose more elevation and reach the bottom of the switchbacks, where a use trail leads left and back to Chief Lake. The grade is easier now, and you soon reach the junction (0.9 miles; 10,510 feet; 8.5 miles) where you leave the PCT-JMT, which leads away to the right on a lofty path to Reds Meadow and the Devils Postpile National Monument. Turn left instead to Goodale Pass.

Hiking through a small, sandy saddle, you can see a beautiful tarn ahead. You pass down through subalpine meadows and reenter sparse forest near a campsite by the shore of Papoose Lake on your left. Papoose Lake is very beautiful, as are most lakes in these clusters on the north slope of Silver Pass. The whole group of lakes spawns the headwaters of Fish Creek.

You cross the outlet creek as it first leaves Papoose Lake near large boulders just below the campsite, pass to the right of a rocky outcropping, and within yards reach a junction (0.5 miles; 10,360 feet; 9.0 miles) where you turn left. The right branch would take you to Minnow Lake in 4 miles, and just 0.2 miles down that branch is Lake of the Lone Indian, which you can see below. This is undoubtedly the prettiest of the lakes here, and a fine campsite lies just off the trail by a large boulder near its south end.

Now you begin the ascent of Goodale Pass. A number of knee-straining high steps greet you as you switchback up the east side of the canyon. Soon you reach a gentler slope along a shallow, rounded gully that is partially choked with decomposed granite. Passing windswept whitebark pines, your grade eases even more and you enter a stark, granite-block world where decomposition has rounded the corners of the layered rock around your sandy, little draw.

Just before reaching the apparent crest of this draw, your trail makes an abrupt, 90-degree turn to the left and begins to ascend through a small cut in red-tinted granite. This very sandy path leads across sandy meltwater streambeds that seem out of place this near a summit. Soon you reach the summit of Goodale Pass (1.1 miles; 10,960 feet; 10.1 miles), from which you have a good view down the Cold Creek drainage.

As you switchback down from Goodale Pass you have a wonderful walk among cliffs of pink granite, as you tread upon more sandy decomposed granite. You soon work your way across a bench and down toward a long, emerald-green meadow. You drop in elevation until you reach the level of the meadow near its downstream end (1.4 miles; 10,095 feet; 11.5 miles). Note the avalanche damage to the resilient young trees here. Apparently a powder snow avalanche, moving at high speed downslope, has abraded needles and bark on these hardy colonizers.

Your tread switches back and forth and continues to descend, moving into forest for a while, before delivering you onto a grassy flat with willows and large lodgepole pines. There are good camping possibilities here near a cabin-sized boulder. Traversing and switchbacking lower along a slope with short willows, you can see more young trees along the slope on your right that were resilient enough to snap back from avalanches. The more rigid trees have been uprooted.

In less than a mile you enter a beautiful, open meadow of sedges, grasses, and wildflowers. Then the trail leaves this gem behind and enters forest again, only to break into the open soon as it crosses the head of a smaller meadow along a log and dirt causeway. Soon you reach a junction

MAP 4B

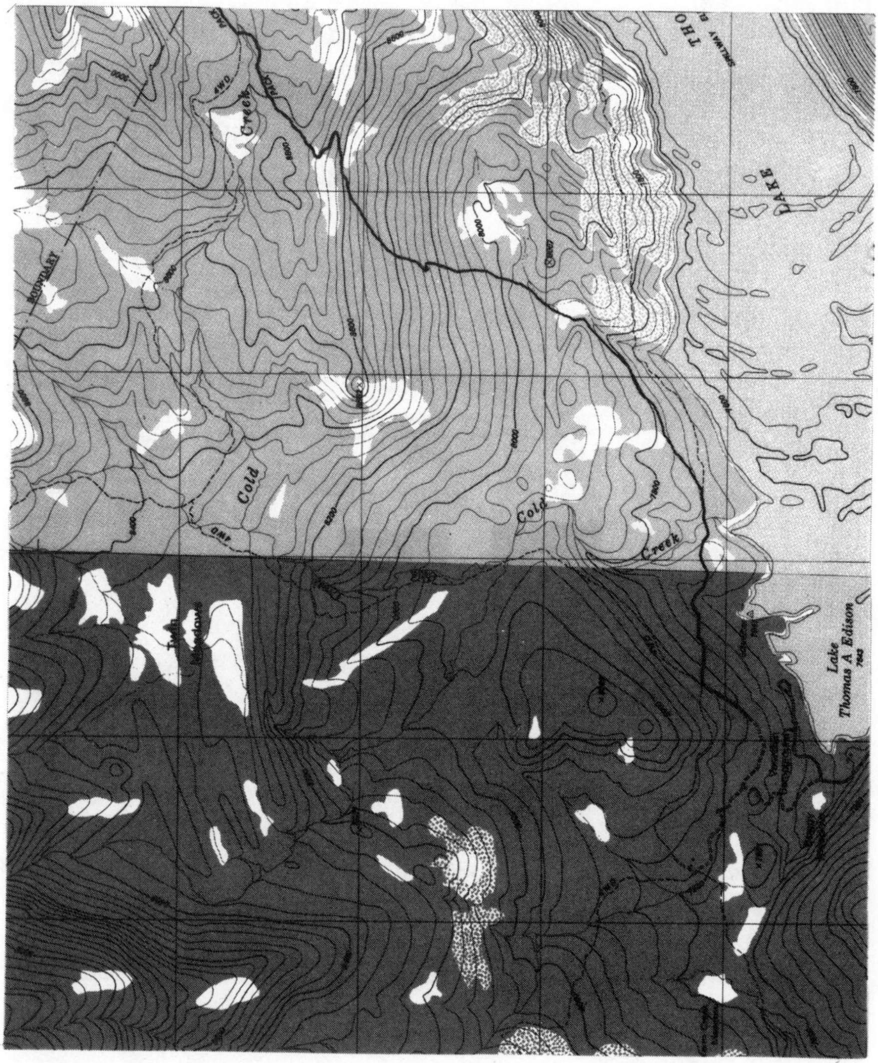

(1.7 miles; 9,425 feet; 13.2 miles) with a trail that receives much use branching right to Graveyard Lakes. Continue straight on your trail down the hill.

You follow a little creek on your right and descend through the small openings of upper Graveyard Meadows, separated by forests of lodgepole. Then, 0.4 miles below the junction, you pass through the track of an avalanche that descended from your left and deposited a jumble of uprooted trees on both sides of the trail.

Your long, downhill stride brings you to what appears to be a junction but is actually just an intersection with an abandoned trail alignment. Your trail now meanders through the forest and crosses Cold Creek, which then runs on your left. Soon you reach a confusing junction with a trail branching right. This is an old trail used by horsemen, and to help you keep on the main track, a sign points left. Take this left branch, and within yards you recross Cold Creek. You can usually do so by rock hopping or using a log.

MAP 4B

Once you reach the edge of the bench (3.6 miles; 8,800 feet; 16.8 miles) you've been following, you are treated to a view of Lake Edison through the trees. Now your trail descends on a well-chosen grade, and you can step downward easily through a forest that is mostly lodgepole pines, with occasional very large ponderosa pines. Snowflowers abound here in the duff of decayed logs in early season.

Switchbacks are present, although the slope is gentle here and it should not be necessary to switchback because of grade. As you descend, you can catch occasional glimpses of Lake Edison. An old trail alignment soon joins from your left. Continue ahead and down, and you shortly reach a 5-acre meadow abounding with wildflowers, sedges, and grasses.

The trail takes you through forest again for a mile or more before you come upon a sign identifying your route as the Goodale Pass Trail and stating that this trail is maintained by the Sierra Club under the Adopt-a-Trail Program. Just beyond the sign is a junction (2.2 miles; 7,720 feet; 19.0 miles) where you take the right fork, which leads to the trail head. The left fork leads east along the north shore of Edison Lake and is the trail you used if you did not take the water taxi earlier.

You reach a junction just before crossing Cold Creek. Equestrians may turn left here and ford the stream, while those on foot should follow the sign to an arched, wooden bridge over the flow. Yards after you cross the bridge, the horse trail rejoins your tread. Your undulating route now leads westward through mixed conifers and reaches the Mono Creek Trail trailhead (1.0 mile; 7,800 feet; 20.0 miles), the end of this hike.

5 ♦ REDS MEADOW—PURPLE LAKE—FISH CREEK HOT SPRING

Distance:	30.3 Miles
Low elevation:	6,340 Feet
High elevation:	10,560 Feet
Class:	Difficult
Hiking time:	20 Hours

Reds Meadow, adjacent to Devils Postpile National Monument, is a private resort of long standing located in the Inyo National Forest and famous for its hot-spring baths. East of Merced, California, and halfway between Yosemite and Kings Canyon National Parks, this area offers great variety and interesting features.

Reds Meadow was begun by "Red" Sotcher, an 1870 entrepreneur with a bright beard that gave him his name. The establishment probably supplied Mammoth Lakes miners with home-grown vegetables at inflated prices during boom times.

At present, Reds operates a store and accommodations, and offers trail rides and packing. The hot-springs bath house, built many years ago, is now nearly surrounded by Reds Meadow campground, which is operated by the Forest Service. The old bath house still is in fair condition, with a functioning water system and warm water. Most through hikers on the PCT and John Muir Trail over many decades have stopped at the bath house, and you cannot use these historic facilities without feeling strong ties to the past.

Geothermal areas are fascinating, and nothing quite matches soaking in a clean hot spring after a day of hiking. The Reds Meadow region also offers the opportunity to observe land formations and areas of recent volcanism. Hot magma is present not too far below the surface, raising the questions whether continued volcanism is a probable future event here and whether the earthquake fault near the town of Mammoth Lakes is in any way related to volcanism in the area.

This area, poised close to the eastern fault of the Sierra, differs from more southerly regions of the range by virtue of its volcanic and thermal activity. Volcanic eruptions here were recent in geologic terms. Red

Cones, two cinder cones that initially poured out basaltic lava, were formed just 1,200 years ago. Less than a mile apart, the twin vents ended their last activity with explosive eruptions of pumice, which formed the present features. Well-preserved craters crown each cone's summit.

Another feature is Devils Postpile National Monument, where basalt columns with three to seven sides stand vertically as they were fractured from a solid lava flow. That flow filled the entire canyon of the Middle Fork San Joaquin about 100,000 years ago. Stress fractures, formed as the lava cooled, produced these very symmetrical columns. Ice and water have removed most of the flow, leaving only a small portion, part of which is the Devils Postpile. The top surface of the formation was polished smooth by glaciation. Erosion has pitted this polish in places, but much remains.

Volcanic activity has been going on for a long time near the eastern fault of the Sierra block. Volcanos around Mono Lake, roughly 30 miles north, are up to 13 million years old. Negrit Island, a California gull nesting site in the middle of Mono Lake, was formed volcanically just 2,000 years ago and experienced additional volcanic activity less than 300 years ago. It is not likely that the region is now dormant.

Though volcanic areas are common during this hike, Sierra batholith granites are present over much of the route. In fact, in order to construct a trail passable to livestock, a footpath had to be blasted in slick, glaciated granite for hundreds of feet. The Middle Fork of the San Joaquin River and tributary Fish Creek flow through glaciated, granitic canyons. But nowhere else along the eastern crest does the PCT hiker experience close proximity to so much recent east-side volcanism.

Differences in elevation and slope aspect on this routing allow for great variety in wildflower and wildlife species. During midseason we noticed snowflower, lupine, marsh marigolds, paintbrush, larkspur,

Crimson columbine

Scarlet gilia

pussypaws, scarlet gilia, wild rose, yarrow, meadow goldenrod, crimson columbine, shooting star, penstemon, shrubby cinquefoil, tiger lilies, mariposa lily, and water buttercup. Wildlife spotted included the golden-mantled ground squirrel, lodgepole chipmunk, yellow-bellied marmot, pine marten, mule deer, coyote, junco, robin, raven, northern goshawk, Stellar's jay, white-crowned sparrow, rufous hummingbird, and white-breasted nuthatch.

Heavy snowfalls are common in this region of the Sierra. Summer weather is quite mild, and afternoon and evening thunderstorms may be less frequent here than among the higher Sierra crests to the north and south.

DESCRIPTION

This is a loop route, returning you to the same trailhead from which you began the hike. Plan to experience this hike in leisurely fashion, for the volcanic features and hot springs deserve to be enjoyed.

Beginning in the Inyo National Forest, the route also spans parts of the Ansel Adams and John Muir Wildernesses. At this latitude, the Pacific Crest Trail and the John Muir Trail are coincident. At the southernmost point, you are deep in remote country, with the only bail-out possibility a strenuous climb over the crest near Duck Lake and eastward to the well-used Mammoth Lakes group.

By the time you reach Duck and Purple lakes, you have been climbing along a definite ascending bench for several miles, with the yawning canyon of Fish Creek alongside to the south. Cataracts can be seen descending the far side of this broad, glaciated canyon, draining hidden tarns. An unusual sense of scale is provided by the view, beginning with 12,099-foot Mount Izaak Walton in the southeast and Devils Peak and Double Peak to the southwest.

The classification of difficult has been assigned for two reasons. First, there are the elevation gains involved in climbing from Reds Meadow and again from Fish Creek northward to Reds Meadow on your return. Second, there is a crossing of Fish Creek that requires either fording or crawling over the stump end of a fallen log and sliding down slanted poles. Few people have real difficulty here, but a slip or a broken pole could deposit you into swift current. The ford is not deep, except possibly during early-season runoff.

Near the middle of this loop route are Fish Creek Hot Springs on Sharktooth Creek. These springs, with water around 102° Fahrenheit issuing from a crack in a house-sized boulder and flowing into a small pool, are favorites with hikers who have the discipline to reach them. There are several campsites here on a series of benches that appear to be calciferous deposits from earlier hot seeps. The growing season for many wildflower species is extended by ground warmth in the area, and some specimens here are unusually large, due to possibly favorable ground mineralization and readily available moisture.

Angling is good in Fish Creek, as its name might imply. Dropping in small cataracts and rapids, the stream with its granitic bed may appear sterile, but fish can be seen in the clear water from the trail. Access along the stream bank is difficult in places where the flow squeezes between slick granitic banks or runs through dense alders.

Lower Fish Creek, at 6,340 feet, is warm in the summer and has good campsites, as well as remnants of sites heavily used in times past. The size of this creek mandates the substantial bridge that has been constructed.

The ascent from the canyon is across a south-facing slope in montane chaparral. Many wildflower species are present here that are not usually seen on a hike in the high Sierra. Keep in mind that western rattlesnakes may be present. Once you reach the pine forest, the ascent eases as the route climbs along Crater Creek, parallel to the Middle Fork San Joaquin in the deep canyon to the left. Glacial rounded cliffs, slick granitic expanses, and forest fingers lead you toward the end of the route.

Rainbow Falls, so named because there is often a striking rainbow in the mist at the bottom, are worth taking time to view. The rainbow effect may be best at midday or in the early afternoon. Just a short distance from the trail as you near Reds Meadow, these falls are visited by large numbers of people. The throngs of people you encounter here may seem incongruous after the solitude you just experienced in a wilderness paradise.

Administrative Agency: USFS

Inyo National Forest	Mammoth Ranger District
873 N. Main Street	POB 148
Bishop, CA 93514	Mammoth Lakes, CA 93546
(619) 873-2400	(619) 934-2505

USGS map: 7.5' series, Crystal Crag, Bloody Mountain, California

Declination: 15½ degrees

MAP 5A

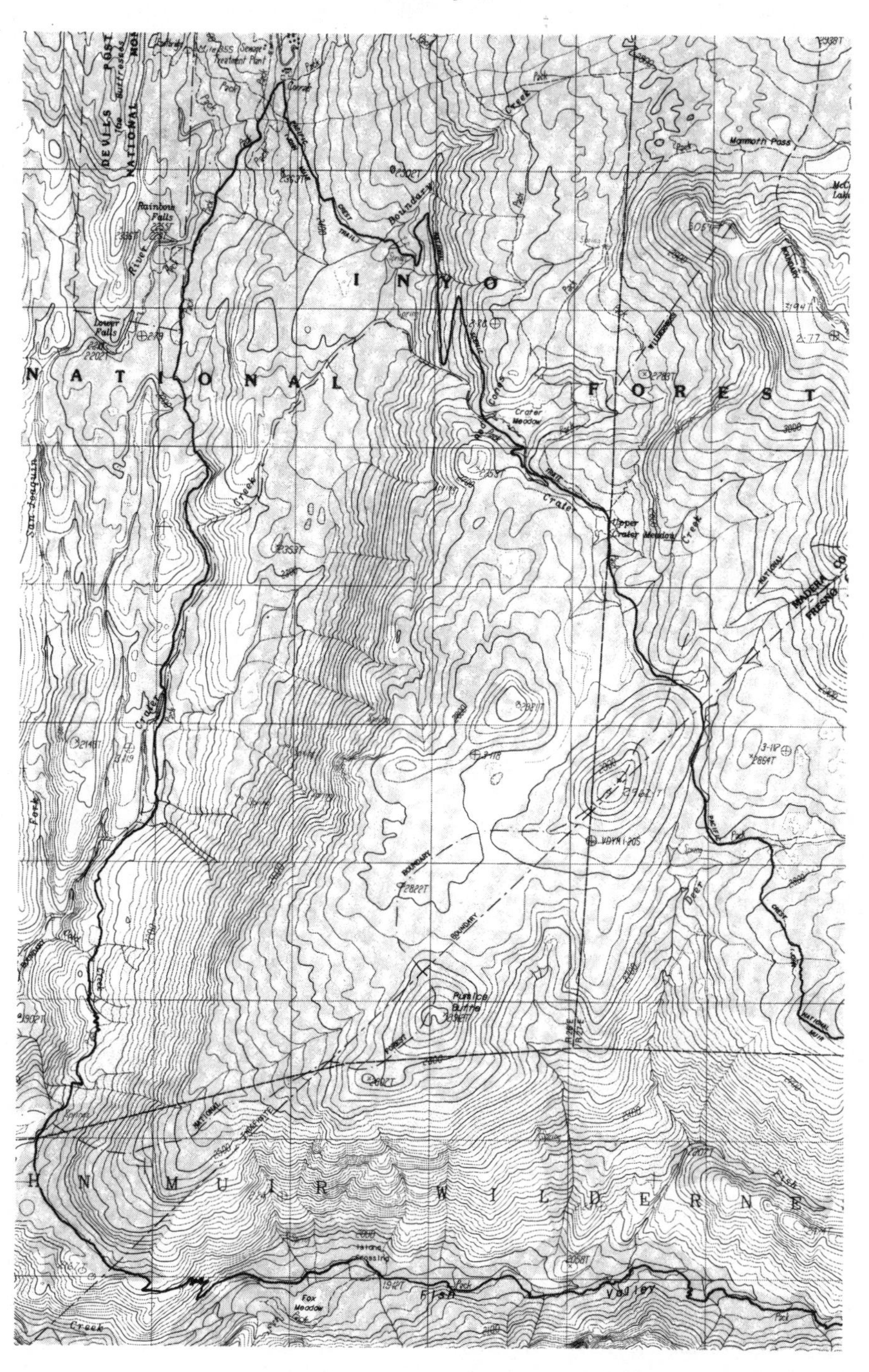
Mammoth Pass
Rainbow Falls
INYO
NATIONAL
FOREST
Crater Meadow
Upper Crater Meadow
Pumice Butte
MUIR WILDERNESS
Fish
Valley
Fox Meadow
MADERA
FRESNO
San Joaquin

DIRECTIONS TO TRAILHEAD

From the Mammoth Lakes junction on State Route 99, 39 miles north of Bishop, California, turn west on road 203 and continue 3 miles to Mammoth Lakes. At the west end of town, turn right at a stop light on the Minaret Summit road, which also leads past the Mammoth Mountain Ski Area and Lodge. Proceed past Minaret Summit, with its fantastic view of the Minarets and the Ritter Range to the west. The road narrows and descends to the north for about 3 miles before turning abruptly south at the Agnew Meadows Pack Station junction. Continue south on the main, paved road, past Devils Postpile National Monument to Reds Meadow. The excellent twenty-eight-space Reds Meadow campground is found here, as well as the resort and the Rainbow Falls trailhead.

TRAIL ROUTE DESCRIPTION

If you begin at Reds Meadow Resort and Pack Station, at an elevation of 7,660 feet, hike south from the store past cabins to the main horse corral. Pass to the right of the corral, and meet the junction with the PCT in about 200 yards.

If you begin at the Rainbow Falls trailhead, elevation 7,640 feet, hike south less than 300 yards to the PCT.

No matter which parking area you are coming from, turn left (southeast) on the PCT, which is also the John Muir Trail at this point. In another 200 yards, you will spot an old road below and to the left. A horse trail drops down to this road and also leads to the left up the hill. A few yards farther you cross this road; continue straight ahead on the PCT.

The trail takes you on a gentle ascent through mixed conifer forest, with ponderosa pine and red fir. Along this section of the trail, PCT emblems burned into oak blocks are attached to trees. Often the burned emblem is faint, but the blocks suffice to mark the route.

Look for snowflowers in this area in early season, especially where there is thick organic material around larger trees and rotting logs and stumps. Their brilliant red, unusual shapes are instantly identifiable.

The sandy tread enters Ansel Adams Wilderness (0.6 miles from last point; 7,870 feet above sea level; 0.6 total miles) and passes through an open conifer forest that now is predominantly fir, both red and white. The trail then levels and continues across small, open pumice flats before crossing a small spring stream.

Soon you come upon a spring (0.7 miles; 8,010 feet; 1.3 miles) boiling up from a 20-foot-diameter pool immediately to the left of the trail. Note the bubbling gases released periodically from the bottom. Though mineralized, the water is cold. The route switches back in a northerly direction here, and shortly you pass two spring flows issuing forth just above the trail. Just beyond, you cross an early season meltwater flow that runs on top of granite.

Traversing along a steep sidehill, you are treated to a fine view of the Minarets and Iron Mountain to the northwest and the canyon of the Middle Fork San Joaquin as it flows south to join with Fish Creek before turning abruptly west into a narrow canyon.

You can hear the sound of rushing water, but the trail first switches back north before reaching the flow. Soon you switch back again, and this time, just after a fine view of the southerly Red Cone, you reach the flow. At a junction (1.9 miles; 8,650 feet; 3.2 miles) just before crossing Deer Creek, a trail to Mammoth Pass branches left. Continue south, crossing the creek on nearby logs, and ignore the faint trail that heads west just beyond the creek. There is a large campsite here. At this point, you have just left the Ansel Adams Wilderness and entered the John Muir Wilderness.

You are heading southeast now, across a large, flat area where lodgepole pines are well established. Note the lodgepole pines and firs that are attempting to grow on the slopes of the recently active Red Cones. These pumice cones have challenged vegetation with loose surfaces and moisture that percolates immediately. Trees have managed to become established, however, and as their organic material builds up, soil is being formed.

As you pass along the left flank of the cinder cone, you can see many good camping possibilities along Crater Creek below as it flows through the flat. As you gain elevation and look back, you are treated to a view of the northerly Red Cone, its crater opening to the west. Just beyond, you again cross Crater Creek (0.4 miles; 8,800 feet; 3.6 miles). As you continue ahead, you come upon signs identifying this as the Pacific Crest Trail, placed here to prevent confusion with several old trail alignments that cross the tread. You will see many abandoned sections of old trail along this route as you move southward.

Your trail levels and approaches a beautiful grassy meadow, only recently intruded upon by short, struggling lodgepoles. Crossing this meadow on a long causeway built to prevent trail erosion, you reach a junction (0.5 miles; 8,880 feet; 4.1 miles) where a trail to Horseshoe Lake branches left. Continue south, completing your crossing of Upper Crater Meadow on more causeway. Excellent drinking water is available from the two spring flows where a tributary of Deer Creek is born near the upper end of these meadows. Look for buttercups and other water-loving flowers, depending on the season.

The sandy tread continues for 0.4 miles, then dips slightly to cross one small stream and soon another. On an easy ascent, the trail undulates among lodgepole pines. More old trail alignments are visible along this section. You cross a trickle and continue up the meadow on deeply rutted trail. Curving away from the meadow, you next cross a broad pumice flat that is actually a saddle between two creek drainages and is being colonized by lodgepole pines. Coming to the second stream, the trail follows its grassy oxbow meanders downstream until a crossing (1.4 miles; 9,180 feet; 5.5 miles) just after an old trail alignment that branches right to stay on that side of the stream. Look for deer in this area.

Soon you'll be able to spot a clear, year-round spring welling up just yards below the trail, running down among mossy rocks and wildflowers. Next you begin a descent, and undulating trail leads you out to a short section with southwestern exposure. Manzanita has been quick to take advantage of this minienvironment.

Good campsites adjoin Deer Creek (0.6 miles; 9,085 feet; 6.1 miles), which you can cross by rock hopping or on convenient logs. Campsites are on either side of the creek. Watch for lupine, shooting stars, buttercups, and other flowers in this spot. A causeway minimizes damage to the meadow as you enjoy the various flowers.

Your trail now ascends alongside a marshy meadow on your left, then through a lodgepole forest with a scattering of western white pines. Your elevation allows you a good view of the southern side of Fish Creek canyon, which we can see through the scattered trees. Much of the far side of the canyon is bare granite. If you glance back down at the trail, you'll see that the glacial moraine over which you are now treading has mixed granitic and metamorphic rock.

MAP 5B

Kinnikinnick appears in favorable places as you continue on the now eased route. You cross several early-season meltwater streams in rapid succession. At a crossing of one seasonal stream (0.8 miles 10,170 feet; 6.9 miles), you can see the massing of downed trees and other debris that indicates you are standing near the end of an avalanche track. Your trail now undulates, with little change in altitude.

On southwest slopes you can observe bush chinquapin, a partner of manzanita in montane chaparral. Look for paintbrush, phlox, and sun-loving flowers here. The trail gently descends, then soon takes the form of switchbacks and curves eastward into the drainage of the outlet to Duck Lake. It climbs again as it parallels the creek below, then crosses a broad avalanche chute that has a lot of timber debris lying about. The rocks here are interesting, and the contact zone between granitic and metamorphic rock is easily seen.

You cross Duck Creek (1.6 miles; 10,040 feet; 8.5 miles), then continue upstream a short distance to a campsite beside a large rock. After passing the campsite, the PCT switches abruptly to the right and begins

MAP 5B

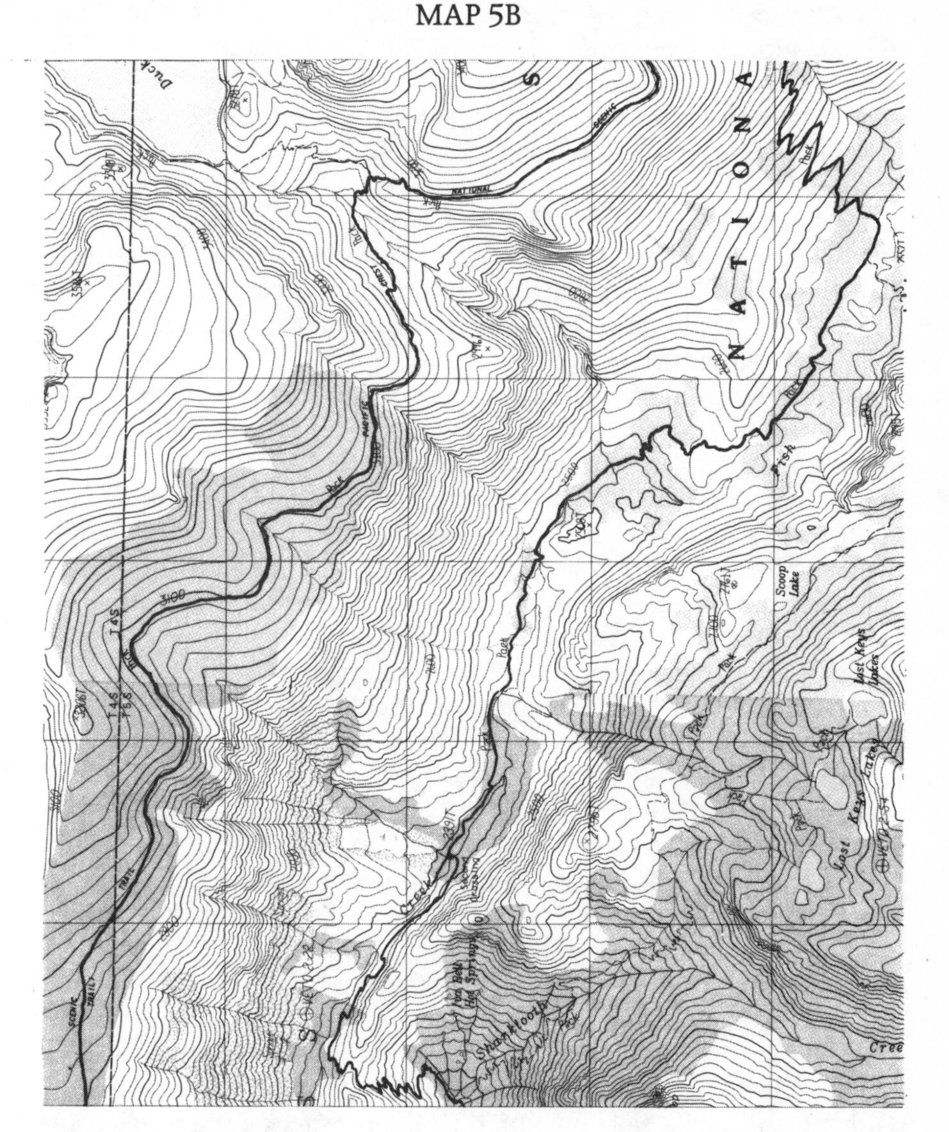

the ascent out of this drainage. You pass a junction (0.2 miles; 10,170 feet; 8.7 miles) where the Duck Lake Trail branches left. Continue on the PCT up the incline. Moving up through willow-bordered switchbacks, you turn right to traverse a small, last-gasp successional moraine left by a dying glacier. The trail now heads up the side of the mountain in serious switchbacks that eventually turn into a long, climbing traverse topping out at 10,560 feet before beginning the descent into Purple Lake. The highest peak visible to the southeast is Mount Izaak Walton, at 12,099 feet.

After descending 0.4 miles, you reach a gate with a hiker pass-through, intended to restrain the movement of loose pack animals. Your descent leads you to a junction with a trail just above Purple Lake, which leads to a camping area on the northwest shore of the lake. There is sometimes a ranger stationed here at Purple Lake.

Continuing above the shore of the lake, you reach another junction (2.2 miles; 9,920 feet; 10.9 miles) at Purple Creek as it leaves the lake. Here, you turn right (southwest) toward Cascade Valley and Fish Creek Trail, leaving the PCT as it continues southeast to Virginia Lake. Camping is not allowed in this area, but there are some fair campsites a short distance down Purple Creek.

The descent to Fish Creek traverses glaciated granite, littered with rubble dropped by the glacier. Switchbacks soon turn to an amble through open forest of lodgepole and western white pine. Soon you start to descend on serious switchbacks beginning near Purple Creek, here noisily cascading over rocks. You may spot a scraggly Jeffrey pine beside the trail, the outrider of others of its kind you'll see as you drop lower into the belt where these trees become a part of the forest.

MAP 5B

Your descent alternates between open, dry slopes with purple sage and moist, riparian ribbons where spring streams trickle downslope among thick alders. Rather abruptly you reach the level of montane chaparral, where you can spot greenleaf manzanita, buckbrush, and stately junipers.

You reach the floor of Cascade Valley at the junction (3.0 miles; 8,395 feet; 13.9 miles) with the Fish Creek Trail. Turn right (west) and continue alongside beautiful green meadows that are now mostly restored after having been overgrazed by horses in years past. You can see Fish Creek wending its way through the meadows. Looking upward on the south wall where Minnow Creek tumbles down to your level, you can begin to understand why this has been named Cascade Valley.

Within 100 yards, you reach a fine, large campsite near a granite boulder. There are several campsites on the left in the next few hundred yards, as well as the junction with the Minnow Creek Trail, which turns left. Continue straight ahead, downstream. Your track leads among lodgepole, thick in spots with gooseberry along the trail. After 0.4 miles in this wonderland, you come upon the remains of an old stock-control fence and, in minutes, another wire fence with a gate to control horses.

Now your trail leads to a beautiful falls where Fish Creek begins a cascading drop. You leave the bottom here, turn right, and gain enough elevation to bypass a steep cliff. If you look up, you can see the glacial polish on rounded cliff surfaces rising hundreds of feet above you. You are soon walking on polish and can feel the slick surface just before you drop down to near creekside.

MAP 5C

Duck Creek faces you next, a rock hop in early season only because the channel here is split into several branches. There are also logs to make crossing easier and drier.

Beyond Duck Creek you enter a stand of quaking aspen among the lodgepole pines and are treated to a pleasant meander just above the rushing cascades of Fish Creek.

You pass a series of cascades and then experience a close-up of one of Fish Creek's spectacular falls. Then the trail leaves the creek momentarily to lead into more quaking aspens. Soon you are back by the creek however, and can watch the flow slide down over granite smoothed by glaciers. The creek has not had the time, nor does it carry sufficient abrasive sediment, to cut its own channel deeply; it uses the existing glaciated surface, which is why the falls are wide and smooth flowing.

Along this stream, colorful Davidson's penstemon grows from the rocks, adding brilliant splashes of magenta to the gray of the granite.

Soon you reach Second Crossing (3.4 miles; 7,840 feet; 17.3 miles), where your trail crosses Fish Creek. The track leads abruptly to the water, and horsemen will have no trouble fording here. Neither will you, if you don't mind strong, icy current up to your knees. As an alternative, downstream 100 yards is an island, access to which is gained across the top of an old logjam. Then, from the far side of the island, tipped tree roots and two slim poles serve as a dry crossing. This spot, however, is hazardous at any season and especially so during high runoff times.

Immediately across Fish Creek your route turns right (west) and begins a series of climbing switchbacks—traverses and descents that take you half a mile downstream along Fish Creek, crossing several lively tributaries in the process. Sunny pitches alternate with descents into welcome shady forest near the creek. A series of switchbacks takes you south, ascending onto the summit of a ridge 1.5 miles from Second Crossing.

Looking to the south, you can see and smell Sharktooth Creek drainage and on the near side, upstream, spot various signs of mineraliza-

Vertical Profile of Hike 5

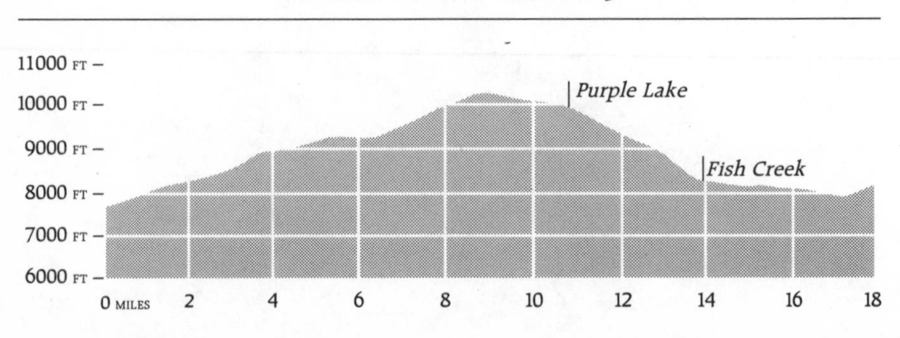

tion. Dead areas of salt grass and yellow mineral stain give away the location of Iva Bell Hot Springs. Heated deep in the earth's crust, the waters make their way to the surface along joints, or cracks, in the granite.

Crossing a saddle, you immediately enter a southern exposure basin, which has created cozy conditions for a chaparral community. Wild rose and blue penstemon dot the trailside. You abruptly enter forest 0.8 miles from the top of the saddle. Within 150 feet a use trail branches left, crosses two small spring streams, heads for a granite boulder that you pass on the right, and continues east 150 yards to the hot springs. The water, averaging around 102° Fahrenheit, issues from a fault in a large granite boulder and is channeled through a short section of pipe into an 8-foot-diameter pool. A warm soak here can give you a new outlook on your hike!

There are campsites just down the hill from the hot-springs area, and using them will reduce the considerable impact visitors have had on the immediate area.

Be sure to look at the wildflowers growing in the mineralized area. Early summer or late, you are sure to see some wonderful specimens, as many species react favorably to the minerals and warmth of the locale. Don't be surprised if you see plants in this natural wildflower nursery that are two or three times larger than in other locales.

Note also that of the cedars and the pines—the two trees competing in the area—the cedars appear to be less tolerant of the extreme mineralization, for there are many dead cedars and few dead pines. Is it possible that the former's seedlings are just more aggressive, taking root in locations that later prove to be inhospitable to them?

Back on the main trail, you switchback down through the forest, past a number of use trails that lead left up into various campsites. Soon you cross a creek and, immediately after, reach a junction (2.4 miles; 7,120 feet; 19.7 miles) where the Goodale Pass Trail branches left and your trail turns right to Fish Valley. Look for crimson columbine and vio-

Vertical Profile of Hike 5

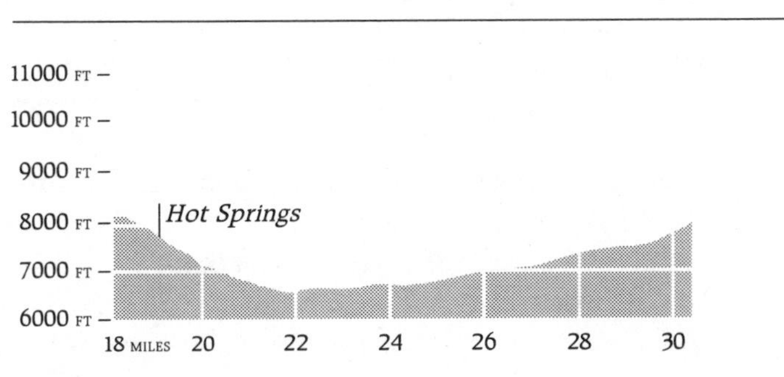

Porcupine

lets as you leave the junction. After you cross a small stream, take note of a very large red fir just to the left of the trail.

Twenty minutes later you switchback off an elevated rocky area. There is a small camping area on the right, just before the route ascends again. Shortly you are led close to Fish Creek, larger here because of tributary contribution; farther along you come still closer to the cascading flow. After passing another stock-control gate, your sandy path meanders on the level through scattered large trees, now joined at this lower elevation by white firs. Perhaps you will see skyrockets, which grow profusely in this area.

You reach a junction (2.2 miles; 6,360 feet; 21.9 miles) where the Fish Creek Trail turns left while your branch, the Reds Meadow Trail, leads to the right. You cross Fish Creek on a sturdy bridge and immediately pass through a stock-restraining gate before addressing the switchback ascent of this south-facing slope. Montane chaparral plants like this spot, and you will soon see live oak as well as California black oak trees dotting the area. Early or late season, many wildflowers grace this favorable but dry slope. You are treated to this hillside botanical garden for just under a mile before you enter the welcome shade of trees, round a corner, and arrive at the top of a granite knob for momentary relief from the climb.

Soon you pass by low, columnar andesite cliffs to your right. A mix of plants grow here, enabled by concentrated water runoff from the rock. Notice also the succulent plants growing from the rock faces.

Soon your elevation provides fine vistas across the Middle Fork San Joaquin River, with distant waterfalls to help you along the upward traverse. Before long you are meandering along a bench among mixed conifers; then you descend and cross a small flat thickly populated with mule's ears. Shortly after, you cross a sharp, manzanita-cloaked point that offers a fine view up and down the canyon.

After a series of descending switchbacks, you cross a dual-channel creek (3.5 miles; 6,770 feet; 25.4 miles). Soon you begin a traverse over sloping, glaciated granite, where your trail has been blasted into the sloping surface to provide better footholds. Completing this traverse, you enter a group of small ponderosa pines, then break out into the open and negotiate more trail blasted into granite. You round a corner to find a small stream crossing the rock slope, after which it cascades down a cliff and then slides in a wide sheet down the sharp incline into the river out of sight below. You ascend along a crack in the granite, passing a small stream on the left, which is also descending along an eroded joint in the bedrock to join a larger stream and make up the waterfall you just witnessed.

You cross several spring seeps that run out on top of the bedrock before crossing the main creek (1.3 miles; 6,830 feet; 26.7 miles) and following your sandy path along rounded granite ridges among scattered ponderosas. You leave the bench and descend into a cool forest of fir and pine, then pass solid carpets of bracken among quaking aspen.

You leave the John Muir Wilderness (0.5 miles; 6,920 feet; 27.2 miles) after crossing a creek on convenient logs. The trail ascends gently and then more steeply beside the creek. You leave the creek, climb some more, and soon pass the base of a sheer cliff just yards away on your right.

The trail undulates in a rolling ascent over pumice knobs. Large trees cast welcome shade in this area. Soon your trail surface is sandier than you might like, and you come to a junction (2.3 miles; 7,440 feet; 29.5 miles) where the left fork leads to Rainbow Falls, the sound of which reaches you plainly. By all means walk the short distance west to view these inspiring falls, which face west.

From the Rainbow Falls junction, your trail branches right, and immediately you have a choice of two treads. Take the left; the right is the stock trail to Reds Meadow. In 0.4 miles, you pass a junction where a clearly signed trail branches left, leading to Devils Postpile National Monument. Continue straight and you soon reach the junction (0.8 miles; 7,640 feet; 30.3 miles) with the PCT where you began this hike.

If you need to return to the Rainbow Falls roadhead, turn left here on the PCT, go a short distance to the Rainbow Falls Trail, and turn right to the trailhead. From this PCT junction, Reds Meadow is across the PCT and 200 yards straight ahead, up the hill.

6 ♦ AGNEW MEADOWS—THOUSAND ISLAND LAKE

Distance:	19.9 Miles
Low elevation:	8,030 Feet
High elevation:	10,115 Feet
Class:	Moderate
Hiking time:	14 Hours

"Mount Ritter is king of the mountains of the middle portion of the high Sierra, as Shasta is of the north and Whitney is of the south sections," wrote John Muir. He was probably the first person to ascend to the summit, taking a route that cannot be recommended to anyone who has longevity in mind. Muir was struck by the views from this highest peak in the Ritter Range, especially by the in-line perspective of The Minarets just 2 miles away. These peaks form the western horizon over much of the course of this hike. Of them, Muir also observed, "The most complicated clusters of peaks stand revealed harmoniously correlated and fashioned like works of art."

Just to the south is Devils Postpile National Monument. A few miles northwest lies that portion of Yosemite National Park that spawns the Tuolumne River. This hike's routing circles inside the Middle Fork San Joaquin River drainage system, surrounding that area buffering the Ritter Range from the Sierra crest, east of which lies the Owens Valley and Mono Lake.

In this region the presence of the intruded Sierra granites, and the older metamorphic rocks that lie above them, are easily observed. The Ritter Range is composed of ancient seabed sediments, metamorphosed into rock. Remnants of comparatively recent lava flows can be seen, the most notable being the glaciated flow remains at the Postpile.

The Sierra crest bends westward around the headwaters of the Middle Fork San Joaquin River. It is thought that this river once had headwaters eastward, perhaps as far as Nevada. Later, uplifting and tilting caused the abrupt eastern escarpment and an accompanying change in drainage systems.

The rustic footbridge spanning the outlet of Garnet Lake was constructed of logs from trees carried into the water by avalanches.

Deep snows are the rule in the higher elevations here. Meltwaters originating to the north of Ritter flow into the Tuolumne, and those from the east side into the San Joaquin. Just a few miles west are the headwaters of the Merced, while to the east of the San Joaquin drainage are east-flowing waters leading to the closed Owens Valley system.

Because this hike visits several life zones, it offers a great variety of flora and fauna. Late-summer wildflower species include azure penstemon, shooting star, skyrocket, pennyroyal, false Solomon's seal, sulfur flower, mule's ears, larkspur, golden star, crimson columbine, lupine, goosefoot violet, corn lilies, pink heather, white heather, and alpine goldenrod. Wildlife includes the yellow-bellied marmot, chipmunk, northern goshawk, mountain quail, white-crowned sparrow, junco, robin, and Stellar's jay.

DESCRIPTION

This loop hike, after leading through some fantastic scenery, returns to the trailhead from which the route began. From the high trail along the eastern portion of the loop, the views at sunrise have no equal; as sunlight first brushes the summits of Banner Peak, Mount Ritter, and The Minarets, they glow gold against a pink sky. Seemingly within seconds the light speeds down their bulky outlines like a liquid flow, and the emotional experience is over. It cannot, however, be forgotten.

While the very fit hiker could complete this route in one day, it is much more enjoyable as an overnight hike. With good trail throughout and reasonable ascents, the hike is classified as moderate.

The verdant traverse outbound from Agnew Meadows soon gives way to a route through sparse forest as the trail negotiates the elevated bench above the river. A long descent leads through montane chaparral before crossing the Middle Fork San Joaquin River. Look for those species of flora and fauna that you would expect to see in this community, and you won't be disappointed.

The loop route ascends through more chaparral on the southwest slope of the canyon until it reaches beautiful Shadow Lake, where a summer ranger may be stationed. The Shadow Lake area has been extremely popular in the past, but now many of the overused areas are closed for restoration and usage seems to be more reasonable. It is best not to camp here so that the restoration has a chance to take hold.

Above Shadow Lake, a lodgepole and red fir forest blends into subalpine as the trail crests a ridge and drops down to Garnet Lake, a body nearly 2 miles long occupying a glaciated basin. Banner Peak, only a mile to the west, glowers over the basin when cloud-shrouded, just as it smiles benevolently in the sunshine. Beyond, another ridge crossing leads past striking Ruby Lake, notable for its coloration and for a vertical cliff that drops straight into the water.

At first sight, Thousand Island Lake appears to occupy a basin much like that of Garnet Lake. There is one difference: The former is circled on the north by Agnew Pass and Island Pass, both on the Sierra crest divide. The wide, shallow, glaciated basin of Thousand Island Lake will test your depth perception. The many islands in the lake may make it appear to be much larger than it actually is.

Traversing west from Thousand Island Lake, the route soon leads onto the high trail. A more or less continuous ascent, first through tarns and forest fingers, leads onto the northeast slope of the drainage. The slope has direct southwest exposure, and plant communities that nor-

---

Administrative agency: USFS

Inyo National Forest
873 N. Main Street
Bishop, CA 93514
(619) 873-2400

USGS map: 7.5′ series, Mammoth Mountain, Mount Ritter, California

Declination: 15½ degrees

MAP 6A

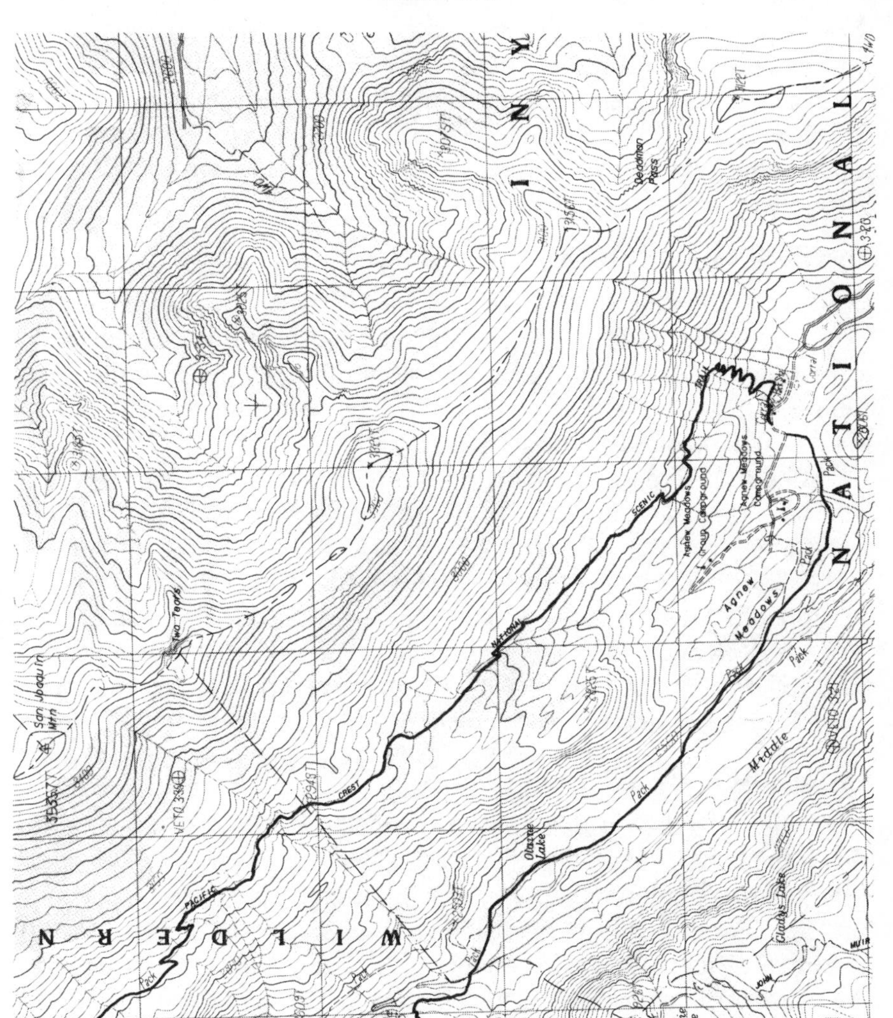

mally would be found at lower elevations are present here. You can experience unforgettable sunrise views of the Ritter Range from anywhere along this segment of the trail.

The near-timberline traverse of this open mountainside is thrilling because of the 180-degree view. You will be able to observe geographic features from different perspectives as you make your way along the trail. You also can readily observe spring flows that begin as seeps from the hillsides near the trail, then tumble downslope while eroding deeper and deeper channels, finally carving deep gullies well below the trail.

The hiking season recommended for this segment is from July 1 through early October, although climatic variations can shorten or lengthen the good-weather window.

Black bears here have been educated in Yosemite, so take care to bear-bag all food. The balanced system, using two bags, is probably best. It has been said that sophisticated Yosemite bears can tell the difference between a square knot and a bowline.

DIRECTIONS TO TRAILHEAD

Northbound on Route 395, 39 miles north of Bishop, California, turn left (west) on Route 203 at the Mammoth Lakes Junction and proceed 3 miles to Mammoth Lakes. Southbound on Route 395, 29 miles south of Lee Vining, turn right (west) on Route 203 and proceed 3 miles to the town of Mammoth Lakes.

Continue through the town of Mammoth Lakes to the west end stoplight and intersection with road 103 to Devils Postpile National Monument and Reds Meadow. Turn right on road 103 and go 8.2 miles to the junction with road 3555 to Agnew Meadows. Turn right on road 3555 and proceed 0.4 miles to the trailhead parking lot. If this lot is full, there is an overflow parking lot a few hundred yards farther. Both parking lots have toilets and piped water. Also at Agnew Meadows is a twenty-two-space Forest Service camp with piped water.

TRAIL ROUTE DESCRIPTION

From the main parking lot, take the trail signed "Shadow Lake," which also is the High Trail route of the Pacific Crest Trail. You soon pass by the overflow parking lot and shortly thereafter can see old fencing posts as you cross the end of Agnew Meadows. Your wide tread crosses a spring stream, and soon you are meandering through a lodgepole forest. Note the metamorphic rock outcroppings on your right. You reach a junction (1.1 miles from last point; 8,260 feet above sea level; 1.1 total miles) where you leave the Pacific Crest Trail as it turns southward. Turn right onto the River Trail, and you soon are traversing along the edge of the canyon on your way to the river below. Big leaf manzanita and a montane chaparral community find this west-facing slope to their liking.

You cross a ledge of gray schist and reach the river bottom, where the elevation is 8,030 feet, the low point on this hike. Crossing a small seasonal stream, you now begin a gentle upslope while paralleling a small stream on your left along which grow tall shooting stars.

Olaine Lake, rimmed with willows and alders, appears on your left just beyond a good camping area. Leaving the lake, you pass through a grove of quaking aspens and enter a mixed forest of red fir, mountain hemlock, and lodgepole pine.

MAP 6B

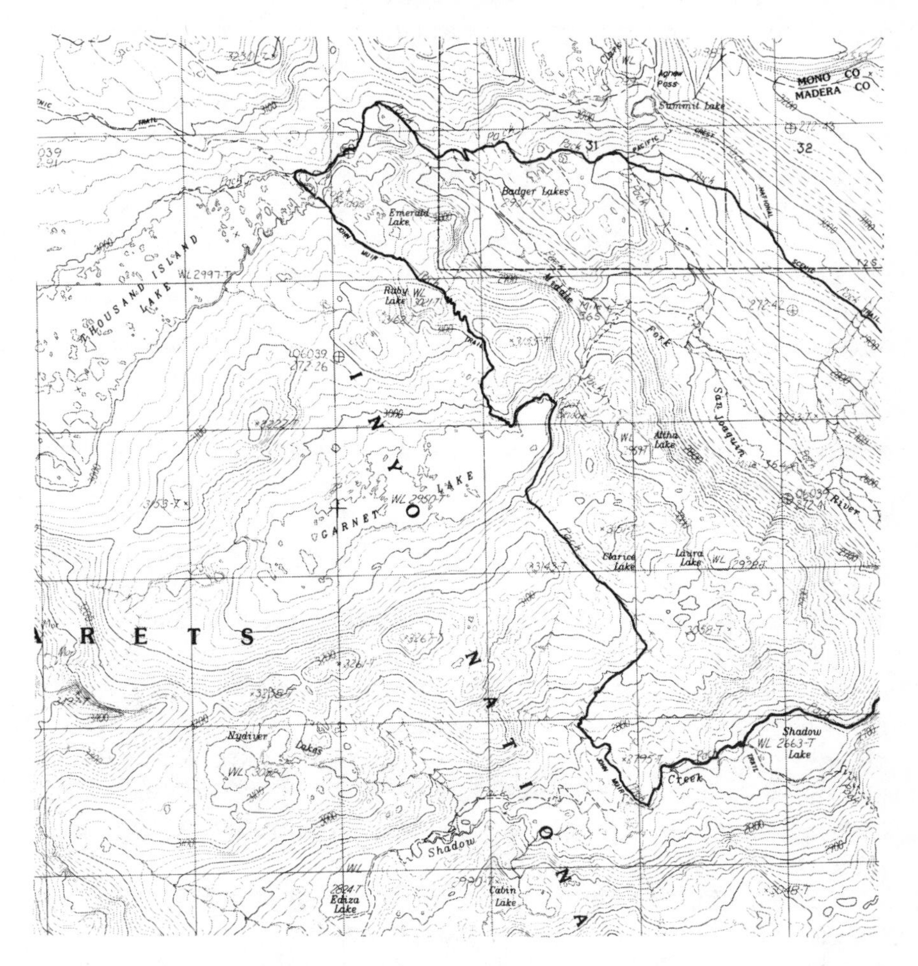

At a junction (2.4 miles; 8,070 feet; 3.5 miles), you turn left on the Shadow Lake Trail, while the River Trail continues up the canyon. The wide track makes a short dip and then narrows as you head toward the river, which you can now hear to your left. The dry, sandy bottom is an excellent spot for many wildflower species.

Soon you pass between large juniper trees on either side of the trail. A small campsite lies to your left. You now approach the San Joaquin River, lined with cottonwoods and quaking aspen. Your trail takes you across the river on an arched timber bridge, then continues downstream. In 100 feet, it switches back to the right and ascends a slope. Note that here sage and wild currant share the same habitat, along with manzanita and buckbrush. Wildflowers favor this slope.

MAP 6B

As you climb upward along the canyon side, dotted with a number of picturesque Sierra junipers, you get a better view of Olaine Lake below. Notice the resistant spine of rock that the glacier carving this canyon was unable to remove; this spine splits the canyon bottom in two at this point.

Switching higher, you can see an avalanche chute on your side of the canyon, just downstream, where trees have been torn from the slopes above and carried into the bottom. Soon you come upon a series of small but beautiful cataracts descending through glacier-polished surfaces of upended metamorphic layers. Originally accumulated on the bottom of an ancient sea, these rocks were altered by heat and pressure, uplifted and folded, and finally ground smooth during the last ice age.

Passing by the upper series of cataracts, you get an eyeball-to-lake-level view of Shadow Lake, just yards ahead. Once you reach the outlet stream of Shadow Lake (1.2 miles; 8,740 feet; 4.7 miles) where, in early season, the rainbow trout spawn in the outlet gravels, you can see an area across the creek where camping overuse in the past has contributed to a camping ban around the lake. The approved camping area is on the south side of the inlet stream. A ranger is sometimes present at Shadow Lake.

The beauty of this spot, rimmed by high peaks, engulfs you as you traverse along the north side of the lake. Near the lake's upper end are many more sites where camping privileges were abused and that are now off limits. You soon reach the inlet creek and then a junction where a trail (0.6 miles; 8,765 feet; 5.3 miles) to the left leads over a bridge to the camping area, dead-ending at Rosalie Lake. Continue up the hill to the right.

The attractive camping area on the flats below is also off limits. Your trail ascends, levels momentarily, and soon gives you a close look at falls to your left. Note that the restoration efforts on the flat below are allowing a return to a more natural state. There is, however, a camp table placed there.

Now, beside the creek cascading over boulders and ledges, your trail continues ascending to a junction (0.7 miles; 8,980 feet; 6.0 miles) where

Vertical Profile of Hike 6

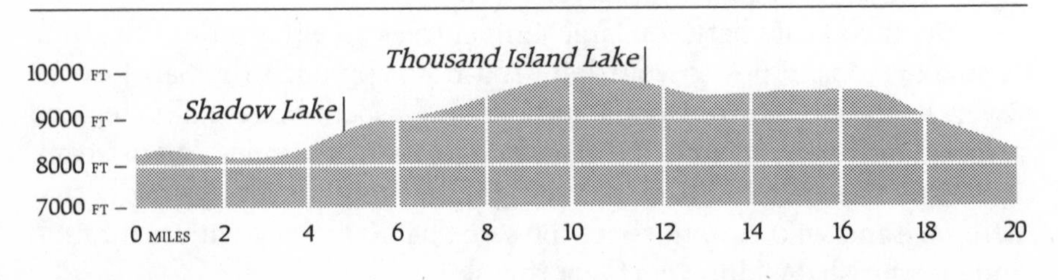

Mountain quail

the left branch leads to Ediza Lake. Turn right and continue along on the John Muir Trail. At this spot, it is okay to camp to the right of the trail in the small grove of lodgepole pines. Just beyond, you pass a small meadow on the left where Shadow Creek meanders in an almost placid flow. A few steps later, you enter a grove of large lodgepoles, with a few mountain hemlocks, which do not achieve large size at this elevation.

You pass a nice camping site on your left as the well-routed trail ascends the hill, taking advantage of natural benches where lodgepoles provide shade. You have an excellent view of a portion of The Minarets behind you. You can see the highest level reached by the glacial ice; everything below that level is rounded, while above, untouched by the grinding ice, projections are jagged and sharp.

You cross a willow-lined seasonal stream and shortly thereafter, creeklet. Soon you pass through the timberline and ascend along a meadow, where causeways of stone and earth help alleviate erosion.

You crest a small pass with a tarn on the far side and are treated to long-ranging views from this 10,060-foot spot. Now, dropping off the summit, you pass the tarn and can see wind-contoured whitebark pines along the exposed ridges; then Garnet Lake comes into view ahead. Imposing Banner Peak and Mount Ritter loom at the lake's west end.

Soon you arrive at the water's edge, where a use trail made by fishermen leads along the shore. You come to a junction (3.2 miles; 9,680 feet; 9.2 miles) a few yards before the outlet creek to Garnet Lake. This trail branches right over a carved gouge in the glaciated rock just 30 feet after crossing onto the surface and leads to the river trail below. Fifty feet beyond, your trail crosses the outlet creek on a bridge made of logs originally carried into the lake by avalanches.

Bear left along the opposite lakeshore. A campsite that is too close to the water lies to your left. Extremely limited camping is possible farther back among the trees.

Now you ascend along a recently reconstructed trail past a small meltwater pond. You come upon a use trail 0.4 miles from the creek that branches left, back toward the lake and possible camping. Continue on your track, which, just 0.2 miles beyond, crosses a pass in a narrow slot at 10,115 feet elevation. A short distance beyond, you can see Ruby Lake below to the left. A fine campsite lies to your left as you descend toward the water. Here a carved wood sign identifies your trail as the John Muir Route.

The vertical headwall of Ruby Lake apparently continues down far beneath the surface, causing the lake to have a deep coloration—not red, however, but blue. Soon you cross the outlet creek (1.5 miles; 9,895 feet; 10.7 miles) after passing a campsite on your right. You climb a bit, traverse along the north shore of Ruby Lake, climb a minute more, and then pass just west of Emerald Lake, which lies in a shallow depression.

You cross the outlet stream from Thousand Island Lake, and a short distance beyond, you reach a junction (0.9 miles; 9,830 feet; 11.6 miles) with the PCT. The left branch leads to Island Pass. Take the right branch, also the PCT, toward the River Trail and the High Trail.

Old trail alignments are visible as you follow along Island Creek for a while, then leave the creek to wend around a small melt pond and meander among alpine meadows crossed by spring streams. Descending a west slope among large trees again, you reach a junction (1.1 miles; 9,570 feet; 12.7 miles) where the River Trail branches right into the canyon along the San Joaquin River and the PCT High Trail continues straight ahead.

[The River Trail is an alternative here. You could turn right onto it and drop down into the canyon 5 miles, passing the Shadow Lake Trail and ascending to the top of the canyon rim to meet the PCT, and then retrace your steps 1.1 miles back to Agnew Meadows.]

Continue straight ahead on the PCT High Trail and begin ascending the ridge to a junction (0.3 miles 9,645 feet; 13.0 miles) where the left branch trail goes to Clark and Summit lakes. Again, continue straight ahead on the PCT. Soon, on a fledgling ridge that runs right, you can see a small lake and campsites. You pass other small ponds, one at the base of an 80-foot-high cliff on your left.

After crossing a small meadow filled with corn lilies, you reach a junction (0.6 miles; 9,520 feet; 13.6 miles) where the left branch also goes to Summit Lake, then to Agnew Pass in 0.5 miles. The right-hand fork drops down to the River Trail. Continue straight ahead on the High Trail, which passes through a mixed-age lodgepole forest and soon crosses above a small meadow containing a snow course depth marker. There are lots of wildflowers here, and the scent of wild onions is in the air.

The slope here is an incongruous mix of sage and bush willow. Above, on the long, open slope, the predominant plant is sage. If you look across the canyon, you can see the outlet creek from Garnet Lake cascading down the granite surfaces toward the river, and you can hear it plainly as well. In a short time you reach yet another junction, where a trail branching left also leads to Clark Lake. There is a suitable campsite at this junction, and water can usually be found in one of the spring streams that originate just above.

Out in the open now, you have a 180-degree view of all the peaks west of you from south to north. Your trail crosses patches of rock that are fissured in a honeycomb pattern and resemble cobblestones, the result of special cooling of molten material causing vertical fractures along columnar lines.

You cross numerous freshets that spring forth from the slope above and develop gullies as they run toward the river far below. This entire slope is one large wildflower nursery, and many varieties are found here all season long. Before long, you come to a surprise series of switchbacks that takes you to a bench higher on the slope. Entering patches of quaking aspens, you soon reach a short segment where your trail heads straight toward Shadow Lake across the canyon. Take a moment to admire the view of this handsome lake and the rushing outlet stream. Clearly visible are the switchbacks you traversed earlier on your climb out of the canyon.

Your open-slope traverse ends as you enter forest (3.3 miles; 9,620 feet; 16.9 miles) again and soon pass a use trail that leads a few yards out to the cliff edge on your right. From this overlook you can again see Shadow Lake and also in early season a long, thin cascade that descends to the river 0.5 miles south of Shadow Creek. Soon you are descending along a small stream on your left. You turn into a gully, cross the stream, and continue your relentless drop.

Lower still, you reach a sign that welcomes uphill hikers to the backcountry at 8,795 feet elevation. Crossing another spring stream, you lose more elevation and can see a portion of Agnew Meadows below. Your route next begins a series of sandy switchbacks along an open hillside, below which you can reenter the trees. Just inside the forest, there is a group of unusually large red firs. A little observation will reveal that this spot has long been home to these behemoths, for on the ground are many rotted logs in various stages of decomposition, and younger trees are also evident.

Before long you cross a water line that takes water down to the stables at Agnew Pack Station, which you can see now on your left. Within minutes you reach the trailhead parking lot (3.0 miles; 8,330 feet; 19.9 miles).

7. TUOLUMNE MEADOWS—VOGELSANG—LYELL FORK

Distance:	21.0 Miles
Low elevation:	8,660 Feet
High elevation:	10,590 Feet
Class:	Moderate
Hiking time:	14 Hours

To most, Yosemite National Park means "The Valley," with Half Dome, waterfalls, and giant sequoias; to others, it means Tuolumne Meadows and the high country. The John Muir Trail begins in Yosemite Valley, then crosses through Tuolumne Meadows, there joining the Pacific Crest Trail as both wend their way, nearly always coincident, 200 miles south to Mount Whitney.

John Muir explored much of Yosemite, and his fervent efforts to conserve it were pivotal in 1890, when the first preservation steps were taken to protect what is today 1,189-square-mile Yosemite National Park. With elevations from 2,000 to more than 13,000 feet above sea level, as well as its glaciers, lakes, streams, and rivers, Yosemite deserves the reverence in which Muir held it. The park now holds 200 miles of roadways and over 700 miles of trail.

Park geological features have the same origin as other high Sierra areas: Sediment layers built up beneath an ancient sea were folded and twisted and thrust up above sea level. Molten rock welled up beneath the sedimentary crust but cooled gradually into granite without ever reaching the surface. Erosion, from water and then glaciers during the ice age, wore away the surface, while at the same time the granitic, sediment-capped block was being uplifted and tilted. Glaciers were responsible for the finish carving of most of the present canyons and lake beds, smoothing monoliths and quarrying the sides of peaks.

The Tuolumne Glacier, spawned on the slopes of Mount Dana, Mount Lyell, and Donohue Peak to the south, carved out the largest subalpine meadows in the Sierra before moving westward to gouge the Grand Canyon of the Tuolumne and Hetch Hetchy Valley. Hetch Hetchy Reservoir today inundates this northern twin to Yosemite Valley.

Heavy foot and pack animal traffic motivated the Park Service to design and construct a stone-and-earthen causeway across the fragile meadows near Vogelsang camp, 10,000 feet up in Yosemite National Park backcountry.

The routing for this hike begins at Tuolumne Meadows, following the Pacific Crest Trail/John Muir Trail up the Lyell Fork of the Tuolumne River. The route traverses the beautiful, nearly level meadow for a short distance, then abruptly ascends Rafferty Creek to Vogelsang High Sierra Camp.

Vogelsang came into existence in 1924 in a location along the shore of Booth Lake. The marshy location proved undesirable because of water supply and mosquito problems, and in the early 1930s a new site was selected at a higher elevation near the junction of Rafferty, Vogelsang, and Lyell trails. Moved to its present location in 1940, the camp lies on Fletcher Creek a short distance downstream from Fletcher Lake. Vogelsang and Fletcher peaks provide the majestic background for the site.

A pass, peak, and lake were all named in honor of C. A. Vogelsang, who presided for a period over the California Board of Fish and Game. A. G. Fletcher, who directed much of the stocking of trout in Yosemite, is commemorated by a lake, peak, and creek.

Vogelsang is one of several Yosemite High Sierra Camps presently operated by the Yosemite Concession Services Corporation. Designed to facilitate a hiking loop, these camps are located from 8 to 10 miles apart and offer meals and accommodations by reservation. Lodging is dormitory-style in tent cabins, and hot showers are provided. Breakfast and dinner are served in a central dining room, and box lunches are available if ordered the previous day.

High Sierra Camps also offer a limited meals-only service by reservation. Information is available from the High Sierra Reservations Desk, telephone (209) 454-2002. You may want to hike to Vogelsang and camp nearby but use the meal services.

The close proximity of several lakes, including Fletcher, Booth, Vogelsang, Hanging Basket, and Townsley, stirs the interest of fishermen. The high vantage point of this routing gives you a view down the Merced River drainage toward Yosemite Valley. Marmots sun themselves, and golden-mantled ground squirrels beg for favors, which you should steadfastly withhold.

A short climb through a narrow pass is all that's necessary to again enter the Tuolumne watershed near Evelyn Lake. The route then drops into the forested zone underlying the subalpine, from which it descends into the Lyell Canyon. From that point, the trail follows the lush, green valley bottom, cut by wandering bends and oxbows of the Lyell Fork, back to Tuolumne Meadows.

Does it seem incongruous that John Muir once herded sheep in these same meadows? Perhaps it was the destruction of fragile subalpine meadows by thousands of sheep, which Muir sometimes called "hooved locust," that helped him decide that Yosemite must be preserved.

On a scouting trip in late summer, we saw twelve species of wildflowers in bloom, seven bird species, and four small mammals. How does this compare with what you saw?

DESCRIPTION

This hike is a loop, backtracking over only 2 miles of the PCT/JMT between Rafferty Creek and Tuolumne Lodge. If suggested as a day hike, which it is not, this hike would be classified as difficult by virtue of the ascent to and descent from Vogelsang. As an overnighter, the route is moderate. The trail is excellent except for a short rocky section east of the ridge before it drops into Lyell Fork.

As soon as you begin the ascent up Rafferty Creek, you'll be able to sense that this hike will be different. Whether or not you have made a reservation to take meals at Vogelsang, it is exciting to approach this camp, which has been touted for many years as the epitome of Yosemite High Sierra Camps.

Though the ascent keeps your mind on the climb, you won't be able to help but notice that the route is passing through one life zone and into another. Trees become smaller, the forest more open, and finally, about the time the gradient begins to ease, subalpine meadows appear. Soon you come to a causeway of stone and earth built to protect the fragile meadows from trail erosion. Several old, eroded trail segments here have been restored and are almost indiscernible.

At Vogelsang Camp, the stone building and tent cabins cluster together on a gentle, boulder-clad slope. A haven to some and a blasphemous development to others, the camp does make it possible for many people to visit the wilderness who otherwise would be unable to experience it. If you care to indulge in the luxury of hiking with a lighter load, the camp offers the way to do this if you can obtain reservations.

Vogelsang is in the Merced drainage. Just upstream from Fletcher Lake is Tuolumne Pass; east of this pass, water flows into the Tuolumne drainage. Cresting the ridge through a narrow slot, this summit marks the extent of wandering by many Vogelsang visitors. By the time you reach open, bleak Evelyn Lake, you have regained solitude.

East of Evelyn Lake the route crosses a granitic ridge, where whitebark pines struggle against the wind and harsh exposure. The trail descends from this ridge in many switchbacks, until it joins the PCT/JMT along the Lyell Fork in the middle of Lyell Canyon.

Fishing is popular in Lyell Fork. Trout often can be seen in the clear water, and this means that the trout also can see the fishermen. The river passage through this beautiful meadow is generally flat and creates a very pastoral scene.

Winter snows are heavy in this region. Even though little of the higher-elevation trail is shaded by forest canopy, patches of snow can linger well into the spring. Travel is usually possible by July 1, while early snowstorms can close trails as soon as mid-October.

Administrative agency: USNPS

Wilderness Permits	High Sierra Camp Reservations
Wilderness Office	Reservations Desk
P.O. Box 577	(209) 454-2002
Yosemite, CA 95389	

USGS map: 7.5′ series, Tioga Pass, Vogelsang Peak, California

Declination: 15 degrees

Mosquitoes can be troublesome here in the early season, so consider using repellent. Sunscreen and sunglasses should also be used because, as with any high-elevation locale, ultraviolet rays are intense.

Yosemite is the grad school for black bears, and these animals are apt pupils. Expect your food supply to be in jeopardy. Don't set your pack down and walk away, even during daylight; it may not be there when you return a few minutes later. These bears are trapeze artists and knot specialists, so be sure to hang your food properly.

DIRECTIONS TO TRAILHEAD

The Tioga Pass Road, California Route 120, is at 9,945 feet the highest-elevation automobile pass in the state. Turn off the Tioga Pass Road 0.3 miles east of the Tuolumne River bridge and the Lembert Dome parking lot, on the road leading south to Tuolumne Lodge. Proceed to the first parking lot. Wilderness permits may be issued at a kiosk here on a first-come, first-served basis.

MAP 7

TRAIL ROUTE DESCRIPTION

From the wilderness permit parking lot, the signed trail leaves to the south and crosses the road. This is both the Pacific Crest Trail and the John Muir Trail, for the two are coincident along much of the 200 miles between Mount Whitney and Tuolumne Meadows and here in Yosemite. Heading upriver, on worn track, you soon reach a junction (0.4 miles from last point; 8,715 feet above sea level; 0.4 total miles) where a trail branches left to Tuolumne Lodge. Continue straight ahead along the river. Multiple tracks are eroded four wide into the soil. Soon you reach another junction, where the left fork also leads to the lodge; take the right fork and cross the Dana Fork of the Tuolumne River on a handsome timber bridge. Shortly you reach another junction (0.3 miles; 8,755 feet; 0.7 miles) where a trail branches left to Taylor Lake. Continue right on the PCT.

Before long you pass a sizable stagnant pond on your left; just beyond, you enter a meadow-restoration project where attempts are under way to help the area heal from excessive use and abusive practices in the past. Stay on the trail here. In about a half mile, you cross the Lyell Fork of the Tuolumne on well-crafted twin bridges that make use of a rock in the middle of the flow. A minute or two past the bridge, you reach a junction (0.6 miles; 8,670 feet; 1.3 miles) where the right-hand branch leads to Tuolumne campground, 1 mile distant. Take the left fork of the trail, which in 0.4 miles, after undulating through lodgepoles, across runoff streams, and over granite outcroppings, leaves the meadow restoration area.

MAP 7

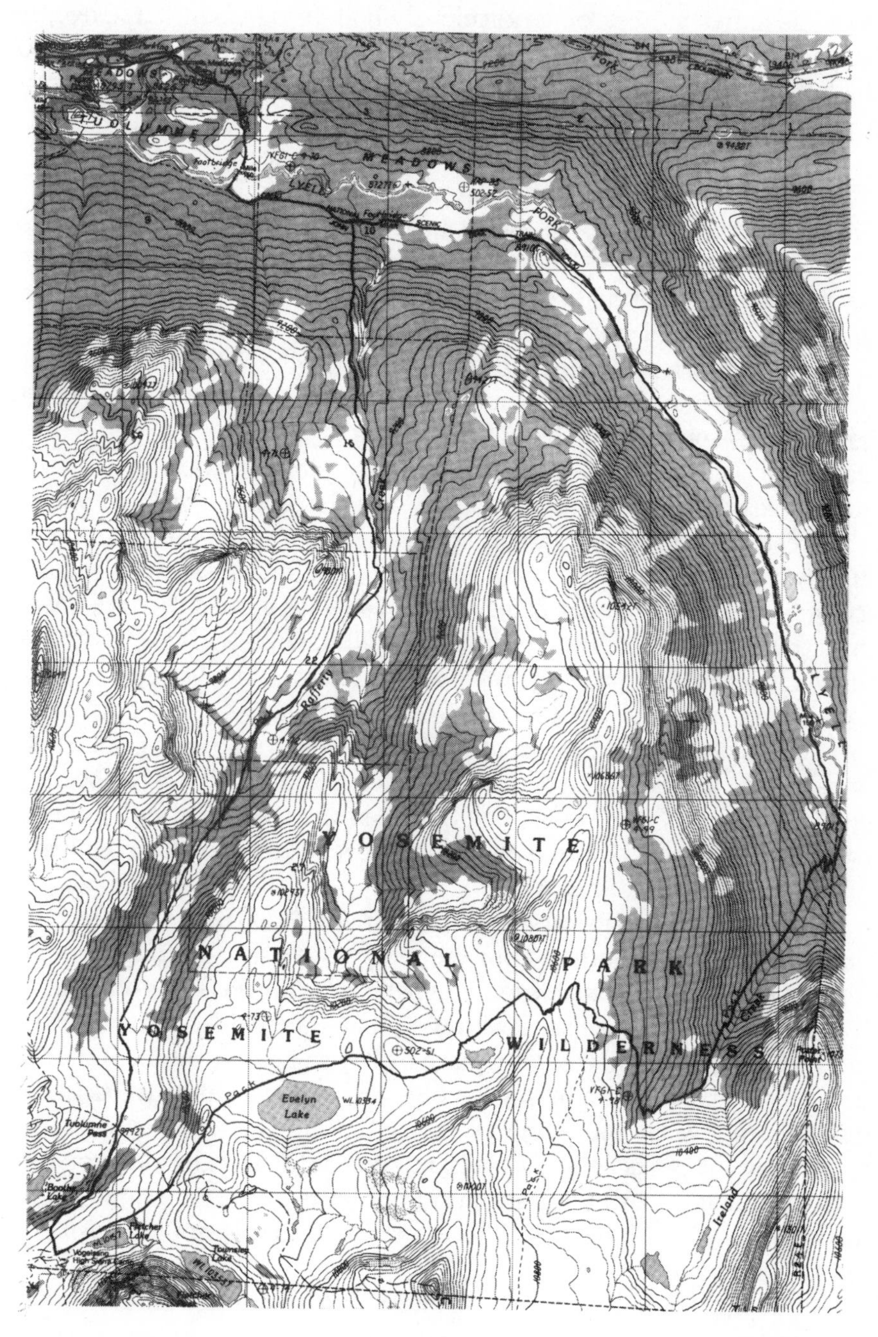
MEADOWS
TUOLUMNE
Footbridge
MEADOWS
LYELL
FORK
Creek
Rafferty
YOSEMITE
NATIONAL
PARK
YOSEMITE
WILDERNESS
Evelyn
Lake
Tuolumne
Pass
Booth
Lake
Fletcher
Lake
Townsley
Lake
Ireland

At a junction (0.7 miles; 8,720 feet; 2.0 miles) the PCT-JMT goes left to cross Rafferty Creek on a ridiculously high bridge, built far above the surrounding terrain. One can't help but wonder what circumstances of high water would require the lofty placement. Turn right at this junction toward Vogelsang.

The alpine experiences that await you now clearly state their cost—the trail begins to climb immediately. Nicely laid with cobblestones on the very steep pitches, the ascent is accomplished without undue erosion, even though horse and pack-string use of this trail is high. As you ascend, passing through the 9,000-foot level, the lodgepoles become more scattered and smaller.

Soon you reach the top of a rounded ridge, which you follow upward for a while before working your way off the left side, where the grade eases somewhat. The undulating trail crosses a two-channel seasonal runoff stream, then leads to a subalpine bench with scattered lodgepoles and granite outcroppings. You descend slightly, paralleling the creek, and continue through open forest. Within 75 feet of the creek finally, you exit the trees onto a beautiful subalpine meadow. A few feet later, you can see that many decades of use have eroded the trail deeply into the meadow. The old track on the right is wide and deep, with two newer alignments in the grass to the left. Restoration work needs to be done here.

Young lodgepole pines are beginning their surreptitious colonization work in the meadow, and before many decades this will not be the open, grassy expanse you now see here. By then the trees that are now mere seedlings will have matured and other, new seedlings will have filled in much of the meadow area.

You cross one tributary stream (3.0 miles; 9,450 feet; 5.0 miles), and in 0.6 miles cross another. Your seemingly endless ascending trail now breaks out into another meadow, where you can see slightly more advanced lodgepole colonization. Now you are greeted by a sturdy causeway, constructed of soil held in place by rows of granite stones on either side. It was placed here by the Park Service and is an effective shield for fragile meadow surfaces subject to horse traffic.

Now the peaks behind Vogelsang come into view ahead. If you turn, you can see into both the Dana and Lyell forks of the Tuolumne behind and below, where lodgepole forests carpet all that is not solid, smooth granite or protruding peaks.

Ascending along the creek on alternating multitrack natural-surface trail and stone causeways, your route climbs higher onto the meadow. Belding ground squirrels scurry about on their daily chores, often stopping upright to stare as you pass. Others dive into concealing dens under the very granite blocks you tread on.

At last your trail breaks over the lip of the meadow, and you can see farther directly ahead. You pass several tarns on either side of the trail and then arrive at a junction (2.1 miles; 9,990 feet; 7.1 miles) where the right branch leads to Booth and Merced lakes. Take the left branch toward Vogelsang. You immediately round the left end of a tarn on an elevated stone-and-earth causeway. This junction could be called Divide Junction, for it marks the point where waters behind you flow east into Lyell Fork, while those immediately ahead flow west into the Merced.

You traverse along the slope, while the meadow you so recently trod drops away on your right. You round a bend, and below you lies a long, narrow, but deep lake occupying a glacial gouge where it gives birth to Emeric Creek. In minutes, you round a corner just above the 10,000-foot level where the trail is backfilled against a laid-up stone wall. Yellow-bellied marmots waddle from your presence here, then stop on boulders to stare.

About when it seems your route cannot climb farther, it does so, but soon you reach a trailside sign directing you to a campground area and toilets to your left. A few yards beyond that, you reach a junction (0.8 miles; 10,130 feet; 7.9 miles) at the Vogelsang city limits, where the right-hand fork leads to Emeric and Merced lakes, straight ahead reaches Vogelsang Pass and Bernice Lake, and the left branch, your route, goes to Fletcher Lake.

Ever since being publicized by early Sierra Club presentations, Vogelsang has been seen as the epitome of high Sierra camps. Buttressed to the south by Vogelsang Peak and its henchmen, the camp occupies a flat area near the outlet to Fletcher Lake. The scenery is as breathtaking as the air is thin. It may be possible to buy a meal here without reservations if the camp load is not too great. Accommodation and meal reservations are required, however, and are detailed earlier in this chapter.

Vogelsang is the ideal spot to camp and to experience a sunset and sunrise. Alpenglow, a reflection of light from the west long after the sun has set, is usually spectacular.

Camp areas are to the east of Vogelsang proper, just to the north of Fletcher Lake. A nice bench runs parallel to and north of the trail opposite Fletcher Lake and provides widely separated campsites with good

Vertical Profile of Hike 7

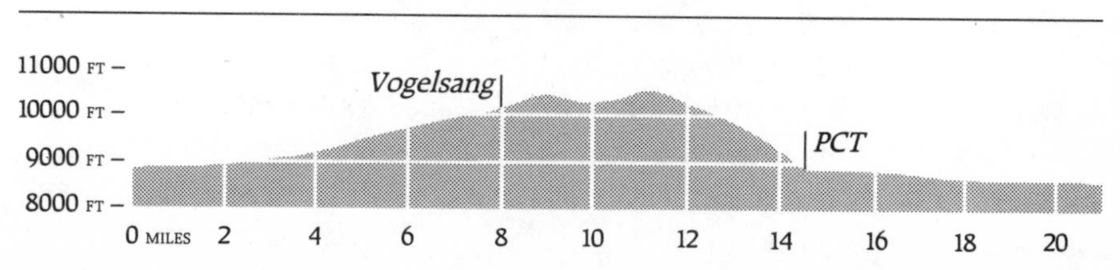

views. While the park service has strung a wire cable between trees near the east end of the lake to facilitate bear-bagging food, camping in the immediate area is limited and much of the shoreline area is a restoration zone. No wood fires are allowed in this area, as is the case in much of the high country in Yosemite. A large, efficient composting toilet has been installed near the west end of the bench for the use of campers.

Now, leaving the stone building and tent frame cabins of Vogelsang, you head east on the Fletcher Lake Trail. Soon you pass that lake on your right, and in a short distance you are greeted by a graphic example of poor trail alignment, maintenance, and use: four trails, side by side, all eroding deeply into the sloping meadow soil. The trail runs straight down the hill, and so does the water, cutting ever deeper into the fragile soil. A few water bars and restoration structures here would be helpful.

If you thought that Vogelsang was at the summit, you now know better as you ascend the rutted, rocky trail. Soon you reach an apparent summit and cross between two low granite walls that form the narrow notch of Tuolumne Pass (1.0 mile; 10,440 feet; 8.9 miles). Ahead and below, you can see alpine fell field around Evelyn Lake. Tarns occupy the northeastern end of the fields. Your trail is plainly visible for more than a mile. To your right, Fletcher and Vogelsang peaks are spread irregularly across the horizon.

Descending now, you soon reach the outlet of Evelyn Lake (0.6 miles; 10,320 feet; 9.5 miles), cross, and amble up a broad ridge. Your climb soon eases along the top of the ridge, among scattered lodgepoles. Trail ducks help point out the way, and in places your trail has been bordered with stones. Before long you cross an intermediate crest at 10,410 feet and immediately see an unnamed lake ahead.

This lake lies in a basin just a few hundred feet below timberline, a fact you can easily affirm by looking up the slopes beyond the lake. Now you cross the outlet of the unnamed lake (1.0 mile; 10,420 feet; 10.5 miles) and begin a steady climb, mostly in sunshine as the more stunted lodgepoles at this elevation provide little shade. These sunny slopes harbor various wildflower species not seen in the more shaded locations, and looking for them will keep you busy as you move upslope.

Once you reach the granite ridgetop (0.5 miles; 10,590 feet; 11.0 miles) take note of stunted, bushlike whitebark pines growing along the exposed spine. Wind and abrasive snow have sculpted these trees to a mere yard-high conformity. The view from this exposed site is striking; you can see Donohue Peak and, just to its right, Donohue Pass to the east, and Mount Lyell and Simmons Peak to the southeast.

A routing along natural ledges and joints in the granite switches you down off the ridge. In minutes you cross a small seasonal stream and reach a junction (0.6 miles; 10,420 feet; 11.6 miles) where the right-hand fork would take you to Ireland Lake in 3 miles. Go left, threading between heather-trimmed boulders as you drop down into larger lodgepoles, which provide good shade. Your trail traverses directly toward Mount Lyell, the opposite of the way you want to go, in order to bypass a steep, rocky area that lies out of sight below the trail. The beauty of this heather-carpeted bench makes up, however, for the additional steps necessary.

In just 0.7 miles, you cross a tumbling stream and continue downhill through the lodgepoles, your trail now heading the way you want to go. Soon, after descending farther, you parallel sizable Ireland Creek as the switchbacks cease and you reach the bottom. An illegal camp too close to the water is on the right here; a better place would be up on the bench to the left. Now you cross a series of tributary streams and descend farther on a generally beautiful traverse through open woods. If you are observant you may spot an occasional mountain hemlock in this area. Old, abandoned trail alignments descend with you, intersecting at intervals.

White-headed woodpecker

You break into more open country as you drop over succeeding benches that offer excellent camping in several locations. Now you reach the junction (3.0 miles; 8,900 feet; 14.6 miles) with the PCT-JMT. To the right, this famous route leads over Donohue Pass. Turn left, down the Lyell Fork of the Tuolumne River. After moving downstream a mere hundred feet you'll see a PCT emblem on a tree to the right of the trail. Shortly beyond the junction, you reach a broad meadow.

This is prime bear country, actually the graduate school of beardom, for large numbers of backpackers use this area and many are not experienced in bear tactics. The results are habituated bears that look upon backpackers as mere vehicles for carrying food. Sow bears teach their cubs, and now there are many bears for whom getting food bags out of trees is no trick at all. If you camp in this area, be sure to use proper bear-bagging techniques.

Here, as in other places on this hike, there are signs of misuse, such as multiple tracks and eroded surfaces. But the beauty of this meadow is overpowering, with its transparent waters, oxbow bends, and granite backdrops. You may be able to spot an occasional trout in the clear water of the river. Late in the day, trout may feed on insects drifting on the surface.

One mile later, you can see dead trees littering the opposite slope of the valley, the site of a 1986 avalanche. That year much of the Sierra received more than a dozen feet of snow in one storm, and many devastating avalanches resulted.

Your trail passes through the meadow, detouring occasionally to cross smooth granite outcroppings too resistant for the glacier to have leveled. Eventually, your trail reaches the north end of the meadow and enters the lodgepole forest. Walking in shade now, you soon reach Rafferty Creek, at the high bridge you saw earlier when you left the PCT to climb to Vogelsang. You now cross over the timber bridge and in 200 feet arrive at the junction (4.3 miles; 8,720 feet; 18.9 miles) where you left the PCT to climb to Vogelsang.

From this point you retrace your steps northward along the PCT-JMT, past the junction in 0.7 miles where the trail to Tuolumne Campground branches left. In 500 feet you cross the Lyell Fork on twin bridges. In 0.3 miles more, you pass the junction where the right trail branch leads to Taylor Lake. Keep straight ahead, and in another 0.2 miles you pass a junction where the right branch leads to Tuolumne Lodge. You then pass the Dog Lake parking lot, 200 feet to your right, and in minutes pass the ranger station and residences and arrive at the wilderness permit parking lot (2.1 miles; 8,660 feet; 21.0 miles).

8 ♦ TUOLUMNE MEADOWS—GLEN AULIN—WATERWHEEL FALLS

Distance:	17.6 Miles
Low elevation:	6,950 Feet
High elevation:	8,610 Feet
Class:	Moderate
Hiking time:	8 Hours

John Muir described Tuolumne waterfalls as "spreading over glacial waves of granite without any definite channel, gliding in magnificent silver plumes, dashing and foaming through huge boulder dams, leaping high into the air in wheel-like whirls, displaying glorious enthusiasm. . . ."

The idea that Yosemite Valley was carved by glaciers was first advanced by Muir and later adopted by noted geologists of the time. Perhaps no evidence of ice-age carving is so accessible as that around Tuolumne Meadows, particularly as you travel downstream. The Tuolumne Glacier, at more than 60 miles the longest in the Sierra, gradually ground away rock until the canyon conformed to the present-day shape. In places the Tuolumne River hasn't eroded at all, still flowing over glacial polish on the rock. It is these polished ledges and chutes, over which the river drops into the Grand Canyon of the Tuolumne, that make this area the land of waterfalls.

Tuolumne Meadows had long been the site of summer sheep grazing; in fact, Muir himself had shepherded a band there. John Lembert homesteaded 160 acres at the soda springs in the meadows and built a cabin on that site. Two brothers named McCauley bought the homestead and rebuilt the cabin in 1898. Purchased by the Sierra Club in 1912, the homestead became a campground and the cabin was occupied by a caretaker. In 1915 the Sierra Club constructed Parsons Memorial Lodge, honoring Edward Parsons, who helped Muir in the failed effort to stop Hetch Hetchy Dam and who later had become a director of the club. Used as a base for Sierra Club outings, the soda springs property was sold to the National Park Service in 1923, making it public land once again.

Sediments, deposited as glaciers melted and accreted by water, provide the broad, flat portions of Tuolumne Meadows. Downstream, below the first waterfall series where the river meanders peacefully, Glen Aulin is a glacier-gouged lake bed that has been filled with sediment and now supports a forest.

Glen Aulin High Sierra Camp, part of the chain of High Sierra Camps in Yosemite, is located at the confluence of Conness Creek and the Tuolumne River, below White Cascades. The Pacific Crest Trail turns away from the Tuolumne along Conness Creek in its ever-northbound quest, deserting the Tuolumne drainage.

"Waterwheels," features of the Tuolumne River and especially Waterwheel Falls, are not wheels at all, but streams of water that are projected out into the air to fall in long, curving arcs back into the flow. Angled ledges, cuts, and glacial grooves that end in an outward-projecting surface produce the waterwheels. Many of these mechanical surfaces in the streambed were carved by glaciers and have undergone little stream erosion in the last 10,000 years.

The 8,500-foot elevation of Tuolumne Meadows is high enough to receive substantial snowfall, but weather influences in the valley are less harsh than on higher windswept ridges and mountain slopes. While typical high Sierra summer afternoon and evening thunderstorms do affect the meadows, lightning strike hazard is considerably less than on more exposed locations. Spring snowmelt turns the meadows into a bog, and at that time mosquitoes are numerous.

Much has been made of the flora and fauna of Yosemite. Scouting for this hike, we were impressed with the variety of animals and birds seen. Most notable was a pine marten, a particularly frisky individual that crossed the trail a mile west of Parsons Lodge. The season determines which wildflowers are in bloom. Consider keeping a list to compare with species given in park brochures.

DESCRIPTION

This is not a loop hike; rather, you return along the same route. It is designed as an easy, two-day ramble that provides plenty of time to explore and enjoy the area. While the trail does involve some sections with considerable gradient, much of the walking is over very gentle terrain. It is only because of the elevation change that the hike is classified as moderate.

Early in the route is an excellent opportunity to explore the Parsons Lodge complex and taste the soda water bubbling up from nearby underground springs. For years campers have concocted beverages with this carbonated water plus powdered drink mix.

The trail remains mostly in the forest for the first few miles and affords good wildflower viewing. You get some fantastic vistas of river and meadow, with Cathedral and Unicorn Peaks as backdrops. Then the track leads across several polished expanses of granitic rock, where feldspar crystals, cut and wearing glacial polish, are evident in the surface.

Farther into the hike you become conscious of the accelerating current, and the Tuolumne River begins to murmur with impatience. On the south riverbank just before the bridge crossing, careful observers can spot Little Devils Postpile, kin to the larger, more famous monument to the south. These formations are glaciated remnants of a basaltic lava flow that intruded the granite 9 million years ago and cracked into columns, and they are easily identified by their dark color. A use trail from the bridge follows along the south riverbank to this feature. Perhaps you will notice a large granitic boulder on top of the basalt. This is an "erratic," balanced here when the glacial ice carrying it melted.

The trail takes on more character here, switching and rounding domes as it struggles to lose elevation as rapidly as the river. You first encounter Tuolumne Falls and then White Cascades as the route descends to another bridge across the river, which leads to Glen Aulin High Sierra Camp on Conness Creek. This route as far as Glen Aulin is a popular day hike. You can also expect to meet a pack train taking supplies to the camp or a group of riders with that destination, or both.

Glen Aulin is part of the evenly spaced chain of High Sierra Camps operated by the Yosemite Concession Services Corporation. Services include overnight lodging, showers, breakfast and dinner, and box lunches. All services are by advance reservation, awarded by lottery. Applications are accepted between October 15 and November 30 for the following summer. More information can be obtained by calling the High Sierra Reservations Desk, telephone (209) 454-2002. Hikers often camp near Glen Aulin and use the camp facilities for meals. It is worth considering if you wish to minimize your backpack load. This, too, calls for a reservation, although it may be possible to secure a meal here without a reservation, depending on how near capacity the camp is operating.

The real elevation drop begins as the trail parallels, with switchbacks, the 500-foot-long cascades just below Conness Creek. At the bottom of this descent, you enter the "glen" of Glen Aulin. Note the fine soil of this now-filled lake, so appropriate for evergreens, quaking aspens, and cottonwoods. Recently a fire passed through and killed many of the trees in this locale. Though it will take many years before the devastation of the burn is no longer visible, eventually the area will again be shady and wooded.

Administrative agency: USNPS

Backcountry Permits	High Sierra Camp Reservations
Wilderness Office	Reservations Desk
P.O. Box 577	(209) 454-2002
Yosemite, CA 95389	

USGS Map: 7.5′ series, Tioga Pass, Falls Ridge, Vogelsang

Declination: 15 degrees

The now peaceful Tuolumne comes alive again at the end of the glen, at plunging California Falls. Below this is Le Conte Falls, named after Joseph Le Conte, friend of John Muir and an early convert to Muir's glaciation theories.

A steeper descent, among house-size boulders, leads below 7,000 feet to impressive Waterwheel Falls. Several huge waterwheels spurt endlessly along the 200-yard sluice of the falls. During early season when flow is great, the wheels are drowned by the volume of water passing over them, and in late season the wheels are weak and thin due to greatly reduced flow and less velocity. During a considerable range in between, however, Waterwheel Falls put on a fantastic show.

At this point, well inside the montane chaparral plant community, the route turns around and backtracks to the beginning point in Tuolumne Meadows. After this hike, you will have striking mental images whenever you recall Tuolumne Meadows.

The hiking season can vary. Late June through mid-October will usually afford reasonable weather. Remember that mosquitoes can be troublesome in the early season.

Black bears are plentiful here, and not just any bears, but Yosemite bears, probably the most experienced animals anywhere at pilfering food. Be sure to take proper precautions with your food supply.

DIRECTIONS TO TRAILHEAD

From the Tuolumne Meadows store, drive west 1 mile on State Route 120 (Tioga Pass Road) to the Tuolumne Meadows Visitors Center. There is parking here, and there is additional parking at the Lembert Dome parking lot, 0.5 miles east of the store; at the pack station, 0.3 miles north on a gravel road from the Lembert Dome parking area; and at the wilderness

MAP 8A

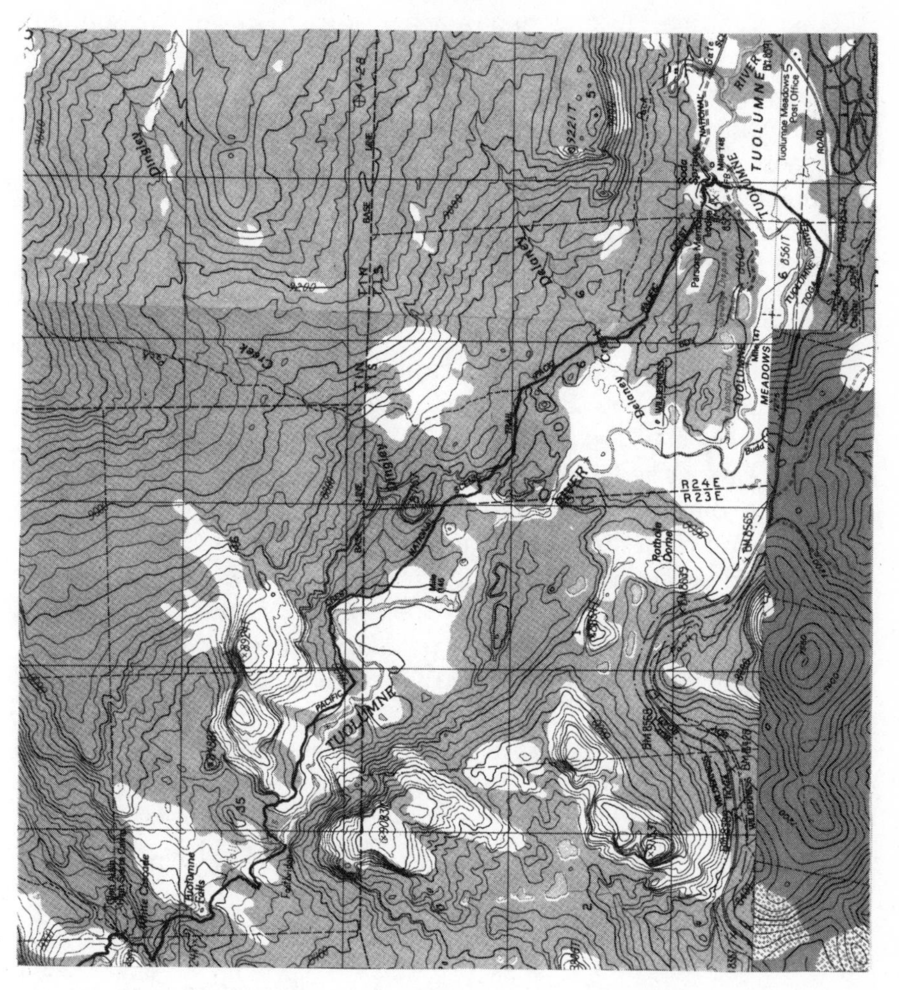

permit station, immediately on the right after you turn off the highway to Tuolumne Lodge.

TRAIL ROUTE DESCRIPTION

MAP 8A

Beginning at the Visitors Center parking lot, walk out the approach drive and turn right onto a trail paralleling the Tioga Pass Road. In just 1,200 feet, you reach the pedestrian lane where the Tuolumne Meadows trail crosses the Tioga Pass Road. Turn left (south) and traipse along the broad, sandy path, which soon becomes two or more treads. The meadow here is presently undergoing restoration to correct damage of earlier heavy, and improper, use.

Immediately you are treated to beautiful meadow views of lush grasses and sedges, meandering drainage streams in early season, and clumps of lodgepole that seem unable, after centuries of trying, to colonize the meadows proper. Soon you cross a drainage stream that flows beneath your trail in metal culverts. Belding ground squirrels scurry off, then pause to sit upright and watch you with curiosity. Soon you cross the Tuolumne River (0.3 miles from last point; 8,570 feet above sea level; 0.3 total miles) on a picturesque timber bridge. One hundred feet past the bridge is a junction with a little-used gravel road that leads to Parsons Lodge, and here you turn left. This road used to lead to a campground that the Sierra Club maintained in this area some years ago.

In 50 yards, turn right onto a tread leading to Parsons Lodge. The inspiring design of this natural-stone structure encourages reading the interpretive signs placed at this historic spot. Some information on the history of Parsons Lodge is given in the hike description.

You rejoin the trail as it crosses a gravel road 100 yards east of the lodge, and climb briefly up a rocky trail past signs with conflicting mileages and permit information. The route levels after a few yards and crosses a boggy meadow, and you can soon spot a stagnant, grassy pond on your left through the lodgepole pines now covering the landscape. Just 0.2 miles farther, you pass another stagnant pond on the left just yards from the trail.

This semiopen forest is wonderfully carpeted with grasses and sedges, an obvious comment on the health of forest understory when livestock grazing is not a factor.

Your trail crests a small rise, then drops down pleasantly to undulate through inspiring open glades and lodgepoles. You cross the twin branches of Delaney Creek in 0.5 miles, by either rock hopping or using logs. In a few minutes you cross a seasonal stream that runs to your left out into the lower Tuolumne Meadows, from which point you are treated to a view of the carved and smoothed peaks that guard the meadows to the west.

The trail now gently ascends along a seasonal stream on your left that provides moisture for shooting stars, buttercups, and lupine. Minutes later, the horse trail from the Tuolumne Meadows stables joins your track from the right. Then at another junction (1.7 miles; 8,605 feet; 2.0 miles), the Young Lake Trail branches right and leads 4.7 miles to Young Lake. Continue straight ahead on the trail signed "Glen Aulin."

Swinging along this delightful route, you are soon treated to a view of more granite monoliths, and you can hear the roar of water on your left, the first indication that this hike will expose another side of what has up until now been the placid Tuolumne River.

Following rock ducks across a broad, glaciated granite sheet, you soon reenter the forest to undulate over the almost imperceptibly descending slope. Here, on our hike, we heard a drumming on a dead snag that turned out to be a black-backed, three-toed woodpecker advertising his presence to any females of his species within hearing.

You soon reach more open areas and can enjoy the view of the lazy, meandering river passing through the meadows. Ground squirrels busily line nests or feed in the open. Various wildflowers add their cheerful colors to the idyllic scene.

Your wide trail crosses two broad, stony meltwater channels that in early season flow into the river. Then the sandy track leads very close to the river and into welcome shade from scattered lodgepoles. The raised, boulder-lined causeway stretching 300 feet in this area is an attempt to avoid trail erosion and mud caused by standing water. Shortly thereafter, more sections of causeway do their work, and soon another causeway marks your way through a marshy meadow dotted with shooting stars.

Before long you are very near the river. Instead of having cut its own channel, the river here spreads out in thin sheets over the smooth, 10,000-year-old granite surface. That time span notwithstanding, cutting has not occurred because of the relative youth of the channel and because, even in flood stages, the river at this point transports little abrasive sediment.

You reach a broad expanse of gently sloping granite (1.7 miles; 8,410 feet; 3.7 miles) beside the river. The sometimes rounded, sometimes angular pinkish crystals in the granite are feldspar, an aluminum silicate. Here, a seam of intruded material runs through the granite nearly parallel to your route. Drop below this seam and rejoin the trail close to the river at the far side of the rock expanse. The campsite immediately on your left as you reenter the trees is much too close to the water to be used.

After a few yards through the trees, you break out again onto another sheet of granite, this one 200 yards wide, and follow trail ducks that turn slightly toward the river, which is noisily cascading over short drops on your left. Soon you are back among trees, and you can look

Vertical Profile of Hike 8

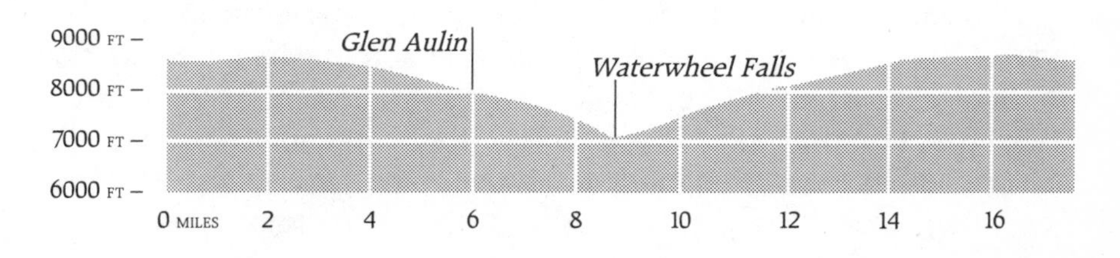

Black bear

down through an opening on your left to see the river descending over sharp breaks.

Now the trail switches abruptly left, descends a short distance, and then begins climbing along the base of a trailside cliff on the right. Whoever blasted the footholds here must have taken giant steps, but the surface holes provide good footing, anyway. In a few yards, you are led out onto a rounded saddle that projects ahead 40 feet.

This is a good place to look left, across the river, and view Little Devils Postpile, a 9-million-year-old volcanic intrusion that penetrated the Cathedral Peak granite pluton, which rose beneath the surface some 80 million years ago. Looking closely at the dark gray, rounded formation, you can see that the basalt has cooled into long, columnar shapes. The glacier has smoothed the top of this outcropping, and the columns are breaking into short pieces. The granite boulders lying on top of the basalt are glacial "erratics" that were carried within the ice flow and deposited at random as the glacier melted.

From the rounded saddle, the trail crosses sharply to the right and immediately descends over cobblestones. This type of trail surface is designed to fill in voids of more-than-comfortable stepping height in the trail, prevent erosion, and provide traction for horses. It is not always easy to walk on, but there is no disputing its effectiveness in erosion control.

Swinging down alternately on natural granite surfaces and trail tread, you soon reach the bottom of the short switchbacks. Before long, you reach the river and cross (0.8 miles; 8,345 feet; 4.5 miles) on two attractive stone-and-timber bridges. This would be a poor choice of places to swim, as the strong current flows swiftly to drop over a succession of granite ledges. A short distance downstream you can hear the roar of a much higher cascade. Do your swimming elsewhere.

[To visit Little Devils Postpile, cross the second bridge and turn left sharply, moving upstream along a wooded, sandy floodplain. Within a few hundred feet the plain ends, and you can see various use trails climbing the rocks just above the water. Use caution here, for loose pine needles, sand, or rotting materials on top of slick rock surfaces can be very slippery. Within a few hundred yards, you will reach the volcanic basalt columns.]

Leaving the bridge, you climb up onto a granite ridge, then start down on partially cobblestone tread. The trail switchbacks up and away from the river in order to traverse a steep cliff on your right. Passing this obstacle, you descend the far side in easy switchbacks, coming out onto a wide trail on the flat. You can hear the rumble of more rapids ahead and to the right.

After coming into view of the river again, you turn abruptly left and cross more bare granite, following rock ducks. Penstemon flowers from unlikely locations in cracks in the granite. Descending to the bottom of the outcroppings, you turn onto a broad trail that leads left along the level. In season, heather blooms along this section of the trail.

Cresting a rounded knob under the trees, you can hear a much deeper roar from the unseen river to your right. Then you descend an eroded, straight path and finally reach Tuolumne Falls (0.9 miles; 8,050 feet; 5.4 miles). The power of this falls, tumbling down a nearly sheer drop, is awesome, especially in early season when the water volume is heavy. The falls create wind, and the air is damp with mist and spray. When the light is right, rainbows frolic in the spray, creating a light and unreal prismatic mosaic, belied by the reverberating thunder of the falls.

Leaving the spectacle, you continue on down the trail to a junction (0.3 miles; 7,975 feet; 5.7 miles) where the trail to McGee and Tenaya lakes turns left. Keep to the right on the PCT, heading toward Glen Aulin. Continuing down over mostly cobblestone trail, you soon reach the broad pool at the bottom of White Cascades. A water ouzel often makes repeated trips under and behind the falling torrent, seemingly unperturbed by thundering tons of liquid pounding into the pool. Passing the pool, you can see a campsite above the trail on your left. Immediately ahead is a steel bridge across the Tuolumne River.

You cross the river on the steel bridge and progress straight ahead up Conness Creek 200 feet to a bridge on your right that crosses the creek. Immediately across this bridge is Glen Aulin High Sierra Camp (0.2 miles; 7,890 feet; 5.9 miles). Toilets for hikers are located here. Reservations at Glen Aulin High Sierra Camp, for just meals or accommodations with meals, are detailed in the "Description" section of this chapter.

It may be advisable to camp in the Glen Aulin area and complete the downstream portion of this hike without your pack. Besides the campsite already mentioned, there are barely adequate sites around the High Sierra Camp, as well as many spacious campsites within the first half

MAP 8B

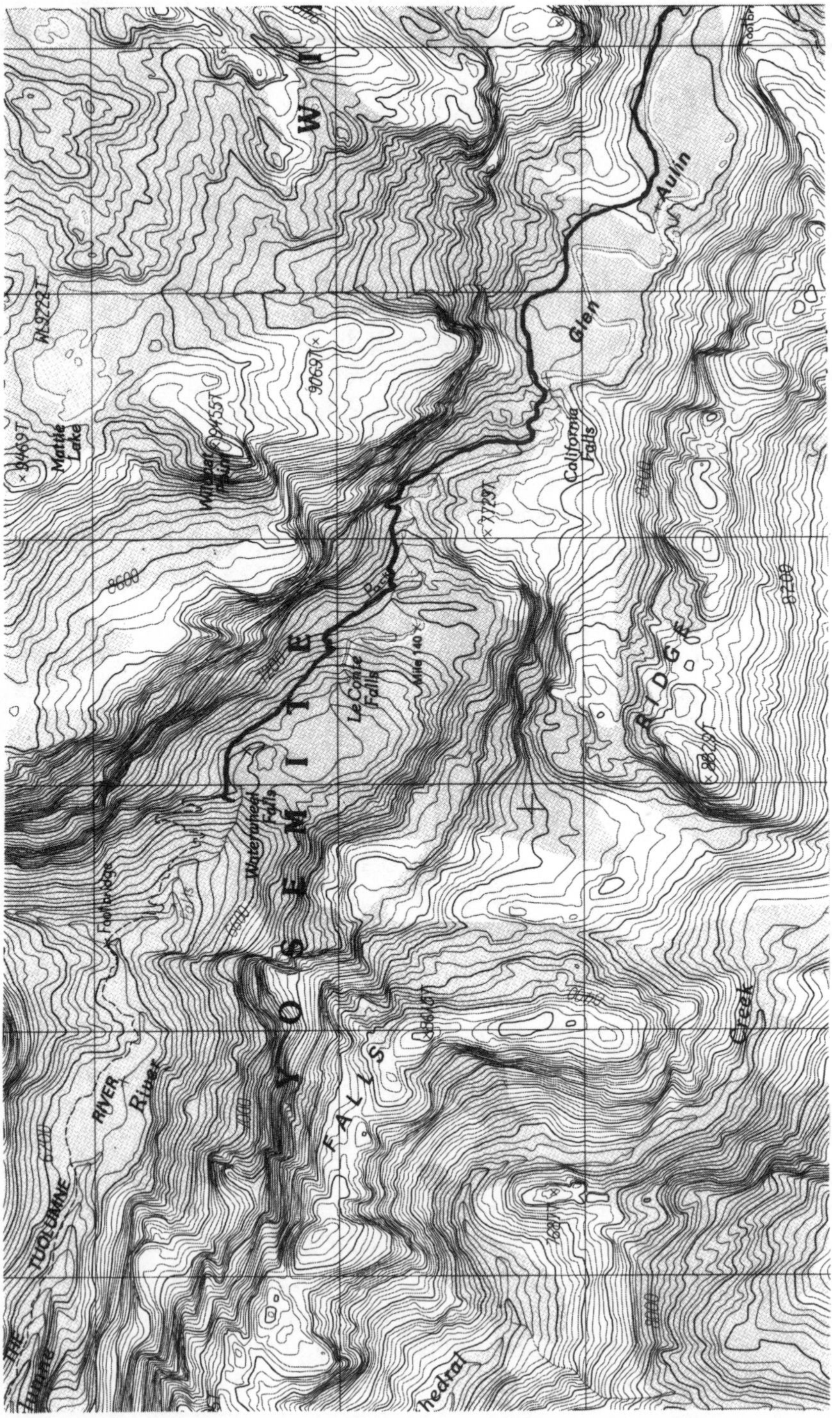
YOSEMITE
Waterwheel Falls
LeConte Falls
California Falls
Glen
Aulin
Mattie Lake
RIDGE
Mile 140
TUOLUMNE
RIVER
River
FALLS
Creek
9069T
8200
8600

mile of Glen Aulin itself. Unfortunately, lightning started a fire that ravaged much of the glen in 1987. Most of the lodgepole pines here were killed; many still stand. It may be several decades or more before this scar is even partially healed.

To reach Glen Aulin, exit the High Sierra Camp on the Conness Creek bridge, turn right, and proceed 50 feet to the junction with the Waterwheel Falls Trail, which turns left. At this point you leave the PCT, which goes straight ahead up Conness Creek. After turning left, you round a rocky promontory and switchback down on natural and cobblestone tread, closely paralleling a rushing chute that culminates in a large pool at the bottom. Soon you reach flat Glen Aulin below.

MAP 8B

Glen Aulin, once a glacial lake, has the dubious distinction of having been filled in with natural waterborne sediments. This is why there is sand here, as well as soil that is more highly developed than in most other subalpine locales. For a mile or more the river winds in lazy fashion across this now-filled lake bed. Grasses and sedges have recovered nicely here since the fire, and the emerald green floor of the valley helps offset the starkness of the dead lodgepoles and quaking aspen. While crossing the flat, you can also see bracken and bush chinquapin. Note the campsites and wires for bear bagging that the Park Service has provided.

Soon the trail leads you close beside the river, which here is quite deep. A sharp left bend of both trail and river has you crossing a granite protrusion. You descend the far side on cobbles laid at right angles down a natural joint in the granite, apparently to provide traction for horses. Once beyond this protrusion, you again leave the river and meander on through forest. You cross a small stream on logs; the same stream can be seen cascading down vertical cliffs 500 feet above and to your right.

You get visual notice of the impending California Falls as the smooth, placid flow you follow seems to disappear at a hard, level line some distance ahead. Soon you also can hear the falls, as you climb up onto granite and drop off the edge to follow along a strong series of cascades. You switchback down on mostly cobblestone trail, losing the same elevation that the river loses, only doing it much less noisily and spectacularly.

At the base of California Falls (1.5 miles; 7,535 feet; 7.4 miles), there are a large Sierra juniper and a western white pine beside the trail, the first time you encounter these species on this hike, as you have just dropped down into their zone. The sharp-eyed will spot red fir here as well. Ponderosa pine and white fir soon appear, and the conifer community becomes much more varied.

As you once again meander along a section of placid water, take note of other changes the drop in elevation has brought about. There are a lot of bush chinquapin. And if you gaze skyward, the cliffs rising to either side of you seem awesome against the deep blue sky or billowy afternoon thunderheads.

A distinct roar greets you as you approach Le Conte Falls, and soon you are able to see the cataracts themselves. The trail veers sharply to the right and leads you almost under a granite overhang as you make your way down the cobblestones. Large mica sheets in the granite shine like mirrors as you descend among house-size boulders. The trail levels momentarily, then you pass a serviceable campsite immediately before a large boulder on your left.

Leaving the base of Le Conte Falls, you wend your way downward between boulders. Here the river channel has split in the thundering rush to lose altitude. A small-volume fork flows beside the trail, away from a much larger fork that flows toward the opposite side of the canyon, ending in a distant, calm pool.

Soon you see big-leaf manzanita and buck brush beside the sometimes brushy trail. And then to your left you can both see and hear Waterwheel Falls, the most spectacular falls on the river. At a junction (1.4 miles; 6,950 feet; 8.8 miles), a use trail branches left toward the midsection of the falls, while the main trail continues downward toward Hetch Hetchy. There is a less-than-adequate campsite at the junction that should not be utilized, because this is a heavy-use area.

As you break out of the trees near camp and walk toward the falls to view the full display, proceed with caution, because the slope is steep and the rock very slick. What has not been smoothed by glaciers has been worn by water, and though the surface has good traction where it is dry and clean, any moisture, pine needles, dirt, or algae will start you on a trip courtesy of gravity that could be quite serious. Be careful!

Ahead of you, the water is sliding downward at a rapid rate, as huge waterwheels reach skyward and then curve into a downward fall that becomes indistinguishable from the frothing torrent from which they originated. At least five waterwheels display along the 200 yards of torrent—one of the most unusual falls anywhere and certainly the scenic high point along this "hike of the waterfalls."

MAP 8A

This is the turnaround point; from here you retrace your steps to the trailhead in Tuolumne Meadows.

9 ♦ ROUND TOP LAKE—MOKELUMNE WILDERNESS—FOURTH OF JULY LAKE

Distance:	15.1 Miles
Low elevation:	7,475 Feet
High elevation:	9,420 Feet
Class:	Moderate
Hiking time:	10 Hours

Designated by the Eldorado National Forest as Round Top Geological and Botanical Area, the environs south of the Carson Pass crossing of the Sierra are extremely accessible. The Pacific Crest Trail crosses State Route 88 at the Carson summit, in a striking, high Sierra setting.

Carson Pass earned a place in California history when scout Kit Carson guided John C. Fremont over the Sierra on a government exploring expedition. Carson took advantage of this crossing to carve his name in a tree near the summit. Today, this tree is in Sutter's Fort museum near Sacramento, while a bronze replica of the Kit Carson tree stands beside Route 88.

Little has changed in the high Sierra since that 1844 event; new trees have matured, but the mountains and valleys are virtually the same. Boulders and outcroppings of granodiorite, the salt-and-pepper rock that makes up much of the Sierra, have weathered slightly but are basically just as the glaciers left them as the ice melted 10,000 years ago.

Ash, mud, and lava originating from volcanism that began 30 million years ago once covered this section of the Sierra. Then, during the ice age, glaciers ground away at the volcanic rock to expose the granitic rock you see today at Carson summit. But when the ice age ended and the land was uplifted to nearly the present level, some of the volcanic material remained. Round Top and Elephants Back were once a volcanic vent and a lava dome, and The Sisters and Fourth of July Peak are of volcanic origin. A small but conspicuous moraine exists on the east slope of Elephants Back, and recessional moraines form the north and south shores of Round Top Lake. Also, contact zones between volcanic and granitic rocks are recognizable in many places, even by those without training in geology.

The soil types derived from different rocks vary widely, as do the plants that thrive in those soils. Because of this, plus such variables as elevation and slope aspect, the area's botanical diversity is such that the Round Top Botanical Area was established. During a late-summer hike we noted these wildflowers: mule's ears, alpine lupine, lupine, skyrocket, dandelion, rabbit brush, paintbrush, mullein, cliff penstemon, azure penstemon, meadow goldenrod, water hemlock, Sierra sedum, low bush penstemon, Lewis monkeyflower, seep-spring monkeyflower, explorer's gentian, California fuchsia, and cushion buckwheat. In mid-season there is no doubt even more variety.

Area wildlife includes the mule deer, Douglas squirrel, coyote, golden-mantled ground squirrel, chipmunk, Clark's nutcracker, flicker, meadowlark, robin, and junco.

Ideally positioned to extract moisture from marine air reaching the crest, Sierra peaks and ridges in the vicinity of Carson Pass receive more than adequate snowpacks during normal winters. Since some slopes are kept virtually snowfree by winds and many south-facing areas melt free early, the great plant diversity is facilitated even more.

DESCRIPTION

At a few locations in the Sierra, it is possible to leave a motor vehicle and immediately step into a true high Sierra environment. Carson Pass is one of those places. This loop hike retracing only a mile or so of trail begins on the PCT, which at this point holds to its namesake crest with fidelity.

A visitor station is maintained at Carson Pass during the summer season. A new visitor building, accomplished in no small part through private donations and with the help of volunteers, is nearing completion at the summit. Here also are located a paved parking area and toilets.

This hike is most enjoyable when done in two days. This will allow you adequate time to investigate geological features, identify wildflowers, and get the most out of your trip into such interesting country. You can camp at or in the vicinity of Fourth of July Lake in a classic subalpine environment. A stay here is memorable, with impressive headwalls, a moraine with spacious camping area, and a view into deep Summit City Canyon.

The first 2 miles of this hike along the PCT are very easy, as is much of the trail. If done as an overnight, the hike would be rated as easy except for the ascent from Summit City Canyon, past Fourth of July Lake, to Round Top Lake. Portions of this trail section have a steep gradient, so the hike is classified as moderate.

The change as you proceed southeast from Elephants Back, away from the subalpine environment that extends from Carson Pass, is dramatic. You traverse sage and boulder fields, conifers virtually disappear, and you enter a xeric, east-side, high-desert community.

At the same time, you will see signs of early mining exploration and activity, such as old roads crossed by the trail. As the route swings farther south before turning west, a low ridge composed of colorful rock is paralleled by a mining road.

Soon the trail crests in a rolling saddle, and the routing turns to follow the Summit City Canyon. The canyon's south-facing slope provides conditions favorable to plants that thrive in warmer, drier areas. Along this segment the trail traverses granodiorite one minute and volcanic rocks the next. Evidence of rapid water erosion and avalanche activity abounds. In several broad avalanche runout areas, only the young, resilient trees survive. Mature trees, being rigid, break off and are carried away.

Montane chaparral borders the trail along the ascent to Fourth of July Lake. Here the routing enters the forest again before climbing higher to subalpine Round Top Lake, a glacial cirque lake that seems tightly squeezed between two moraines.

The enjoyable downgrade routing to Winnemucca Lake provides views northwestward into the American River drainage. An easy ramble is all that separates this area from the trailhead.

The hiking season normally runs from late June until mid-October. Precipitation patterns can affect these dates, so be sure to check with the Forest Service if your schedule dictates very early or late timing.

Administrative agency: USFS

Eldorado National Forest
Information Center
3070 Camino Heights Drive
Camino, CA 95709
(916) 644-6048

USGS map: 7.5′ series, Carson Pass, Caples Lake, California

Declination: 16½ degrees

MAP 9

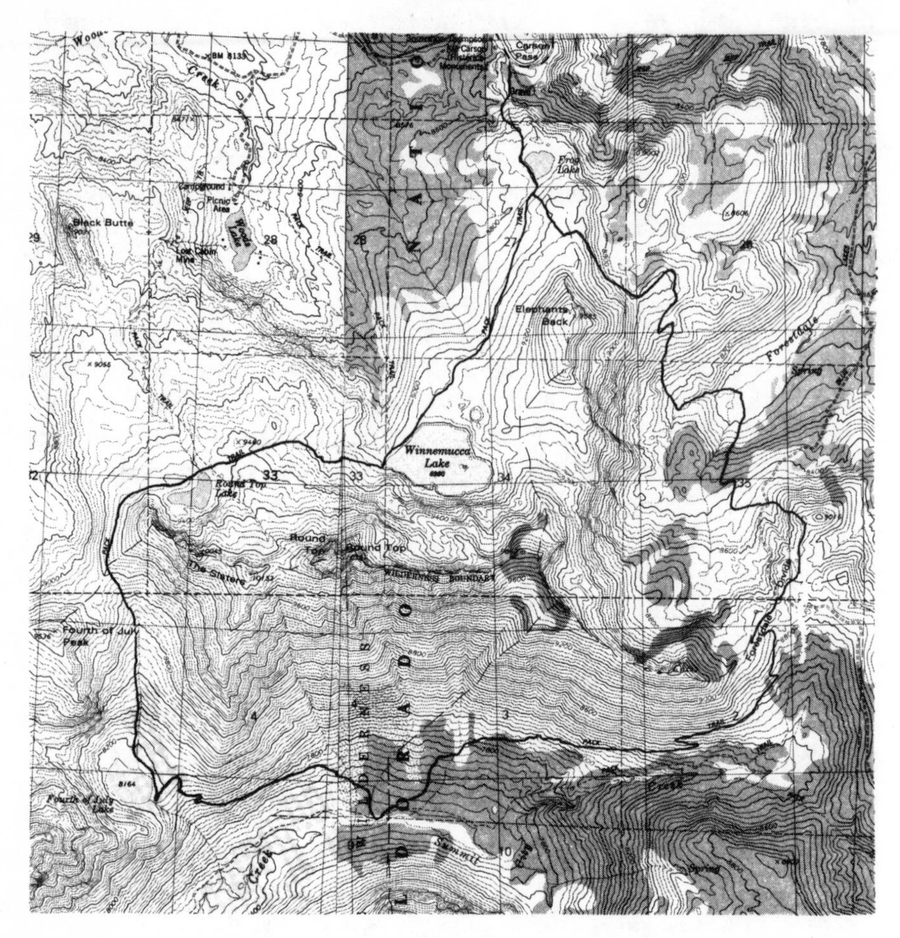

Black bears are common in the Carson Pass area. While not tenacious in terms of food thievery, bear-bagging your food is advisable here.

DIRECTIONS TO TRAILHEAD

The trail begins beside the Forest Service information building at the paved parking area on the south side of California State Route 88 at Carson Pass summit. Carson Pass summit is 28 miles west of Minden, Nevada, and 64 miles east of Jackson, California. There are toilets and an emergency phone at the parking area.

TRAIL ROUTE DESCRIPTION

MAP 9

From the trailhead bulletin board, just to the right of the Forest Service information building, you begin this hike at 8,573 feet elevation, heading south on the Pacific Crest Trail. Notice the boulders of coarse granodiorite, one rock type that makes up much of the Sierras. As your trail undulates among rounded knobs, you can see that many of these exposed rock surfaces have been ground smooth by glaciers. You pass a small tarn as the route winds among western white pine and red fir.

You enter the Mokelumne Wilderness (0.5 miles from last point; 8,580 feet above sea level; 0.5 total miles) at a sign identifying the area as such, after which your track negotiates a series of low ridges made up of resistant rock that was not glaciated as rapidly as the softer material between. In 0.5 miles you reach a rolling, open, sage-covered flat. Shortly, after more easy ascending, you reach a spur trail that turns left to Frog Lake. The lake occupies a glacier-gouged ridgetop basin a short distance from the trail.

Now you reach a junction (0.8 miles; 8,840 feet; 1.3 miles) with the Winnemucca Lake Trail, which branches right. This is the junction at which you will return to the PCT near the end of this hike.

Moving out of the granitic rocks, you reach an area where volcanic rock is to the right of the trail and glaciated granitic knobs are to the left. This is a contact zone, where older volcanic rocks remain on top of the comparatively younger granite that intruded beneath, hardened, and has now been exposed by erosion and glacial action.

The mountain on your right is Elephants Back, carved nearly vertical on the east side by glacial action. As you begin a descending traverse of the east face of this volcanic relic, several small tarns, which may be dry during late season, lie to your left and below. Moving now from scree to talus, you switchback down to a lower alignment and continue 100 yards above a successional moraine left by the most recent small glacier to inhabit the east face of Elephants Back.

Now you tread upon granite again as your trail leads northeast along a hummocky ridge covered with sage, boulders, and occasional clumps of whitebark pine. After leaving the wilderness, you cross a jeep road (1.0 miles; 8,750 feet; 2.3 miles) as your route leads east and then descends via switchbacks. Now curving back westward, you descend past a clump

Vertical Profile of Hike 9

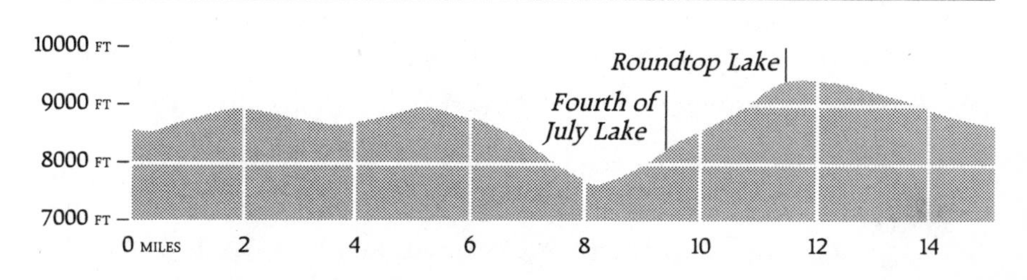

Pocket gopher

of western white pine. Occasional wind-swept junipers cling to this slope. Shortly, you descend into a willow-lined draw where a spring emerges from beneath a large rock.

Southbound now, you continue a descending traverse across a bouldery hillside. Below, to your left, is a grassy meadow where water stands in oxbow bends. At a fine spring flow originating beneath a talus slide, you reach the end of your descent and reenter a scattered hemlock and lodgepole forest. Several causeways of stone or logs and earth help prevent erosion of the trail at this point.

Climbing now over glaciated volcanics, you turn south and ascend in looping traverses toward a volcanic ridge of green, purple, and ochre tuff that lies to the south. You pass a small tarn on the right, and just above at the end of a long, curving ascent, you reenter trees (2.3 miles; 8,720 feet; 4.6 miles). At this point you also reenter Mokelumne Wilderness. Below, to your right, are two beautiful lakelets nestled in a willow-choked basin.

Soon leaving the scattered trees, you turn your back on the granitic headwall above the basin you've just traversed and cross a broad, open volcanic ridge. Leaving the wilderness again momentarily, you cross a jeep road at 8,885 feet elevation. You soon reach a junction (0.4 miles; 8,845 feet; 5.0 miles) where the Summit City Canyon Trail turns right, while the PCT continues south to Ebetts Pass. This junction is just inside the wilderness; there are signs 100 yards eastward along an unsurfaced road. Leaving the PCT, you turn right and descend the gravelly Summit City Canyon Trail. After an open area, switchbacks drop you down to the level of scattered trees. Soon you are ducking in and out of willowy draws, each with a spring flow.

Abruptly you leave volcanic rocks and enter a granitic area where the volcanics have been scoured away. Your trail will lead you over several such zones in the next mile or so. This south-facing slope suits a number of different plants; you can see junipers and some of the montane chaparral species. Deer browse heavily on some plants in this area that especially appeal to them. You are definitely below the subalpine zone.

Long traverses, punctuated with switchbacks that allow your descent to match that of the canyon bottom below, mark this section. Deadwood Peak lies across the canyon to the south, a study in glaciated granite. You enter a grove of large red firs and switchback again while in this forest. Soon you cross a dry wash area, where meltwaters or thundershower runoff has roared down the slope, carrying mud and gravel. The buildup of alluvium for some distance shows that this has happened many times in the past.

Now you come across a concrete sign base with steel posts but no sign. Near this is a stainless steel Forest Service toilet. Beyond is a camping area and a trail junction (3.0 miles; 7,505 feet; 8.0 miles.). Here a trail to Blue Lakes turns sharply left and a fork branches right to Horse Canyon. Turn right on the Horse Canyon Trail, and in 0.1 miles you reach another junction. Here the Horse Canyon Trail continues straight ahead to Camp Irene. Turn right on the Fourth of July Lake Trail.

The shade of larger trees is left behind as you cross an avalanche area where only small trees resilient enough to flex before onrushing snow and debris survive. The traverse is easy, punctuated now and again by short, steep pitches. Soon, however, the steep pitches become the rule as you labor upward through boulder-studded montane chaparral. The climb eases again as you cross the lip of the cirque and reach a junction (1.4 miles; 8,175 feet; 9.4 miles). A spur trail leads to beautiful Fourth of July Lake 100 yards away. Many fine campsites occupy the gently sloping moraine to your left. Turn right here, taking the trail to Round Top Lake.

Rufous hummingbird

Leaving Fourth of July Lake, your track ascends gently along a slope among scattered mixed conifers. As the grade steepens, switchbacks allow easy ascent among occasional western white pine, some of which are 4 feet in diameter. Soon you enter a sloping basin enclosed by high, jagged ridges above timberline. On the far side of the basin, an old trail alignment is visible. You cross a spring stream (1.1 miles; 8,760 feet; 10.5 miles), then switchback and traverse your way to the ridgetop, which is marked by another curious stone signpost base with steel posts but no sign.

Your route, now at 9,215 feet elevation, turns right and ascends the ridge diagonally, crossing over to the north side and passing through occasional clumps of whitebark pine. You move along the hummocky glacial till beneath the north face of Round Top Mountain ridge. A persistent snowfield remains from the most recent glacier at this site.

Before long you reach a spur trail branching right to Round Top Lake (1.1 miles; 9,325 feet; 11.6 miles). The lake lies in a gouge created by glacial action, between two roughly parallel recessional moraines. The newer, southernmost moraine looks almost like an island in the lake. On the northern moraine are many good campsites, each with a view of impressive Round Top Mountain as a backdrop to the lake.

Crossing the outlet stream of Round Top Lake, you pass a well-used campsite and, just beyond, a junction (0.2 miles; 9,325 feet; 11.8 miles) with a trail leading left (northwest) to Woods Lake. Continue straight ahead (east) to Winnemucca Lake. In 0.2 miles, you cross a broad, glaciated ridge at 9,420 feet elevation, the high point of this hike.

Dropping down along your sandy tread, you reach the outlet creek (1.0 mile; 9,000 feet; 12.8 miles) of Winnemucca Lake, which has been visible for the last half mile. Passing through several campsites, you reach another junction where yet another trail branches left to Woods Lake. Continue straight ahead to Carson Pass. Other campsites are evident along both sides of the trail as you skirt Winnemucca Lake. Some are closed to camping to allow restoration of compacted soil and trampled vegetation.

Walking along a broad, gravelly trail, you soon wind your way through a flat, bouldery meadow dotted with clumps of pines. After a pleasant ramble along the level, you reach a junction (1.2 miles; 8,840 feet; 14.0 miles) with the PCT.

Turn left at this junction, descending northward on the PCT, and retrace your steps 0.1 miles to the Frog Lake spur trail. Then, keeping left on the PCT, retrace your earlier route to the Carson Pass trailhead (1.1 miles; 8573 feet; 15.1 miles).

10 ♦ CARSON PASS— ROUND LAKE—MEISS LAKE

Distance:	14.4 Miles
Low elevation:	8,037 Feet
High elevation:	8,720 Feet
Class:	Moderate
Hiking time:	8 Hours

The Truckee River begins as a trickle and attains an imposing adolescence in a long, high valley just north of the Carson Pass summit. The landscape is gentle, the result of smoothing by glacial action. This friendly topography allows the Truckee's birth as a smooth-water stream, flowing in oxbows through meadows before beginning a more boisterous drop northward toward Lake Tahoe.

This valley and the surrounding hillsides were once richly covered with native grasses, sedges, and forbs. More than a century of livestock grazing has altered the native plant communities over the area. Riparian areas show the effects of grazing, too. Forested areas show little impact by comparison, although understory characteristics have no doubt changed.

The buildings and corrals observed near Meiss Meadow are located on Eldorado National Forest land that is overseen by the Lake Tahoe Basin Management Unit by virtue of being in the Truckee drainage. Used jointly by the permittee and the Forest Service, these facilities are allowed to remain on the location. This would not be the case in an established wilderness.

Volcanic eruptions beginning around 30 million years ago buried the Sierra in this area under thick layers of lava, mud, and ash. Most of this volcanic rock was eroded away by water and glaciers, but on some of the higher ridges and mountaintops, much volcanic material remains. The pond-blessed pass just north of Carson summit is volcanic, as are the north-trending ridges to either side. Layers of volcanic material are plainly visible on the east side of Round Lake. Boulders from cliffs of autobrecciated lava, broken pieces cemented together with fine material, have tumbled down to the lakeshore, where they may easily be inspected.

The glacial gouging that created Round Lake also uncovered the granodiorite that lay beneath volcanic and sedimentary rock. The rocks now exposed along the east shore of Round Lake are volcanic, while the west shore is granodiorite boulders and outcroppings. The routing will be on granitic rock and soils from that point to Showers Lake.

At Meiss Lake, resistant domes of granodiorite, which forced glacial ice to mold around them, were not worn away as fast as other areas of softer materials. Such domes are visible in and around the lake.

Hike routing maintains an even elevation over most of the distance. A red fir and mixed conifer forest community shades much of the route, while some sections lead through subalpine meadows. During an early-season hike, when the wildflowers were just beginning to bloom, we saw mule's ears, lupine, paintbrush, mountain violet, bluebells, skyrocket, desert parsley, and cliff penstemon. Wildlife we spotted included the coyote, mule deer, golden-mantled ground squirrel, chipmunk, black-backed woodpecker, Audubon's warbler, Clark's nutcracker, raven, red-tailed hawk, and the ever-present junco and robin.

Sierra weather patterns differ here only in that conditions are perhaps more mild. Still, snowfall is considerable during normal years, and the area is popular for cross-country skiing, in part because of the gentle topography of the upper Truckee drainage.

The PCT in this area is also sometimes known as the Tahoe to Yosemite Trail. Not as heavily used as the PCT/JMT segment between Whitney and Tuolumne Meadows, this routing offers solitude and a pleasant environment.

DESCRIPTION

This hike is a partial loop, retracing a portion of the route on the return. Routed along a gentle portion of the PCT, it has been classified as moderate because elevation gains are not great and the trail is, for the most part, excellent. The conditioned hiker can complete this route in less than a day, but doing so will not allow time to fully appreciate the area or observe this particular ecosystem. For this reason it is recommended that, if possible, you make this an overnight hike.

This is not a wilderness hike; rather, it penetrates into a subalpine environment above 8,000 feet elevation where humans have had an impact on the flora and fauna. Livestock grazing has caused much of the impact, as permittees have been using the region for more than a century. In many ways, much of the area does not appear to have been affected. For example, the heavily forested areas appear much like other places at similar elevations where grazing does not take place.

But on the open slopes above the forest patches, few of the native grasses are present. Forbs, sage, and similar plants have become dominant. If you look closely at these slopes, you can see the maze of grazing trails where hooves have cut into fragile soils. At present, a disproportionate amount of the surface on these slopes and ridges is bare mineral soil. A lack of native grasses means that little natural reseeding occurs, and some grasses that do take root are destroyed the same season by grazing.

The more obvious effects of grazing at high altitude are especially revealed in the riparian zones, which are generously sprinkled along the route. Damage can be seen along the headwaters of the Truckee River, which is the main inflow into Lake Tahoe. Many studies have been done on the effects of livestock concentrations in riparian zones. The erosion of streambanks caused by thousand-pound animals with sharp hooves is obvious. When there are dozens or hundreds of animals occupying one small area, it is easy to see why there is sparse native vegetation remaining to stabilize streambanks. Bank erosion and downcutting are the result, and if the proceed to even moderate degrees, the ability of the zone to heal itself within a reasonable time is doubtful.

Downcutting of the moisture-supplying stream brings about the drying of riparian areas. When downcutting no longer allows streamside vegetation to reach the surface water and slow its flow, the rate of erosion accelerates. Then the exposed banks allow groundwater in the adjoining flat areas to drain off into the stream, further increasing erosion and making it even more difficult for vegetation to become established on bank areas.

Once the stream has dropped a few feet by this process, it is no longer possible for regrowth of vegetation to reverse the cycle. Hikers often see sagebrush growing right up to the edges of streams that now

Administrative agency: USFS

Eldorado National Forest
Information Center
3070 Camino Heights Drive
Camino, CA 95709
(916) 644-6048

USGS map: 7.5′ series, Carson Pass, Caples Lake, Echo Lake, California

Declination: 16½ degrees

flow in deep gullies—the final result. Returning the health of such damaged riparian areas awaits fortuitous action of beavers, or the next ice age.

The observant hiker will see at least one area along this route where the Forest Service has done streambank repair. In another spot, fencing has been used in an effort to limit streamside grazing.

This route begins on the PCT, heads north, then branches east on a loop to visit scenic Round Lake and Meiss Lake. Returning to the PCT, it leads northwest for 3.5 miles to Showers Lake before completing the hike southbound on the PCT to the starting point.

The upper Truckee watershed, like most of the Sierra, has experienced heavy glaciation. While the contact area between volcanic and granitic rock is usually hidden by sediments or debris, you can see several spots where the change takes place within a few yards.

Snow is usually off the trails by mid-June, and the area remains pleasant to hike until the middle of October. Typical afternoon thunderstorms can be experienced here. Generally, though, the climate is quite benign for an area at this elevation.

Mosquitoes are present, especially in early season, with their numbers tapering off by midsummer.

Black bears in moderate numbers inhabit this region. For the most part, they have not yet learned to perceive hikers' packs as a source of food, but you should still be sure to bear-bag your food and keep a clean camp.

DIRECTIONS TO TRAILHEAD

The trailhead is at the Carson Pass summit, on State Route 88, located 28 miles west of Minden, Nevada, and 64 miles east of Jackson, California.

At the summit, there are a paved parking lot, toilets, and a Forest Service information building, which is staffed during the summer season.

TRAIL ROUTE DESCRIPTION

MAP 10

At the paved parking area on the south side of Route 88, at the Carson Pass summit at 8,573 feet elevation, there are two bronze historic markers. Cross from there to the north side of the highway, watching carefully for traffic. Then move a few yards to your left (west) and take the yards-long trail that leaves the roadside and leads up onto the old highway right-of-way. Continue down the old pavement for a few hundred feet to a wide spot, from which the route becomes a real trail and heads west at a signboard. Notice the remarkable old junipers in this area—scattered, thick of trunk, but not very tall. The trail climbs, undulating through granite boulders and lodgepole pines.

Still heading westward, you can see a few firs and then brushy colonies of quaking aspen. At a junction (1.0 mile from last point; 8,360 feet

MAP 10

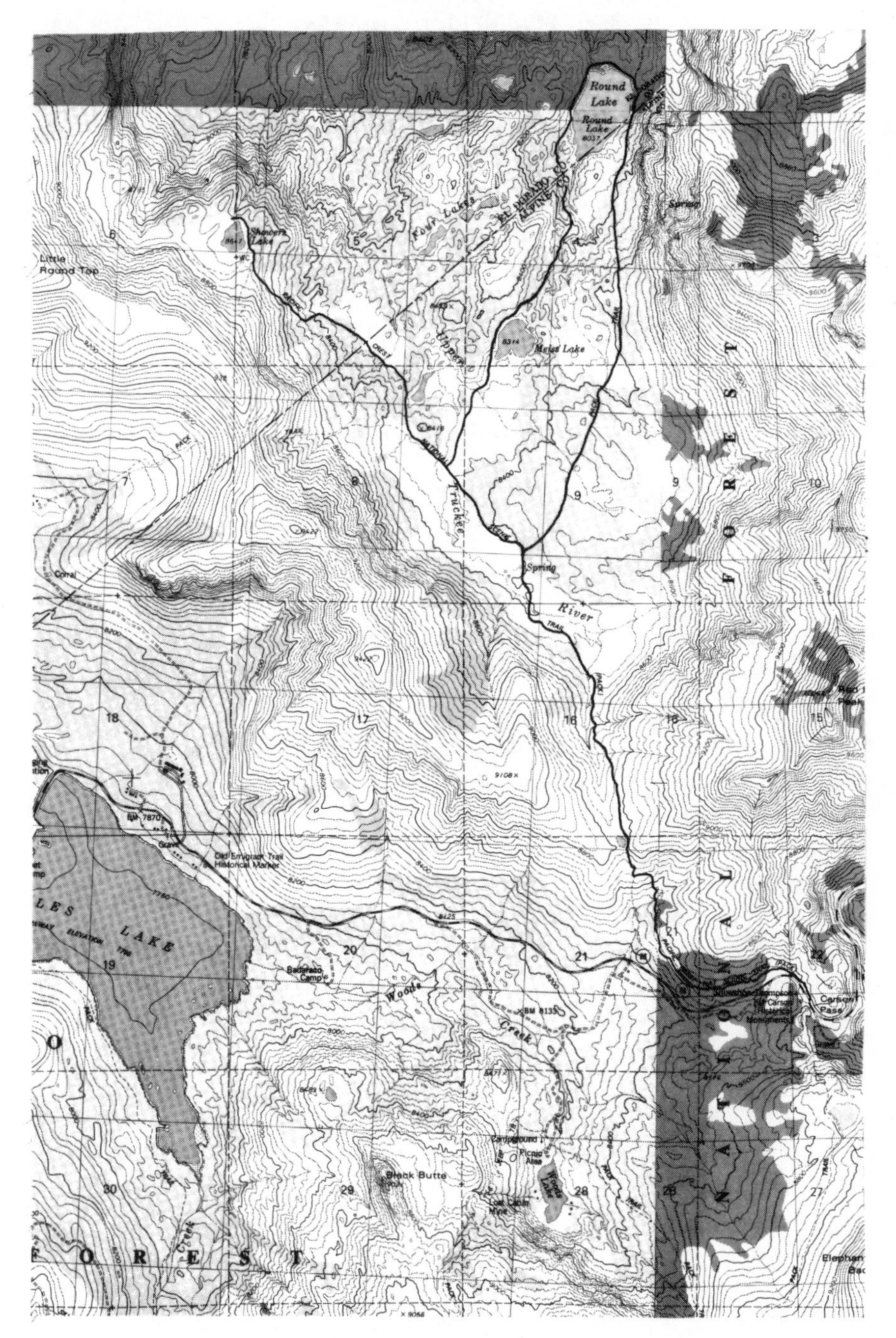

Round Lake
Four Lakes
Showers Lake
Little Round Top
Meiss Lake
Upper Truckee River
Spring
Coral
Old Emigrant Trail Historical Marker
BM 7870
Badlands Camp
Woods Creek
BM 8135
Campground
Picnic Area
Black Butte
Lost Cabin Mine
Carson Pass
F O R E S T
N A T I O N A L

above sea level; 1.0 total mile), a trail branches left down the hill to the old Meiss Lake trailhead on Route 88. Continue straight ahead. You leave most of the trees and enter a bowl where your trail crosses willow-lined gullies. You wind among them and then begin a steady, switchbacking ascent. This open south slope is favored habitat for a number of wildflowers. Phlox, buttercup, and woolly sunflowers spring up quickly shortly after the snow leaves. Later bloomers follow all through the season.

Near the top of this hill, your trail, which is now quite wide, is joined by an old, no-longer-used road that appeared from myriad eroded tracks on your left. Soon you reach level trail again at a small, half-acre pond (0.5 miles; 8,760 feet; 1.5 miles) that is fed entirely from meltwater from large snowdrifts on the east and west. From this spot, if you turn and look south, you can see Woods Lake just south of Route 88 below, as well as the entire ridge that borders Carson Pass to the south, Elephants Back, and Round Top. It is interesting to note that the Roundtop Glacier, spawned on the northeast slope of that mountain, became so immense that part of it overflowed and crossed the saddle on which you now stand to move down the Truckee River drainage.

Now you move north through a gate structure in a drift fence by the pond, and within a few yards you come to the beginning of the Truckee River drainage. A minute or two later, you are on the best viewpoint of this route at 8,535 feet elevation, looking north into Lake Tahoe in the distance. You may spot mountain violets in this area.

Descending now along the dual track, which is the old road the permittee used for access, you soon enter the west side of a beautiful bowl meadow, where you can cross the embryonic Upper Truckee River in a single bound.

A level meander among scattered lodgepole brings you to an old drift fence (1.2 miles; 8,400 feet; 2.7 miles). A campsite is located in a lodgepole clump on the right just past the fence. Soon after, you can see restoration work on the streambank just before your route crosses the stream a second time.

A short time later, after traversing subirrigated meadows, you reach another old fence crossing. A cabin, shed, and corral 100 yards to the west are used in season by the permittee and occasionally by the Forest Service.

A few yards north, you reach a junction (0.3 miles; 8,400 feet; 3.0 miles) where your trail to Round Lake branches right from the PCT. You turn right and move basically north through a forest of lodgepole and occasional California fir. There are lots of dead trees in this area, and with luck you may see more than one species of woodpecker. This is an open, friendly woods—one of those places where one shouldn't hurry.

At a small meadow on the right, you can see more evidence of the effects of livestock grazing in riparian areas. Two surface levels, separated by bare earthen banks, are clearly present in this meadow where numbers of cattle sometimes congregate. Don't be confused by the cattle trails that converge on this meadow; continue ahead, cross the seasonal outlet from the meadow, and again enter the pleasant forest.

Soon you cross a creek (0.9 miles; 8,380 feet; 3.9 miles) that ceases to flow during dry periods. Just beyond, notice a log structure that prevents cattle from grazing along the streambank. There has already been damage here that will not self-repair.

After making a short ascent, you can view a narrow, twisting meadow to the left and below; then you level out to cross openings and pass quaking aspens. Now you enter an older age class forest of lodgepole and red fir. Some of these trees reach 4 to 5 feet in diameter. Soon, the dark outlines of volcanic cliffs are visible through the trees above and to your right.

Your descent continues to Round Lake (1.2 miles; 8,000 feet; 5.1 miles), where a camp on your left is too close to the water. Some distance along the lake, note four huge boulders lying to the left of the trail near the water. These have come from the cliffs above, and their makeup of autobrecciated volcanic materials tell you of the cliffs' composition. Near the boulders is a legal camp among trees up the hill to your right, on sloping ground.

On the north shore you reach a junction (0.2 miles; 8,000 feet; 5.3 miles) where the Meiss Meadow Trail continues north to a roadhead in 3.5 miles. Stay left (west) along the shore, past an illegal camp at the junction, and note picturesque trees growing from the volcanics along the trail. You walk over the moraine here that formed at least some of Round Lake. Narrow peninsulas of deposited volcanic materials support a few trees and make this end of Round Lake quite different from the upper end, where glaciated granite outcroppings are evident.

Crossing the outlet, you can see a small dam that was installed years ago to raise the water level a few feet. When you clamber up the opposite bank, you enter a world of granite. The volcanic material that covered this granite has been eroded completely away, now most likely reposing at the bottom of Lake Tahoe.

Vertical Profile of Hike 10

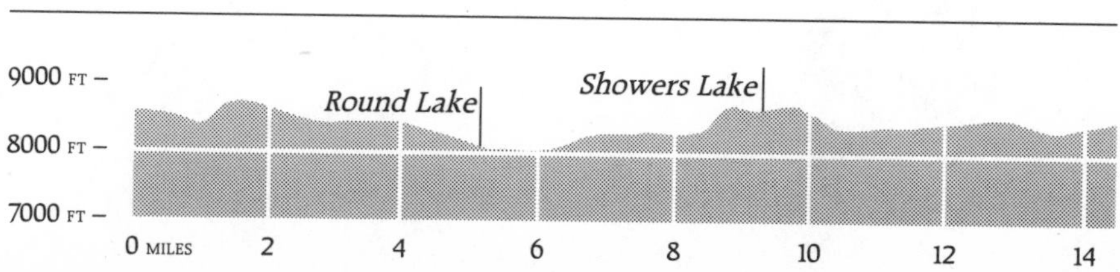

Take your pick of trails to follow through the granite boulders as you make your way south along the west shore, always secure in the knowledge that the routes parallel the lakeshore. Use trails are plentiful, and some lead to more than one excellent, legal campsite from which the views of the lake against a backdrop of rugged, stratified cliffs are impressive. Near the extreme south end of Round Lake, at a small inlet and rocky point (0.6 miles; 8,040 feet; 5.9 miles), these trails all converge.

When you leave the lake, you follow along the right side of a long, narrow, swampy pond that is usually dry except during runoff periods. You traverse an obviously damp area with willows; here the tread is again obvious. Toward the lake from this spot, beavers have cut quaking aspens. The beavers sometimes did so while atop several feet of snow, resulting in stumps 6 or more feet high.

Continuing south, your trail follows along the top of a lateral moraine and gains altitude quite rapidly. You pass a series of ponds ringed with willows on your left. These ponds, connected by a small seasonal stream, provide little water during the dry season. Now your ascent is gentle as you cross the resistant granite that forms the elevated northeast shore of shallow, glacier-carved Meiss Lake (0.8 miles; 8,320 feet; 6.7 miles). About 25 acres in extent, this lake offers good swimming because the shallow waters warm easily. The boulders jutting out of the water were dropped by a receding glacier. When the water level is high, a resistant, tree-studded formation becomes an island. There are several good campsites along the north shoreline of Meiss Lake.

The trail becomes faint again as you leave Meiss Lake and head west-southwest up the meadow. You can use any of the various cattle trails, staying in the meadow with the lake at your back. This will soon bring you to the twin-track PCT at the head of the meadow, with the north-flowing Upper Truckee River just beyond (0.8 miles; 8,320 feet; 7.5 miles).

Turn right (north) a few yards to the river crossing, where you can rock hop across just to the right of the trail crossing or, if the water is

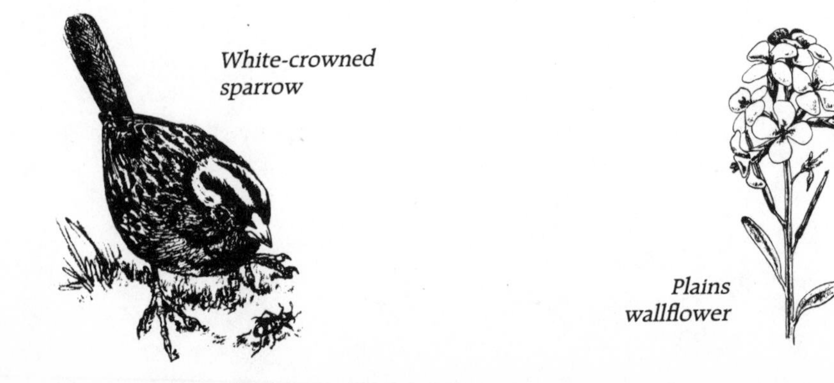

White-crowned sparrow

Plains wallflower

high, remove your boots and wade across any of the shallow areas just upstream.

A few hundred yards of gentle ascent northwest on the PCT brings you to a saddle, just before which you can see a large Jeffrey pine on the left. At this point a faint trail branches left to ascend the ridge and lead eventually to Schneider's Camp. Move ahead across the broad saddle to begin a gentle descent through a scattered forest of lodgepole. A small unnamed lake lies on your right. Your old road, while apparent in some areas, has largely disappeared now, and only trail tread beckons ahead as you leave the meadow, turn noticeably left (northwest) (0.8 miles; 8,320 feet; 8.3 miles), and begin an ascent through mixed conifers.

A few short, steep switches move you upward onto open slopes shared with brushy willows and lonely firs. Moving northwestward across more of the same, you soon reach the top of this spur ridge (0.5 miles; 8,720 feet; 8.8 miles). In a slight depression on the ridgetop, a trail branches left (southwest) to join with the trail leading to Schneider's Camp. Pretty Showers Lake lies at the foot of the lush, seeping hillside to your left.

Proceeding down to Showers Lake (0.4 miles; 8,650 feet; 9.2 miles), you enter an area where mountain hemlock are present. Rounded granitic outcroppings along the west shore make it evident that Showers Lake lies in a glaciated, granite bowl. As with Round Lake, a small dam has raised the water level of Showers Lake. Pleasant camping areas are found here under lodgepole, hemlock, and western white pine. Trout fishing is usually good, although the fish are small.

Dropping down and across the outlet creek to climb the other side into a minienvironment of granite should definitely be on your exploration list for this turnaround point, the northern terminus of this hike. From Showers Lake, the PCT continues north about 10 miles to Route 50 and Echo Summit. You turn around, however, and head south, back the way you have come.

In 0.9 miles, you reascend the ridge, complete the descent, and turn south along the meadow edge. In another 0.4 miles, you pass the unnamed lake you saw previously, and 0.3 miles farther, cross the Upper Truckee River, and continue south along the trail on a section you bypassed previously.

These 0.6 miles pass quickly as you stroll through scattered lodgepole along the meadow fringe and find yourself at the junction with Meiss Meadow Trail, where you previously turned to Round Lake. Passing by the cabins on your right, you move south up the meadow, cross the fledgling river twice, and arrive at the divide pond in just 1.5 miles. Dropping onto the south slope, you descend switchbacks for 0.4 miles to the Old Meiss Lake trailhead junction, then continue left the way you came along the PCT 1.1 miles to the Carson Pass trailhead.

11 ♦ DESOLATION WILDERNESS—ECHO LAKE—EMERALD BAY

Distance:	21.9 Miles
Low elevation:	6,580 Feet
High elevation:	9,400 Feet
Class:	Difficult
Hiking time:	16 Hours

The Desolation Wilderness lies directly west of the southern end of Lake Tahoe, an 8x13-mile expanse of exposed granitic ridges and valleys straddling the present-day crest of the Sierra. Seldom does so much unspoiled territory lie so close to a burgeoning area like populous South Tahoe. Needless to say, Desolation Wilderness is a popular place; beauty and ease of access see to that.

The wilderness is named for the scoured Desolation Valley, which is occupied by Lake Aloha. The word "desolation" is a fitting description. So completely did glaciers remove preexisting soils and rock, and so slowly is the exposed rock weathering, that little soil is being formed and few trees thrive. Most patches of forest in this wilderness grow on moraines or debris deposited by glaciers, and meadows are scarce above 7,000 feet.

Nearly 130 lakes of all sizes dot the 100-square-mile wilderness. There is no place on this route more than a few hundred yards from a lake, or at least the view of one. Most of the route, with the exception of the drop into the Lake Aloha basin, is along east-slope drainage. Streams here flow into Lake Tahoe via Fallen Leaf Lake, Cascade Lake, or directly. The Truckee River outflow from Tahoe leads to Pyramid Lake in Nevada, part of the Great Basin closed system.

The land area between the Sierra and Carson ranges subsided along faults, which resulted in Lake Tahoe. Volcanism and ensuing lava flows 2 million years ago changed stream flows, diverting their water into Lake Tahoe. Glaciation, at its most active here 200,000 years ago, deposited sediments in the lake, along with the likely calving of icebergs. Much of this sediment was redistributed by Tahoe's currents, and no terminal moraines survive, but it is estimated that the glaciers may have extended as much as a mile into the lake from the present shoreline.

Trees you will encounter on this hike include ponderosa, Jeffrey, western white, and whitebark pines; red fir; mountain hemlock; incense cedar; and western juniper. The cedar is found at lower elevations.

While hiking this trail shortly after snowmelt, we saw a variety of wildflowers: crimson columbine, lupine, alpine lupine, paintbrush, corn lily, woolly sunflower, spreading phlox, yarrow, wandering daisy, snowflower, western meadowrue, Davidson's penstemon, larkspur, and shooting star. Many other species were not yet in bloom. Early-season wildlife includes the mule deer, Belding's ground squirrel, golden-mantled ground squirrel, chipmunk, Stellar's jay, white-headed woodpecker, Clark's nutcracker, black-capped chickadee, white-breasted nuthatch, robins, and junco.

A low coastal range here allows winter storms to proceed northeastward while still carrying large amounts of moisture, guaranteeing heavy precipitation for the Tahoe area. Most of that precipitation falls as snow, and monumental depths result. This is good news for the many winter sports areas and their aficionados. Winter sport activities within Desolation Wilderness have become common, and traveling there during that season can be rewarding. During the late 1980s and early '90s, however, snowfall was far below normal.

DESCRIPTION

This is not a loop hike. The route has been selected based on scenic considerations and to allow you to truly experience the Desolation Wilderness area. The beginning trailhead is at Echo Lake resort, just north of U.S. Route 50 at Echo Summit, and the exit trailhead is on State Route 89 at Emerald Bay, some 900 feet lower in elevation. Both areas are very busy, and hitchhiking possibilities are good into and out of South Tahoe, which lies in between. If you can position transportation at both ends, so much the better. The hike is classified as moderate because of the distance involved, as well as elevation changes.

The Pacific Crest Trail negotiates the wilderness almost from end to end, entering just 2.5 miles north of the southernmost extent. The high usage of the Desolation Wilderness means this portion of the PCT is well traveled. This is also the terminus of the Tahoe-to-Yosemite trail designation; the Tahoe-bound north segment branches from the PCT north of Middle Velma Lake, reaching Tahoe at Meeks Bay.

The topmost 12 feet of water in Echo Lake is owned by Pacific Gas and Electric Company, because the company constructed a dam to raise the level by that amount. Before the dam, Upper and Lower Echo Lakes were joined by a flowing stream. Now, when the dam is closed, there is a single, larger lake. By fall, the power company usually has drawn down its quota of water and the two lakes are again separated.

Echo Lake Resort, located at the dam, operates a water taxi on the lake during much of the summer. More than 2.5 miles of this hike can be covered by boat, if you're so inclined. From the boat dock at the north end of Echo Lake, it is but a short ascent to the PCT. A telephone is located at the boat dock. Make arrangements for boat rides at the resort.

One of the more striking aspects of this hike is the bleakness of the wide, glaciated, granitic basins. Whether the city of Sacramento heightened or lessened the appeal of Desolation Valley by constructing a dam to create Lake Aloha depends on the observer—and the time of year. A sparse lodgepole forest that was beginning to colonize the bare expanses of granodiorite was summarily drowned; their corpses are the gray, broken snags projecting from the water that you can see today. Actually, more than one dam was necessary: So shallow and level was the valley that without a plug dam, water would have overflowed into Heather Lake and down Glen Alpine Creek to increase the contribution of Fallen Leaf Lake to Lake Tahoe.

The route from the Aloha Valley to Heather Lake takes you across the Sierra Crest. Here, waters spill tumultuously down toward Tahoe. You left the granitics of Echo Lake to walk on metamorphics at Haypress Meadows, and you now leave granite-cupped Aloha to again encounter colorful metamorphic rocks around Heather Lake and the projection from Jacks Peak.

You experience typical east-side Desolation lakes and landforms as you pass Susie, Gilmore, Dicks, and Velma lakes. Then you begin the same downcanyon trip taken by the glacier that carved beautiful Emerald Bay and deposited the lateral moraines on either side.

During this hike, you cross life zones beginning with montane chaparral, which gives way to a red fir–subalpine forest, which higher

---

Administrative agency: USFS

Eldorado National Park	Desolation Wilderness
Information Center	Lake Tahoe Basin Mgmt.
3070 Camino Heights Drive	P.O.B. 731002
Camino, CA 95709	South Lake Tahoe, CA 95731
(916) 644-6048	(916) 573-2600

USGS maps: 7.5′ series, Echo Lake, Pyramid Peak, Rockbound Valley, Emerald Bay, California

Declination: 17½ degrees

still becomes a true alpine vegetation zone. There is much blending of zones, with many species present in two and sometimes all three. Many plants have rooted in the poor soils, making this a good area for wildflowers in season.

Hiking is usually possible, without fighting too many snowdrifts, July 1. The 8,000-foot average elevation is high for this latitude; snow can begin to build up on the passes by mid-October.

At present, you need a permit for overnight stays in Desolation Wilderness. Wilderness rangers do check permits and often issue citations to those without the necessary permission. Be sure to contact the Lake Tahoe Basin Management Unit for current conditions and regulations.

Black bears are present in Desolation Wilderness, but compared with those in Yosemite, they are timid. Still, it is a good idea to use care with food and bear-bag it at night if you wish to be certain of having it in the morning.

If the bears are somewhat timid, the mosquitoes are not. These insects can be very persistent, especially as the snow is melting and for a few weeks after. Take repellent.

DIRECTIONS TO TRAILHEAD

Two roadheads are used for this hike. The entrance roadhead is at Echo Lake Resort. The signed turnoff to Echo Lake is on Route 50, 0.5 miles west of Echo Summit and 0.25 miles west of Little Norway. Turn north here and proceed 0.3 miles to a junction signed "Echo Lake." Turn left and drive 0.5 miles to a large, paved parking lot on the left. Just below this spot is the resort, where parking is reserved for guests and homeowners. Besides the lodge facilities, there is a store and a telephone here. The resort also runs a boat taxi the length of the two lakes.

The exit roadhead is on State Route 89 at Emerald Bay, on the west side of Lake Tahoe. Located on the west side of the highway where Eagle Creek drops into the head of Emerald Bay, this popular roadhead serves hikers going to Eagle Falls and Eagle Lake. Parking is provided for about thirty vehicles. There are toilets and a few picnic tables, as well as a trailhead register for self-issued day hike permits. There is considerable traffic on Route 89, as well as visitor parking just north of this spot for visitors to Vikingsholm. Securing a ride to South Tahoe and then Echo Summit may not be difficult.

TRAIL ROUTE DESCRIPTION

The PCT here at Echo Lake Resort begins at a trailhead signboard and day hike register at the walkway over the dam. You can get a head start on this hike by taking the water taxi to the end of Echo Lake; the resort operates this service from Memorial Day to Labor Day.

MAP 11A

From the trail register, walk across the dam. The trail immediately switchbacks upward to gain a bit of elevation in a landscape of montane chaparral sprinkled with ponderosa and lodgepole pines. You are in a world of granite, and glacial polish is evident on many surfaces. You'll see many cabins around Echo Lake. On the north side of the lake, most of these cabins are on land that has been privately owned for many years. On the south side, the cabins are on land leased from the USFS. On the latter you must incinerate or use pack-out toilets, while on private land outhouses are allowed. The water quality in Echo Lake is not pristine, and the dense population along the shore might be one reason for this.

The trail is wide and heavily used as far as the last cabin. It soon moves away from the lakeside clutter, however, and a runoff channel provides enough moisture for mountain ash and willows. At a junction (2.6 miles from last point; 7,500 feet above sea level; 2.6 total miles) a trail branches left, down to the west end of the lake and the water taxi. If you have used water transportation, this is where you join the PCT.

At a junction (0.5 miles; 7,670 feet; 3.1 miles) with the Triangle Lakes Trail, which branches right, you continue straight ahead and enter Desolation Wilderness. Trekking on past occasional lodgepole pines, you ascend to still another junction (0.3 miles; 7,860 feet; 3.4 miles), at which the Tamarack Lake Trail branches left. Tamarack Lake is soon visible in a granite bowl carved into the canyon bottom. As you go straight and ascend on a good grade, you'll leave behind all the day hikers but a hardy few who are going to Lake Aloha. Before long you reach a third junction (0.6 miles; 8,240 feet; 4.0 miles), where the Lily Lake Trail branches right. Continue straight ahead. Willows and corn lilies grow around a marshy area here, as well as large western white pines.

In 0.4 miles the trail branches left to Lake of the Woods, in a broad saddle where red fir and mountain hemlock are the dominant species. Keep to the right here. Note several elevated causeways constructed to keep the trail above runoff during snowmelt times.

Soon you approach another junction (0.6 miles; 8,160 feet; 4.6 miles) in another saddle where yet another trail to Lake of the Woods branches left near the west end of Haypress Meadows. A few hundred feet beyond this junction another trail branches right, the beginning of a loop that winds around Lake Margery and returns to the PCT 0.5 miles farther on. Continue straight on the PCT, descending through mixed conifers to a junction with the Aloha Trail, which branches left to Lake Aloha, rejoining the PCT more than a mile ahead. Again continue straight ahead on the PCT, still descending through shady forest. Shortly you pass a small pond on your left, as well as the point where the Lake Margery Trail rejoins the PCT. Stay on the PCT, which continues straight ahead. You pass another small pond, this one on the right.

Finally, reaching campsites and the level of Lake Aloha, you come upon the junction (1.4 miles 8,160 feet; 6.0 miles) where the Lake Aloha Trail rejoins the PCT on your left. Heather flourishes in this area, and you can find it growing trailside as well as from cracks in the granite. Note the dead tree skeletons in Lake Aloha waters—the telltale sign of a man-made lake.

The breadth of this basin attests to the power of the glaciers that formed it. Consider the amount of material that has been scoured away. Islands in Lake Aloha are made of more resistant rock, and the large boulders lying about were dropped as the glaciers melted.

The trail passes a meltwater pond on the left, then leaves the lakeside briefly and traverses through a grove of large western white pines

MAP 11B

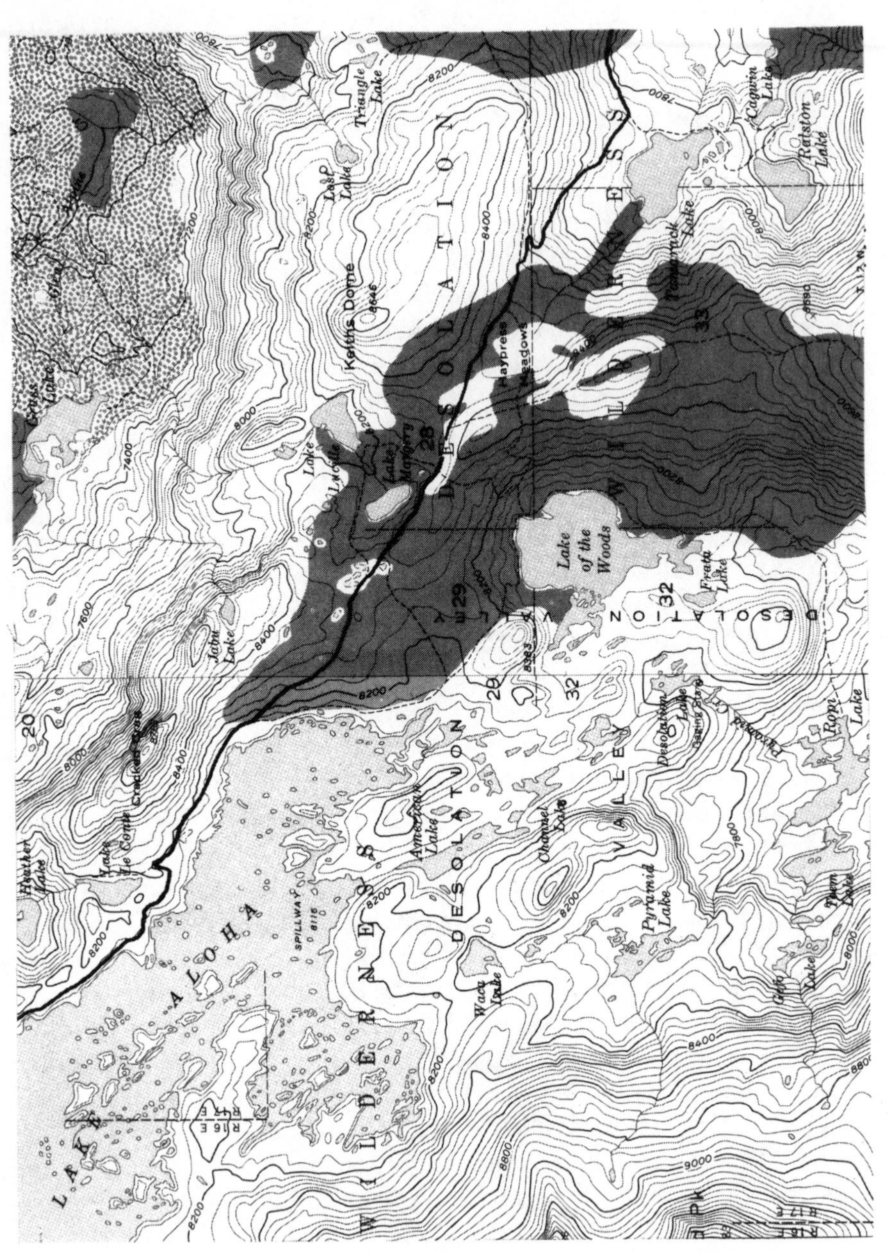

with scaly, orange bark. Just before the PCT crests a small spur ridge, a faint trail branches off to the right, leading to beautiful Lake Le Conte, which lies nestled in a small basin above the main trail. By all means visit this picturesque lake.

The PCT now wends northwestward through granite boulders and ledges, once again along the shore of Lake Aloha. Just beyond low rock dams on each side of the trail, you reach a junction (1.5 miles; 8,140 feet; 7.5 miles) where Trail 16E05 branches left to Mosquito Pass. Turn right on the PCT, which here is signed "Dicks Lake." Several sharp switchbacks take you quickly down and across a wooden causeway. The scattered debris and skinned trees here are signs that this is an avalanche runout area.

You descend still farther and cross a creek. On your right are a small wooden bridge and a pond. There are beautiful waterfalls here, especially in early season when runoff is heavy. Shortly you reach Heather Lake at its inlet creek (0.6 miles; 7,950 feet; 8.1 miles). Just across the creek are a large rock and a western white pine that is 6 feet or more in diameter. This is an excellent area to find uncommon wildflowers.

The trail continues along the rocky slope above the lake; in places your track has been blasted from the rock. You soon descend to Susie Lake, located in a basin of volcanic rock. The glaciers here melted before stripping away all of the volcanic rock from atop the underlying granite, and from this point to Gilmore Lake and Dicks Pass, you often will be treading on metamorphic and volcanic rocks and soils derived from them.

Your track winds around the sparsely wooded south end of Susie Lake to the outlet creek (1.2 miles; 7,720 feet; 9.3 miles) and a small water-regulating structure. A good campsite is on the right just across the creek, above the cascading falls of the outlet. This site is superior to the tiny, heavily used sites along Susie Lake itself.

Crossing over a rocky ridge, you pass two melt ponds on your left and descend to a marshy bottom. You ascend gently into the woods on the far side and reach a junction (0.7 miles; 7,790 feet; 10.0 miles) at which the right-branching trail leads to Glen Alpine in a little over 4 miles. Continue straight ahead, ascending the brushy hill on switchbacks. A pond lies ahead, then your trail switches away from it. You soon arrive at a four-way junction (0.5 miles; 7,815 feet; 10.5 miles). The right-hand fork leads a short distance to join the trail to Glen Alpine, while the left branch leads 1.5 miles to Half Moon Lake. Hike straight ahead, up a trail well maintained with timber water bars and rails.

In 0.5 miles, you approach a cascading stream 150 feet to your right and soon reach the junction (0.6 miles; 8,300 feet; 11.1 miles) with a trail signed "Gilmore Lake." This trail passes by the southeast shore of that lake as it leads to the summit of volcanic-capped Mount Tallac. Go left on the PCT, and in a few hundred feet you can see Gilmore Lake 200 yards to your right. There is fine camping on the broad, open-forested moraine between the lake and trail in this area. Gilmore Lake occupies a large bowl formed by moraines on the south. Impressive headwalls complete a half circle above the lake. A small cirque to the north looks as though it

MAP 11C

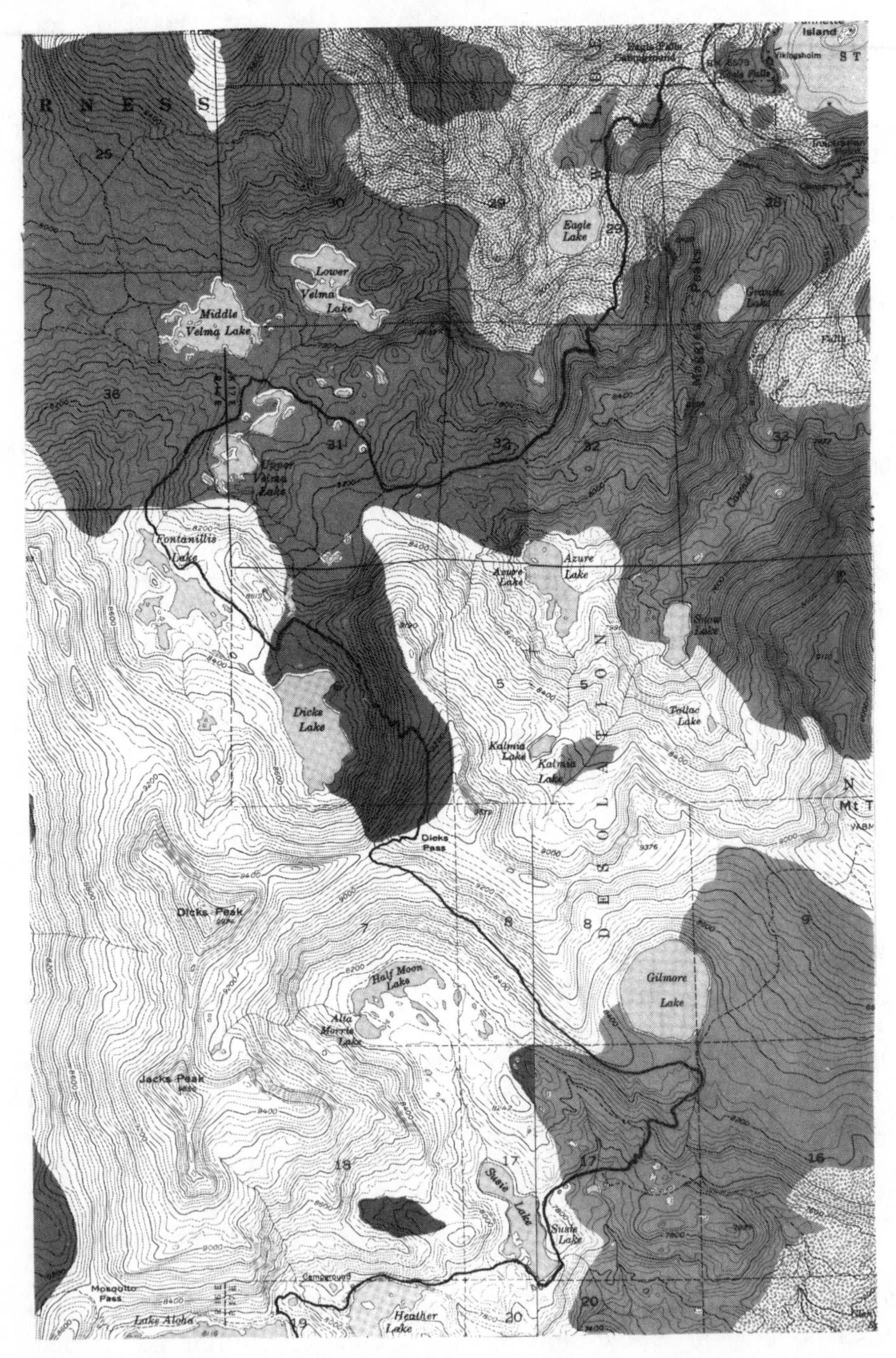

Eagle Lake
Lower Velma Lake
Middle Velma Lake
Upper Velma Lake
Granite Lake
Fontanillis Lake
Azure Lake
Snow Lake
Dicks Lake
Tallac Lake
Kalmia Lake
Dicks Pass
Dicks Peak
Half Moon Lake
Alta Morris Lake
Gilmore Lake
Jacks Peak
Susie Lake
Mosquito Pass
Lake Aloha
Heather Lake

may contain a lakelet, but it does not. You may see Belding's ground squirrels and blue grouse here.

As you ascend a bench paralleling a ridge to your right, numerous pondlets come into view in the granite to your left and below. The glacier that put the finishing touches on this valley 10,000 years ago must have been immense. Note that where you stand, near its origin, the glacier was moving in a southeasterly direction. Resistant ridges caused the ice mass to curve to the east, where it carved the bed of Fallen Leaf Lake and carried large amounts of sediments northward, to later deposit them in the waters of Lake Tahoe. If you examine the low point in the ridge between Heather Lake and Lake Aloha, you surmise that some ice from the flow in the Aloha Basin spilled through that gap to add mass to the abrasive forces flowing down Alpine Creek toward Tahoe.

Even Pyramid Peak to the south of Lake Aloha, at 9,983 feet elevation, wash carved smooth on all but its highest facets by glaciers, which created its present-day rounded projections as well as those of Mount Agassiz.

Before long you can see Half Moon Lake below, shaped roughly like its namesake. Continuing upward through miniature meadows and picturesque, gnarled pines, you soon reach Dicks Pass (2.1 miles; 9,210 feet; 13.2 miles), from which you have excellent views north and south. From the pass, a faint trail leads west to 9,974-foot Dicks Peak. A few whitebark pines struggle on these windswept ridges.

You jog east here and may chose either of two trail alignments that rejoin 0.25 miles up the ridge. You enter sparse forest and traverse the top portion of a northwest slope high above Dicks Lake, at 9,400 feet, before dropping in several switchbacks. Fine views entertain you to the left. The Forest Service has blasted shallow trenches in the granite to serve as a trail in some sections. At least these spots will be slow to erode, something that cannot be said for the old trail alignment, which is visible in several places nearby.

You continue to descend and reach the junction (1.9 miles; 8,350 feet; 15.1 miles) with the Bay View Trail, which branches right and leads to the

Vertical Profile of Hike 11

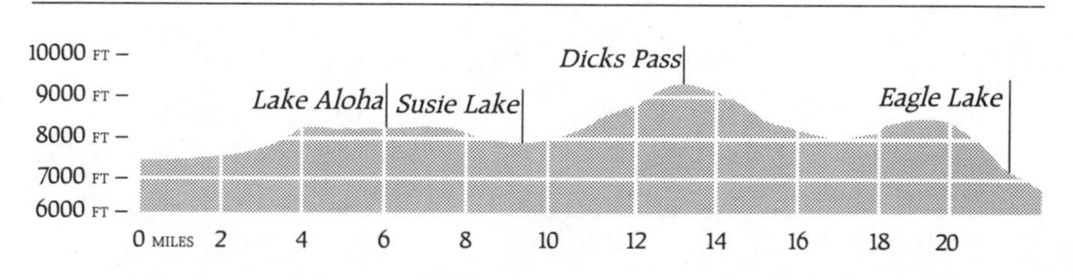

Bay View roadhead along Route 89 on the south ridge above Emerald Bay. Your trail branches left, and in 0.2 miles you arrive at another junction, where a short spur trail branches left to the outlet of Dicks Lake.

Taking the PCT to the right, you soon pass a snowmelt pond on the left, beyond which you can see the waters of Fontanillis Lake. A short distance farther, there is another pond on your left, for which your trail serves as an outlet during runoff. Before long you are walking along the shoreline of pretty Fontanillis Lake. You can cross the outlet stream on a logjam. Note that you once again are standing in an avalanche runout area, evidenced by the scarred, bent trees damaged by snow avalanches that swept across the frozen lake surface.

Beldings ground squirrel

Now you tramp onto a broad moraine and almost immediately begin a descent down the sloping surface. A few minutes later, Upper Velma Lake is visible through the trees on your right. In a few yards you cross a seasonal creek and begin a pleasant, level meander through cathedral-like mountain hemlock and red fir. All too soon this leads you to another descent along a lateral moraine to the junction (2.1 miles; 7,935 feet; 17.2 miles) where you bid farewell to the PCT, which continues to the left and past Middle Velma Lake to Phipps Pass. It is well worth hiking the few hundred yards down to the shore of beautiful Middle Velma, with its picturesque islands, good fishing, and camping.

Leaving the PCT, you turn right at this junction. Observe the glacial striations in the granite over which you stride. In little more than 0.1 miles, you pass a junction where the trail to Upper Velma Lake branches right. Just beyond this, you cross the outlet creek from that lake. Your route now takes you upward into rocks, past two melt ponds on the right and left, and then past the northern end of one of the Upper Velma Lakes.

You climb now via sometimes badly washed out switchbacks through scattered forest favored by the red-breasted nuthatch. Nearing the saddle, you pass a small melt pond on the right and in a few yards reach a junction (1.2 miles; 8,200 feet; 18.4 miles) where the right fork leads back to Dicks Lake. Take the left fork. Your trail undulates for a few hundred yards, gaining little if any elevation before beginning a descent.

Soon you have a classic view of Lake Tahoe, framed in a notch between 8,499-foot Maggies Peak on the right and its 9,195-foot companion to the north. You then stroll along a broad ridge to a junction (0.8 miles; 8,200 feet; 19.2 miles) with a trail leading right to the Bay View trailhead. You turn left, drop off the ridge, and begin a steep descent to a nearly level traverse along the slope of a ridge to your right. A narrow meadow lies below, just upstream from a small pond. You can both hear and see cascades across the canyon, just below your level.

At the end of this pleasant traverse, you move sharply upward over a routing that the trail builders put there just to get your attention, then immediately begin losing elevation again among old-growth western white pine, hemlock, and red fir.

A rushing creeklet on your right is flanked by creek alder, mountain ash, and currant. You enjoy this moist environment for a few yards, then cross this flow, round a small knob, and again descend. Now you can view deep Eagle Lake only a few hundred yards below to your left, hemmed in by steep granite walls on both sides. Arriving at the junction (1.8 miles; 7,000 feet; 21.0 miles) with the short spur trail left to Eagle Lake, you can see the better camp spots on a bench across the outlet creek. Continue straight ahead down the canyon. The trail here is well used and close to the roadhead, but this won't prevent you from enjoying the sweet, pungent odor of the blooming chaparral that surrounds you.

The stream fisherman will enjoy the pools and rapids below the trail along this segment, although they are hard to reach because of vegetation and boulders. You have reentered the ponderosa pine zone, and here there are two large specimens beside the trail. Now losing more elevation, you cross a causeway constructed over a boggy area. Note showy lowbush penstemon with its striking magenta flowers in this area.

Before long you reach the boundary of the Desolation Wilderness. A few yards outside of the wilderness, you cross Eagle Creek on a wood-decked, steel bridge. Beyond this a spur trail branches left to Eagle Falls.

Quite close to the roadhead now, you are treated to stone masonry steps that seem out of place. Then you reach the roadhead register and parking lot (0.9 miles; 6,580 feet; 21.9 miles). If you do not have transportation waiting here, this is an active trailhead during the hiking season and you should be able to find a ride.

12 ◆ LASSEN PARK—BUTTE LAKE—SWAN LAKE

Distance:	18.6 Miles
Low elevation:	6,100 Feet
High elevation:	6,720 Feet
Class:	Easy
Hiking time:	10 Hours

Lassen Volcano, the southernmost volcano of the Cascades, is the world's largest plug dome volcano. Geothermal activity here indicates to geologists that there is an active magma chamber present. Lassen, then, is not extinct as a volcano. The last eruption of Lassen itself was in May 1915 when, after a year of emitting steam blasts, lava welled into the crater for six days and formed a small dome. On the night of May 19, a single explosion removed the dome, after which lava filled the crater and spilled over the west rim.

The afternoon of May 22 saw another explosion, which formed a new crater and produced a pyroclastic flow, pumice bits lubricated by hot gases, down Lost Creek. Sporadic volcanic outbursts continued until 1921. These events were well documented and photographed, and roadside exhibits explaining the geological history of the area are found at various locations within the park. Samples of the work done by B. F. Loomis in documenting the most recent eruptions are displayed at the Manzanita Lake information station. Lassen Volcanic National Park was created in 1916.

Archaeological data indicate that Native American peoples have used the Lassen area periodically for at least four thousand years. In 1911, a party of surveyors spotted three members of the Yahi tribe, who, like their ancestors, had frequented this area in the summer and fall to hunt and gather. Two women bolted into the forest, but the lone male, Ishi, left his ancestral way of life and joined the white men, with whom he had had no previous contact. The fate of the women is unknown, and Ishi would not speak of them because to do so was taboo in his tribe. These three individuals were the last known stone age beings in the forty-eight states. Ishi contributed much knowledge of the Yahi culture as he lived out his life at the University of California.

Protected by the surrounding forest and reflecting the area's beauty in its calm surface, Swan Lake offers good campsites.

DESCRIPTION

This is a loop hike with no backtracking. It takes you into one of the most diverse volcanic landscapes imaginable, where you will walk upon and view a great deal of evidence of volcanism that occurred within the past two centuries. While the strong hiker can make this loop easily in one day, it is most enjoyable as a hike with at least one overnight.

Beginning at Butte Lake, you immediately see a stark, black, basalt lava flow that is very young, from an eruption at the base of Cinder Cone believed to have occurred in the late 1700s. Your trail winds along pumice flats, climbs up saddles and broad ridges that have been volcanically deposited, and negotiates the mostly buried remains of old lava flows. Nowhere else can you see so many recent volcanic features in such a compact area.

The lakes you visit on this hike have good fishing, especially Snag and Horseshoe lakes. Both depend heavily on runoff water for their existence, as there are few springs in this volcanic world. The other lakes, such as Swan and Rainbow, occupy bowls in the middle of forests and are often studies in reflections of the shorelines. There also are many small seasonal ponds along the route.

Streamflows here vary dramatically, depending on runoff from snowmelt, and many of the streams are outlets from one lake running down to supply another. Don't expect much in the way of stream fishing along the route.

You will view several forest types and observe succession replacement in volcanically denuded areas, as well as instances where lodgepole pine is establishing itself directly in these areas. This is possible mostly because the volcanism that last altered these areas left great areas of pumice, which will support the growth of lodgepoles. Consequently, as natural seeding takes place, the lodgepoles slowly move into such bare areas. Where volcanism has left bare rock, as in the lava flows, it is often necessary for lichens and the smaller plants to establish and form soil from the rock before other plants, shrubs, and finally trees can begin colonization.

The last quarter of the hike takes you over the most recent cinders and lavas ejected from Cinder Cone. A side hike to the summit of Cinder Cone is well worth the effort; from that viewpoint you can see the double crater at the top as well as the extent of the recent flows. The added elevation provides an excellent view of Mount Lassen about 12 miles to the west.

You will traverse an area hit heavily with lava bombs during the most recent eruption, traveling a route once taken by the Noble emigrant train and later used by settlers and miners moving into California shortly after the eruption changed the landscape in that region.

Here, what has happened over the past two centuries can be plainly read. The remains of forests, in the form of rotting logs and stumps, lie where they were when the pumice descended. During volcanic eruptions, chunks of viscous lava are often thrown from the crater, to fly through the air and land some distance away. These chunks are called lava bombs, and many lie where they landed on the pumice beside the trail. You can feel the desolation of the area. Then you see a few small trees taking root on the edge of the lava flow and realize that before too long, this also will be covered with forest.

Since Lassen marks a change point for many vegetation species, you are treated to great diversity in plant life here. Roughly two hundred more species are represented in the Lassen area than are found on and around Mount Shasta, the next of the linear volcanos to the north. The most common wildflower species here is lupine, a plant well adapted to pumice soils. You will see many others, especially along the damp areas where streams flow into or out of lakes.

While the Lassen region is not known for unique wildlife species, you can expect to see a good assortment here. While making an early-season hike, we spotted mule deer, pine martens, Douglas squirrels, lodgepole chipmunks, and the tracks of black bear and coyotes. Birds we saw included

MAP 12A

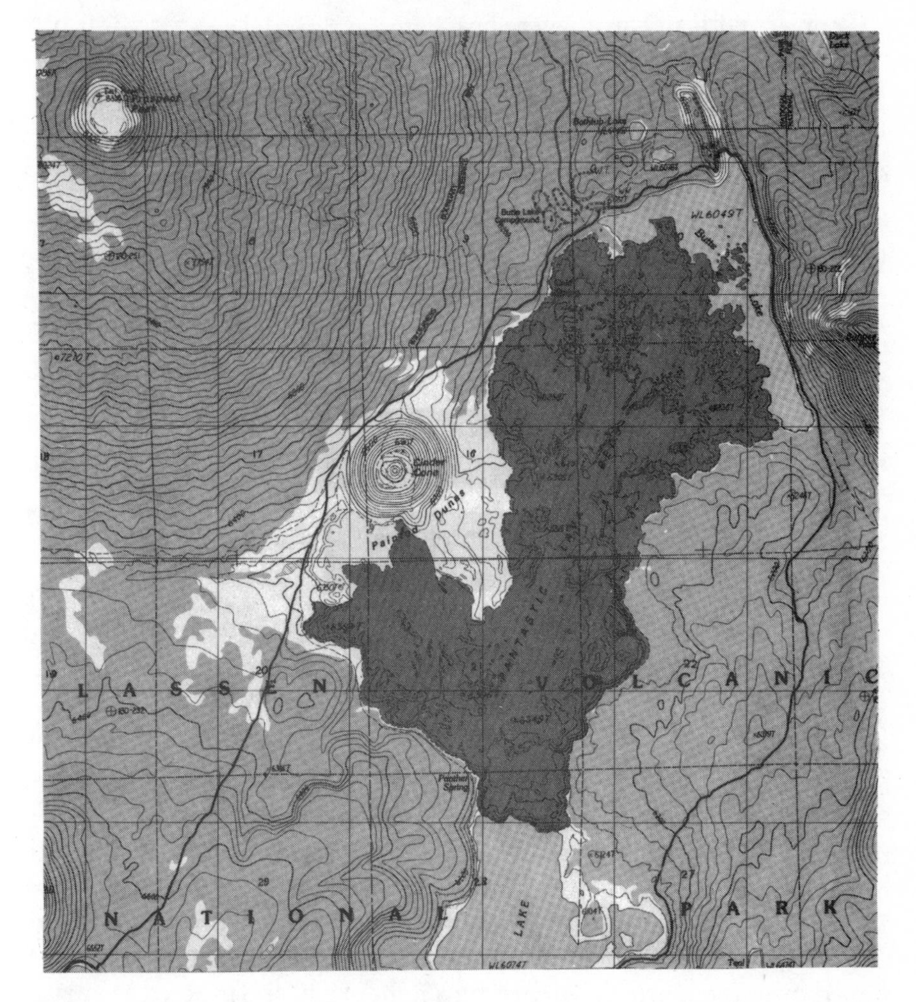

bald eagle, red-winged blackbird, mourning dove, Stellar's jay, gray jay, Oregon junco, robin, Townsend's warbler, raven, Canada goose, common merganser, black-backed woodpecker, and flicker.

In the summer, temperatures can be quite warm and storms, except for short-duration thundershowers, are not common. This tendency to the mild offers a very enjoyable area in which to hike and backpack. Trails are generally free of snow, except for a few patches, by mid-June, and hiking is enjoyable into mid-October. Usually snowfall on the eastern side of the park is lighter than on the western side.

Mosquitoes can be very numerous during the three or four weeks after the snow leaves. Be sure to carry repellent, even after the "bug season."

Black bears are not particularly numerous in the park, but they are present. As with any area where bears are suspected, be sure to bear-bag your food.

The campground at Butte Lake has all the usual facilities except that as of this writing, because of continuing drought, water is not available, so be sure to carry along a supply.

Administrative Agency: USNPS

Lassen Volcanic National Park
Superintendents Office
P.O. Box 100
Mineral, CA 96063
(916) 595-4444

USGS map: 7.5′ series, Prospect Park, Mount Harkness, California

Declination: 17½ degrees

DIRECTIONS TO TRAILHEAD

Northbound on State Route 44, from the junction with State Route 36 5 miles west of Susanville, drive north 34 miles to the signed turnoff to Butte Lake. Turn left (west) here on a gravel-surfaced road and proceed 6 miles, entering Lassen National Park and arriving at Butte Lake Ranger Station trailhead parking lot. From the north on State Route 44, proceed from the junction with State Route 89 at Old Station, 11 miles south to the signed turnoff to Butte Lake, then turn right (west) and proceed as above.

TRAIL ROUTE DESCRIPTION

MAP 12A

From the parking lot just east of the ranger station, the trail begins on the east side, at 6,100 feet elevation, with an easy stroll through magnificent ponderosa pines. Then, in a few hundred yards, you begin an ascent to a viewpoint (0.6 miles from last point; 6,225 feet above sea level; 0.6 total miles) near the north end of the lake. Notice the mountain mahoganies favoring the dry, south exposure of this rocky point. From here you can see much of Butte Lake and a half dozen cinder cones to the south. Steep switchbacks that were poorly engineered then drop you down to Butte Creek (0.2 miles; 6,040 feet; 0.8 miles), the outlet that flows when the lake is full.

Crossing the creek, you turn south just above the shoreline of Butte Lake. Keep a lookout for common mergansers, often seen here. Cottonwood

MAP 12B

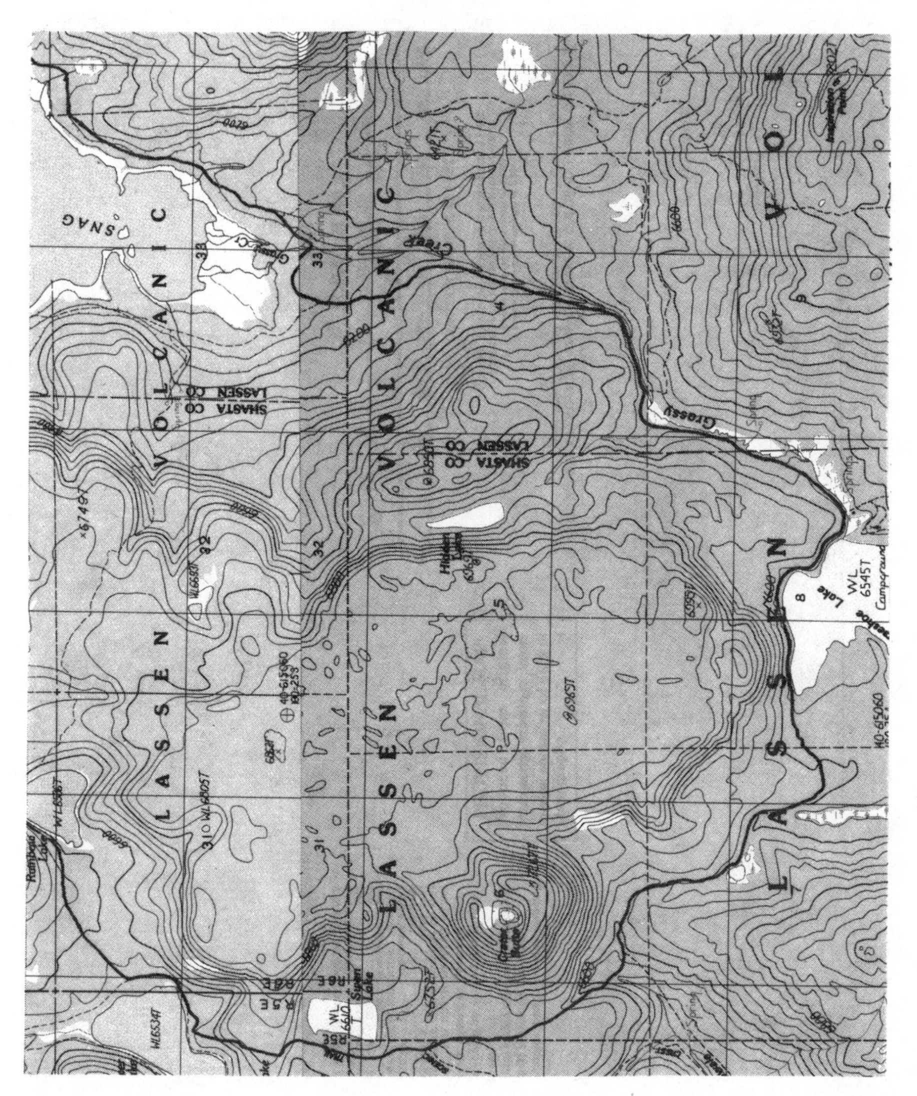

trees favor the shoreline, and you can also find gooseberries, wild raspberries, wild rose, and mullein here. Near the south end of the lake, the cottonwoods give up in favor of quaking aspen, and you leave the lake amid a grove of these trees (1.4 miles; 6,070 feet; 2.2 miles), but not before you get a fine view of Mount Lassen and Cinder Cone to the west.

Continuing a few hundred feet, you reach a junction with a trail that branches left, leading to Widow Lake in 1.4 miles. Take the right fork. Here the Park Service has replaced the old wooden signposts, which bears liked to chew, with steel, no doubt to the bruins' chagrin.

MAP 12B

You ascend gently now, over pumice soil that nourishes a predominantly lodgepole forest. Currant bushes are scattered here, as are mule's ears. There are red, 2.5-inch metal discs nailed to trees along this stretch, from days when park administrators had proportionately larger budgets. In Lassen, hundreds of metal discs and diamonds, usually red or yellow, were used to mark trails.

As you travel through more lodgepole, notice the lupine that flourishes in many of the sunny spots. Your trail is finally level, and it reaches a broad crest at 6,370 feet elevation, then descends through mixed conifers. Soon quaking aspen appear, and in minutes you have reached Snag Lake (2.6 miles; 6,080 feet; 4.8 miles).

This section is actually an eastward-protruding bay of Snag Lake. It sports an island—maybe even more than one at low water levels. Your tread leads along the lake, always back a respectful distance from the water, as you pass areas that received heavy impact from improper camping many years ago. Happily, these spots have largely restored themselves. Corn lilies grow in the damp areas here. At the north end of the lake, to your right, you are treated to a glimpse of the lava flow.

Soon you pass a narrow peninsula (1.1 miles; 6,175 feet; 5.9 miles) jutting several hundred feet out into the lake, an area that was camped almost to death two decades ago but has nearly recovered. To camp here, select a site at least 200 feet from the water. Five hundred yards beyond, you cross a creek that empties into the lake. There are good camping possibilities just beyond. The campsites along the high-water lakeshore here are illegal when the lake is full.

Continuing along this lakeshore trail, you reach a junction (0.3 miles; 6,120 feet; 6.2 miles) with a trail that branches left (east). Taking it would bring you to Juniper Lake in 2.9 miles. Your trail continues straight ahead before dropping down a few yards to parallel Grassy Creek on your right. This creek is the outlet for Horseshoe Lake, emptying into Snag Lake. You reach a boggy area, which you can cross on log structures, and continue upstream to reach a wooden bridge crossing (0.1 miles; 6,120 feet; 6.3 miles) over Grassy Creek.

Vertical Profile of Hike 12

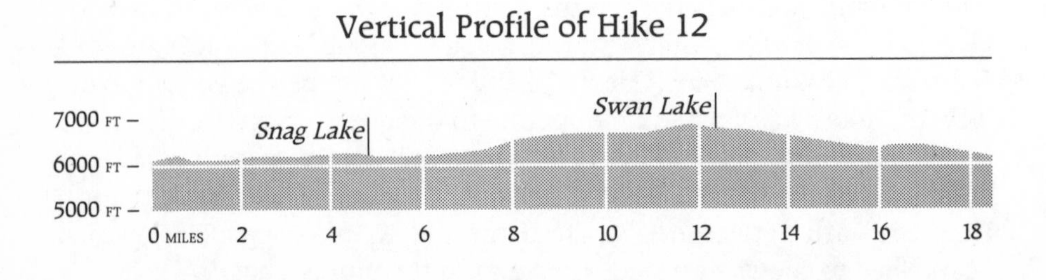

Merganser

Once across the bridge, you enter a pumice meadow, sprinkled with phlox and lupine. Here conditions have been just right for lodgepole reclamation, and there are also a few small firs.

Your trail now takes you west a suitable distance from the creek, then curves back to head south. Soon you reach a junction (0.3 miles; 6,120 feet; 6.6 miles) with a trail that branches right to Rainbow Lake and Cinder Cone.

[If you wish to cut your hike short, this trail is one of the routes you could consider.]

Take the left trail, which ascends through an area where western white pines are flourishing. You can identify these trees by their five-needle bundles and by the cones, which are up to 8 inches in length. The sugar pine also has five-needle bundles, but the needles are comparatively short and the cones are much longer.

Before long, you are back following the creek (0.8 miles; 6,240 feet; 7.4 miles), which parallels on your left. Note the edge of an andesite flow exposed on the far bank. Presently you pass a small trailside spring. You can soon cross the creek via a log bridge or by rock hopping. If the water is high, the right-hand bank may be easier to negotiate. The streamside environment is damper and the noise of the creek is soothing and relaxing.

You reach a junction (0.6 miles; 6,570 feet; 8.0 miles) with a trail branching left to Jakey Lake via Cameron Meadows in 3 miles. Continue straight ahead along the now-tamed creek that begins meandering through narrow meadows, then skirts a somewhat larger meadow along the right side. You may find water plantain buttercup, corn lily, and hound's-tongue here. Upstream, the creek slows even more between flower-lined banks, looping from one side to the other in adolescent oxbows. You can see evidence of old oxbows curving through the meadow.

The peaceful feeling of this area ends all too soon at a junction (0.8 miles; 6,620 feet; 8.8 miles) with a trail that branches left, across a log bridge, to the Horseshoe Lake Ranger Station. This rustic log outpost is manned during the peak season. If you followed the trail beyond, you would reach Juniper Lake in 1.4 miles. Continue straight on the main trail.

Passing the ranger station on a gentle traverse, you reach Horseshoe Lake itself, and walk along the glistening water on your left. Note that camping is not allowed along the north shoreline. If anything, this regulation improves the views along the trail. Beyond the restricted area, there are primitive camping possibilities just past the lake. A quarter mile after leaving the lake, you pass a seasonal pond on your right, ringed by a lodgepole forest, and then ascend gently along a seasonal creek on your left. You then pass a series of seasonal ponds, which may not exist during the dry season, in the widening meadow and approach a shallow, 2.5-acre lake from which the streamlet you've been following flows.

Shortly you come to a deeper, 3-acre lake on your left. Good camps lie in the saddle just beyond, at an elevation of 6,720 feet. Crossing the saddle and descending now through lodgepoles, you pass a shallow pond on the right and descend along its outlet, which flows during early season.

Soon the Corral Meadows Trail branches left (2.2 miles; 6,645 feet; 11.0 miles). Take the right fork, signed "Twin Lakes." Note the magnificent stand of old-growth western white pine and Shasta red fir at this junction. A short distance beyond, you cross a creek and ascend toward the northwest.

At a junction (0.8 miles; 6,720 feet; 11.8 miles), turn right onto the Pacific Crest Trail. The left branch here again leads to Corral Meadows, 3.7 miles distant. Within 0.4 miles, you reach Swan Lake, evidenced first by the apparent gap in the timber on your right. Then you see the lake itself through the trees as you approach the outlet creek, which flows during high water. Fine camping is available at Swan Lake in open lodgepole stands between the trail and the lake. Swan Lake seems especially reflective, with the opposite shoreline often mirrored in the still waters. To help preserve this special place, take care to leave no trace of your campsite.

A minute beyond Swan Lake, you reach a small lakelet on the right and cross its usually dry outlet. A deep blue lake lies to the left. A few hundred yards later you reach a junction (0.5 miles; 6,615 feet; 12.3 miles) with a trail branching left to Upper Twin Lake just 0.5 miles distant and Summit Lake beyond. Keep to the right-hand branch, and you are soon

Pine marten

ambling along the shore of Lower Twin Lake. There is good camping along the northeast shore of Lower Twin Lake, the proper distance from the water, in lodgepole pines and with a view. At the next junction (0.3 miles; 6,540 feet; 12.6 miles), the PCT branches left to Cluster Lakes. Take the right fork, signed "Rainbow Lake and Cinder Cone."

This section of trail, well routed up a pleasantly broad ridge, takes you through a mixed-age forest with many large red firs, then descends to Rainbow Lake (0.5 miles; 6,590 feet; 13.1 miles). Held carefully in an irregular, forested bowl, Rainbow rivals Swan Lake in its striking shoreline reflections. The campsites between the lake and trail are too close to the water; better sites can be found on the saddle at the north end of the lake. The sharp-eyed hiker will spot an old, bear-chewed wooden signpost projecting a few inches above the ground next to the lakeside trail. As you leave the lake you reach a junction (0.3 miles; 6,600 feet; 13.4 miles) with a trail to Snag Lake that branches right. Had you chosen to shorten your hike by taking the shortcut trail at Snag Lake, this is the spot you would have reached.

MAP 12A

Continue straight ahead (northeast) onto a broad plateau where rotting red fir logs lie on the ground. In various stages of decomposition, these logs demonstrate the return of nutrients to the soil and show that likely the loose pumice soil here allowed growth of an even-age stand of red fir that matured as the climax species without competition from understory trees or plants. These huge trees reached the end of their life span more or less at the same time, then yielded, one or several at a time, to the strong winds of winter storms, which toppled them toward the northeast. Few of the oldsters remain standing; most of the old forest lies before you as rotting logs, all pointing in one direction.

The trees that replaced the old growth have a century to go to maturity, allowing you to glimpse Cinder Cone as you descend from the plateau onto open pumice slopes where ponderosa pine again makes an appearance. Only a few widely scattered plants have a foothold on the loose pumice. The few large logs you see are from ponderosa pines that stood here before the volcanic event that covered the terrain with pumice. The most recent volcanic activity here was long thought to have occurred around 1851, but new theories place it a full century earlier. Chronodendrology, the dating of tree rings, should be able to pinpoint the year in which the pines that once stood on this site were killed.

Also notice the small, conical-shaped depressions in the pumice. It is thought that as the roots of trees that once stood here decay and leave voids, the sandy pumice fills these cavities, creating the reverse-cone depressions.

You continue to a junction (2.7 miles; 6,200 feet; 16.1 miles) where a right-branching trail follows around the west side of Fantastic Lava Beds to Snag Lake. Take the left fork, and in a few yards you cross a flat bottom, which has held water in recent years. When the inlet from the west delivers more water than can percolate into the coarse sand, there will be water there again. As you ascend from this bottom, you are rewarded with a view of Mount Lassen to the west.

The few trees growing on and near the lava flow are an example of direct colonization on bare rock without the prior succession of lower plants. Many ponderosa pine cones have rolled down the slope from the forest edge above, effectively delivering seeds to new locations.

Just after a spur trail branches right to climb Cinder Cone (0.5 miles; 6,380 feet; 16.6 miles), you join the alignment of the Nobles Emigrant Trail, created by William Nobles in 1851. This trail led from just north of the Great Salt Lake through this spot on the way to the rich valleys of western California. You will hike along the historic route from this point to the roadhead.

Note the lava bombs beside the trail; they were ejected from Cinder Cone during an active period. From this more elevated position, you can see the true extent of Fantastic Lava Beds and Painted Dunes, which surround Cinder Cone on the south and east. There is much to see here, and because this point is but a short walk from the roadhead, interpretive signs have been installed. Now you drop down to a junction (0.2 miles; 6,320 feet; 16.8 miles) where the main trail to the top of Cinder Cone branches left.

[This is the closest point from which to make the 450-foot climb up Cinder Cone, here up a broad, loose cinder trail. From the summit at 6,907 feet, you can view Butte and Snag lakes, the lava flows that issued from the base of Cinder Cone, and the secondary crater built up inside the original at the top. While catching your breath at the top, reflect upon the relative youth of the landscape. Cinder Cone is a tephra cone, composed of many layers of ash and cinders, and probably formed within the last 500 years. The vast Fantastic Lava Beds, basaltic lava that formed Snag Lake, issued from vents on the south and east sides of the cone's base.]

From the Cinder Cone Trail junction, continue northeast on the broad, sandy trail, which navigates an almost exclusively ponderosa pine forest. You parallel the north extent of the lava flow here and soon reach a junction (1.2 miles; 6,150 feet; 18.0 miles) where a trail to Prospect Peak, 2.8 miles away, branches left. Just beyond this junction, 100 yards to the right of the trail at the base of the blocky lava flow, is Cold Spring, a reliable flow that surfaces at this point. Just 100 yards past Cold Spring is a junction with an equestrian trail that skirts the campground on the south. Proceed a few hundred feet along the left branch to the rear of the theater, cross the campground bearing to the right, go past the ranger station, and you arrive at the parking lot (0.6 miles; 6,100 feet; 18.6 miles).

13 ♦ TOAD LAKE—DEADFALL LAKES

Distance:	18.1 Miles
Low elevation:	6,200 Feet
High elevation:	8,060 Feet
Class:	Difficult
Hiking time:	11 Hours

Mount Eddy lies 9 miles due west of the city of Mount Shasta, on Interstate 5 in Northern California. Toad Lake and Deadfall Lakes lie just south and west of the 9,025-foot peak, all in the Shasta-Trinity National Forest. A few miles south is Castle Crags Wilderness, popular with climbers. This region is part of the Klamath Mountains, made up of the Trinity, Salmon, Marble, and Siskiyou ranges.

Immediately west of the hike region, odd-numbered sections of land are owned by Southern Pacific Land Company (SP), acquired as railroad grant lands. The PCT has a right-of-way agreement with SP, and every other mile for many miles north and south, the trail crosses over these private lands. This agreement allows the PCT to continue to follow the crest route as closely as possible through this segment.

The early prospectors and cattlemen who penetrated the Upper Trinity area came south from Scott Valley in the mid-1800s. Sisson, a town on the lower slopes of Mount Shasta, was the nearest outpost of civilization, and an east-west trail was established for access to the Trinity drainage. In 1911 the newly created Shasta National Forest improved and reconstructed the established trail. This Sisson-Callahan Trail provided a link between Forest Headquarters in Sisson and the Callahan Ranger Station. For a time, a telephone line was also maintained along the trail. The Sisson-Callahan Trail was used for access to the Forest Service lookout on Mount Eddy until the lookout was abandoned in 1931.

The Shasta National Forest and the Trinity National Forest were combined in 1954 for administrative purposes and today are one, called the Shasta-Trinity. Don't spend time searching maps for Sisson—the town was renamed Mount Shasta.

Mount Shasta, one of the world's largest stratovolcanos and the second highest in the Cascade chain at 14,192 feet, dominates the landscape in the central part of Northern California. Naturalist John Muir ascended the mountain in 1874 and again in 1875 as he attempted to find a site for a monument to be set by the Coast and Geodetic Survey. Muir and a companion were caught by a sudden storm, and they took refuge in a muddy, sulfurous hot spring a few hundred feet from Shasta's summit. The mud temperature was much too hot for comfort and the storm was well below freezing, so the two men spent a very uncomfortable night. The next morning they made their way off the mountain, at the cost of freezing to Muir's feet—damage that would be with him the rest of his life. But the naturalist undoubtedly owed his life to the fact that Mount Shasta was still an active volcano.

The west slope of this hike area is Trinity River drainage, waters of which reached a confluence with the Klamath River about 25 miles inland from the Pacific. East-slope drainage is into the Sacramento River. Since the 1960s completion of Lewiston and Trinity dams, part of California's Central Valley Project, upper Trinity waters have been diverted via the Clear Creek Tunnel into Whiskeytown Lake and eventually the Sacramento River. The Trinity River Hatchery, operated by the California Department of Fish and Game, was constructed to mitigate loss of steelhead and salmon runs.

Plainly observable along the segment of the PCT traversed on this hike is peridotite, an ultramafic rock common in the Klamath Mountains. Ultramafic rocks are very heavy and are a black color when freshly broken. Rich in iron and magnesium, ultramafics weather to a rusty red color that makes them easy to recognize. These rocks are believed to originate on the undersides of oceanic plates as these plates are driven beneath the continental plate, melted, and intruded as a rising, molten mass, and then solidified beneath the surface. Some such rocks, in the process, are altered into serpentine, also common in the Klamath Mountains.

Serpentine rock weathers into serpentine soils, which possess characteristics conductive to growth of the California pitcher plant, rarely found outside the Klamath Mountains. Pitcher plants derive part of their nourishment from insects that are lured by scent into the plant's hollow stem-like leaves. Once the insect follows the wafting lure down into the pitcher, fine, down-pointing hairs prevent its climbing back out. The insect is eventually digested by bacteria and other organisms, and the pitcher plant absorbs the juices. You can observe several colonies of this unique, insectivorous plant along the hike route.

Late-summer wildflowers we noted along this hike included lupine, rabbit bush, paintbrush, partridgefoot, scarlet gilia, sulfur flower, thistle, yarrow, bluebell, explorer gentian, and pitcher plants. Area wildlife includes the deer, chipmunk, Douglas squirrel, red-tailed hawk, American kestrel, Stellar's jay, cedar waxwing, robin, junco, and white-breasted nuthatch.

There are high amounts of snowfall in the hike area, as it is located within 80 miles of the coast and is at an elevation sufficient to condense much of the moisture from winter storms. Coastal proximity has a modifying effect on temperature, however, creating a climate less harsh than you would expect from the amount of snowfall. This relatively mild climate is evidenced by the plant life found in the area.

DESCRIPTION

This is a loop hike, but if you position extra transportation at the North Fork Trail trailhead, you can shorten the hike by the nearly 5-mile walk on gravel road back to the Toad Lake trailhead.

The last 0.1-mile stretch of the road leading to the Toad Lake trailhead is very rough and rocky; all except high-clearance vehicles will have difficulty. As a result, most people park at the onset of the bad road. It is but a short walk to the trailhead.

The barn you see at the roadhead was probably constructed in the early twentieth century in conjunction with Toad Lake Cabin, which was built by the Cattle Company of Callahan but destroyed by arsonists in 1989. You will see additional evidence on this hike of the impact of livestock grazing in the area.

Formerly, the Forest Service allowed motor vehicles to drive to Toad Lake; in fact the generous camp tables seen there are leftovers of that era. As a result, the trail to the lake is actually along an old roadway. The road is gradually fading in the area, however, leaving only the track followed by the trail. Along this section, growing in a bog south of Toad Creek, are the first pitcher plants you'll encounter on the hike. Toad Lake is a popular camping spot due to its accessibility, but its beauty is certainly another factor. From the lake, the routing climbs up onto the crest and joins the PCT.

The route negotiates rocky slopes and cliffs along the divide, where many wildflower species can be seen if cattle have not devoured them. A crossing from east slope to west leads you into a mixed forest with a rich understory community, which near Deadfall Lakes gives way to more sparse conditions as you ascend to Mount Eddy's southern ridge.

Several rare plant species are found in this locale. Stay on the trail, for the plants are fragile and might be damaged. Unfortunately, cattle are grazed here, and they ingest forbs and cut the fragile soil to dust under their hooves in some areas. Late season finds range cattle gathered on small, soft bogs and meadows, where grasses and sedges remain green the longest. This results in severe overuse of riparian areas in a sensitive segment of national forest. Grazing here may not be in the public interest.

Administrative agency: USFS

Shasta-Trinity National Forest 2400 Washington Avenue Redding, CA 96001 (916) 246-5222	Mount Shasta Ranger District 204 West Alma Mount Shasta, CA 96067 (916) 926-4511

USGS map: 7.5′ series, Mount Eddy, South China Mountain, California

Declination: 18 degrees

From Deadfall Lakes eastward, the route follows the Sisson-Callahan Trail. You may be able to spot remnants of the telephone line that once paralleled the trail, usually in the form of wire anchors in trees, and sometimes insulators. In places the trail is wide and much eroded, as if from overuse as a stock route. It is easy to imagine early forest rangers making the lonesome ride over this connecting link between Sisson and the remote Callahan station.

Exiting from the North Fork Sacramento involves crossing a ridge and dropping south to the North Fork Trail trailhead at the end of a logging road. This segment of the trail is somewhat obscure, not evident on the ground in some areas and marked only by widely separated tree blazes. If you are not a confident route finder, it may be best to make a modified loop hike and return to the Toad Lake trailhead as described earlier. If however, you have experience in route finding, you will have little trouble following the North Fork Trail.

The best hiking season is from mid-June to mid-October. In high-precipitation years, the trails may not be completely snowfree until the first of July. Occasional summer thundershowers may occur in the area, but otherwise precipitation during the hiking season is rare.

Black bears are certainly present here, but they are very shy. It makes good sense, however, to bear-bag your food when camping wherever bears are present.

DIRECTIONS TO TRAILHEAD

From the Central Mount Shasta exit (Lake Street) of Interstate 5 in Northern California, proceed west 0.3 miles to North Old Stage Road, signed "Siskiyou and Castle Lake." Turn left (south) on North Old Stage Road, and in 0.1 miles

MAP 13

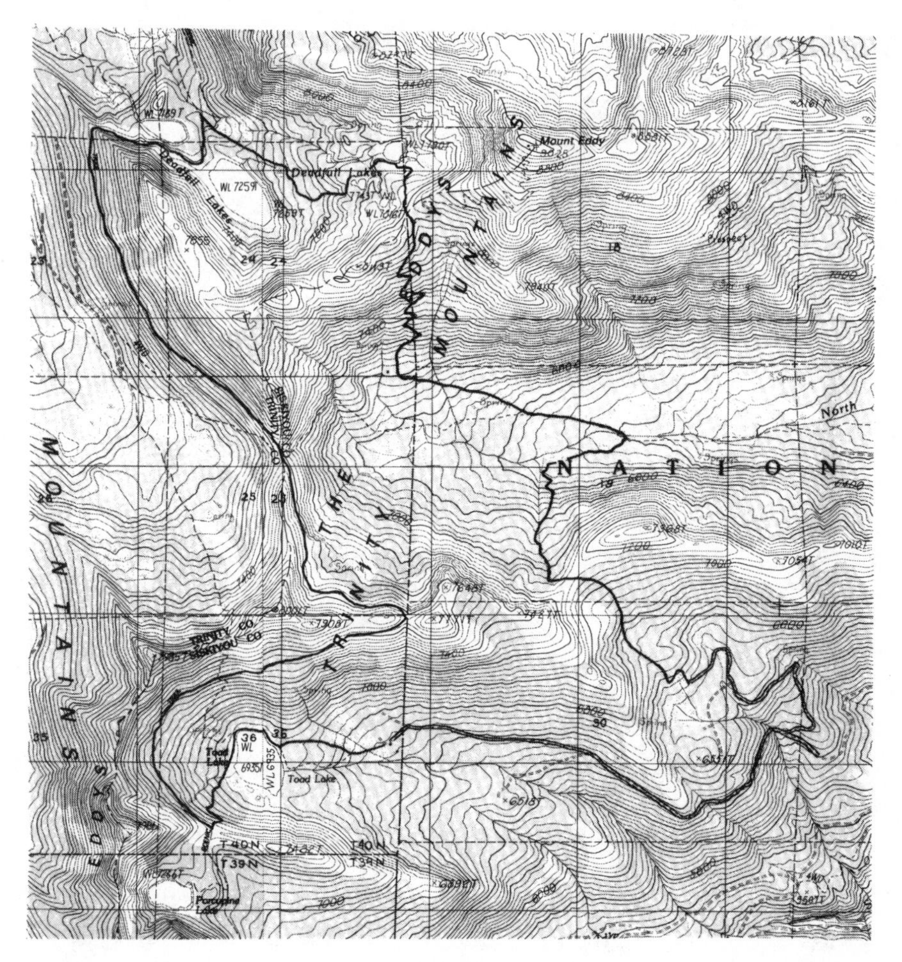

turn right on W. A. Barr Road. Continue around Siskiyou Lake on a paved, two-lane road that becomes forest road 26. Proceed 8.4 miles west on road 26 to forest road 41N53, signed "Toad Lake." Turn right here onto gravel surface, and go 0.2 miles to a junction where forest road 40N64 turns left. Go left on 40N64, and in 5.9 miles cross a bridge over the Middle Fork Sacramento River. After 2.9 miles, you reach a sign reading, "Toad Lake, 2; North Fork Trail, 3; Sisson-Callahan Trail, 4." Keep left here and proceed 1.1 miles over sometimes rough road to a road that branches left. Keep to the right here and go 0.6 miles, until you reach the beginning of some very bad road. You can park here, or if you have a high-clearance vehicle, you can drive 0.3 miles farther to the actual trailhead. If you wish to position transportation at the North Fork Trail trailhead, turn right at the "North Fork Trail, 3" sign.

MAP 13

TRAIL ROUTE DESCRIPTION

From the parking area, walk up the road 0.3 miles to the trailhead elevation, 6,720 feet. Note the old barn, all that is left of the Toad Lake Cabin complex. From the bulletin board your route passes through scattered lodgepole pines. Almost immediately you cross a year-round spring flow. Your trail here was once a road, before the Forest Service banned four-wheel-drive access. You soon come alongside Toad Creek, outlet for Toad Lake. Look for a colony of California pitcher plants growing in a bog on the far side of the creek.

At beautiful Toad Lake (0.3 miles from last point; 6,935 feet above sea level; 0.3 total miles), your tread approaches the water at a campsite and then follows close to the north shore. There are several well-spaced campsites with large tables at this popular lake. At the west end of the lake, you skirt more camps, then pass a small, rocky knob immediately to your left. Just beyond this knob is a flat, grassy meadow, dotted with trees. At this point your trail turns to the right and angles up the hill to the southwest, soon crossing a rushing spring flow.

The ascent steepens, and shortly you reach a sign signifying a junction with an old trail, which, if you could find it, would branch to the right. With the construction of the PCT, this trail is no longer heavily used, so continue to ascend via switchbacks to the Pacific Crest Trail (1.0 miles; 7,320 feet; 1.3 miles). To the left (south), the PCT passes near Porcupine Lake and to points south. Turn right (north) onto the PCT, which immediately begins a curving traverse around the Toad Lake basin. Portions of this route had to be blasted from the rock.

Your gentle ascent continues, giving you plenty of time to enjoy the view of oval Toad Lake below. On the horizon to the southeast, you can see Mount Lassen and, much nearer, the jagged pinnacles of Castle Crags. Now your shade is provided by red fir and western white pine, and soon you pass a use trail (1.2 miles; 7,440 feet; 2.5 miles) that leads down to Toad Lake.

Nearing the northeast tip of the ridge, your ascent steepens as you leave the trees and traverse open slopes. Here you can see wooden posts in which are burned the PCT trail emblem and numbers, but these numbers have little value to the hiker. Soon you cross through a saddle (0.9 miles; 7,650 feet; 3.4 miles) and view a long traverse of the trail ahead as it passes around the head of the North Fork Sacramento drainage.

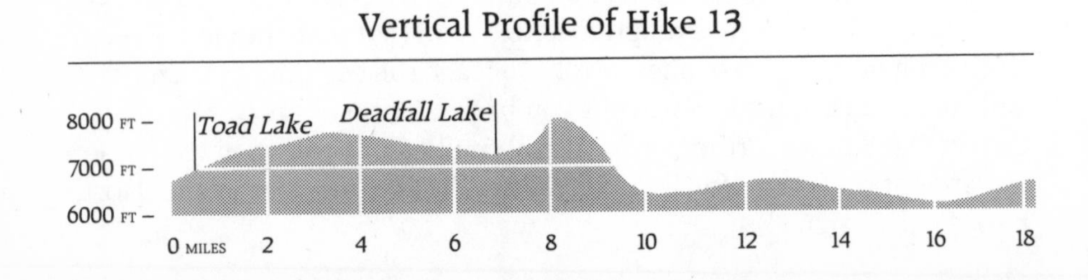

Red-breasted nuthatch

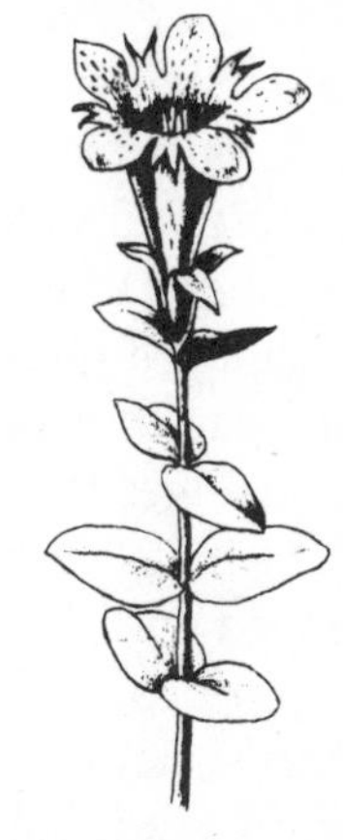

Gentian

A rust-colored rocky knob immediately on your right has that appearance for a good reason: It *is* rust. The knob is peridotite, an ultramafic rock from deep below the earth's crust. High iron content causes this rock to weather to a rusty red when exposed to moisture and air. Freshly broken surfaces of this rock appear black, requiring some time to rust. On this hike, you often will be walking on ultramaffic rock.

Your route leads along a beautiful, nearly open traverse through occasional western white pine. You reach a narrow crest ridge and wind along it to a junction (1.5 miles; 7,440 feet; 4.9 miles) where a spur trail turns right to intersect the Sisson-Calahan Trail. A left turn here leads toward the Trinity River. Cross this branch of the Sisson-Calahan Trail and continue north on the PCT.

[If you are not going to exit this hike on the North Fork Trail, this is the PCT junction to which you will return after crossing the ridge south of Mount Eddy.]

Traversing now along a southwest-facing slope, you enter private land owned by Southern Pacific Land Company. Soon your trail becomes shaded as you enter a nearly pure red fir forest with chartreuse staghorn moss adorning the tree trunks. Rounding a point of the ridge to head eastward, you traverse across a talus slope, ascend, and round another rocky promontory to view Lower Deadfall Lake (1.9 miles; 7,225 feet; 6.8 miles) below and to your left.

After 0.2 miles, you pass a use trail branching right to the main Deadfall Lake, which lies just out of sight. A short distance beyond, you cross the Deadfall Lake outlet. A few steps later, a sign identifies Lower Deadfall Lake, which you have already passed, to the left and below.

At a junction (0.2 miles; 7,180 feet; 7.0 miles) beside a small stream, the Mount Eddy trail turns right (east), while the PCT continues north. You leave the PCT here and turn right onto the Mount Eddy Trail, which is also signed "Sisson-Calahan Trail."

Ascending eastward, you are soon able to look down into Deadfall Lake. Shortly thereafter you pass on your right a spring flow and bog area that contains many clusters of pitcher plants. Crossing the upper end of the bog, your trail heads southeastward for a short distance before resuming its steep climb. A lakelet (0.8 miles; 7,750 feet; 7.8 miles) on your right occupies a glacial depression, and its fine gravel bottom and small size make it an ideal place to swim. Barely adequate campsites can be found on the west end and on the east near the trail.

In 0.2 miles you reach a lakelet, another of the Deadfall Lakes. This one, ringed with a grassy shoreline, is extremely picturesque. Here too, camps might be made to the east or west. Note the imposing, above-timberline ridges that cradle this basin to the north and east. The greenish rock in the north ridge is a form of serpentine. Mount Eddy, to the east, rises to an elevation of 9,025 feet.

Now you can see more wooden posts; these once held National Recreation Trail markers, but most have been removed by vandals. Ignore a spur trail that leads left to possible camp areas above the lakelet, and instead follow the trail up and to the right. Shortly you see a shallow tarn and marshy area to your left, and just beyond, your trail turns directly up the hill. You ascend to the top of the ridge and reach a junction (0.2 miles; 8,060 feet; 8.0 miles). Here the Mount Eddy Trail branches left, up the ridge, to ascend to the summit.

Your trail is faint for several yards just beyond the junction sign but generally follows just left (north) of the bottom of the shallow draw leading eastward. Within 50 yards the track again becomes easy to follow, and you begin a long, switchbacking descent of the southeast slope. Switchbacks eroded by range cattle lead you off the ridge, and in 1.5 miles you encounter the first of many large incense cedars, some up to 4 feet in diameter. Shortly thereafter, you reach a junction (1.6 miles; 6,660 feet; 9.6 miles) with the spur trail that leads west to the PCT.

[If you are not accomplished at route finding, you may wish to turn right here and complete a shorter loop that will return you to the Toad Lake trailhead on well-established trails. To do this, turn right (west) at this junction and proceed westward, ascending along the north slope to the junction (1.2 miles; 7,440 feet; 10.8 miles) with the PCT at the crest ridge you negotiated earlier. Here, turn left (south) on the PCT and retrace your route to the Toad Lake Trail junction, turn left again, and swing past Toad Lake to the trailhead (total distance, 15.0 miles).]

Just beyond this junction, you cross a small spring. Continuing your descent, you soon reach another junction (0.4 miles; 6,500 feet; 10.0 miles), where a trail turns back sharply right (west). This junction, an old alignment of the Sisson-Calahan Trail, is very obscure when approached from the west. Continue straight ahead (east) and in 0.3 miles you cross a spring and bog where another colony of pitcher plants thrives.

Soon you pass a grassy meadow on your left, sprinkled with lodgepole pines. Just beyond you can rock hop across a larger creek and reach a trail junction. (0.5 miles; 6,400 feet; 10.5 miles). Here the North Fork Trail turns sharply right, while the Sisson-Calahan National Recreation Trail continues downstream to the east. Turn right onto the North Fork Trail 5W05. Watch closely for this junction, which turns immediately after you cross to the south bank of the creek.

Ascending gently to the west along the bottom just south of the creek, you pass among scattered ponderosa pines and soon are following blazes on trees as the trail crosses a grassy area. Beyond a small wash, you find the trail by looking for sawed cutouts in fallen logs. The trail turns left (south), 30 yards beyond the meadow and directly addresses the sidehill. Watch for blazes ahead, as the trail is quite obscure in this section.

After 100 yards of direct upslope, you follow a switchback to the left; 100 feet later you switchback right to a small spring seep, at which point you switchback again. Then you again address the slope directly, up a broad, loose dirt-and-gravel section. After this slope eases, you cross one creeklet (1.2 miles; 6,775 feet; 11.7 miles) and then another, the second of which may be dry in late season.

Now your trail is easier to make out on the ground, and tree blazes are supplemented by rock trail ducks. Watch carefully for tree blazes when the trail is not evident on the ground. Soon you arrive at a broad, semiopen ridge (0.4 miles; 7,140 feet; 12.1 miles) with scattered ponderosa pines.

Descending now, you follow scanty blazes down the hill until your trail turns abruptly to the right, crosses a dry wash, and then swings left down the hill. Curving now to the right, you cross a grassy flat—watch for tree blazes on the far side—and then descend down a wide draw where the trail is again obscure, to the North Fork trailhead (0.8 miles; 6,550 feet; 12.9 miles). Just to the south is a 50-yard-wide, sloping bog that is home to hundreds of pitcher plants. Southeast of the trailhead, the bog dries and widens to form a broad, grassy meadow, nearly flat and well supplied with scattered trees. If you find yourself on this grassy flat, you may have bypassed the roadhead.

Once you have arrived at the North Fork trailhead, if you have not positioned a vehicle here, walk 3 miles southeast along the dirt-and-gravel road 40N64A, which soon turns west, to a junction with gravel road 40N64. Turn right on gravel road 40N64 and walk 2.2 miles west to the roadhead.

14 ♦ SKY HIGH LAKES—MARBLE MOUNTAIN WILDERNESS

Distance:	14.7 Miles
Low elevation:	4,160 Feet
High elevation:	6,560 Feet
Class:	Medium
Hiking time:	12 Hours

The Marble Mountain Wilderness is located in Siskiyou County, Northern California, a little south of halfway between Yreka, on Interstate 5, and Crescent City, on the coast. The wilderness is centered in the Klamath Mountains and bordered on the north by the Siskiyous, which reach well into southern Oregon, and on the south by the Trinitys. Both ranges are part of the Klamath chain. There are many Sasquatch legends surrounding this region.

With the area's abundant summer precipitation and mild winters, many different plant species that in less hospitable locations would be separated by temperature and latitude here grow side by side. Thus the plant communities are more diverse than in most other areas along the PCT. Some plants, such as the California pitcher plant, are more or less limited to the Klamath Mountains. Several other plant species are endemic to this area, not surprising when more than five hundred species have been identified here. In his book *The Klamath Knot,* David Wallace observes, describing the diversity and singularity of species in the Klamaths, "I was seeing a community of trees at least 40 million years old."

Wildflowers here can be spectacular. Mid-summer flowers include fireweed, checkermallow, tiger lily, white clover, Copeland's owl clover, Indian paintbrush, cascade lily, narrow goldenrod, lupine, azure penstemon, dandelion, shooting star, crimson columbine, larkspur, Mariposa lily, skyrocket, candystick, pinedrops, sulfur flower, pussypaws, cow parsnip, coyote mint, and wandering daisy. Many other varieties have by now finished blooming, and still others have not yet begun.

Along this route, you first walk on metamorphic rocks, cross a few outcroppings of marble, descend Red Rock Valley on ultramafic serpentinite, and finish again on metamorphic soils. This mosaic began more than 350 million years ago, when the ocean floor began receiving sediments from the western edge of the North American continent. In addition, and important to your understanding of what you see in this area, skeletons and remains of numerous sea animals in the form of a coral reef contributed to the layers building up on the ocean floor. Pressure and cementing agents changed clays into shale, sand into sandstone, and the marine skeletons into limestone. The area was repeatedly raised, followed by inundation.

About 150 million years ago, plate movement brought about a period of mountain building, metamorphosing the shale into slate, while other sedimentary and volcanic rocks were converted to quartzite, gneiss, and schist. The formation from which the present-day wilderness receives its name metamorphosed into marble. Much of the Klamath Mountains has its origins in a collection of scrapings from ancient sea floors and adjoining formations.

Faulting of surface layers occurred as the Pacific plate dove deep beneath the continental plate, subducting deeply enough to melt into magma, which then rose slowly toward the surface. The granite plutons of Wooley Creek and English Peak were intruded about this time. Ultramafic rock, from deep within the earth's superheated mantle, also intruded to near the surface. Some of the magma reached the surface and cooled as volcanic rocks, mostly basalt. The andesite and schist of today metamorphosed from this beginning.

The Klamaths became an island again until 50 million years ago, when the waters receded and the mountains were again subjected to periods of uplifting. Finally, exogenous forces began to tear at the mountains, eroding the entire surface. Still later, glaciers rounded peaks, carved cirques, deposited moraines, and carried sediments to the melt streams at their terminuses. The metasediments above much of the marble were removed by these processes, leaving the exposed layers you can see. Black Mountain is a cap of sediments that were deposited on top of the coral reef.

The lower levels of these glaciers reached nearly to Lover's Camp at about the 4,500-foot level, near where this hike begins in a healthy, dense old-growth forest nourished by deep soils derived from glacially deposited sediments.

DESCRIPTION

The Lover's Camp trailhead provides easy access to some of the most scenic parts of the Marble Mountain Wilderness. You enjoy excellent views of Marble Mountain itself within the first 5 miles. This is a loop hike, with only a single mile of trail traversed twice. The loop makes use of 2 miles of the PCT, on a high crest with outstanding views. However, a round-trip hike just to Sky High Lakes and back is a very enjoyable outing covering 12.2 miles. If further wilderness experience is desired on either the loop or round-trip hike, you are positioned to make extension hikes to several other major lake groups in the Marbles, as well as to Marble Mountain, Black Mountain, and The Castle.

One feature of this hike is that you travel in old-growth forest for most of the distance. Beginning in mixed conifer forest at the 4,200-foot level, you may observe Douglas fir, white fir, incense cedar, western white pine, sugar pine, and Pacific yew, as well as bigleaf maple, cottonwood, chinquapin, vine maple, and dogwood. You are in the shade for much of the hike, sometimes walking under a forest canopy so thick it nearly obscures the sky.

Snow can linger in the Marble Mountain Wilderness. Generally, drifts have melted by the end of June and the trails remain usable until mid-October. Check with the rangers at the Scott River Ranger Station to make sure that the trails are usable.

Black bears are quite common in the Marble Mountain Wilderness and unfortunately, in some areas of high use, have learned that backpackers and campers can mean obtainable food. Make sure you bear-bag your food when camping in this wilderness.

Administrative agency: USFS

Supervisor's Office	Scott River Ranger Station
Klamath National Forest	Fort Jones, CA 96032
1215 S. Main St.	(916) 468-5351
Yreka, CA 96097	

USGS map: 7.5′ series, Marble Mountain, California

Declination: 18½ degrees

DIRECTIONS TO TRAILHEAD

Leaving Interstate 5 at the intersection with State Route 3 at the south end of Yreka, drive west on Route 3 for 17 miles to Fort Jones. Turn right on Scott River Road at the south end of town, and follow that road 14.2 miles to the junction with signed Forest Service road 44N45. Turn left on 44N45 and cross the bridge over the Scott River. Here you'll find Indian Scotty Campground, a USFS fee facility with thirty-six campsites and a

MAP 14

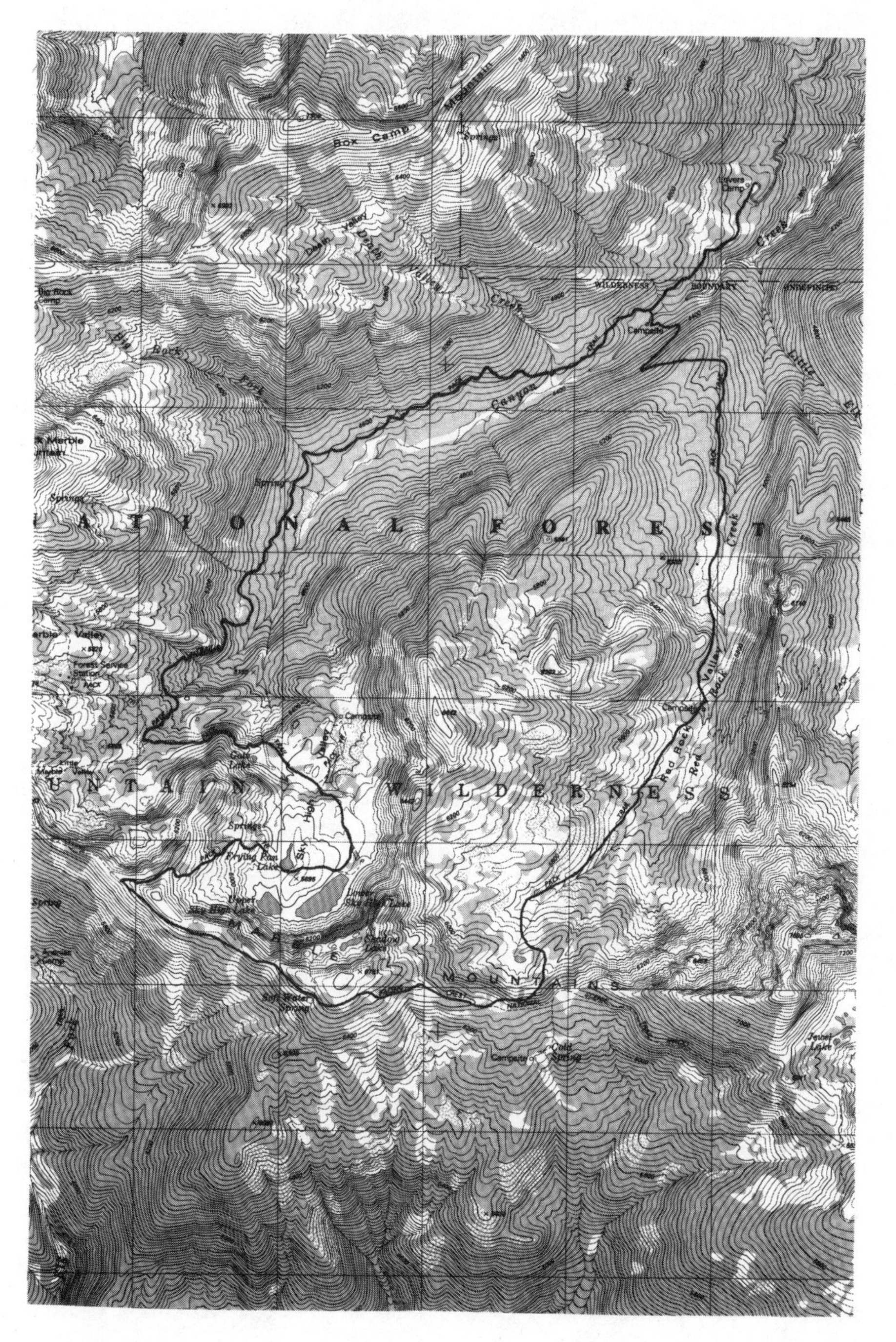
Box Camp
Spring
Death Valley
Creek
WILDERNESS
BOUNDARY
Campsite
Big Rock Camp
Big Rock Fork
Canyon
Spring
Valley
Forest Service Station
Campsite
Frying Pan Lake
Upper Sky High Lake
Lower Sky High Lake
Shadow Lake
Soft Water Spring
Campsite
Cold Spring
Red Rock Valley Creek
Red Rock
Jewel Lake
MOUNTAINS

telephone. Ascend on gravel-surfaced 44N45 for 5.5 miles to a junction with Forest Service road 43N45. Turn left at this junction, and follow 43N45 for 1.7 miles to the trailhead. The first parking area you reach is for pack stock; just a short distance beyond is the hikers' trailhead, which has a few tables and campsites. The water system may not be in service, so if you wish to camp here, be sure to bring sufficient water for your stay at the roadhead.

MAP 14

TRAIL ROUTE DESCRIPTION

From the upper parking lot, the trail begins immediately behind the large signboard and meanders south, crossing a small creeklet and then emerging onto a dirt road. Turn left on this road, soon crossing 43N45A, and in a few yards you reach a trail register kiosk at the junction of the trail from the pack stock parking lot. Your trail continues past the right side of the kiosk, offering level going along an old roadbed with water seeps. You then cross a creeklet (0.5 miles from last point; 4,270 feet above sea level; 0.5 total miles) flowing eastward into Canyon Creek, which is out of sight and parallel below on the left. Gentle undulations lead through mixed conifer old growth with heavy canopy. Some trees along the trail are in excess of 6 feet in diameter; such growth has resulted from the rich volcanic soils scoured from the peaks above and deposited at the terminus of glaciers at around the 4,500-foot level.

Before long, the Red Rock Valley Trail forks left (0.5 miles; 4,300 feet; 1.0 mile), while your trail continues southwest, reaching a creek (0.4 miles; 4,325 feet; 1.4 miles) 0.25 miles up which is located the remains of Grindstone Camp. According to one account, this was the campsite of an itinerant who sharpened axes and tools. Look for Pacific dogwoods, which are numerous along this segment. The ancient forest experience continues along gentle grades and a short descent, soon reaching Death Valley Creek (0.5 miles; 4,425 feet; 1.9 miles) and the easy climb beyond to Big Rock Creek (0.7 miles; 4,645 feet; 2.6 miles). Though intermittent, Big Rock Creek has branched into many channels that cross the trail.

Traversing easy terrain still, your trail reaches an unnamed creek (0.3 miles; 4,770 feet; 2.9 miles), also with multiple channels. Here the grade becomes steeper, at the beginning of what some call the "Marble Staircase": steps of marble laid in the trail to prevent erosion. Ascending this short staircase segment, you soon cross a north fork of Canyon Creek (0.8 miles; 5,215 feet; 3.7 miles) on a shelf with beautiful cascades above and a respectable waterfall below. Within minutes you arrive at a trail junction, the right-hand fork of which leads to the Marble Valley Guard Station less than 1 mile away.

[For a side trip to Marble Mountain, Black Mountain, The Castle, Big Elk Lake, or Paradise Lake, turn right here and follow the ascending trail

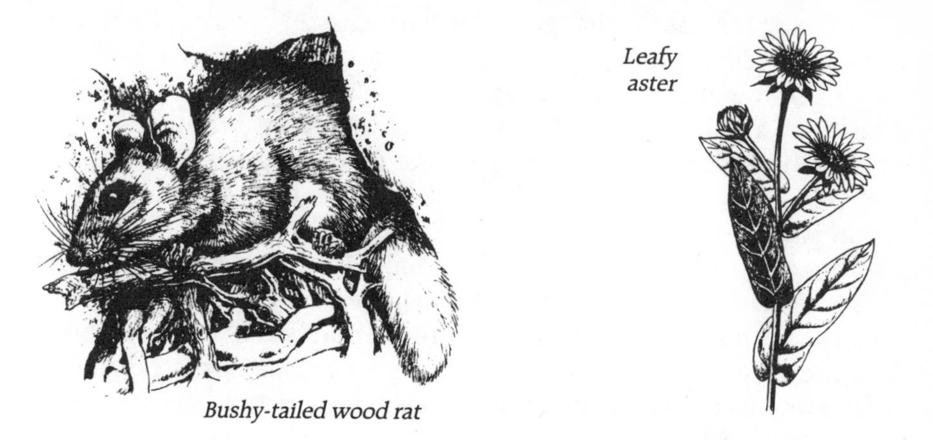
Leafy aster

Bushy-tailed wood rat

west to Marble Valley Guard Station (0.6 miles; 5,690 feet). From this point, features to the south, west, and north can be visited easily.]

Go left and within 0.5 miles, the trail officially becomes the Sky High Valley Trail at another junction of a spur that leads right (northwest) to intersect the trail to Marble Valley Guard Station. Take the left branch, which levels and turns east. A short time later Gate Lake, actually more shallow pond than lake, comes into view. Your trail descends short, steep switchbacks to a creek draining a marshy area to the south (1.2 miles; 5,545 feet; 4.9 miles).

[Just beyond this creek, a faint trail branches left to a camping area 0.3 miles east near the creek draining the Sky High basin.]

Continuing southeast in gentle undulations among willows and corn lilies, the trail next ascends gently through broad meadows graced with many wildflowers. Here you encounter old trails that have worn through the sod and eroded deep into the soil. Some of these have been blocked off and water barred to deflect runoff water; you can observe the meadow slowly healing the damage. Several trails branch off the main trail to various locations within the basin, while the main trail continues up the meadow and reaches Lower Sky High Lake (0.8 miles; 5,770 feet; 5.7 miles).

An Adirondack shelter, once scheduled for removal but granted reprieve as it is studied for historic classification, lies a short distance down and across the outlet creek. Several campsites are located on the near side of the outlet creek just downstream from the lake.

Use trails lead toward a little, sloping campsite under small conifers on the lakeshore and continue on around the north shore not far from the water's edge. The main trail branches right and ascends westerly to the top of a knoll (0.4 miles; 5,760 feet; 6.1 miles), which separates Upper Sky High and Frying Pan lakes. This knoll has several excellent campsites in medium conifers—all legal and observant of the 200-foot rule.

Frying Pan Lake is shallow and will not sustain fish. Both Upper and Lower Sky High lakes have eastern brook and rainbow trout, with the larger fish found in the much bigger Lower Sky High Lake. Lower Sky High, with a nearly vertical headwall rising 1,000 feet at the eastern end, is a beautiful water body, filling a glacial gouge over 50 feet deep.

From the camp area atop the knoll, the main trail makes a short descent, passing by the shore of Frying Pan Lake, beyond which you find another camp 100 yards up the trail. Climbing now northwesterly, the trail ascends on a moderate grade through meadows as it leaves the Sky High Basin and enters forest again. Note the numbers of mountain hemlock at this spot. From this point you can enjoy one of the better views of Marble and Black mountains, each about 2 miles distant to the northwest and easily identified.

The trail levels to a gentle southwesterly traverse until reaching a junction with the Pacific Crest Trail (1.4 miles; 6,415 feet; 7.5 miles). Two short spur trails serve the northbound and southbound hiker at this point, forming a triangular "traffic island." Take the left fork 50 yards, then turn left again at the junction with the actual PCT.

[Several interesting features of the Marble Mountain Wilderness, such as Marble Mountain, Black Mountain, The Castle, Big Elk Lake, Paradise Lake, and the Marble Valley Guard Station are within easy hiking distance of this junction.]

For the next 1.8 miles you enjoy very gentle grades, as the PCT has been constructed just below the crest of a long, straight ridge running to the southeast. Your location just southwest of the crest affords excellent views over several large, forested canyons that constitute much of the western and southwestern portions of Marble Mountain Wilderness. Also visible on the southern horizon are Thompson Peak and Sawtooth Ridge and their attendant glaciers, which cover portions of the north slopes of these Trinity "Alps" some 37 miles away.

You can enjoy these vistas as the well-routed trail crosses talus slides of marble and passes through a montane chaparral community of tobacco brush, chokecherry, greenleaf manzanita, and chinquapin alter-

Vertical Profile of Hike 14

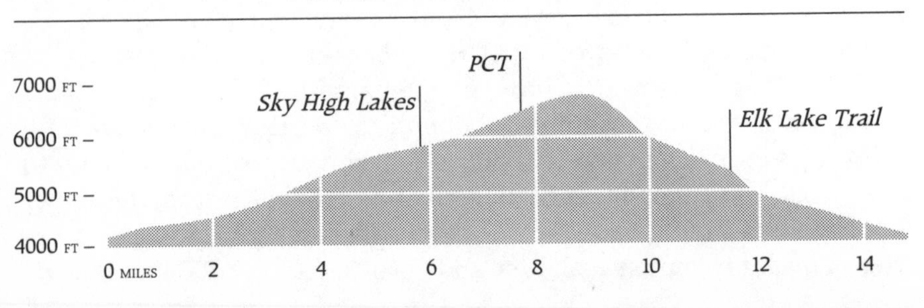

nating with patches of forest and meadows. Your heading gradually changes to just north of east and you reach a junction (1.3 miles; 6,560 feet; 8.8 miles), easily missed, where a spur trail leads left (northwest) down to Shadow Lake, 0.4 miles and 400 feet below.

From the Shadow Lake Trail junction, proceed straight ahead (east) to the junction with Red Rock Valley Trail (0.6 miles; 6,280 feet; 9.4 miles). Here you leave the PCT, having just completed one of the more scenic segments in the Marbles. The PCT continues straight ahead while your trail turns left to descend into Red Rock Valley.

[Heading right at this same junction is a spur trail to Cold Springs, 0.4 miles south.]

Leaving the PCT behind, you descend short, steep switchbacks on sometimes loose gravel and soon you can see a small, shallow, unnamed lake, more like a pond, below and left. You then cross the apparent lake outlet (0.6 miles; 5,880 feet; 10.0 miles), which is actually the beginnings of Red Rock Creek very near its headwaters in the marshy pond area to the left. Continuing the descent, your route passes through sedge meadows, patches of corn lilies, and willow thickets for nearly a mile, mostly in open meadow where the small streamlet flows crossing the trail are born. Note the quaking aspen at the northwest meadow edge before entering a small patch of large conifers next to which stands a large western white pine.

Now you cross a small creeklet that usually boasts a water flow and continue past sizable cottonwood trees on your right. Reentering old growth, you soon pass a campsite on the left, then cross a tributary of Red Rock Creek (0.9 miles; 5,605 feet; 10.9 miles). Within 0.5 miles, your track crosses the creek and then reaches a campsite on the right. Within 100 feet you cross the creek for a third time and arrive at a junction (0.6 miles; 5,240 feet; 11.5 miles) with the Elk Lake Trail, which branches right.

[To visit Little Elk Lake, take this right fork, switchbacking up steeply the first mile or so, to Little Elk Lake (2.3 miles; 5,400 feet). The trail crosses Little Elk Lake Creek at the outlet of Little Elk Lake. Just across the creek, the trail to Summit Lake branches right. If you wish to visit Deep Lake, one of the better fishing lakes in the Marbles, take Deep Lake Trail, the left fork at this point, and ascend northeasterly to a creek crossing (0.5 miles; 6,420 feet). Beyond, the trail contours gently northward for 1.5 miles, rounds the shoulder of the ridge to the east, turns south again crossing Deep Lake Creek (2.7 miles; 5,780 feet), and 0.4 miles farther, encounters a trail junction. The left fork is Deep Lake Trail, which continues eastward to the Wright Lakes, but you turn right, up the valley, and go 0.5 miles to Deep Lake at 6,380 feet elevation. Just 0.5 miles above, at 7,200 feet elevation, lies the ABC lake group, in a glaciated granite basin that looks for all the world exactly like so many Sierra lakes.]

Occupying a deep glacial gouge, Lower Sky High Lake offers many good campsites where subalpine beauty abounds just a few miles from the trailhead.

From the Red Rock Valley/Elk Lake Trail junction, take the left fork downstream (north). You soon pass through a gate designed to limit cattle grazing in the Sky High Valley. Soon the trail crosses a creeklet and then the junction of a side stream from the west with Red Rock Creek (0.4 miles; 4,965 feet; 11.9 miles). There is an old cabin of historical interest 100 yards west of this confluence.

Passing on through essentially the same meadow in which the cabin is located, you cross a creeklet (0.3 miles; 4,895 feet; 12.2 miles), reenter forest, and begin a short ascent that gains only 30 feet elevation as you traverse northwest around the shoulder of the ridge separating Canyon Creek and Red Rock basins. Note the many large ponderosa pines in this area, graphic examples of a species migrating to higher elevations when topography and other conditions create a warmer environment. Your descent is accomplished via several switchbacks as you make your way down to Canyon Creek (1.5 miles; 4,310 feet; 13.7 miles).

Depending on water levels, a dry crossing here may require using a huge log that has spanned the watercourse for several years. Except during very high runoff, however, Canyon Creek at this point is a shallow ford or a rock hop.

Once across Canyon Creek to the west side, you find several campsites under large trees, and continuing, you come to the junction with the Canyon Creek Trail within 100 yards. This is the trail upon which you started, so turn right. Retracing your steps 1 mile northeast leads to the roadhead (1.0 mile; 4,160 feet; 14.7 miles).

15 ♦ COLD SPRINGS—SKY LAKES WILDERNESS

Distance:	20.4 Miles
Low elevation:	5,820 Feet
High elevation:	6,800 Feet
Class:	Easy
Hiking time:	12 Hours

This loop hike, one of four along the Pacific Crest Trail in Oregon, penetrates into the Sky Lakes Wilderness. Sky Lakes stretches 27 miles along the crest of the southern Cascades from Crater Lake National Park south to and including 9,495-foot Mount McLoughlin near State Route 140 between Medford and Klamath Falls. The wilderness is mostly covered with untouched forest, with the exception of volcanic outcroppings, talus and scree slopes, and some volcanic pumice flats. The west slope of the wilderness spawns the headwaters of the Rogue River. The lowest elevation in the wilderness, about 3,800 feet, is found where the Middle Fork of the Rogue River flows out from the west boundary.

True to form for the Cascades, this region is of volcanic origin. It is also very young. The composite volcano Mount McLoughlin probably began building 1 million years ago, at the same time Mount Mazama to the north was lifting its mammoth bulk. Rising above the rocky crest of the Cascades, which had been formed 4 million years previously, the two volcanos then endured the ice age, during which glaciers eroded their slopes. North and east slopes bore the brunt of the carving, while in lower elevations, basins were scoured and the deep canyon of the Rogue Middle Fork was scraped to nearly present depth.

By the end of the ice age 10,000 years ago, much of the south portion of the wilderness had been formed. Brown Mountain, a short distance south of Mount McLoughlin, had spewed out extensive lava flows to the west just a few thousand years previously, accompanied by the last eruptions from McLoughlin.

In the northern portion of the wilderness, however, there was more minor volcanism after the ice receded. Goose Nest, Goose Egg, Ethel, Ruth, and Maude mountains are cinder cones that were formed during that period. A catastrophic event, the explosion of Mount Mazama, occurred 6,700 years ago, collapsing that composite volcano and forming the caldera of Crater Lake. Ash and pumice rained down on the northern part of the wilderness, forming the pumice flats known today as the Oregon Desert.

Within the 113,000 acres of wilderness are about two hundred bodies of water, ranging in size from small ponds to glistening lakes of more than 40 acres in surface area. Some of the lakes are quite deep, and many of the larger ones support trout populations. Also present are marshes, like Big Meadow and Sevenmile, where eutrophic demise has turned shallow lakes into meadows-to-be.

Nearly two dozen species of trees are found in the Sky Lakes forest. Mixed conifer stands cover most of the terrain, with white and Douglas fir in the lower elevations giving way to lodgepole pine upslope. The lodgepole is found in nearly pure stands in some areas just above 5,000 feet. It is also much at home in the pumice of the Oregon Desert. At higher altitudes, mountain hemlock mixed with California red fir predominate, and subalpine fir is also found. Whitebark pine grows near timberline on Mount McLoughlin. Sugar pine and ponderosa pine occur as scattered specimens.

Understory is scattered or lacking in many areas, but you will certainly notice the low and high huckleberry, especially in the fall when these plants bear their tasty fruit. Wildflowers are typical of the Cascades. Look especially for members of the lily family and red columbine, that wide-ranging member of the buttercup family.

The Cascade crest receives much of the moisture the coast ranges miss when winter storms pass. As a result, snow depths in this area reach several feet. Snow often remains into early June, and by late September or early October, the first snows often dust the higher ridges, with serious storms possible thereafter. Summer weather is mild, with occasional afternoon thunderstorms. Such disturbances can be accompanied by gusty winds and lightning strikes, usually on the peaks and high ridges.

While evidence remains of prehistoric use of the Sky Lakes area by Native Americans, much of what can be seen today of human activities dates from the early 1900s. A few shelter and cabin structures remain in the wilderness today. After its birth in 1906, the U.S. Forest Service built both trails and fire lookouts within the wilderness; however, none of the lookouts are active today.

The Twin Ponds Trail, running between Fourmile Lake and the base of Mount McLoughlin, was an old Native American travel route. The grade was good, so in 1863 it was widened and used as a military wagon route between Jacksonville, a gold-mining town in the Rogue Valley, and the military camp at Fort Klamath, just north of Klamath and Agency Lake.

In 1888 a far-sighted Oregon conservationist, Judge John B. Waldo, in a party with four other men, journeyed from Waldo Lake in the central Cascades to Mount Shasta along essentially the same route taken by the present-day Pacific Crest Trail. You may see the names of that party carved into a California red fir near the southeastern end of Island Lake along the Blue Canyon Trail.

The Oregon Skyline Trail, established in the 1920s, parallels the Cascade crest and in some sections is coincident with the PCT. Generally, though, the PCT has been kept as close as possible to the true crest and often routes hikers away from lakes that the Skyline Trail visited. In the 1930s, the CCC built the present shelter at Cold Springs, which is now slightly askew.

Deer are common in all areas here. Winter snows cover available browse, so the deer migrate to adjoining lower elevations then. In the spring, deer move upward into the wilderness often before snow has completely left the forest floor.

Elk also are present in fair numbers. The presence of this animal is one of the success stories in wildlife management, for the historic herds had been killed off completely before 1900. Reintroduction was accomplished near Crater Lake in 1917. The herd multiplied slowly at first, but now numbers appear to be at the maximum for the available winter range. Like deer and most other ungulates in mountainous habitat, elk follow a vertical migration pattern, merely moving down in elevation just ahead of the winter snow. Dropping as little as 3,000 feet means available winter food for these large cervids.

Coyotes are numerous in the wilderness. You may hear their chorus at night and certainly will see their scat, matted with the fine hair of rodents, on the trail. Other area wildlife includes the pine marten, black bear, mountain lion, and many small rodents. Bobcats hunt snowshoe hares here, and fishers, those black, darting phantoms of the deep woods, are present also. If you see a fisher, we would appreciate learning about the episode.

DESCRIPTION

This loop hike has been rated easy because of the good trail and an elevation gain of only 980 feet. Most of the area is in the low 6,000-foot range, a most pleasant altitude for leisurely hiking. Yet there is plenty of dramatic topography, long-range views, and real wilderness solitude. If one lake is being used by campers, it is a simple matter to move to the next. Plan to spend at least one overnight during this hike.

The route is designed to move northwest to intercept the Pacific Crest Trail, along the crest northward to the high elevation point at the north end of Sky Lakes basin, there leaving the PCT and dropping in elevation eastward into the basin. The route southward, along so many lakes and ponds that it's a challenge to keep count, is seldom equaled in wilderness hiking.

The well-maintained trail closes the loop just 0.6 miles from the roadhead, leaving only that very short segment to backtrack.

Much of the way is shady, as you pass through forests where mountain hemlock predominates. You will be seeing several ages of trees, naturally classed, with many beautiful specimens of California (Shasta) red fir. Most of the way, though, this trail could be aptly named "The Way of the Hemlocks."

You may see gray jays, also known as "camprobbers" or "whiskey-jacks," and are almost sure to spot Oregon juncos. You will probably see and hear ravens and, with a bit of luck, spot a golden eagle or one of the buteo hawks soaring above.

The preferred time to make this hike is between June 15 and September 15. In early season, be sure to take along insect repellent.

Black bears are common in Sky Lakes, but most have not yet become bold enough to steal food from camps. Just the same, it is highly recommended that you bear-bag your food and keep a clean camp.

Before you leave, be sure to check for current wilderness permit requirements.

Administrative agency: USFS

Rogue River National Forest	Winema National Forest
Supervisor's Office	Supervisor's Office
P.O. Box 520	P.O. Box 1390
Medford, OR 97501	Klamath Falls, OR 97601
(503) 776-3600	(503) 883-6714

USGS map: 7.5′ series, Pelican Butte, Oregon

Declination: 18½ degrees

DIRECTIONS TO TRAILHEAD

Access is from Oregon State Route 140, between Medford and Klamath Falls. Eastbound from Medford, turn left (north miles) at the Cold Springs trailhead sign, which is 3.1 miles east of the junction of Route 140 and Dead Indian Road. Westbound from Klamath Falls, turn right

MAP 15

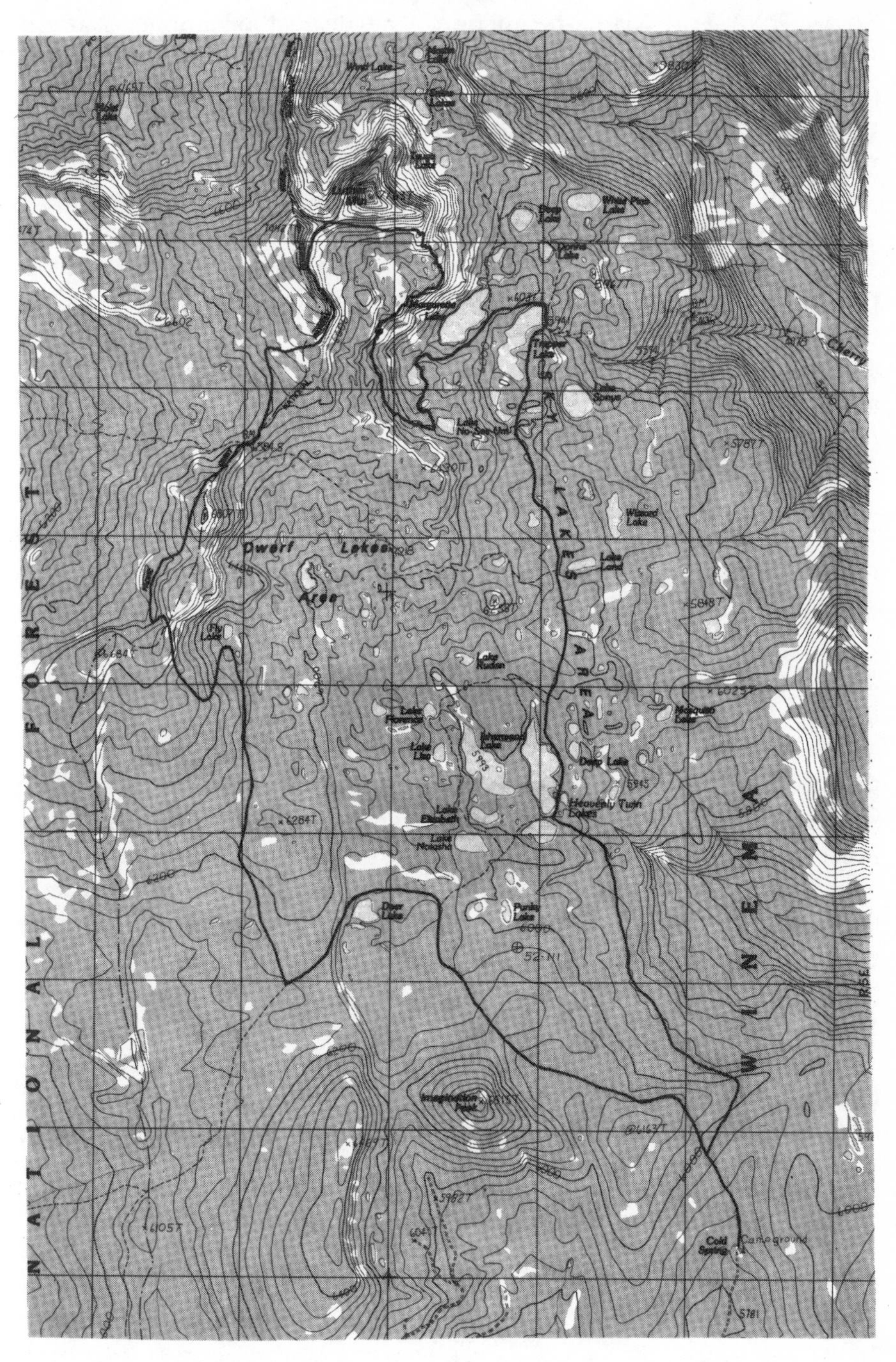
Lake No-See-Um
Wizard Lake
Lake Land
Dwarf Lakes Area
Lake Florence
Lake Elizabeth
Deep Lake
Heavenly Twin Lakes
Lake Notasha
Deer Lake
Imagination Peak
Cold Spring
Campground
Cherry
SKY LAKES AREA
NATIONAL FOREST
WINEMA

(north) at the Cold Springs trailhead sign, which is 2.7 miles west of the Rocky Point–Fort Klamath junction. The nearest telephone is at the Rocky Point resort. Forest Service road 3561 to Cold Springs trailhead is gravel surfaced. You pass a road forking right to a gravel pit at 0.1 miles, then at 1.4 miles you pass another road that forks left. Stay on the main roadbed, climbing gradually up and onto a broad saddle that stretches westward from Pelican Butte, the mountain to your right. If you look carefully, you can see an old fire lookout on the summit.

The Forest Service has placed mile markers along the road, and just past mile 10 you reach the trailhead, with a circle turnaround, several campsites, fewer tables, one outhouse, and parking for several vehicles. The old CCC shelter is here, with its eastward list, close by the namesake spring that now delivers water through a pipe. The spring area is fenced to keep livestock away from the source proper. We recommend treating this water for drinking purposes.

MAP 15

TRAIL ROUTE DESCRIPTION

From the Cold Springs trailhead, elevation 5,820 feet, the track goes north, just to the east of the fenced spring area, on a gentle incline. Many windfalls have been cleared here, and in places the forest floor resembles a game of pickup sticks. A short causeway and culvert have been installed to keep the trail dry during periods of high runoff.

Moving north-northwest now through mixed conifer forest, you pass the junction with South Rock Creek Trail, which branches right (0.6 miles from last point; 5,880 feet above sea level; 0.6 total miles). This is the junction to which you will return near the end of the hike.

Continuing on the left fork, you can see mountain hemlock and lodgepole pines, along with white fir. The trail climbs almost imperceptibly, swings to the west around hill 6163, and tops a small knoll (1.0 mile; 5,940 feet; 1.6 miles), then descends a few feet and continues westward 1 mile to the shoulder of Imagination Peak, which lies 0.5 miles south.

Undulating gently, the trail heads northwesterly through a forest inhabited by Douglas squirrels, which may scold as you pass. Soon, without gaining elevation, you reach the Sky Lakes Trail (2.4 miles; 6,080 feet;

Vertical Profile of Hike 15

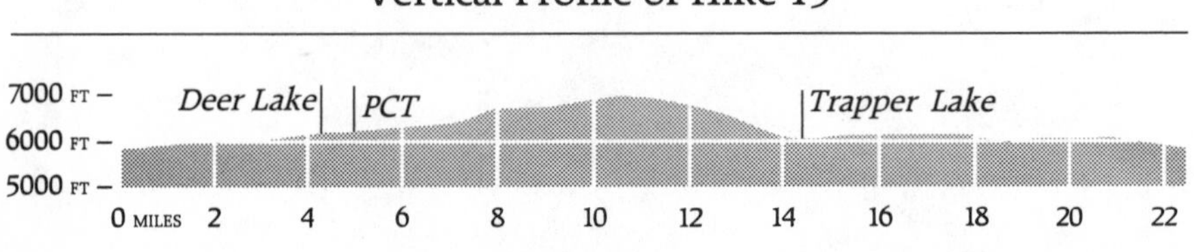

Coyote

4.0 miles). This was one of the older trails, and a main north-south route before the Pacific Crest Trail was built in this area in the 1970s.

[A right turn at this point will cut the hike short by about 6 miles total. After you turn right, proceed to a junction from the left with the Isherwood Trail near Lake Natasha (0.6 miles; 6,000 feet), then continue on to the right between arms of the two Heavenly Twin Lakes to the South Rock Creek Trail (1.1 miles; 6,000 feet). Turn right on South Rock Creek Trail and head south along level contour to a junction (2.4 miles; 6,000 feet) with the Cold Springs Trail, then turn left and hike 0.6 miles to the roadhead.]

Take the left fork of the Sky Lakes Trail. In a few feet you turn westward and then south around Deer Lake on the left (0.3 miles; 6,040 feet; 4.3 miles). There are a few small ponds beyond and to the south.

For the first time here you may become aware of gaining altitude, as the track leads up and then onto the broad crest that divides the east and west flows from the Cascades. Note the older age class of the forest as you make this short climb. Shortly you come to a junction with the Pacific Crest Trail (0.6 miles; 6,160 feet; 4.9 miles).

[A left turn here leads along the PCT some 14 miles to the junction with, and parking lot on, State Route 140.]

Turn right (north) on the PCT and meander gently almost due north, gaining little elevation. The true crest is somewhat to your east along this section. You may get the feeling of wanting to see out of the thick forest, something that is impossible.

When the Pacific Crest Trail was conceptualized and built, it was aptly named. This is not the only segment where hikers are kept in the timber along a crest, while grand views are possible just on either side. Trailside water along the PCT is scarce on this segment, one supply being at Fly Lake just ahead. The old Oregon Skyline Trail traveled the crests but dropped down into the many lake basins. This was both a blessing and a curse, as routing all traffic to the lakes led to overuse.

Continuing northward, you can finally see Fly Lake (2.4 miles; 6,240 feet; 7.3 miles) directly ahead. There the trail bends left, reverses directions, and heads south, climbing up short switchbacks to move along the east side of a rocky spine to a saddle (0.4 miles; 6,640 feet; 7.7 miles). From this section you are treated to some of the views you have been missing. South and east, Pelican Butte is dominant, and immediately below you the south half of the Sky Lakes Basin spreads its timber carpet, punctuated by enticing, sparkling hints of lakes.

Deer and elk often cross the crest in the very saddle where you stand. A rocky knob just south and a slightly higher one to the north offer excellent views.

The trail now switchbacks down into forest, and 0.2 miles beyond there is a viewpoint to the west of the trail that overlooks the headwater drainage of the Rogue River.

The downhill soon ends and you climb again, still in forest, and shortly pass just to the west of hill 6807. A few minutes of downhill striding brings you to a saddle junction with the Wickiup Trail, now abandoned (1.3 miles; 6,584 feet; 9.0 miles.) This abandoned trail leads both east and west from the saddle.

[A right turn (east) here would take you, in 2.5 miles, to the Sky Lakes Trail on the east side of the basin. Though easily followed, the abandoned Wickiup Trail has had no maintenance, and there are many, many windfalls. Even if you desire to shorten the route, continuing around the north end of the basin may be just as fast and easy even though it is more than twice the distance.]

Continue straight ahead (north) at this junction. You have been able to enjoy occasional views of Klamath Lake in the far distance, with its abrupt, eastern scarp shoreline hundreds of feet high. Now views of Agency Lake, the northernmost in the distance, and the Sky Lakes Basin right below end for a while as forest closes in again. You shortly negotiate easy switchbacks, leading from the east side of the crest gently upward to cross onto the steep talus headwall slopes of a glacial cirque that opens eastward. Note the amount of material that the glacier must have carved from this mountainside, for less than a hour ahead you will see vivid evidence of the movement of abrasive-laden ice.

At a saddle along the northwest edge of the cirque, you reach a junction (1.8 miles; 6,800 feet; 10.8 miles) where the Divide Trail branches west from the PCT. Luther Mountain, with its glacier-resistant core reaching 7,163 feet, is northwest 0.4 miles from this point. Devil's Peak is 3 miles north along the PCT.

Here you leave the PCT and turn right (east) on the Divide Trail, traversing downward along a rocky spur ridge that protrudes eastward from Luther

Mountain. Soon switchbacks ease the descent through typical montane chaparral, and you reach the bottom of the cirque whose sides you've traversed for nearly 300 degrees of the compass. An unnamed pond lies right, immediately beside the trail, and more ponds can be seen through trees to the southwest.

Before long, your trail leads to a cliff top overlooking Margurette Lake. Here, ground into the large basaltic blocks along the trail, are striations caused by passage of the glacier from the cirque above, vivid testimony to the shaping power of millions of tons of ice on the move.

The trail now leads southward along a bench. Be sure to appreciate the wonderful specimens of tall fir and hemlock in this section, which rise from steep hillsides, reaching well up toward the canopy before any limbs appear. Then an eastward-trending trail abruptly turns north at Lake No-See-Um (2.4 miles; 6,200 feet; 13.2 miles). Two illegal camps that are too close to the lake are found here, but backpackers can find suitable camping spots the appropriate distance away from most of the lakes in the basin.

You pass Lake No-See-Um on the right, then soon pass an unnamed pond on the right and, a few minutes beyond, another on the left. Margurette Lake, which you viewed from above, now appears on the left (0.6 miles; 6,000 feet; 13.8 miles). A restoration site lies 0.2 miles beyond. Here severe camping damage to soil, trees, and plants has led to the prohibition of camping. Just north of the restoration site, the easy-to-miss Sky Lakes Trail junction leads left (north) to Deep Lake and beyond.

Junco

Turn right (east); you are now on the Sky Lakes Trail, which leads to the north end of Trapper Lake, then follows the shoreline south to a junction with the Cherry Creek Trail (0.6 miles; 5,940 feet; 14.4 miles), which turns left and leads downhill 4 miles to a roadhead.

Continue south past the south end of Trapper Lake, at which point Lake Sonya lies 0.3 miles east of the trail. On generally level tread, now passing through a younger age class forest that again contains lodgepole and white fir, you pass a pond on the left and another on the right before reaching Lake Land to your left (1.5 miles; 6,000 feet; 15.9 miles). At various points along the next few miles, you may see insulators hanging from trees on short pieces of wire. These insulators were part of a telephone system once used for communication with fire lookouts.

A hundred yards beyond, coming into your trail from the right, is the junction with abandoned Wickiup Trail. You earlier passed this trail's junction with the PCT. A junction with Isherwood Trail (0.7 miles; 6,000 feet; 16.6 miles), which branches left, offers a short alternate route through this scenic lake cluster.

[To take this alternate route, turn right (west) on Isherwood Trail and continue west 0.6 miles, at which point Lake Ruden lies a few hundred yards north of the trail. Continuing on Isherwood Trail, you pass Lake Florence and Lake Liza (0.6 miles; 6,000 feet; 17.2 miles) on the right, as well as Isherwood Lake on the left. Continue south to Lake Elizabeth (0.6 miles; 6,000 feet; 17.8 miles) on the left and Lake Natasha on the right, pass between them, and proceed to the Sky Lakes Trail junction. (0.3 miles; 6,000 feet; 18.1 miles). Turn left at this junction and hike eastward along the narrow land strip between Heavenly Twin Lakes to the junction with the South Rock Creek Trail (0.4 miles; 5,960 feet; 18.5 miles).]

Continue south at the Isherwood Trail junction, and soon the north twin of Heavenly Twin Lakes lies on your immediate right and Deep Lake just to your left (east). You move along the shore of north Heavenly Twin Lake, past areas that have been destroyed by heavy and improper campsite usage and are now protected restoration sites. Soon you reach a trail junction on the narrow neck of land between the two Heavenly Twin Lakes (0.7 miles; 5,960 feet; 17.3 miles). At this point, Sky Lakes Trail heads right (west); here you leave it, turning left on South Rock Creek Trail.

A gentle downslope leads you past two ponds on the left, and then more level traverses lead through the mixed conifer forest until you reach a junction with the Cold Springs Trail (2.5 miles; 6,000 feet; 19.8 miles). Turn left and proceed south on Cold Springs Trail. Soon you pass the wilderness boundary and arrive at the roadhead (0.6 miles; 5,820 feet; 20.4 miles).

16 ♦ MINK LAKE—LUCKY LAKE—THREE SISTERS WILDERNESS

Distance:	30.5 Miles
Low elevation:	4,700 Feet
High elevation:	6,000 Feet
Class:	Moderate
Hiking time:	20 Hours

This hike enters the south portion of Three Sisters Wilderness in the central Oregon Cascades, located just west of Bend, Oregon, on U.S. Route 97 and east of Eugene, Oregon, on Interstate 5. The 283,402-acre wilderness occupies 29 north-south miles along the Cascade crest and contains the North, Middle, and South Sister volcanos as well as the heavily glaciated remains of a fourth, Broken Top. Within the wilderness boundary are cinder cones of various sizes and heavily glaciated basaltic formations. Most of the area is forested, with the exception of outcroppings, meadows, and the more recent flows and pumice deposits. The peaks reach well above timberline and hold numerous glaciers.

The scenery and volcanic evidence found here are almost unparalleled and gained early recognition for the area. Protection began in 1937, when Three Sisters Primitive Area was established. In 1957 the area was classified as wilderness, and finally in 1964 Three Sisters was included in the National Wilderness Preservation System established by Congress.

There are extreme contrasts in this landscape, where the high point is 10,358 feet and the low is 2,300 feet, as it is along Horse Creek in the far westerly corner of the wilderness. This landscape crosses the Cascade divide, where rain forests influence vegetation from the west while semiarid conditions of the Great Basin affect eastern slopes. Hence there are numerous species of plant life. It is this diversity of both flora and landforms that makes Three Sisters Wilderness interesting.

This hike is routed through the southern portion of the wilderness, where elevations of the volcanic landscape range from 4,000 to 6,000 feet. Much of the surface here is pumice, and outcroppings of andesite, hard enough to resist ice-age glaciation, are common even at lower elevations. Volcanic-derived soils have formed in many spots and support various plant life, including lodgepole pines, which thrive in pumice deposits. But this southern portion is mainly a land of lakes, and hundreds of lakes and ponds dot this 10-square-mile area.

The Pacific crest is not well defined in this southern portion of the wilderness, often crossing broad saddles and following ridges so gentle that contour is difficult to discern. The whole area seems more like a plateau than a dividing ridge. This leaves the region open to storms from the southwest, and snowfall is often heavy during the winter months. Summer weather is usually mild, but evenings can be cool. Afternoon thunderstorms do occur, and snowstorms during summer months are not unheard of, so be prepared.

Early-season wildflowers include larkspur, trillium, avalanche lily, and violets, and later varieties include lupine, paintbrush, crimson columbine, elegant cat's ears, and in shady areas of abundant duff, the chlorophyll-lacking candystick. Many others bloom here, and you will be challenged as some western species, near the extreme edge of their range, are not easily recognized.

Fishing is often good in the larger lakes. Check with the Oregon Department of Fish and Wildlife for current regulations and also as to which lakes have the larger and more numerous fish, as conditions change. Be sure to secure an Oregon fishing license.

DESCRIPTION

While the elevation changes on this hike aren't great enough to cause much diversity in plant growth, you encounter several conifer habitats as you walk this 30-mile loop. Only 2 miles of backtracking are involved here to accomplish the loop, and if you establish transportation at the Lucky Lake trailhead, about 6 miles can be cut from the total distance. This hike is rated moderate but received that rating because of distance and not because of topography or elevation gain.

While few will attempt this routing in one day, it makes a fairly easy overnight hike for those in good condition. But in order to have time to fully explore the prettier lakes and to enjoy the sylvan environment and a fine, subalpine meadow, you'll probably want to spend three days.

The route begins in typical lodgepole forest on pumice soil, then begins to parallel watercourses that run in all except the dry season. Here you can see Engelmann spruce, which are all along the route wherever there is sufficient moisture. When the trail crosses dry pumice flats, the lodgepole is again the dominant, if not the only, conifer.

The crest ridge system here is not obvious. The route trends northwest to intercept the Pacific Crest Trail, then turns northward through the Mink Lake group. At the northern end of this lake cluster, your routing leaves

MAP 16A

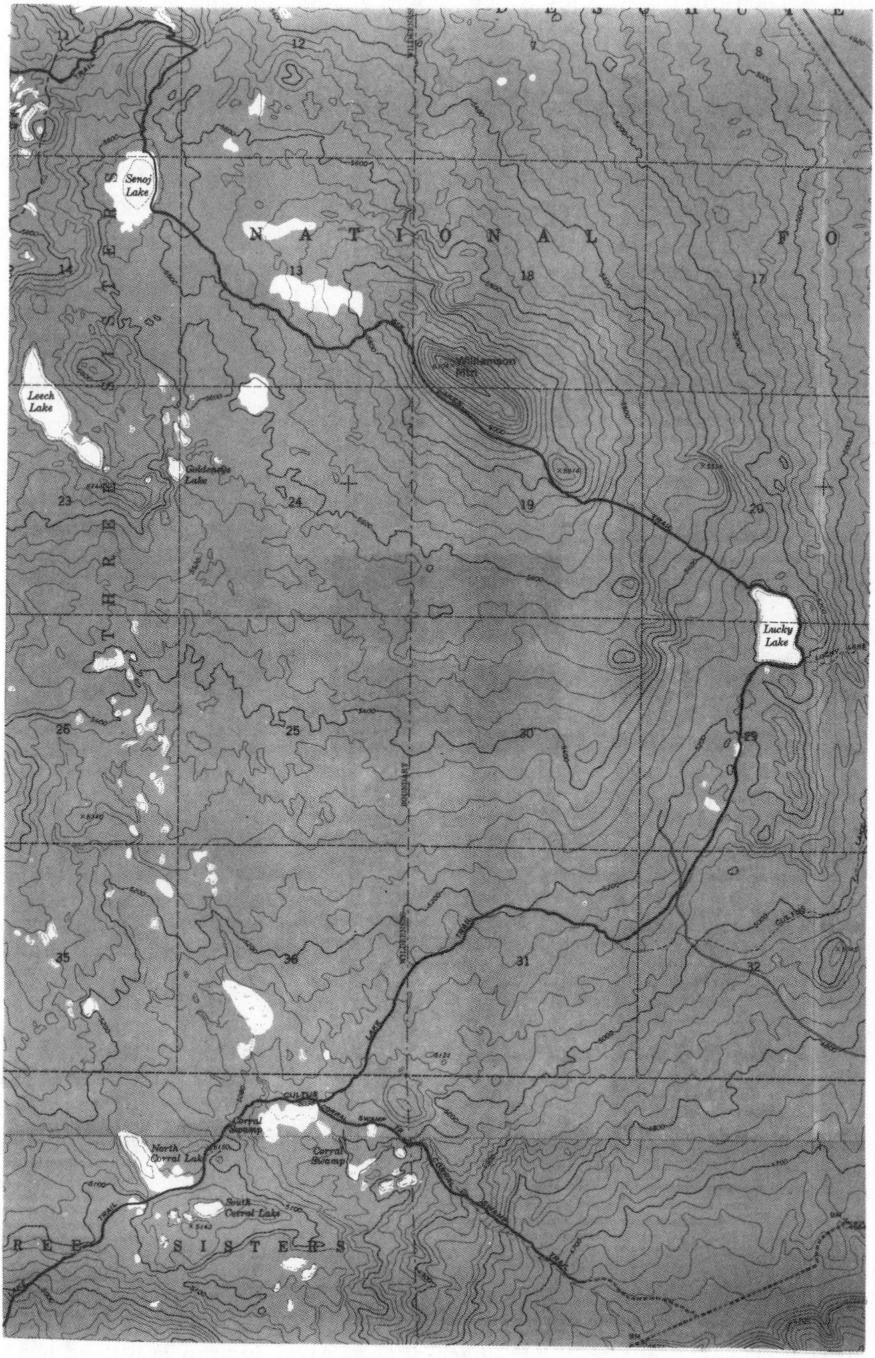
Senoj Lake
Leech Lake
Williamson Mtn
Lucky Lake
North Corral Lake
South Corral Lake
Corral Swamp
N A T I O N A L F O
R E E S I S T E R S
TRAIL

the PCT to head eastward, gently climbs to a 6,000-foot-high meadow where the only broad, long-range views on this hike can be found, then drops gently southeast and south to return to the trailhead.

The trail is usually free of snow by mid-June, except for occasional drifts in shady spots. The hiking season lasts until the onset of winter storms, which can occur around October 1.

As in most conifer zones, there are black bears in Three Sisters Wilderness. While numbers are not unusually high, you should bear-bag all food every night while in the wilderness. Luckily, the abundant suitable trees make it easy to do this.

Mosquitoes can be very persistent in this area. Be sure to carry repellent, especially in the early season.

Be certain to check the latest wilderness permit requirements and trail conditions before entering Three Sisters Wilderness.

Administrative agency: USFS

Deschutes National Forest
1645 Highway 20 East
Bend, OR 97701
(503) 388-2715

Willamette National Forest
P.O.B. 10607
Eugene, OR 97440-2607
(503) 465-6521

USGS map: 7.5′ series, Crane Prairie Reservoir, Irish Mountain, Packsaddle Mountain, Elk Lake, Oregon

Declination: 19½ degrees

DIRECTIONS TO TRAILHEAD

The trailhead is reached from U.S. Route 97. Northbound on this highway, turn left at Crescent, which is 94 miles north of Klamath Falls and 10 miles north of the Route 58 junction. From Crescent, drive 10 miles west on paved, two-lane highway leading to a junction with the Cascade Lakes Highway. Turn right (north) here, past Davis Lake, Wickiup, and Crane Prairie Reservoirs. Continue north on Route 46 (the Cascade Lakes Highway) approximately 25 miles, until you reach a signed junction with Forest Service road 2055 leading to Cultus Lake Resort; 3 miles past that, you come to a right-turn junction with Forest Service road 2016 to Deschutes Bridge. At this point, turn left (west) at the Corral Swamp Trailhead junction. Within yards of your turn, the gravel-surfaced Forest Service road 4628 is blocked by a gate, but dirt road 4632 forks left. Take this road, usually passable even in wet weather, 1.8 miles to the circular turnaround and trail register at the trailhead.

Southbound, from Bend on U.S. Route 97, turn west on the Cascade Lakes Highway (sometimes called Century Drive), which leads past the Mount Bachelor Ski Area. About 33 miles out, now heading south, you pass the Elk Lake Resort on your left, and 5 miles south of that, also on the left, you pass the junction to Lava Lake Resort. Continue heading south for an additional 2.2 miles, then turn right (west) at the Corral Swamp Trailhead junction onto gravel Forest Service road 4628, which within yards is blocked by a locked gate. At this point, turn left on dirt road 4632 and proceed 1.8 miles to the trailhead.

The trailhead has no facilities, other than parking for a few vehicles. Camping is possible here in the surrounding woods, but be sure to bring sufficient water. The improved Forest Service camp and the resort at Lava Lake are your nearest facilities.

TRAIL ROUTE DESCRIPTION

From the trailhead, at 4,700 feet elevation, the broad trail leads northwest over a level pumice flat on which grows lodgepole pine. This tree is highly successful in taking over these areas, which are extremely dry because of rapid percolation of moisture through the loose soils. Lodgepole in this respect is a true pioneer species.

Your trail continues over nearly level ground for about 0.6 miles. Look for gooseberry and squaw carpet beside the trail. The route then begins a gentle ascent as it parallels a seasonal stream on the left. This stream has insufficient staying power for the dry season but adds enough moisture to host white fir and some ponderosa pine.

You cross another seasonal stream (1.2 miles from last point; 4,950 feet above sea level; 1.2 total miles), where the presence of even more moisture encourages growth of a few Engelmann spruce. Note this tree's characteristic cones and dry twigs. Your trail continues on to the boundary of Three Sisters Wilderness (0.4 miles; 5,040 feet; 1.6 miles). A seasonal swamp-pond here can be crossed on logs or by rock hopping.

You soon reach Corral Swamp, an elongated, shallow pond 0.2 miles into the wilderness. The trail crosses the right end, but during the early spring or wet periods you may have to pass around the standing water by going through the woods bordering the right end.

Just 0.3 miles farther, you reach a junction with a trail branching right (east) to Lucky Lake (0.5 miles; 5,038 feet; 2.1 miles). This is the junction where you will rejoin your present trail at the hike's end.

Continuing straight ahead, you soon can see a seasonal lakelet on the left. Nearby grow mountain hemlock and white fir in a mostly lodgepole pine forest. A few minutes later, a 25-acre lake lies on your right a

MAP 16B

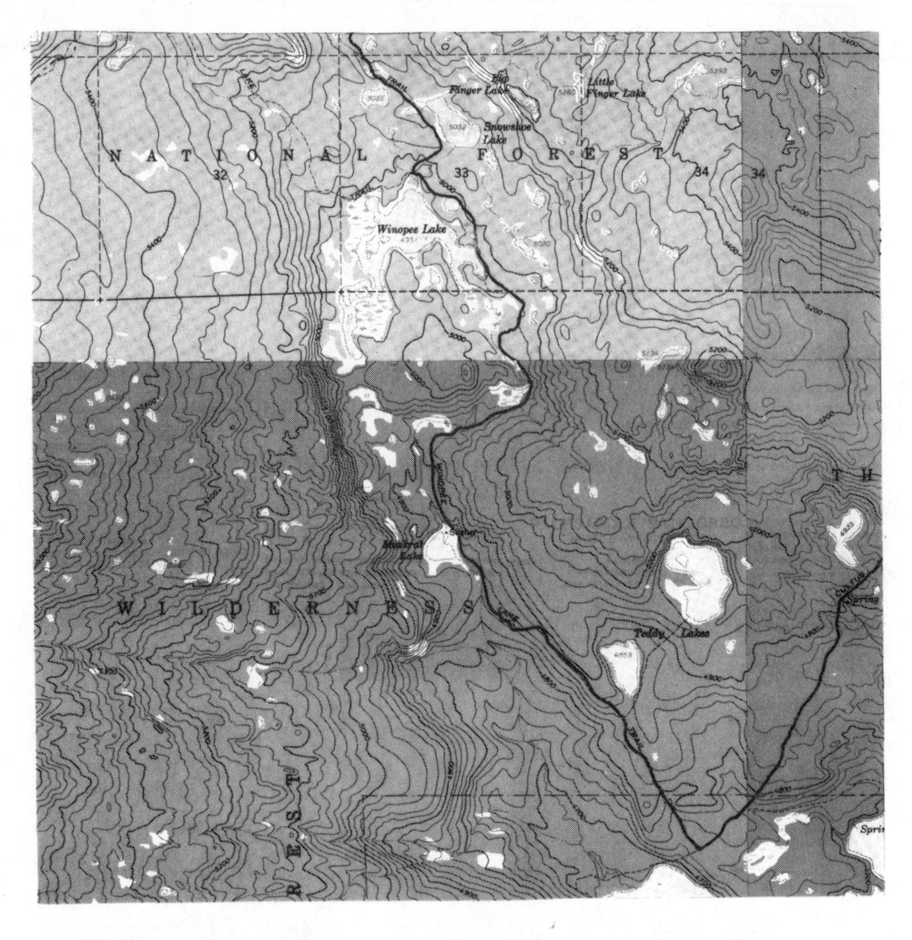

few yards from the trail, with a campsite on the near shore. This camp is too close to the water, but legitimate spots can be found nearby. A minute or two beyond the lake, you pass a seasonal pond on your left.

MAP 16B

Now kinnikinnick and low huckleberry appear beside the trail as you reach a seasonal pond, crisscrossed with windfalls (2.1 miles; 4,920 feet; 4.2 miles).

A short distance beyond, a spring upwells just 10 feet to the left of the trail. Here you can watch white pumice sand boil in the incoming flow. This spring has a good flow in early season, but it is not reliable during dry years. A few yards downstream, most of the flow disappears mysteriously into a hole in the streambed. Farther along the trail, you cross another seasonal flow, and soon after, the forested bulk of Cultus Mountain becomes visible to the left (south). Next you reach a junction where the Deer Lake–Cultus Lake Trail joins from the left (1.5 miles; 4,770 feet; 5.7 miles). Proceed straight ahead (west).

Along this section, moss pinks and tiny, yellow stream violets grow in very early season. Cultus Lake, about 2 square miles in area, lies about 0.5 miles due south. Continue west through lodgepoles along this well-used trail to a junction (0.2 miles; 4,770 feet; 5.9 miles) with the Winopee Lake Trail, which branches right (northwest). In the spring, you can sometimes hear sandhill cranes calling.

In 0.2 miles, you turn right and reenter Three Sisters Wilderness at a sign and a day-use permit register. You had exited the wilderness briefly during your close approach to Cultus Lake. Continuing northwest, you soon come to a junction (0.7 miles; 4,830 feet; 6.6 miles) where the Teddy Lakes Trail branches right (northeast) to these twin lakes, one just a few hundred yards away and the other 0.6 miles.

Continue straight ahead, and in a few feet you cross a log bridge over a small creek. During wet years, this stream could flow all season. Soon you hear the sound of rapids and emerge from the forest at the outlet to Muskrat Lake. A few hundred yards farther is Muskrat Cabin (1.1 miles; 4,860 feet; 7.7 miles), built in 1934 on the meadow beside the lake's inlet stream. The craftsman who constructed the cabin was working for the Forest Service, and his skills are displayed in more than a hundred structures throughout the Cascades. During the last years of the Depression, the lake and surrounding marshy areas were fenced in an attempt to raise muskrats. The attempt failed, but you can see an occasional fence post in the meadow, and the lake received its name from the effort.

The trail now heads upstream, and it frolics along on your left for nearly 0.5 miles. There is enough moisture along the creek to enable spruce, hemlock, and pine to grow quite large. After 0.6 miles, you cross a creeklet on a log bridge. The main flow, still on your left, here meanders through continuous meadows in tight oxbow bends. These meadows are the result of innumerable beaver dams along the stream in this area. Another .6 miles brings you to another creeklet, which you cross via a log bridge similar to the last.

The meadow you are following has occasional dams of volcanic rocks, which no doubt have helped prevent rapid downcutting and aided in the meadow's formation. Note that the trees in this area are larger than those you have come through, and now mountain hemlock is dominant, while Englemann spruce and sugar pine are also present. In 0.4 miles you pass a 15-acre shallow lake on the left, part of Winopee Lake. Here, tall huckleberry is beginning to appear.

A few minutes later, you pass a lakelet to the left of the trail and soon reach a log bridge crossing the stream joining Snowshoe and

MAP 16C

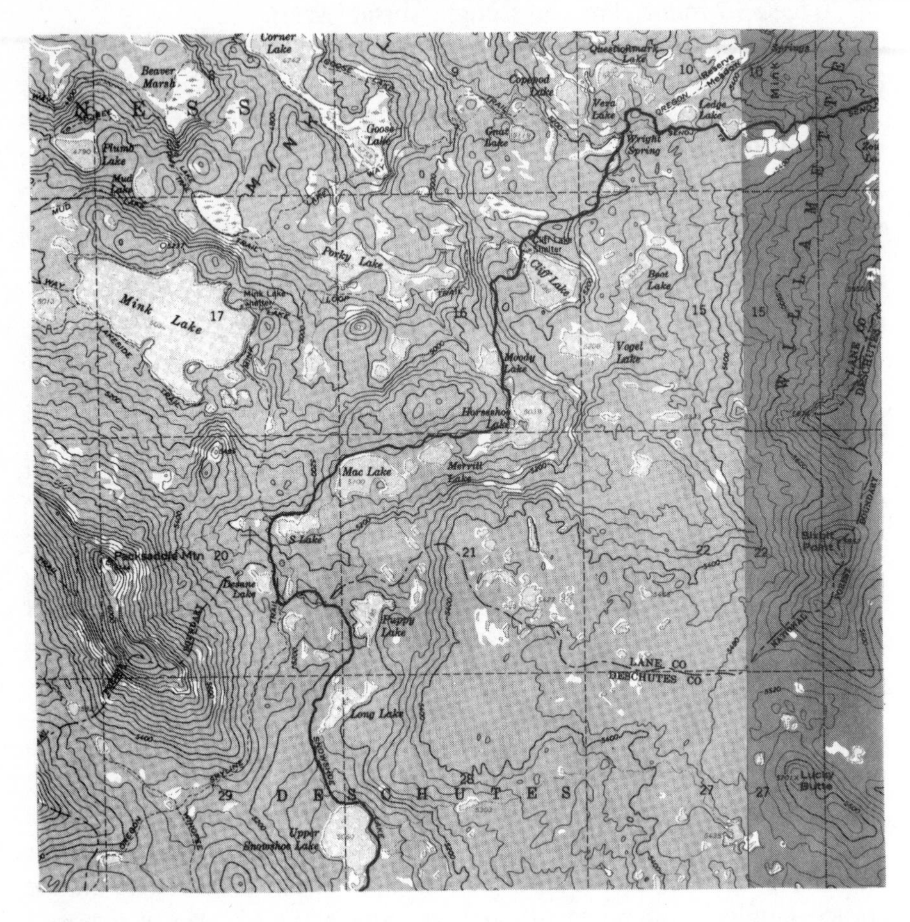

Winopee lakes. Just after, you reach a junction with a spur trail that branches left (west) to join the PCT in 2.1 miles. Continue right (northeast) to Snowshoe and Upper Snowshoe lakes. Notice isolated clumps of beargrass, which in midsummer have creamy, white flower heads on top of yard-high stalks.

Now you climb up a short but steep stretch and find Snowshoe Lake on your right (2.9 miles; 5,032 feet; 10.6 miles). This beautiful lake is bor-

Vertical Profile of Hike 16

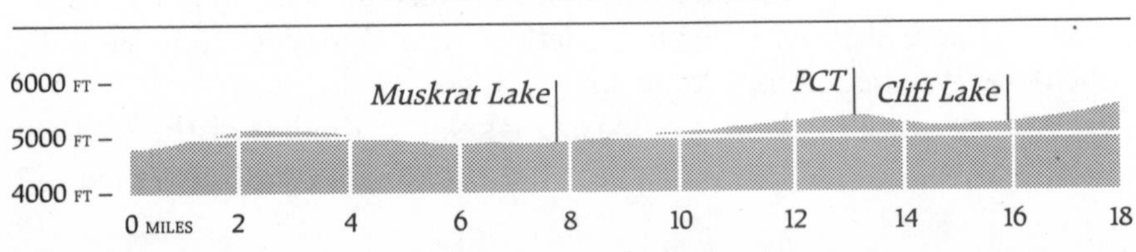

Blue grouse

dered with three distinct andesite cliffs, which break away into a jumble of talus leading down to the water. It has been popular to camp beside the trail on the bluff overlooking the lake, but the Forest Service discourages this. Camps may be made in adjoining areas a sufficient distance from the water. On Snowshoe Lake in early season we saw nesting pairs of buffleheads, small ducks that rarely breed this far south.

MAP 16C

Continue past Snowshoe Lake, and you soon cross an outlet creek that ceases flowing in dry years. Then, 0.25 miles beyond, you cross another creek on a 120-foot-long log bridge. Note how your boots make the bridge deck ring; imagine what a string of pack animals would sound like. Your tread next crosses an inlet stream, and you arrive at Upper Snowshoe Lake (0.6 miles; 5,060 feet; 11.2 miles).

Still northbound, you pass a seasonal pond in fifteen or twenty minutes, then reach 15-acre Puppy Lake on the right. Continuing beyond this lake 0.5 miles, you pass a seasonal, 1-acre pond on the right. The forest here is predominantly mountain hemlock. Soon you reach the junction (1.9 miles; 5,275 feet; 13.1 miles) with the Pacific Crest Trail. A left turn (south) on the PCT would take you to Irish Lake. Turn right (north), and in a few yards you pass Desane Lake on the left. Your trail levels, then begins a perceptible drop.

Soon you pass another seasonal pond on the left, then come to the junction (0.4 miles; 5,215 feet; 13.5 miles) with the Mink Lake Trail 3526. A left turn here would take you to 60-acre Mink Lake, the largest in the group, just 0.4 miles to the west. Continue north on the PCT, and in a

Vertical Profile of Hike 16

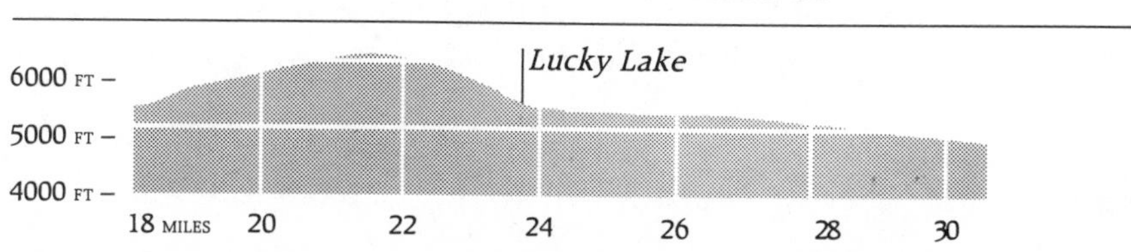

few yards you reach South Lake on the right. An old, abandoned trail branches left 0.2 miles beyond.

Continue on to Mac Lake (0.5 miles; 5,100 feet; 14.0 miles), another jeweled lake appearing through the dense forest. You pass an area of heavy camping that is too close to the water. Use trails branching to your right lead to the lakeshore. Mac Lake is a beautiful aquamarine and appears deeper than some of its companions. Note a large Douglas fir on the right side of the trail here. Near the north end of Mac Lake, you can see the old trail alignment branching left and blocked with logs. You will see segments of the old alignment several times along this section.

In just over 0.5 miles, Merrill Lake lies 100 yards to the right of the trail, and in another fifteen minutes, you pass Horseshoe Lake on the right. Note a restoration area where improper camping has caused damage to the site. You leave this lake on a wooden bridge over the outlet creek.

Soon your trail leads past small Moody Lake, barely visible through the trees some 200 yards left. You cross a seasonal spring flow welling up on your right and draining left into the partly hidden lake. You are moving north here along the west slope and begin a gentle ascent along which grow more Douglas fir. Shortly you are treated to a view of Porky Lake on your left (west), 0.5 miles distant and below, hiding in the timber. Note wild roses along the trail in this area.

A few moments later you can hear running water to your left; a few steps left off the trail would bring you to the top of a bluff overlooking rapids in a small stream that runs there. Shortly you reach a junction (1.8 miles; 5,138 feet; 15.8 miles) with a trail branching left to Porky Lake. Continue straight ahead for few yards, then turn right from the PCT to visit Cliff Lake via a use trail along the base of the talus jumble on your right. Within a 100 yards you will see Cliff Lake ahead.

Nestled in timber surroundings, Cliff Lake is one of the prettier members of the Mink Lake group. Three andesite outcroppings spill talus blocks down to the water. Growing from the stark rock on the north shore are three large quaking aspen, their trunks elephantine and swollen. Initials have been carved into their bark by inconsiderate hikers.

A shelter has been installed here, built of poles with short walls laid up of dry jointed stone, a few yards back from the lake at the outlet. This shelter is too close to the water, having been built before this was of concern. The best campsites are across the outlet creek from the shelter and up on a finger ridge. Some of this area is designated as a restoration site, but there is plenty of room farther back on the ridge. You may see blue grouse in this area.

When ice age glaciers gouged the bed of Cliff Lake, they met the andesite ridge lying just south of where the outlet is today and were forced up and over this resistant formation. You can see evidence of this in the striations cut into the lake-facing end of this ridge.

Retracing your steps westward to the PCT, you turn right (north) and almost immediately cross the outlet creek from Cliff Lake. On the bank of this stream you can spot a large rhododendron, one of the outrider plants of the species in this area.

Your trail rounds the toe of a spur ridge. Note that the bear grass is becoming thicker here. Skirting a rocky outcropping on your right, you can see an older, eroded track immediately beside your improved tread. Your route continues through the forest; with few exceptions so far, you have been surrounded by forest on this trip. Other than across lakes, distant views are rare.

MAP 16A

You pass a shallow, seasonal water body 100 yards to your left and after a bit reach a round lakelet on your right, complete with a pretty outlet flow that you cross via a short causeway. Before long, you reach a four-way junction (1.6 miles; 5,360 feet; 17.4 miles) whose left branch goes to Vera Lake. Straight ahead the PCT goes north, but instead you turn right on the trail to Doris Lake. You are still on the west side of the Cascade crest and should be able to spot another rhododendron or two.

Varying hare

You head east for a mile up a gentle ascent, then top a 5,690-foot ridge. Another ridge, 0.2 miles farther along your trail, appears to be the crest, then the trail descends to a junction (1.8 miles; 5,600 feet; 19.2 miles) where the trail to Doris and Blow lakes branches left. Take the right fork toward Senoj Lake, hiking through an east-slope forest where lodgepole have already become dominant, or at least very close to it.

You reach Senoj Lake (0.4 miles; 5,570 feet; 19.6 miles), which has a gently sloping shoreline. Moisture from the lake has enabled spruce and hemlock to grow quite large.

Now begins a gentle climb that becomes noticeably steeper as you approach Williamson Mountain. Your trail leads upward, to finally traverse the south slope of the mountain at 6,000 feet elevation, and you enter onto a hillside mountain meadow upon which elk sometimes graze. This airy, delightful section is a treat after so many forest-bound miles. Views out to the south from several spots give you glimpses of forest-clad flats, rocky outcroppings, and the snowy ridge of Diamond Peak Wilderness many miles away.

Descending now back into a lodgepole forest, you eventually reach Lucky Lake (4.0 miles; 5,200 feet; 23.6 miles) and enjoy the beautiful walk along its shoreline. There are improper campsites right on the shore, and across these the Forest Service has laid small logs. At its southeast end, the lake is obviously deeper and the water is a rich blue. Spots of white on the lake bottom just offshore are areas where the pumice sand is kept clean by upwelling springs. Past the lake, you soon reach a junction (0.3 miles; 5,200 feet; 23.9 miles) with a trail branching left (east) to the Lucky Lake trailhead.

[If you have decided to cut your loop hike short, take this left branch to the trailhead in 1.3 miles.]

Take the right-hand fork, which leads around the extreme southeast end of the lake. From there you will be able to see the snowclad top of South Sister 15 miles to the north. You will probably see gray jays in abundance around Lucky Lake.

You pass a small seasonal pond on the left as you leave the lake, and then within yards you leave Three Sisters Wilderness. Continue on the gently descending trail, which soon joins an old woods road that becomes your route for more than a mile. Finally your dual track reaches Forest Service road 4628, a graveled spur (2.1 miles; 5,110 feet; 26.0 miles) that is usually kept gated and locked.

Directly across the spur road you again reach trail tread and almost immediately pass a seed tree on your right. This particular lodgepole has been fitted with a metal collar so foresters can harvest the cones before the squirrels do.

Now heading southwest, your tread, Trail 996, undulates and wanders through a lodgepole forest. About 2 miles later, you reenter Three Sisters Wilderness. Shortly you reach the junction (2.4 miles; 5,038 feet; 28.4 miles) with the Corral Swamp Trail, the junction you passed near the beginning of the hike. Turn left (northeast) here and continue 2.1 miles to the trailhead (2.1 miles; 4,700 feet; 30.5 miles).

17♦ DEVILS LAKE— LE CONTE CRATER— THREE SISTERS WILDERNESS

Distance:	11.6 Miles
Low elevation:	5,440 Feet
High elevation:	6,280 Feet
Class:	Easy
Hiking time:	8 Hours

Wilderness is defined the following way in congressional writings: "A wilderness, in contrast with areas where man and his own works dominate the landscape, is an area where the earth and its community of life are untrammeled by man, where man himself is a visitor who does not remain."

Three Sisters Wilderness, astride the Cascade Crest in central Oregon, is famed for its beauty and variety, and only some of its trails are "trammeled." The area's landforms illustrate the volcanic forces that were at work in the creation of the Cascades. This wilderness is described in more detail in Hike 16.

Especially interesting in the central portion of the wilderness are the Le Conte Crater and the Rock Mesa obsidian flow. The short climb up the sides of Le Conte cone reveals a small lake in the crater at the top in all but the dry seasons.

Rock Mesa obsidian flow, probably produced about 1,300 years ago, originated from a vent northeast of Le Conte Crater on the lower southwest slopes of South Sister. Look at the contact zone between the obsidian flow and the pumice from Le Conte Crater and try to determine for yourself which feature was produced the more recently. The clifflike edge of the obsidian flow is within a few hundred yards of the Pacific Crest Trail at the northernmost section of this hike. The area is made up of the original shield cone and the later steep cone. There are signs that not only is this landscape new, but it is also still in the formation process.

There is little zone change during this hike, because elevation changes are slight. Soil and rock types are the major deciding factors in the varieties of vegetation. There are nearly pure stands of lodgepole pines that have colonized large areas of pumice and are attempting to colonize

As you cross Wickiup Plain on the PCT, views of South Sister compete for your attention with nearby Rock Mesa obsidian flow, where a glassy topping dozens of feet thick oozed down the mountain before cracking into millions of shiny boulders.

still more. On some of the most recent pumice emplacements, this is progressing very slowly. On much surface area, little or no plant life has yet taken hold.

Lodgepole is the common tree here, but other species are also present, notably mountain hemlock. Wildflower species are numerous, with some blooming during much of the hiking season. While on a fall hike we saw pinedrops, alpine lupine, sulfur paintbrush, fireweed, pussypaws, heather, Cascade aster, buttercups, and partridgefoot. Wildlife we spotted included the mule deer, Douglas squirrel, chipmunk, Clark's nutcracker, red-tailed hawk, mountain bluebird, junco, and robin.

In central Oregon, much moist air overrides the coast ranges and is carried northeastward over the Cascades. The Three Sisters peaks and the crest to the south of them intercept a lot of this moisture, which falls as snow in the winter. During the spring months, the west side of the crest has frequent rain showers. This moisture, along with snowmelt, quickly percolates into the rock and soil, and surfaces as springs in unexpected places.

DESCRIPTION

The first segment of this loop hike passes through lodgepole and hemlock forest as the trail gains in elevation on the way to the stark volcanic landscapes that predominate. The hike is classified as easy because of the excellent trails and the lack of severe altitude change. As an overnight hike, recommended for all but the strongest trekkers, this is an enjoyable route. Two days will give you more than adequate time to detour up the slopes of Le Conte Crater and poke around the huge blocks of obsidian that have tumbled from the face of the Rock Mesa flow.

The Pacific Crest Trail, which passes through viewless forest to the south of this area for scores of miles, comes out into the open at Wickiup Plain, one of the largest sparsely vegetated plains along the PCT in Oregon. Views of South Sister and the relatively new volcanic landscape on its southwest slope are startling.

Good camping is possible at Sisters Mirror Lake, the first source of water on this hike. With care, you can find a campsite that provides a backdrop of snowclad South Sister rising above the forest that surrounds the lake. Other lakes near the trail offer camping possibilities and, in late season when the water has warmed, good swimming. You will encounter little running water on this hike other than at Blacktail Springs, except during early season or particularly wet years.

Because of the area's relatively low elevation, the hiking season is from mid-June through early October. Mosquitoes can be very troublesome during the early season, so be sure to carry repellent.

Black bears are present in fair numbers in the wilderness. These bears are quite shy, but be sure to bear-bag your food at night and take all precautions to prevent bears from associating food with backpackers.

Administrative agency: USFS

Deschutes National Forest
1645 Highway 20 East
Bend, OR 97701
(503) 388-2715

Willamette National Forest
211 East 7th Ave.
Eugene, OR 97440
(503) 465-6521

USGS map: 7.5′ series, South Sister, Oregon

Declination: 19 degrees

DIRECTIONS TO TRAILHEAD

From Bend, Oregon, on U.S. Route 97, turn west on Century Drive (this becomes Forest Service road 46). Continue west past the Mount Bachelor Ski Area at mile 21. Turn left at the Devils Lake Campground sign just past

MAP 17

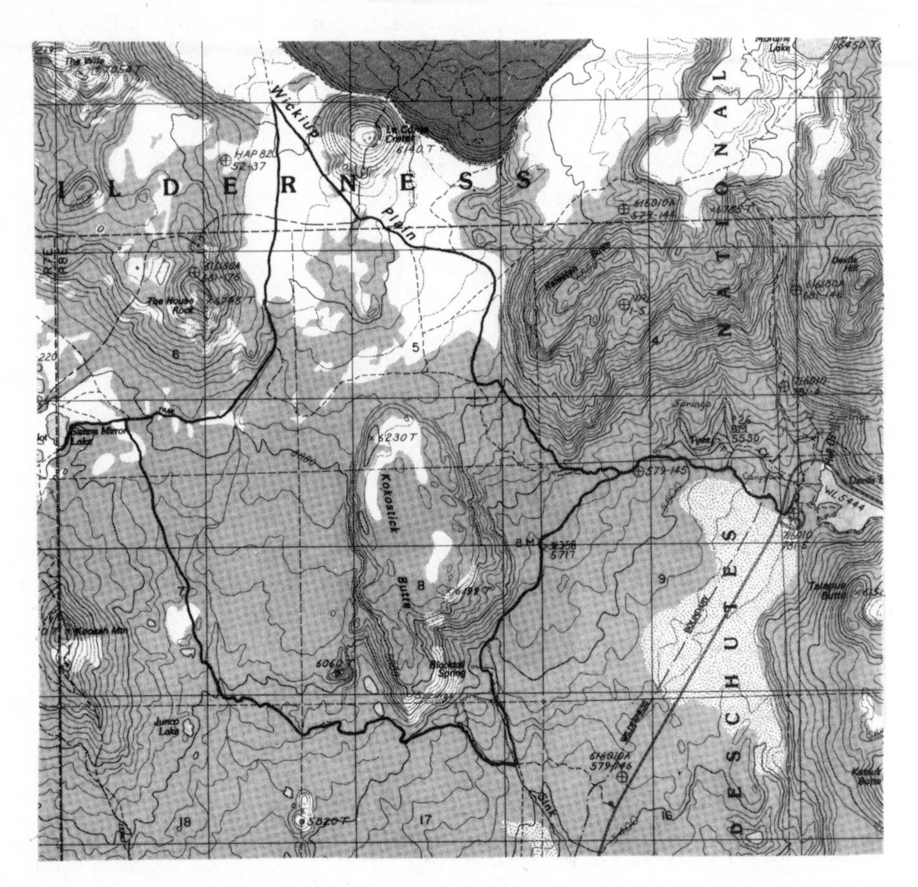

milepost 28. Go past the horse parking area to the hikers' trailhead. Note that there are two trails whose heads are at this loop parking area; your trail, signed "Elk–Devils Lake Trail," is located at the southwest corner. There are two pit toilets here, as well as six walk-in campsites with tables and fire rings. The stock parking area has toilets, loading ramp, and hitching rail.

TRAIL ROUTE DESCRIPTION

MAP 17

From the trailhead, at which is a registration and permit box, your tread leads southwest. Within 500 feet, it is joined by a trail from the stock parking lot, after which you cross under Forest Service road 46 by means of a huge culvert. You skirt the edge of an old lava flow on your left, then climb onto this outcropping and proceed in a sparse forest of lodgepole pine, hemlock, and the occasional red fir. In a short distance you enter Three Sisters Wilderness, and 0.3 miles beyond that, your trail turns left as it joins with the old, long-abandoned Devils Lake–Elk Lake Road. This road provides you with a broad, sandy track with good gradient.

Now flanked by some larger hemlocks, you soon reach a junction (1.0 mile from last point; 5,700 feet above sea level; 1.0 total mile) where the road-trail turns left to Elk Lake. You turn right, however, onto Trail 12A, which is here signed as leading to Sisters Mirror Lake and the Pacific Crest Trail. Ascending gently now on this trail, you enter a forest that is predominantly larger hemlocks, with the occasional lodgepole and red fir. Understory is sparse, giving the area an open feeling. There is some low-ground huckleberry, as well as clumps of conifer seedlings.

The trail makes a winding, ascending traverse generally along a southeast slope, with some flat areas that are usually studded with lodgepole pines. On just such a flat you reach a junction (1.0 miles 5,900 feet; 2.0 miles) where Trail 12A, signed "Sister Mirror Lake" and "PCT South," turns left. Take the right-hand branch, signed "PCT North and Moraine Lake." The trail heads out across the edge of Wickiup Plain. Kaleetan Butte lies 0.5 miles to your right.

Note that few plants have succeeded in colonizing the well-drained pumice of this flat. A few lodgepole seedlings manage to gain a foothold along the edges each year, however, slowly shrinking the size of the open plains. Before long you reach a completely treeless plain, with just a few sedges and forbs that have managed to colonize the surface.

You soon reach another junction (0.4 miles; 6,100 feet; 2.4 miles), where the Moraine Lake Trail branches right and the Sisters Mirror Lake Trail branches back sharply to the left. Continue straight ahead (north) toward a resistant basaltic plug that projects skyward a few hundred yards away. You can often see elk tracks on the trail in this area. The animals graze on scattered forbs on the plains at night and head back into dense forest at daybreak.

Ahead of you to the northwest you can see Le Conte Crater, a cinder cone that contributed a great deal of the pumice over which you are now walking. To the right of it you can see the leading edge of the Rock Mesa Obsidian Flow and, in the background, the rounded, red pumice summit

Vertical Profile of Hike 17

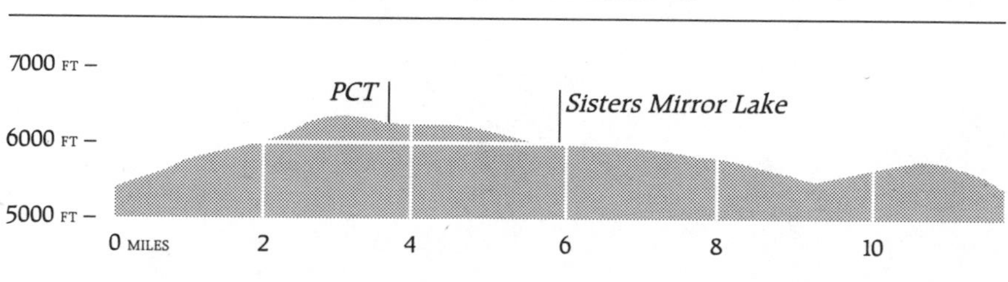

of South Sister. Your trail climbs more steeply as you approach ridges where hemlocks have successfully colonized. Soon you join the faint tracks of an old road, used before wilderness status was granted to the area. Your trail follows this road onto a ridge (0.6 miles; 6,280 feet; 3.0 miles) that marks the boundary between Deschutes and Lane counties, then leads down the north side. Here the pumice holds moisture closer to the surface, and sedges thickly carpet the low areas.

[Le Conte Crater lies on your immediate right to the north, and if you wish to climb to the top, this is the best spot to turn off. Stay to the highest ground from the above-mentioned ridge and head north. Upon reaching the slopes of the cone itself, you will be able to remain in the shade of hemlock groves most of the way to the summit. Keep to the highest ground as you ascend, and you will come to a worn use trail about 200 yards from the top. Follow this trail to the rim, a vertical climb of 350 feet. In early season and during wet years, Le Conte Crater sports a small crater lake, from the rim of which you have excellent views.]

Continue northwest along the worn trail, descending gently as you traverse the open plain. You reach a junction (0.6 miles; 6,160 feet; 3.6 miles) with the Pacific Crest Trail, although it is not indicated by signs. To the right (north), this trail leads to Mesa Creek, while the sharp left branch (south) is signed "Sisters Mirror Lake." Due west of this junction lies The Wife, nearly vertical on the north side and sloping on the south, reaching to 7,054 feet.

[If you wish to visit the base of the Rock Mesa Obsidian Flow, this is the best place from which to do so. It lies to the east about 0.25 miles distant.]

At the junction, turn left (south) onto the PCT, here a well-defined track that ascends gently across the open expanses of Wickiup Plain. Entering

Larkspur

the forest again (0.7 miles; 6,160 feet; 4.3 miles), you begin a descent through a dense, hemlock-dominated stand with little understory. The trail then levels, and you traverse the densely wooded southeast slope of House Rock, finally turning west to meander along its south slope in alternating patches of grass and clumps of trees.

You reach a junction (0.9 miles; 6,020 feet; 5.2 miles) where the Moraine Lake Trail branches left, while the PCT continues right toward Sisters Mirror Lake. Remain on the PCT, crossing a small drainage coming from a tiny meadow on your right. Water can be found here in early season.

Your easy trail soon leads to another junction (0.3 miles; 5,970 feet; 5.5 miles). The right-hand fork is Nash Lake Trail 3527, the left-hand trail leads to the Mirror Lake trailhead, and the PCT goes straight ahead. Continue on the PCT, which leads west, and within 500 feet you come across a sign informing that you are on the PCT. Two old, abandoned trail alignments join at this spot.

You reach Sisters Mirror Lake (0.3 miles; 5,960 feet; 5.8 miles) at a rehabilitation area where no camping is allowed. There are adequate campsites farther along the shore. Be sure to walk to the south end of the lake and look northeast; you will see the summit of South Sister skylined above the lake. If you are making an overnight hike, consider camping near Sisters Mirror Lake, for this is the first reliable water source in 5 miles.

Now retracing your steps back along the PCT to the previous junction, you leave the PCT and turn right toward the Mirror Lake trailhead. You gradually descend on loose trail surface among lodgepoles with scattered hemlocks. Your route follows a wash that is usually dry; on the far side is the edge of an old lava flow. You curve away from the wash and ascend onto a slightly higher bench before turning again to the south.

A small, unnamed lake (1.4 miles; 5,840 feet; 7.2 miles) lies to the right of the trail and makes a pleasant spot to stop for a while. Just 0.25 miles south and some distance west of your trail lies Junco Lake.

As you progress southeastward, you again cross the creek that has been paralleling you on the left. This stream could run water in early season during the melt. Like many such streams in porous and volcanic soils, this sometimes watercourse begins at the green meadow you passed just south of Wickiup Plain and runs generally southward for about 3 miles, with any water that reaches the terminus flowing into a small lakelet that has no outlet. It is a closed system, at least on the surface.

Within 0.5 miles you pass a small, stagnant pond on your left, likely to be dry in late season during drought years. You follow along a lava flow on your left, finally crossing an arm of this flow, which has been contained by a pumice ridge. Soon you reach the southernmost of the two Bristah Lakes (1.2 miles; 5,690 feet; 8.4 miles), passing it to the south. These lakes, without an outlet, are also fed by a short, closed-system stream.

You now enjoy a level meander through large hemlocks, then begin to descend gently, and shortly parallel a stream on your left that flows water in early season. You cross a cold, clear creeklet, the first good flowing water you've come to, and 100 feet beyond reach a junction (0.7 miles; 5,440 feet; 9.1 miles) with the Devils Lake–Elk Lake Trail. A right turn here leads to Elk Lake, and straight ahead Trail 20 leads to the Mirror Lake trailhead. Turn left toward Devils Lake on the road-trail; you immediately begin a moderate ascent along a small creek just to the west.

Within 100 yards set in the ground are two steel rails that acted as anchors for a gate when this old road was still used as such. Your wide track ascends steadily, then crosses over a small branch of the creek it has been paralleling. The trail next traverses a small, wet meadow, easing your ascent temporarily. A painted right-of-way post still remains in the meadow. Within a few steps, you reach one of the Blacktail Springs just above the track on your left. A few yards beyond, two other springs to your right form the basic flow of this creeklet.

Your steady ascent finally ends as you break over a broad summit (1.5 miles; 5,720 feet; 10.6 miles) and begin to descend. Within 400 feet you reach the junction with the Wickiup Plain Trail 12A, which turns left. You have now rejoined the trail on which you began this hike. Continue along the Devils Lake road-trail to the east, and ramble about 1 mile east, under the highway, past the horse trail to the stock parking lot, arriving finally at the starting trailhead (1.0 mile; 5,470 feet; 11.6 miles).

18 ♦ OBSIDIAN FALLS—THREE SISTERS WILDERNESS

Distance:	10.9 Miles
Low elevation:	4,760 Feet
High elevation:	6,620 Feet
Class:	Moderate
Hiking time:	8 Hours

The Three Sisters Wilderness in the central Oregon Cascades was last expanded with the passing of the Endangered Wilderness Act of 1977, when the 45,700-acre Pete French Area was added, bringing the total wilderness size to 283,402 acres. The wilderness effect is enhanced here because Mount Washington Wilderness adjoins Three Sisters Wilderness; their common boundary is State Route 242, the McKenzie Pass Highway. This fortunate circumstance benefits both wilderness areas, as it eliminates the need for a wildlife corridor. There is movement between the two even though much of the common boundary area is covered by a veritable moonscape of lava from Belnap and other nearby craters.

The Three Sisters volcanos are part of a linear chain of volcanos that includes Mounts Washington, Hood, and Jefferson to the north and Mount McLoughlin to the south. They are also called Faith, Hope, and Charity, with Charity the southernmost. Glaciers have carved away heavily at North Sister and altered Middle Sister. The youngest, South Sister, has not been glaciated to the degree of its two siblings. It is the most recently active of the three, evidenced by its summit crater, today partially filled by a small lake.

Tucked away at the west base of North Sister is a feature well worth seeing: Obsidian Falls, a waterfall nearly 30 feet high tumbling over a cliff of obsidian. Volcanism in many areas in the Cascades produced generous amounts of obsidian, the "volcanic glass" from which Native Americans made cutting tools and projectile points. Excursions by early peoples into this area to obtain obsidian were frequent. In some areas, obsidian chips are scattered on the ground, indicating that pieces of obsidian were percussion flaked at the site. These "blanks" were then taken to village sites, where they were worked into tools. Blanks also served as trade items as far away as the Pacific Coast.

In 1862 Felix Scott, believing a road across the Cascades would become an important trade route, blazed the Scott Road, which basically followed an old Native American trail. His road was difficult for wagon freighters and was used for only a few years, after which an easier route was found, essentially the present McKenzie Pass Highway. The Scott route exists today as a partial alignment for Trail 3531, passing just north of the Jerry Lava Flow. The newer route began as a toll road, became a county road in 1898, and was made a state highway in 1917.

Templeton Craig, known as the "Pioneer Mailman," carried mail on foot over McKenzie Pass. Shelter in winter was provided by a rustic cabin near the summit. In December 1877 Craig was caught in a sudden storm; he later was found dead inside the cabin, an apparent victim of hypothermia.

Major conifer species in the hike area are lodgepole pine and mountain hemlock. Many wildflower species can be seen on the trail to Obsidian Falls. Wildlife we saw during a fall hike included the Douglas Squirrel, chipmunk, sharp-shinned hawk, Clark's nutcracker, gray jay, black-capped chickadee, and junco.

Weather along this route is much the same as described for Hikes 16 and 17. Snowfall is great enough, however, that Collier Glacier, just 2,000 feet higher than and 1 mile away from the Pacific Crest Trail segment traveled in this hike, is the largest glacier in Oregon.

DESCRIPTION

This is a modified loop hike, retracing a little more than 3 miles of trail. The distance is moderate and the gradients are easy, but the 1,800-foot elevation gain dictates the hike's classification as moderate.

Heavy camping usage at Sunshine, where the Glacier Way Trail 3528A intersects the PCT, has forced the Forest Service to establish restoration plots here in an effort to aid regeneration of natural plant life on bare, compacted, abused areas. Maps are marked with requests to avoid camping in the Sunshine area. In keeping with that request, this hike, the shortest in this book, is recommended as a one-day hike.

The route begins in stands of lodgepole and climbs steadily. There is little forest change except for the appearance of mountain hemlocks as the elevation increases. About 3 miles beyond the Jerry Lava Flow, the plant communities are much affected and dictated by the volcanic activity that has taken place.

The Jerry Flow is being colonized by trees, easily observable along the trail. Considering that the Jerry Flow is somewhere between 500 and 1,600 years of age, the trees have not done badly. Very little soil has been formed as yet.

MAP 18

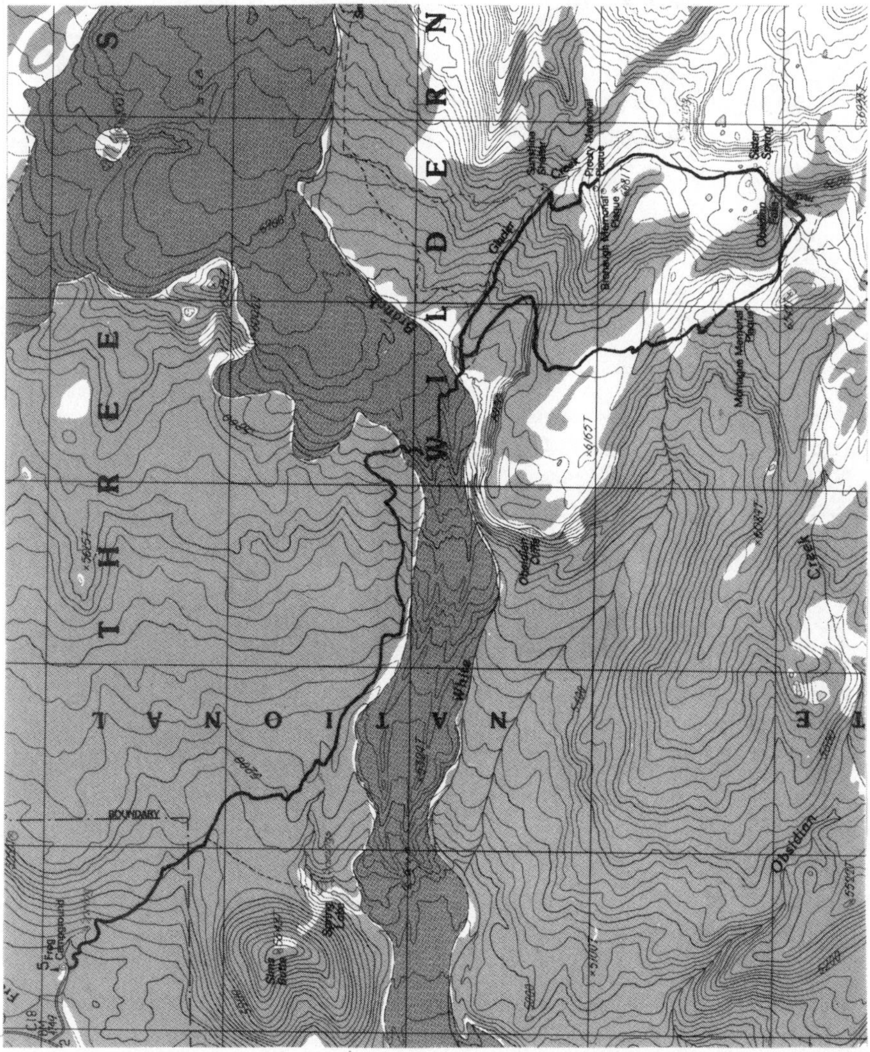

Along the south side of the Jerry Lava Flow is White Branch Creek, crowded out of its original channel by the flow and realigned immediately adjacent. This creek is fed by meltwater from Collier Glacier, which along with adjacent Renfrew Glacier provides water for other creeks and the large springs in the area. Glacier Creek, which the route next follows, begins at such springs.

Looking upslope toward North Sister, it is evident that a great deal of glaciation has occurred. The 7,810-foot Little Brother blocks the view

Administrative agency: USFS

Willamette National Forest
211 East 7th Ave.
Eugene, OR 97440
(503) 465-6521

Willamette National Forest
McKenzie Bridge Ranger Station
McKenzie Bridge, OR 97413
(503) 822-3381

USGS map: 7.5′ series, North Sister, Oregon

Declination: 19 degrees

from this angle, however. The huge moraines at the snout, or lower end, of Collier Glacier are more easily seen from elevated locations to the north of McKenzie Pass Highway.

As you walk southward on the PCT here, you hear sounds like breaking glass. Obsidian chips make up much of the trail surface and are responsible for the sound as you tread on the pieces.

Three memorial plaques were installed along this segment of the PCT, somewhat unusual for a wilderness area. The plaques honor three former presidents of an Oregon hiking club called the Mazamas: H. H. Prouty (1857–1916), J. E. Bronough (1869–1938), and R. W. Montague (1862–1935).

Today it would be quite difficult to secure permission for such memorials in a wilderness area. At the time these were installed, however, such deeds were not prohibited. Nor are the plaques particularly unfitting today; the Mazama hiking club has always been active in conservation measures.

The South Branch of White Branch Creek is spawned at Sister Spring, and within a few hundred yards the considerable flow plunges over black cliffs at Obsidian Falls. Near this point is the southernmost part of the loop route.

Hiking often is possible on this trip by late June, and the season continues until early October. Snowbanks can persist in the spring in heavy snowfall years. Contact the McKenzie Bridge Ranger District of the Willamette National Forest for snow conditions on the well-used trails.

Surprising amounts of surface water are found here, especially during snowmelt in the spring. As a consequence, mosquitoes can be a nuisance during the early season, so carry along repellent.

Black bears are present and, while not particularly troublesome, they will not hesitate to help themselves to any food you leave untended.

Not much food is required for day hikes. Nevertheless, do not cache a daypack with sandwiches or candy bars for later retrieval without making it inaccessible to bears.

DIRECTIONS TO TRAILHEAD

This trailhead is accessed from the McKenzie Pass Highway. From Bend, Oregon, on U.S. Route 97, go north to the intersection with Route 20 near the north end of the city. Head west on Route 20 to Sisters. At the west end of Sisters, take Route 242, which branches left (west), and proceed 21.7 miles. You will find the Frog Camp/Obsidian trailhead at that point, which is also 100 yards west of mile marker 71. Turn left and proceed on the gravel road to the parking area at the trailhead.

From Eugene, Oregon, take Interstate 5 to Route 126. Head east on Route 126 through adjacent Springfield and proceed east approximately 59 miles to the junction with Route 242, 4 miles east of McKenzie Bridge. Turn right on Route 242 and proceed 12 miles. Turn right into the Frog Camp/Obsidian trailhead, located 100 yards west of mile marker 71.

There is a separate horse-parking area at the trailhead, with ramp and hitching rail. Pit toilets are provided by the Forest Service.

TRAIL ROUTE DESCRIPTION

MAP 18

A trail register and bulletin board are found at Obsidian trailhead. Your trail leads eastward from the trailhead, elevation 4,750 feet, and within 100 feet brings you to the junction with Trail 3531A, which turns left and leads to the old Scott party route to the north. Go straight ahead; your trail ascends through hemlocks and subalpine firs with an understory of bear grass and low-ground huckleberry.

Ascending very gently, the trail parallels a watercourse on your right, which runs water during the melt and early season. As you move eastward, note that the Forest Service has placed additional windfall logs across the trail and left a narrow corridor between the cut ends in an effort to reduce trail width, which is considerable here.

You enter Three Sisters Wilderness (0.6 miles from last point; 4,990 feet above sea level; 0.6 total miles) at a sign indicating such and continue your gradual ascent on a dusty track that could become very muddy in wet weather. Old trail alignments are encountered here, but you will have no difficulty in distinguishing these from your well-used tread. You switchback right and in a short time encounter a sign directing you to White Branch Creek, which lies 3 miles ahead on this trail.

Your very gentle ascent along this wide trail is made more enjoyable by shade from the open forest. You continue over a gentle rise, then drop down into a small draw that in normal years runs water until midsummer.

Clarks nutcracker

After 1 mile, your trail climbs more abruptly as you enter a forest with larger trees, mostly hemlock and red fir. Another 0.3 miles farther, the forest is denser, with smaller trees competing for available sunlight and moisture. The result is suppression and very slow growth, causing the trees' small size.

Then, in impressive old-growth forest, your tread becomes carpeted with conifer needles, a welcome change from the dust. The character of your continuous but moderate ascent changes as you reach the edge of the Jerry Lava Flow (2.3 miles; 5,745 feet; 2.9 miles), which vented from Collier Cone some 3 miles east of you. Climbing now onto the lava, you switchback and wend your way across the flow. A few small colonies of trees have established themselves on the lava, but the general lack of vegetation reveals the youth of this formation.

Descending briefly from the lava flow, you come to White Branch Creek, which you can cross by rock hopping. There is a pleasant waterfall just a few dozen yards upstream. Another 200 feet farther along the trail is a junction (0.6 miles; 5,785 feet; 3.5 miles) where Glacier Way Trail 3528A turns left to Sunshine, Minnie Scott Springs, Camp Riley, and Obsidian Falls. Trail 3528 turns right at this junction, to which you will return after completing the loop. Turn left on Trail 3528A to Minnie Scott Springs.

Campfires are prohibited here, and for the next 2.5 miles camping is restricted to areas that are at least 100 feet from water or trails. Several sites damaged in the past by overuse are being rehabilitated.

Your trail parallels tumbling Glacier Creek on your left as you labor up a steep ascent, and it eventually comes within a few yards of this refreshing stream. Now in lupine and sedge meadows, you continue to gain elevation, passing finally through a cut in a large log and reaching a junction with the Pacific Crest Trail (0.8 miles; 6,300 feet; 4.3 miles). This spot, called Sunshine, is a very heavily used area, and the Forest Service asks that tarrying here be avoided. Several rehabilitation areas have been established near this junction. The Minnie Scott Springs Trail continues ahead (east), while the PCT leads both north and south. Turn right (south) on the PCT.

From this spot, looking east, you can see the west face of North Sister and a little to the north, 7,810-foot Little Brother. The Minnie Scott Springs Trail eventually leads to climbing routes of North and Middle Sisters.

Southbound now, you leave the meadow, enter more hemlock stands, and start a switchbacking climb. After a few hundred yards, looking north, you can see Belnap Crater, Mount Washington, and looming large but distant, the bulk of Mount Jefferson. Just after this fine view becomes apparent, as you switchback to the left, you can see a volcanic cliff ahead and, slightly nearer, a house-sized obsidian rock that has been rounded by glacial action. Set into the northwest face of this rock is the bronze plaque honoring Prouty; the other plaques are nearby.

Continuing, you soon enter a wide, glaciated basin with fantastic views of the west slope of North Sister. You pass the Bronaugh memorial, and farther up the valley you see Minnie Scott Springs, the headwaters of Glacier Creek, and nearby, the site of Camp Scott. A use trail leads east from the PCT to Minnie Scott Springs. Camp Riley is located on top of a steep talus slope directly south of the spring, near unseen Arrowhead Lake.

You pass a rehabilitation area beside the trail on a small, flat ridge, and shortly after, a small tarn on your left that often dries up in late season. Wending your way through the volcanic landscape, you cross a grassy area and a tarn on your right. You now surmount a small obsidian ridge and ramble past a small, round tarn on your left.

Then, on your left, at the base of a talus slide, is one of several springs that make up the headwaters of a south fork of White Branch Creek. Flowing 4 yards wide and soon joined by companion springs, this stream flows south and then abruptly turns west. Contrary to normal PCT

Vertical Profile of Hike 18

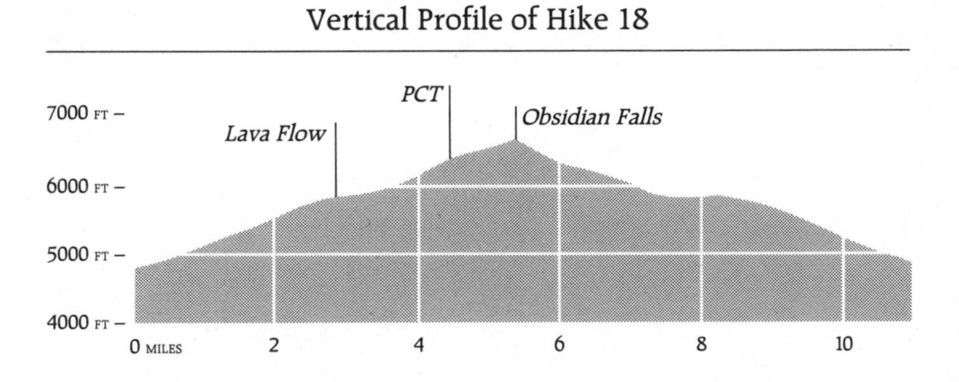

behavior, the trail follows close by the water through this meadow, turns with the creek, and in a short distance crosses on foot stones.

Fifty yards downstream are Obsidian Falls, obscured by a line of trees along the top of the obsidian cliff. This treeline is now a rehabilitation area, because the tying of stock to the trees has resulted in erosion around the roots.

Your trail heads down between the rehab barriers, and you can see Obsidian Falls (1.0 mile; 6,520 feet; 5.3 miles) on your right. The south fork of the creek falls about 30 feet over a nearly vertical cliff largely composed of the hard, black volcanic glass, then drops rapidly along a streambed cluttered with large obsidian boulders. Native Americans visited nearby flows to obtain raw materials for tools.

Switchbacks now allow you to descend as fast as the stream on your right. You can see elaborate stone walls designed to prevent switchback cutting and erosion in this fragile soil. You quickly reach a junction (0.2 miles; 6,370 feet; 5.5 miles) with Trail 3528, which turns right to White Branch Creek while the PCT continues left (south). Turn right here onto Trail 3528, and within 400 feet you cross a tributary of White Branch Creek. The trail follows a small drainage, with the creek to the left, and descends to a small flat, after which you again cross the south fork of White Branch Creek (0.4 miles; 6,205 feet; 5.9 miles).

Now your route leads around a knob of finely layered shale. This short trail segment has been recently realigned, and now you rejoin the old alignment as you move northward. You move through rolling hummocks, pass a resistant, glaciated ridge, and cross another spring stream. Ascending onto a small ridge, you drop off the north side and descend via looping turns across a grassy meadow. Your meadow and finger ridge crossings end now, as you traverse down through a shady forest of old-growth trees.

Following the pathway down a small ridge, you level momentarily and come to the Minnie Scott Springs Trail junction (1.5 miles; 5,785 feet; 7.4 miles), which you passed at the beginning of the loop portion of this hike. At this junction you turn left and retrace your steps, crossing White Branch Creek then the Jerry Lava Flow, and continue down the trail to the Obsidian trailhead (3.5 miles; 4,760 feet; 10.9 miles).

19 ♦ THREE FINGERED JACK—MOUNT JEFFERSON WILDERNESS

Distance:	25.6 Miles
Low elevation:	4,550 Feet
High elevation:	6,400 Feet
Class:	Moderate
Hiking time:	18 Hours

The Mount Jefferson Wilderness is located in the Cascade Mountains northeast of Eugene, Oregon, on Interstate 5 and west of Redmond, Oregon, on U.S. Route 97. This wilderness protects not only the west side of its namesake mountain, but Three Fingered Jack as well. Both peaks are in the linear string of Cascade volcanos that in Oregon begins with Mount McLoughlin near the California border and extends north to Mount Hood near the Columbia River.

The Mount Jefferson Primitive Area was established in 1930 and in 1933 was enlarged to 85,000 acres. It was given wilderness status in 1968 and enlarged to 96,000 acres in 1984.

Along the Cascade crest from the Mount Jefferson Wilderness south are seven wilderness systems, several of which are contiguous, increasing their collective size and the protection they afford. Crater Lake National Park guarantees protection to an additional large area.

It is the beauty and accessibility of the "Jeff" that is responsible for its popularity. Pacific Crest Trail hikers, hungry for scenery after trudging for scores of miles through comparatively viewless forest, here break out into the open parks, with their striking vistas of the lofty peak and its glaciers, and pass through true subalpine areas notable for their openness. In the Jeff, as well as the Mount Hood and Three Sisters areas of the Oregon Cascades, you can walk for hours while enjoying long-distance views.

Three Fingered Jack rests upon a broad volcanic shield that forms the foundation for much of the Cascades. The highly eroded cone reveals inner volcano structure. Resistant enough that they are still in place, the fragmented rocks of the summit peaks are separated into red, gray, buff, orange, and brown layers. Little remains of Three Fingered Jack except these 7,841-foot-high pinnacles.

Isolated snowfields on the north slope of Three Fingered Jack lack only size and permanence in mimicking the glaciers that eroded this massive volcano to its present jagged outline.

Much material has been moved by glaciers down U-shaped valleys to the east and west. Small icefields are even today continuing to gouge into the rock. Look carefully at the northeast slopes and you can spot a tarn at the head of Canyon Creek, as well as at least two small moraines that have been deposited within the last few hundred years.

Though it seems that the low average elevation of this hike would dictate somewhat mild winters, that is not the case. Comparatively low elevations in the coast ranges where storms cross inland allow much moist air to be carried to the Cascade range. As a consequence, snowfall can be quite heavy. This region, located near the forty-fifth parallel, is far enough north that the colder effect of this latitude begins to be noticeable.

Most of the route lies in the lodgepole–red fir zone. This coniferous forest, with its largely huckleberry understory, provides rich habitat for forest creatures and birds. While on a late-fall hike, we noticed the Douglas squirrel, golden-mantled ground squirrel, chipmunk, blue grouse, robin, junco, and winter wren. Late-season wildflowers include Indian pond lily, lupine, asters, scarlet gilia, partridgefoot, fireweed, monk's hood, vanilla leaf, pipsissewa, buttercups, meadow goldenrod, and pearly everlasting. Many other species had bloomed recently.

The portion of the PCT covered in this hike, perhaps more than any other, is representative of what hiking the entire Oregon Cascades section of the PCT is like.

DESCRIPTION

This is a loop hike; the route returns you to the same trailhead with only 1.5 miles of backtracking along the PCT. Almost entirely within the Mount Jefferson Wilderness and with moderate elevation changes, this hike is classified as moderate, mostly because of the distance involved.

While a well-conditioned hiker could easily do this route in one day, it is recommended as an overnight trip. Camping at or near Wasco Lake or at the Bowerman Lake group is best, as they are reliable sources of water in this porous volcanic landscape.

There are at least five routes to the summit of Three Fingered Jack. Several are highly technical rock climbs. The least technical is a route up the mountain's south ridge usually reached from the Square Lake Trail. A scramble route across scree is visible from the PCT and would appear to deliver you to the ridge just south of the southernmost pinnacle, but if you're not an experienced climber, forget it! Regardless, if you aspire to tread on those loose-rock slopes, check first with the Forest Service.

Much of the terrain over which the trail passes is debris left from the long-term erosion of Three Fingered Jack. As a result, there is little surface water, with the exceptions of a few pond areas near the lake groups and a few spring streams. Be sure to carry adequate drinking water on this hike, and do plan to camp near known lakes so cooking water will be available.

Of special interest may be the off again–on again remnant of glacial activity from semipermanent snowfields on the northeast slope of Three Fingered Jack. Young gravel moraines are very noticeable around the tarn 800 yards due east of the summit, at the southern fork of the head of Canyon Creek. Often the snowfield below the north headwall of the summit pinnacles remains all year. Although of no great depth or bulk, this field is likely capable of moving materials beneath it slowly downhill.

Views from the PCT as it negotiates the west and north slopes of Three Fingered Jack are the most expansive of the entire hike. Other volcanos of the Cascade chain stand out on clear days. Westward views are limited only by conditions; it is not unusual to spot the ridges of the coast range on the west side of the Willamette Valley.

The hiking season for this route begins with the melting of snowbanks; the shady route postpones this event until around the last of June. The higher elevations traversed by the trail usually remain snowfree until early October.

Mosquitoes are present in large numbers, beginning with snowmelt and lasting for several weeks after the snow has gone. They are most numerous around the lake groups and other areas where there is standing water in the early season.

Black bears are common in the Mount Jefferson Wilderness. Though they are not accomplished pilferers here, be sure to bear-bag your food at night, don't take food into your tent, and maintain a clean campsite as you would at any location.

Administrative agency: USFS

Willamette National Forest
McKenzie Bridge Ranger Station
McKenzie Bridge, OR 97413
(503) 822-3381

Deschutes National Forest
Sisters Ranger District
P.O. Box 249
Sisters, OR 97759
(503) 549-2111

USGS map: 7.5′ series, Three Fingered Jack, Marion Lake, Santiam Junction, Oregon

Declination: 19 degrees

DIRECTIONS TO TRAILHEAD

From Bend, Oregon, on U.S. Route 97, turn west on Route 20 near the north edge of the city and proceed 21 miles northwest to Sisters. Continue on Route 20 for 20.5 miles to the Pacific Crest Trail parking lot on the north side of Route 20 at the top of Santiam Pass.

From Eugene, Oregon, on Interstate 5, take Route 126 east to the junction with Route 20. From Salem, Oregon, on Interstate 5, take Route 22 east to the junction with Route 20. Once on Route 20, continue east to Santiam Pass and the north Pacific Crest Trail parking lot, located 0.5 miles east of the Hoodoo Ski Area.

The large, paved parking lot has two pit toilets and a horse-loading ramp. The trailhead is at the east side of the parking area.

TRAIL ROUTE DESCRIPTION

From the bulletin board and trail register at the trailhead, elevation 4,820 feet, proceed 200 feet to a junction with the Pacific Crest Trail. Being northbound, you turn left and begin to ascend very gently through a mixed-conifer

MAP 19A

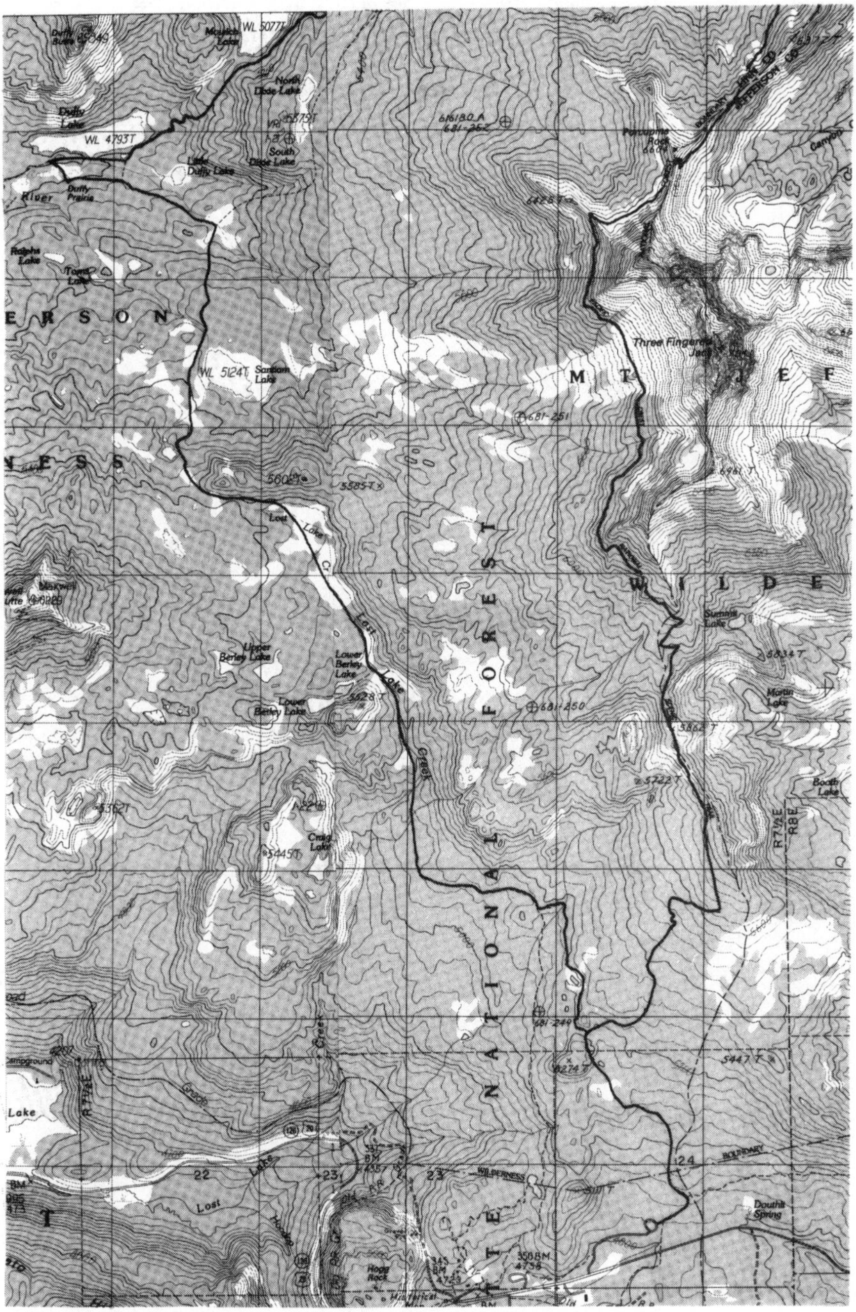

Duffy Lake
WL 4793T
Little Duffy Lake
North Dixie Lake
South Dixie Lake
Duffy Prairie
River
Ralphs Lake
Torrey Lake
E R S O N
WL 5124T
Santiam Lake
N E S S
Lost Lake
Upper Berley Lake
Lower Berley Lake
Craig Lake
5445T
5362T
Lost Lake Creek
Three Fingered Jack
M T J E F
W I L D E
F O R E S T
N A T I O N A L
Porcupine Rock
681-251
681-250
681-249
5834 T
Martin Lake
Booth Lake
5447 T
R7½E
R8E
Campground
Lake
22
23
24
Lost
Hogg Rock
Douthit Spring
BOUNDARY
WILDERNESS

forest. Shortly you reach a junction (0.2 miles from last point; 4,840 feet above sea level; 0.2 total miles) where Trail 4014 turns right (east) to Square Lake. Your easy ascent continues for more than a mile, taking you past a series of stagnant ponds on your right.

Reaching a trail junction (1.0 mile; 5,160 feet; 1.2 miles) at the shoulder of a ridge capped with an outcropping and large andesite boulders, you continue to the right on the PCT. The left fork is Santiam Lake Trail 3491, and it is to this junction that you will return near the end of this hike.

Traversing the same ridge, you pass through open forest with many grassy meadows. The well-graded trail lifts you easily, and in 2 miles you reach an open area where you are rewarded with a fine view to the east. In the right middle distance is Black Butte, a large cinder cone, while a sizable portion of central Oregon is visible beyond and to the northeast.

Wending along your sandy tread onto a ridge, you can see the jagged spires of Three Fingered Jack due north. Continuing your ascent, you pass a sandy use trail that branches left just before your route begins a traverse along the east slope of a ridge, where blasting was necessary to construct the tread. More views of the Deschutes River country around Bend open to you, and if you glance south, Broken Top, North and Middle Sisters, and Mount Washington (left to right) are plainly visible.

Crossing now to the west side of the ridge, you can see the high ridge of Diamond Peak Wilderness far to the south. Your trail then traverses around a rocky ridge point and levels momentarily, giving you occasional glimpses of the south slopes of Three Fingered Jack. Shortly you round another sharp bend and break out of the forest; from here most of the south and west slopes of Three Fingered Jack are visible.

Now your route leads along a curving traverse that parallels the base of the talus slides that form the west slope of the mountain. This airy, nearly level section gives you welcome views after all the forest you've come through. Two lakes lie about a mile distant to the west. The southernmost is Santiam Lake, and the elongated water body farther north is Duffy Lake. Your open traverse ends as the trail again enters scattered forest and heads northward along the side of a ridge paralleling on your right.

A few minutes later you are treated to a view of Mount Jefferson to the north and, closer, the sizable water body of Marion Lake. Closer still is the Eight Lakes Basin, which you will visit a number of miles ahead.

Your trail now crosses from the west to the east slope of the narrow ridge (5.6 miles; 6,400 feet; 6.8 miles), continuing north from Three Fingered Jack. Below to the east is the head of Jack Creek. Nestled in a gravelly cirque below the west ridge of the mountain is a small tarn, and you can see that glaciers are not completely finished with their modern-day remodeling of the mountain. The red and ocher strata running across

MAP 19B

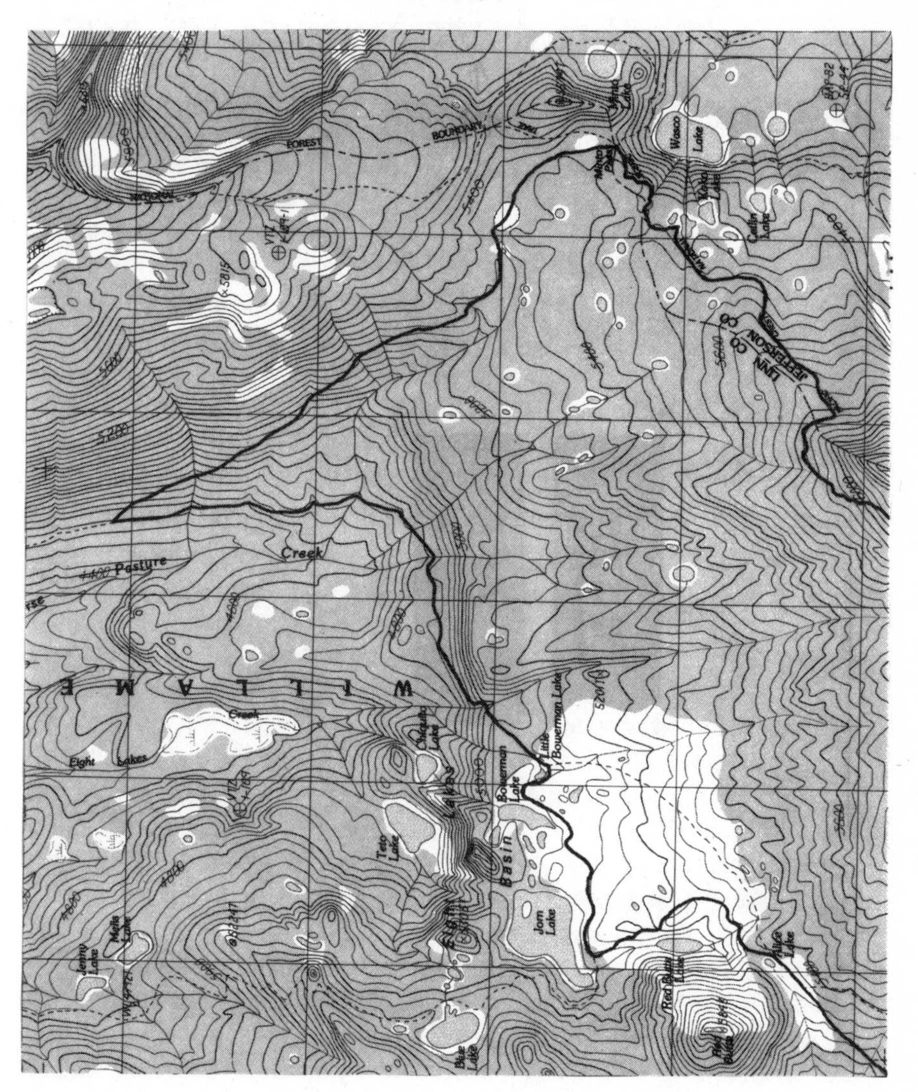

the face of the pinnacles of Three Fingered Jack are ancient ash deposits that have solidified into rock. Note the vertical intrusions of andesite along fault lines.

Then, 0.4 miles farther north, a use trail branches right and leads steeply down into the head of Jack Creek. If you're thirsty and out of water, you can get it here at the cost of a 400-foot vertical climb.

Now your trail heads northward on an undulating descent alongside a ridge and then through shady forest on top of the ridge. Hemlock and white fir make up the forest in this area. Several stagnant ponds lie partially concealed in the forest just beyond a steep switchback. Soon you reach a sister of Koko Lake (2.6 miles; 5,340 feet; 9.4 miles), a smallish lake to the right of the trail that is the first of the Wasco Lake group. You pass a second lake on the right and then another on the left of the trail.

Treading now on striated rock polished by glaciers, you soon arrive on a clifftop (0.1 miles; 5,345 feet; 9.5 miles) overlooking beautiful, 40-acre Wasco Lake. The rugged pinnacles of Three Fingered Jack dominate the view to the south. Your route leaves the promontory and ascends to the northwest, where you soon reach a junction (0.6 miles; 5,240 feet; 10.1 miles) in Minto Pass. The Wasco Lake Trail branches right, reaching that lake in 0.2 miles, while the PCT continues straight ahead to the north. Turn left (west) on Marion Lake Trail 3437.

You follow along a very gentle, almost imperceptible ascent to the northwest and soon crest the saddle of Minto Pass. Following this west-side drainage, you cross a small meadow and then reach a shallow pond on the left of the trail. Farther on, you cross two small early-season streams and then wind through the forest and around volcanic boulders. Before long you are descending and enter a stand of tall, old-growth hemlock and Douglas fir. The presence of several species of ferns and wildflowers in the understory now indicates that more moisture reaches this forest than along the crest proper.

At a junction (2.7 miles; 4,550 feet; 12.8 miles), Marion Trail 3437 turns right, while you turn left (south) on Bowerman Trail 3492. More descent follows, then your trail begins an ascent. Soon you cross several wooden structures bridging seasonal creeklets that are tributaries of Horse Pasture Creek. The trail continues south and then curves southwest, climbing gently as it does so. Shortly after passing an andesite talus jumble on your left, you cross yet another seasonal creek, and your ascent eases as you enter a perfectly flat area dotted with hemlock and red fir.

Beyond, your tread leads in a short, switchback climb. Note sections of the old trail, used before realignment. Now your climb becomes steeper, with short switchbacks that lead to another wooden bridge. After this bridge, your ascent eases, and you parallel a seasonal stream on your right.

Vertical Profile of Hike 19

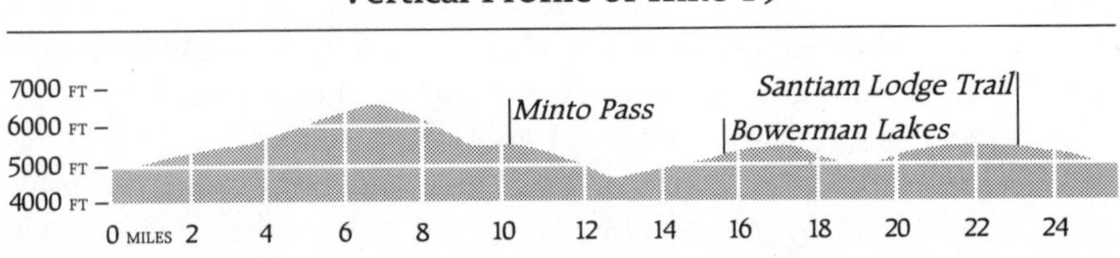

You soon cross this stream on a bridge and follow a raised earthen causeway into a small meadow. To your right is Little Bowerman Lake (2.8 miles; 5,080 feet; 15.6 miles), a small body around which your trail curves to the west. Near a wooden bridge just before this lake, a faint trail branches left on the east side of a seasonal stream. This faint, seldom-used trail loops south and then west to rejoin your trail about 1.9 miles ahead, near Alice Lake.

Elegant cats ears

Winter wren

Now meandering west across a gentle plateau, you reach a point due east of hidden Bowerman Lake just as your trail makes an abrupt turn south. Use trails run west to Bowerman at several points here. Curving now southwest, the tread continues an undulating course with little elevation change and enters a meadow on your right that is several acres in extent. Use trails lead west to Jorn Lake, just a few hundred yards distant over the brow of the hill.

At a junction (0.6 miles; 5,120 feet; 16.2 miles) near the south end of Jorn Lake, Blue Lakes Trail 3422 turns right. Continue left on the Bowerman Trail, here signed "Santiam Pass." An almost imperceptible ascent leads you to a junction (0.6 miles; 5,220 feet; 16.8 miles) where a spur trail turns right to Red Butte Lake, only a short distance to the west. Just 0.3 miles farther is symmetrical Alice Lake, nestled against the southeast slope of Red Butte. The red cinders lying on the top of Red Butte are clearly visible from this point.

MAP 19A

Continuing on an easy grade, you reach a junction (0.6 miles; 5,350 feet; 17.4 miles) at which Dixie Lake Trail 3494 turns left. Turn right onto Duffy Lake Trail 3427, which soon crosses a seasonal stream, dry except in early season. Within 0.5 miles spur trails branch right to larger Mowich Lake, and soon you can see that lake through the trees to your right. Within a few hundred yards you reach the main spur trail that leads to Mowich Lake.

Now your trail leads in a looping descent among small trees interspersed with beargrass. After some time, you reach a grassy meadow in which a spur trail turns right and leads to the north end of Duffy Lake.

Soon you reach a rehabilitation area on your left near a large boulder, where camping overuse in the past caused much damage. Passing another rehab area on the right, you move southwest with the lake on your right. Ignore a cutoff trail that turns left just past camping areas on Duffy Lake. Shortly you reach a junction (1.7 miles; 4,800 feet; 19.1 miles) at which Duffy Lake Trail turns right. Turn left onto Santiam Lake Trail 3491.

Within 0.2 miles, you pass another junction where a different trail branches right to Duffy trailhead. Continue along the left branch here. After ascending somewhat, you reach yet another junction (0.5 miles; 4,940 feet; 19.6 miles), where Dixie Lake Trail 3494 branches left. Continue on the right branch, the Santiam Lake Trail. Before long, you ascend steeply for a 200-foot elevation gain and follow the very sandy trail off the toe of the ridge.

Two use trails soon branch left to Santiam Lake, which shortly comes into view on your left. Passing by this lake on the loose footing of your tread, you then pass a small lakelet 100 feet from the trail on your right. Ascending still, you pass through a 2-acre sandy opening where little vegetation has been able to gain hold. From this spot you meander east, pass through a saddle, and begin a descent.

Now following a broad, sandy path across an equally sandy, open plain, you tramp for some distance before passing a large rock cairn at the south end. Then you duck through a thin line of trees and cross a second similar plain, also with a cairn at its far end. Continuing down a broad, sandy wash past a car-size boulder on your left, you reach a small flat where an unsigned trail branches right to Lower Berley Lake.

Trails in the Willamette National Forest are often difficult to identify, for the Forest Service has removed some identification signs to "enhance the wilderness experience." Present signing is frequently puzzling.

Your sometimes 20-foot-wide, sandy trail undulates through lodgepoles and hemlocks with grassy understory. Soon you pass a grassy, stagnant pond that holds water only in early season. Wending on, you reach a junction (3.9 miles; 5,175 feet; 23.5 miles) where Santiam Lodge Trail 3496 turns right (south) to Santiam Lodge on Route 20 about 2 miles distant. Continue left on Santiam Trail 3491.

From this junction you continue east, and within 0.8 miles you pass a small lakelet on your right. A short distance beyond this lake, you reach the junction (0.7 miles; 5,160 feet; 24.0 miles) with the PCT. Turn right here and retrace your steps to the trailhead (1.4 miles; 4,820 feet; 25.6 miles).

20 ♦ JEFFERSON PARK—WHITEWATER CREEK

Distance:	13.9 Miles
Low elevation:	3,060 Feet
High elevation:	5,890 Feet
Class:	Moderate
Hiking time:	10 Hours

Lewis and Clark first saw this central Oregon Cascade stratovolcano from the west side on March 30, 1806. They named the handsome peak Mount Jefferson in honor of Thomas Jefferson, then president and the man responsible for their expedition. There is little question today that Jefferson Park, a large subalpine plain on the west side of the mountain, is as striking as the mountain itself and one of the most popular places in the Cascades.

The geological history of this area is basically the same as described for Hikes 17, 18, and 19. Mount Jefferson is the largest volcano sitting upon a volcanic plateau that also supports the heavily eroded Three Fingered Jack to the south. Mount Jefferson is considered inactive and possibly extinct, but a lava flow along Jefferson Creek on the south flank is fairly recent in origin.

Mount Jefferson, at 10,497 feet, is a powerful backdrop. The cone itself is not quite perfect, for glaciers have done their work and continue to do it. The mountain now hosts no fewer than five active glaciers. Sizable Whitewater Glacier graces the east and north sides, while Waldo Glacier flows down the southern slopes. Milk Creek, Russell, and Jefferson Park glaciers grind away at the western side of the mountain.

Whitewater Glacier feeds Parker and Milk creeks, among others, as well as the Whitewater River—all east-flowing watercourses. On the west, another Milk Creek is fed by the Milk Creek Glaciers, while Jeff, Russell, and Whitewater creeks are fed by Russell and Jefferson Park glaciers. There is no shortage of water running from the mountain.

As with most all large mountains, Mount Jefferson is quite capable of creating its own weather. In the summer, temperatures are soothingly mild, but at 5,800 feet elevation, Jefferson Park is subject to showers with some frequency. The moist air from the Willamette Valley moves eastward, and the resultant condensation when this air encounters the Cascade ridges causes abundant precipitation. Winter storms, which approach from the southwest, meet the same fate, resulting in heavy snowpacks. The overall effect is that Jefferson's glaciers are active, area streams are healthy, and the lake clusters in Jeff Park are abundantly filled.

The region's plentiful moisture and comparatively low elevation favor rapid conifer growth. The forested areas near the trailhead here have been cut in the past; what you see now are second-growth trees in this area. Along the Craig Trail near the South Fork Breitenbush River grow many large Douglas firs, some more than 6 feet in diameter. Obviously, these stately survivors are old growth.

The temperate rain forest environment also favors rhododendrons, many of which grow near the trailhead. During an early-spring hike, as the snow was melting, we spotted many other wildflowers: bunchberry, vanilla leaf, Solomon's seal, star Solomon's seal, bleeding heart, Oregon grape, azure penstemon, lupine, paintbrush, shooting star, pink heather, buttercups, trillium, and Canada violet. You may also find blackberries at the elevation of the trailhead but rarely higher. By early summer, more species are in bloom, making the slopes and high meadows of the Cascades almost kaleidoscopic.

Wildlife is also plentiful. Species we saw included the coyote, yellow-bellied marmot, Townsend's chipmunk, blue grouse, Clark's nutcracker, Stellar's jay, gray jay, white-headed woodpecker, robin, junco, white-breasted nuthatch, and black-capped chickadee.

A feeling of closeness to the mountain pervades this hike. Jefferson is big, and it is close. It is also awesomely beautiful, with its sparkling glaciers, green fingers of forest, and vari-hued rock. Flirting with the mountain from the inspiring environment of Jefferson Park is popular. The park's close proximity to the populated areas of Oregon sees to that. But if Jeff were more remote, pilgrims would still make the journey. It's worth it.

DESCRIPTION

This is a loop hike in which there is no retracing of route because there are two trailheads located just yards from each other. The hike begins at 3,100 feet in elevation. You will see an exciting variety of plant species on this hike, encountering many species at this low altitude that are not present much higher.

The South Breitenbush Trail begins climbing through second-growth forest. Within 0.5 miles, the route enters Mount Jefferson Wilderness and continues ascending. This hike is classified as moderate, based on the assumption that most hikers will do it as an overnight. The very fit hiker can easily complete the loop in one day and still leave a little time to fully appreciate all the area has to offer.

MAP 20A

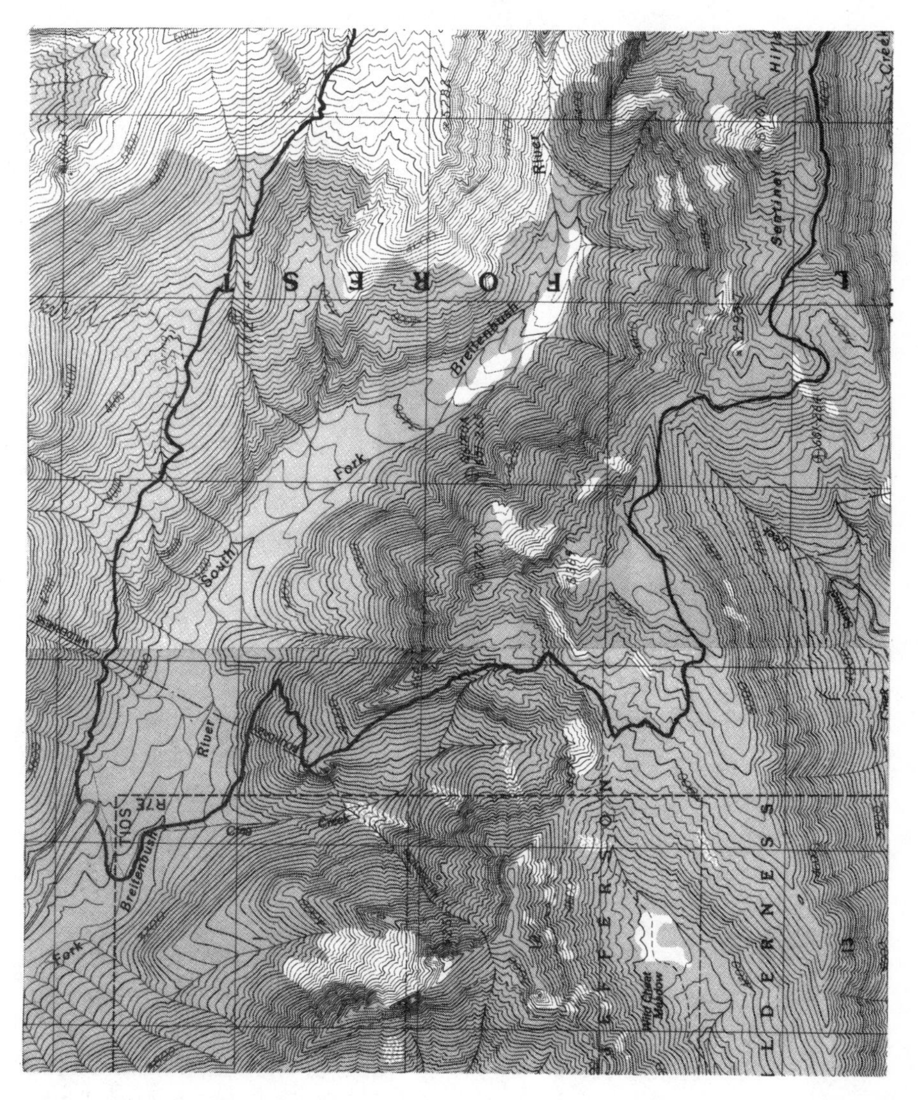

Early in this century, fires devastated a portion of the route on the way to Jeff Park. As a part of the reforestation effort, a "seedling shed" was constructed of poles and split boards at a cool location about 1.5 miles up the trail. The structure provided for safe, cool storage of seedlings stockpiled there in preparation for planting. The shed location showcases bear grass, mountain ash, chinquapin, salal, wild strawberry, salmonberry, and willow in addition to the expected mixed conifers.

Continuing, the route leads through the area that was burned by fire. You can judge for yourself the success of the replanting effort.

Administrative agency: USFS

Willamette National Forest	Detroit Ranger District
P.O.B. 10607	State Highway 22
Eugene, OR 97440-2607	Detroit, OR 97360
(503) 465-6521	(503) 854-3366

USGS map: 7.5′ series, Mount Bruno, Mount Jefferson, Oregon

Declination: 19½ degrees

Next you are led near springs and elk wallows, where wildflowers share meadows with grasses, sedges, and heather. A wandering traverse among huckleberries, heather, subalpine meadows, and mountain hemlock stands leads you closer to Jefferson Park as the route crosses the South Fork Breitenbush River near its headwaters. Glaciers caused the knobby terrain here, just before the trail leads onto the friendly flat known as Jefferson Park and a junction with the Pacific Crest Trail.

Turning south, you come upon hemlock-fingered subalpine meadows and experience the imposing majesty of Mount Jefferson. Possible campsites are everywhere, but good stewardship dictates that you linger here to enjoy only; your camping impact will be better absorbed a mile to the south, where the PCT undulates through forest.

Whitewater Creek Trail gives you the opportunity for fewer over-the-shoulder glances at Mount Jefferson than you might like as you move easily out a long, west-trending ridge. South slopes and microclimates produce unexpected wildflowers, and birds are more plentiful than in the subalpine areas behind you. As you cross this same ridge on Craig Trail, the botanical variety increases, and you soon enter a world of rhododendrons as you lose more than 2,000 feet elevation to the South Fork Breitenbush River.

You cross this river via a solid Douglas fir log, a giant more than 130 feet long that spans the flow with yards to spare. A short romp through numerous wildflowers to the trailhead barely gives your wobbly knees time to recover from the long descent.

The hiking season here begins for most around July 1; the hardiest hikers bob over patches of snow to reach Jeff Park much earlier. In the fall, powder snow often whitens the park by mid-October.

Snowmelt time in the Cascades means mosquitoes, and abundant surface water lengthens their tenancy until midsummer, so be prepared with plenty of repellent.

MAP 20B

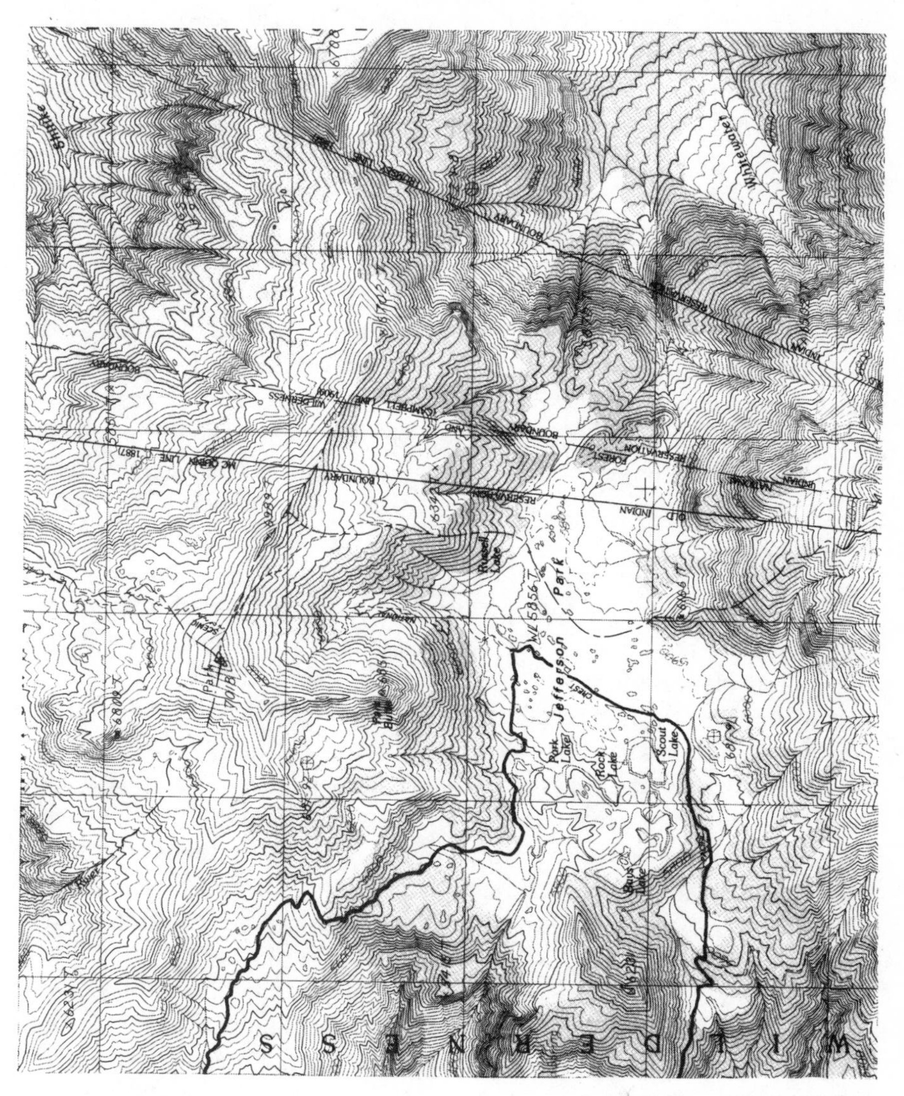

Black bears are present here, and though local bears are not particularly cunning or persistent, good hiking ethics would dictate that you not give these fine animals an education in viewing hikers as a food source. Bear-bag all food.

DIRECTIONS TO TRAILHEAD

From Detroit, Oregon, located on State Route 22, 52 miles east of Salem and 56 miles west of Sisters, turn north on Forest Service road 46 just east of the bridge crossing the inlet arm of Detroit Lake. Continue on road 46 past the old Breitenbush town site, a total of 11.3 miles to clearly signed Forest Service road 4865. Turn right on road 4865, which soon becomes gravel surfaced, and go a total of 4.7 miles to where the road makes a sweeping turn left. At that turn, you will find on the right the trailheads for Craig Trail 3364 and, a few dozen yards beyond, South Breitenbush Trail 3375. One hundred yards before the trailheads, a gravel road turns right into a large, gravel parking area that once was a gravel storage site.

TRAIL ROUTE DESCRIPTION

MAP 20A

From either the gravel parking area or roadside parking, head up South Breitenbush Trail 3375, which begins at an elevation of 3,100 feet. Notice the rhododendrons blossoming beside the road at the trailhead, and be on the lookout for many other species of wildflowers as you progress upward. There is a jumble of large, moss-covered logs that are left over from a logging operation many years ago. Soon you pass several volcanic boulders to the left of the trail, then cross a small spring stream, after which you cross the boundary (0.5 miles from last point; 3,500 feet above sea level; 0.5 total miles) into Mount Jefferson Wilderness.

You are now traversing upward through a thick forest of white and Douglas fir. You round a shoulder and hear a rushing stream below you as the trail levels for a few yards. Soon, at the 1-mile point, you cross the stream, which is the first reliable, year-round water. Then, 0.2 miles farther, you cross another year-round flow.

You reach the seedling shed (0.9 miles; 3,965 feet; 1.4 miles) beside the trail near a bubbling stream. Here you may see rhododendrons blossoming in early season, as well as a number of other flowers present around this 4,000-foot-elevation zone. Striding onward, you soon approach a junction (0.5 miles; 4,300 feet; 1.9 miles) where Trail 3342 branches left to 6,043-foot-elevation Bear Point.

Continue straight ahead, reaching an open saddle that affords a good view of Mount Jefferson to the southeast. Note resistant peaks along Sentinel Hills, a ridge to the south of you that glaciers did not manage to obliterate but merely steepened.

You cross a wooden causeway over a small stream, and just beyond you enter an area where only a scattering of western white pine is visible on slopes covered with chinquapin. These slopes are the location of an old, and very hot, fire. A few lodgepole pines are here also. Beyond, you can hear a bubbling stream on your right, which you cross. You are walking up an old lateral moraine, left by the glacier that extended down the South Breitenbush River.

You pass a large, glacier-smoothed boulder just to the left of the trail, then approach a runoff chute (0.9 miles; 4,920 feet; 2.8 miles) and, a short

Providing excellent camping on its upper slopes, Mount Jefferson hosts active glaciers that, with their glistening snowfields, place the mountain among the most beautiful volcanos in the Cascades.

distance beyond, cross another rushing stream. After a quick switchback, you again move upslope, with the stream tumbling down on your left. Note the old trail alignment to your right, abandoned because it had become quite deeply eroded. Unfortunately, no steps were taken to mitigate the erosion, and the old track continues to deepen.

You closely approach the creek on your left, finally coming to a small meadow (0.8 miles; 5,450 feet; 3.6 miles) above two open, rocky knobs on the opposite side of the creek. Many wildflowers favor this spot in early and late season; added to the fantastic view downcanyon, they make this a special place indeed. The small ponds in the meadow are used by elk as wallows in the fall.

The large springs on the hillside across the creek provide moisture for many kinds of water-loving plants, which in turn reward you visually with brilliant, green stripes down the rocky slope. If you inspect these areas closely, many small botanical treasures await.

Mountain hemlock seedlings dot the open, subalpine area you now enter, with seasonal snowmelt ponds to your right reflecting Mount Jefferson on their smooth surfaces.

You continue through the heather park, eventually climbing the slope above before heading south along the shoulder of a ridge and dropping into forest. Descending farther, you cross a washed-out section among

Townsends chipmunk

andesite talus, after which you continue down through a stand of nearly pure mountain hemlock.

You cross a gentle saddle and head eastward toward the mountain. The trail traverses several subalpine meadows. Note the piled trailside cairns, too large to be called ducks. You then reach a creek (0.9 miles; 5,800 feet; 4.5 miles) and continue your ascent along its left side. Meltwater running down the trail, plus horse traffic, has caused erosion in some places.

You cross the creek (0.3 miles; 5,750 feet; 4.8 miles), which is the outlet of Russell Lake and one of several headwater tributaries of the South Fork Breitenbush River. Then you switch upslope through alternating patches of trees and openings, to arrive in Jefferson Park. Strolling through the heather, you pass small clumps of trees. Mount Jefferson looms just beyond your right shoulder.

Reaching a junction (0.4 miles; 5,860 feet; 5.2 miles) with the Pacific Crest Trail, you turn right (south). Note Russell Lake lying in a shallow depression just east of the junction. The pattern of open parks and clumps of hemlock continues as you head along the PCT toward the mountain.

Jefferson Park has been severely overused in certain spots. The beauty and aura of this place make it desirable to camp and spend time here, so the heavy use is understandable. Because of the pressure caused by comparatively easy access, the Forest Service has restricted camping in certain areas, notably on the peninsula jutting into Bays Lake and the area between Bays and Scout lakes.

If you intend to camp near Jefferson Park, it is recommended that you use either the area near the Russell Lake outlet creek intersection with the South Breitenbush Trail, 0.4 miles west of the PCT junction, or the vicinity of the Whitewater Trail, farther south along the PCT. By doing so, you will avoid further deterioration of Jefferson Park and will still be within easy strolling distance of the park for sunset and sunrise.

Continuing south on the PCT, you pass Scout Lake (0.6 miles; 5,890 feet; 5.8 miles) a short distance to your right. Soon, descending, you join the headwaters of Whitewater Creek. Note an andesite cliff on your right. Then you switchback down through shady forest with the creek on your left. The camps in this area are too close to the creek to conform to guidelines.

Your route crosses Whitewater Creek (0.7 miles; 5,650 feet; 6.5 miles) on a wooden bridge, after which you amble along under shady hemlocks. The bulk of the mountain is never out of mind as you move along, catching glimpses of Jefferson Park Glacier on the near slopes. Straightening, the trail leads through a cathedral-like grove of tall hemlocks upon whose trunks moss grows above the 12-foot line, marking the winter snow depth.

You leave the PCT at a junction (0.4 miles; 5,600 feet; 6.9 miles) where that trail branches sharply left and your Whitewater Trail turns right (west). Immediately after the junction you round the toe of a ridge and head north through more beautiful hemlocks, a very striking spot. Then your wide, well-graded track begins to descend, and you can hear a rushing creek on your right. You cross a small creeklet and soon cross Whitewater Creek (0.3 miles; 5,500 feet; 7.2 miles) on a wooden bridge. Just beyond, you cross another creeklet as it flows through a culvert.

MAP 20A

Mount Jefferson provides the backdrop as you look out over a small wildflower meadow. Notice the tall huckleberries growing along the trail. Now you ascend for a while to level out on a beautiful mountainside traverse among firs and hemlocks. More alluring views of the mountain and the terrain to the south tempt you along this undulating trail. Soon you can spot small Whitewater Lake 1.5 miles away to the south, an alluring green because of finely ground rock called glacial flour in the water.

Passing up a ridge to a saddle that offers good dry camping possibilities, you ascend farther; a ridge lies to your right. Soon you can see the ridge on the north slope of the South Breitenbush drainage up which you climbed on your way to Jefferson Park.

Next you begin to descend along a straight segment that ends in an abrupt switchback left. Out of the larger trees now, you descend a southwest slope covered with young-growth conifers that provide adequate shade.

Vertical Profile of Hike 20

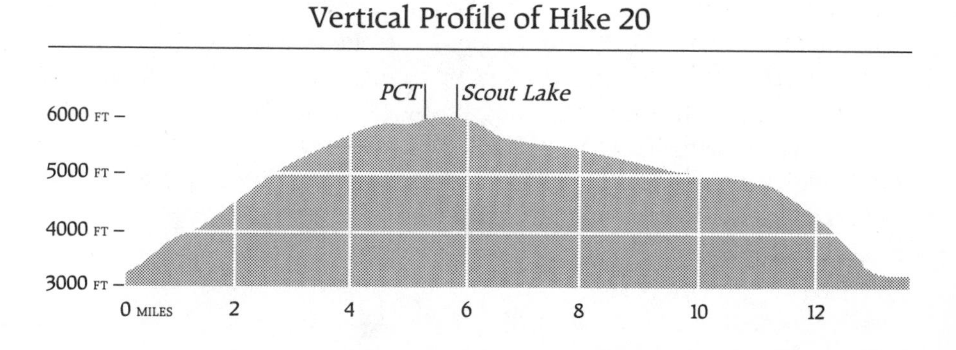

Arriving at the junction (2.3 miles; 5,000 feet; 9.5 miles) where the Whitewater Creek Trail branches left and leads to the Whitewater roadhead in about 2 miles, you go straight ahead on Triangulation Peak Trail 3373, through a veritable jungle of bear grass. The Triangulation Peak Trail does not receive the heavy usage the Whitewater Creek Trail does. Moving along a saddle, you come upon Douglas fir and chinquapin.

Descending along a south slope, with the ridge on your right, you can see Three-Fingered Jack, which although heavily eroded, is the next major volcano to the south in the Cascade range. In 0.5 miles, an old trail alignment turns right. Continue ahead, along the south slope of the ridge. Then the trail levels along the broad top of the ridge, passing through heather and huckleberries.

As you reach the high point of the ridge, you are treated to a long-distance view of Three Sisters, those sibling volcanos that stand guard in another wilderness far to the south.

Reaching the junction (1.7 miles; 4,800 feet; 11.2 miles) with Craig Trail 3364, turn right (north) on this tread, while the Triangulation Trail continues ahead along a saddle. Your trail crosses the same saddle, ascending slightly through a glade on your right. As you enter the forest, note the western red cedars here. A sharp upward slope takes you to a viewpoint west, overlooking the South Breitenbush canyon. There are large rhododendrons growing here. The trail descends past the headwaters of Craig Creek, which soon grows into a musical flow to your left. Then, ending a long descent with a ridge on your right, you cross that ridge and descend farther among rhododendrons and hemlocks, with the same ridge now on your left.

Soon you are switchbacking down a north slope where Douglas firs are more plentiful. On a tiny ridge now, with a small stream on each side, you pass by huge specimens of Douglas fir, rock hop across the small stream, and march along the river. After a few yards on the level, the route makes a sharp ascent up onto a bench. Your undulating trail is overshadowed by huge old-growth Douglas fir, cedar, and hemlock.

You parallel the river for a few hundred yards before dropping down to cross (2.5 miles; 3,060 feet; 13.7 miles) on huge trees that have conveniently fallen across the flow. Without a log to cross on, this would be a wet and certainly hazardous crossing, especially in early season. Steps have been chain-sawed into the log to facilitate climbing onto it while carrying a pack.

As you progress up the far bank, you are now in a riparian environment, with many flowers. Continue to wend your way along the trail, which ascends slightly, until you reach the trailhead (0.2 miles; 3,100 feet; 13.9 miles) on road 4685.

21 ♦ BLUE LAKE—INDIAN HEAVEN WILDERNESS

Distance:	13.5 Miles
Low elevation:	3,990 Feet
High elevation:	5,120 Feet
Class:	Moderate
Hiking time:	9 Hours

About 20 airline miles north of the Columbia River, in the state of Washington, the Pacific Crest Trail elevates gently to the 4,500-foot volcanic plateau that contains the Indian Heaven Wilderness. Mount St. Helens, whose explosion in 1980 gave new meaning for some to the words "dormant volcano," is about 25 miles northwest. Mount Adams, nearly 3,000 feet higher than Mount St. Helens, lifts its imposing bulk above the horizon some 20 miles northeast.

Established in 1984, the 20,600-acre Indian Heaven Wilderness straddles the Cascade Crest, protecting a plateau that includes 5,927-foot Lemei Rock and a number of other summits, as well as rolling and benchy terrain. A small wilderness, only about 10 miles by 4 miles, Indian Heaven is well accessed by trails leading from the Forest Service road system on the east and west sides.

No one knows when Native Americans began using the extensive huckleberry fields found on the plateau, but when Captain McClellan led a military expedition through the area in 1853, they encountered a large Native American encampment near the present Pacific Crest Trail just east of Red Mountain.

Not far from this spot is the Indian Race Track, a worn, roadlike feature about 10 feet wide and 2,000 feet long compacted into the surface of a mountain meadow. It has been fairly well established that Native American horsemen raced on this track and that the site was used for other social gatherings, as well. Of course, horse racing could have taken place only during fairly recent times, for Native Americans had no horses until they procured the animals from Spanish conquerors. The huckleberries, games, and most likely, gambling, attracted Klickitat and Yakima tribes to this area, as well as tribes from as far away as the Warm Springs and Umatillas.

The east end of Blue Lake has many good campsites; the west end has, in a talus slide, a colony of pikas that will whistle, chirp, and stare if you intrude.

If huckleberries were not the main attraction, they certainly made the gatherings possible by providing a relished food source, as well as an excuse to come to Indian Heaven, where the berries were unusually plentiful. This bounty apparently gave rise to the following legend, related on a sign near the trailhead, among the tribes of the area:

> What is the significance of the huckleberry, we ask? The creator named all the fruits that grew in the foothills, and then he was reminded that there were no berries in the mountains. The creator had decreed part of their respect for mother earth was that men were to procure fish and game, and women were to procure the roots. Somehow, he had neglected to include the berries. So then he created the huckleberry and placed it in the high mountains.
>
> The huckleberry is the last food eaten in the ceremonial communion. A long time ago this world was inhabited by animals. They were human, just like we are today. They could talk and understand each other just like we do. One day the creator called all the animals in council and announced that there were new people coming to inhabit this earth. You must make room for these people and select new identities. You have a choice of what you want to be in this new world, and I will help you.
>
> The animals all lined up and declared what they would like to be in the new world. The creator asked each one to perform certain feats to qualify for his selection. If the animal failed, he had to make another selection for which he was more qualified. For example, coyote was monopolizing all the best selections, and each time he failed to qualify. At first he wanted to be an eagle, but he could not fly high in the sky and did not have the keen eyesight the eagle must have. He failed. Then he wanted to be a salmon,

> but he could not swim. Finally, the only thing he could qualify for was to be just a plain old coyote, which he is today.
>
> Each time an animal qualified for what he wanted to be, the creator took part of his own body and placed it in the new creature. This is why the Indian people respect everything that has life, plants, animals, humans; because they are all part of the creator.
>
> When the creator finished his work he discovered he had no berries in the mountains. The only part of his body left over were his eyes, so he took his eyes and put them down into the ground in the mountain. The veins in the eyes bled into the earth and became the roots. The roots became the plant, and the berries sprouted and became huckleberries. Because the huckleberry was the last to be created by God, it is the last food tasted in the religious food communion ceremony in the long house. The foods are all tasted according to their creation. First the waters, then the salmon, then came the elk, the deer, whatever is available. Then the bitter roots, and then the other berries, and huckleberry is last.
>
> It is never forgotten that the huckleberries are the creator's eyes, and they see everything. They watch the new people of the world.

Today the extensive berry patches have diminished because more trees are successfully colonizing the openings where the berries have thrived. There are plenty for the hiker, however, and plenty also for the wildlife, including black bears. Some patches, not far from the wilderness, have been reserved by regulation for continuation of traditional use by Native Americans.

Lemei Rock and East Crater are well-defined craters found in the wilderness, the latter a cinder cone. Other volcanic features include the flows of andesite lava that underlie much of the area and are exposed in various places, especially along the east rim of the plateau. One of these layers enhances the waterfall seen on Cultus Creek.

Indian Heaven receives more snow than you would expect for so modest an elevation. This is due in part to the relatively free sweep winter storms have when approaching from the southwest. The Cascade Crest efficiently wrings moisture from passing storms.

The area supports many different wildflower species. Early-season varieties we saw include yarrow, pearly everlasting, tiger lily, paintbrush, lupine, vanilla leaf, heather, and trillium. Later in the season, many more flowers are evident. Wildlife includes the deer, chipmunk, Douglas squirrel, varied thrush, junco, gray jay, and mallard duck.

DESCRIPTION

This loop hike returns to the starting trailhead on a separate trail; the only backtracking is the approximately 2-mile jaunt leading to Blue Lake at the southern end of the loop. With the exception of the ascent onto the plateau at the beginning of the hike, gradients are very gentle. Since the offending ascent is a short one, the hike has been classified as moderate.

The route can easily be accomplished in a single day by a determined hiker in good condition. An overnight, however, would be much more enjoyable and is recommended. Plan to camp at or near beautiful Blue Lake. This 12-acre lake is the deepest in the wilderness, some 47 feet, and the water color is an exceptional blue.

From the trailhead, you are faced with an abrupt elevation gain. After the ascent, best made at a slow speed, there are no other significant elevation changes on the hike until the descent, on a different trail, back to the trailhead. This is basically a leisurely stroll along good trail, through forest and across subalpine meadows filled with heather and huckleberries. If the weather is clear (the locals say the mountain is "out"), the view of Mount Adams from several spots along the route is spectacular.

Blue Lake, as well as most others of appreciable size and depth, supports trout originally planted by private individuals, most notably sheep herders. Little evidence of the sheep grazing that was widespread in the wilderness in the late 1800s remains today, except for some vegetation change that resulted.

From Blue Lake, located on the PCT, the routing retraces for about 2 miles to Junction Lake, then leads northward along the PCT. Mount St. Helens can be seen from several places along the west side of the wilderness. This trail segment provides opportunities to wander through several stands of large, old-growth forest. All age classes are present in some of these stands, as are obvious examples of the recycling of nutrients contained in rotted logs.

The romp back to Cultus Creek Campground from the lip of the plateau is boisterous as the trail loses elevation quickly. Views from this section, which crosses mountain meadows and basins just below the subalpine zone, are worth stopping for.

Snow remains on the plateau until after July 1. The hiking season extends into October in many years. Weather in the Washington Cascades is extremely unpredictable, with a reputation on the wet side. Carry good rain gear and tents that really keep out water.

Possibly because of the 175 lakes and ponds in Indian Heaven Wilderness, mosquitoes are very happy here. They frolic in large numbers around snowmelt time and continue to be troublesome until mid-August. For that reason, many who have visited this wilderness suggest the month of September as the most enjoyable.

Black bears are present, so always bear-bag your food to minimize the risk of conditioning bears to human's food. These magnificent animals are most healthy when left to forage without food contribution from humans, however unintentional.

MAP 21

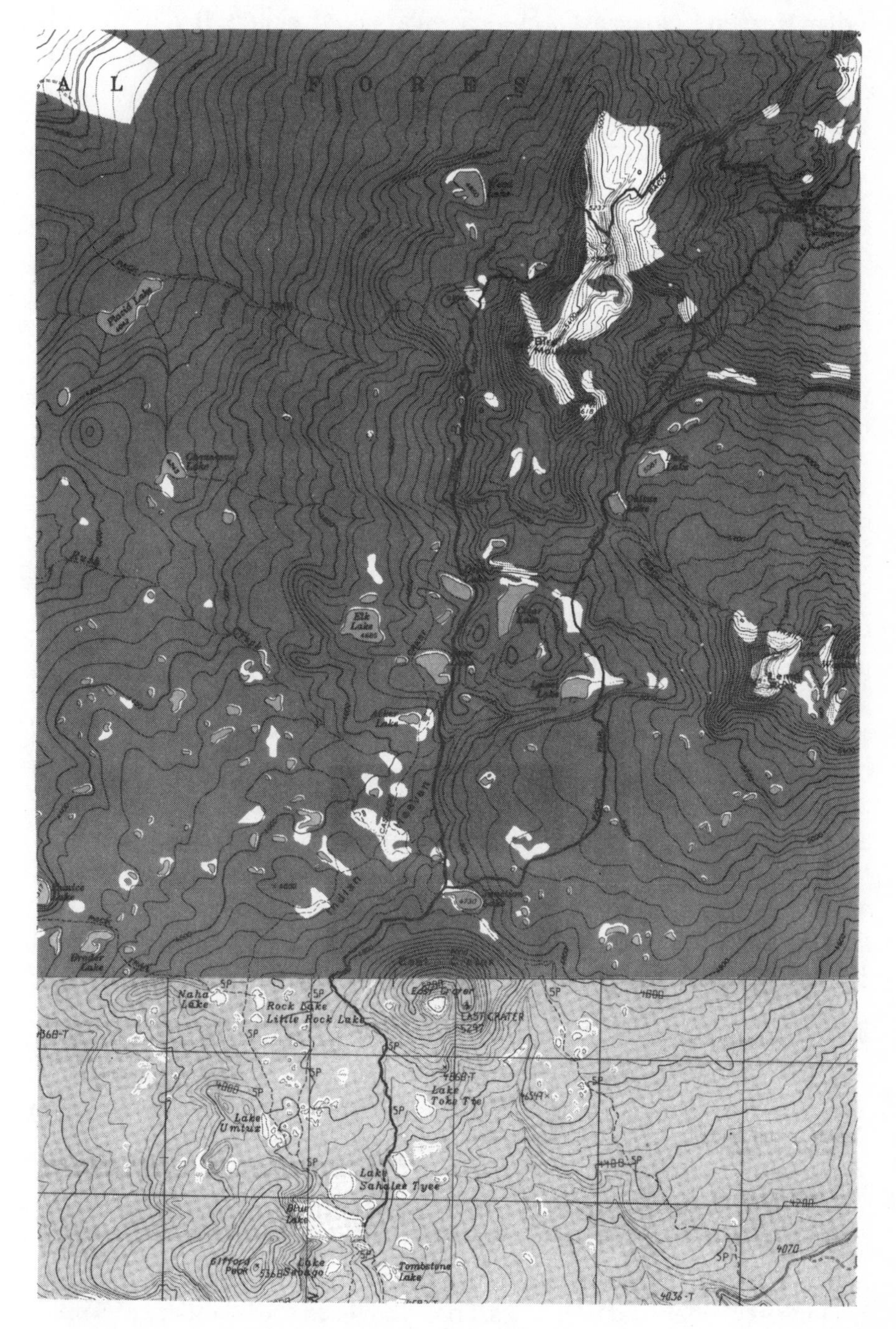
A L
F O R E S T
Naha Lake
Rock Lake
Little Rock Lake
East Crater
EAST CRATER
5297
4868-T
Lake Toke Tie
4654×
Lake Umtux
4800
Lake Sahalee Tyee
4400
4200
Blue Lake
Gifford Peak
5368
Lake Sebago
Tombstone Lake
4070
4036-T
4800

Partly because of its accessibility and partly because of the easy hiking, Indian Heaven Wilderness is quite popular with trekkers. If you enter the area on a weekday instead of a weekend, you will encounter fewer hikers and will help spread out the usage.

Administrative agency: USFS

Gifford Pinchot National Forest
6926 East 4th Plain Blvd.
Vancouver, WA 98668
(206) 750-5000

Mount Adams Ranger District
Trout Lake, WA 98650
(206) 395-2501

USGS map: 7.5′ series, Lone Butte, Gifford Peak, Washington

Declination: 20 degrees

DIRECTIONS TO TRAILHEAD

From Route 14 in Washington along the north bank of the Columbia River 2 miles west of the Hood River Bridge, turn north on State Route 141. Proceed north 7 miles to Hussum, and continue north 14 miles more to the town of Trout Lake. Continue west through Trout Lake, past the Mount Adams Ranger District offices on Route 141, which becomes Forest Service road 24. Stay on this road, whose surface in 7 miles becomes gravel. Nine miles beyond the end of the pavement, you will reach Cultus Camp, where many campsites offer tables. Pit toilets and water are provided. Parking at trailhead 33 may be limited, but you can also park at trailhead 107 a few hundred yards away.

TRAIL ROUTE DESCRIPTION

At Indian Heaven trailhead 33, at 3,990 feet, note the large Engelmann spruce around the parking area. Your trail enters the forested area and within a minute or two crosses an early-season creeklet. Stop to admire the wildflowers growing along the trail.

Within minutes you begin an abrupt ascent and at 0.2 miles reach a self-issue trail permit register. Your climb continues among mountain hemlock, Douglas fir, and spruce, while trailside plants include mountain ash, huckleberry, alder, and bear grass. Soon you reach the boundary (0.3 miles from last point; 4,155 feet above sea level; 0.3 total miles) of Indian Heaven Wilderness as you continue uphill. A short distance uptrail, you pass a jumble of andesite talus, the exposed edge of an old flow. Farther still, you come upon a small cascade to the left of the trail where the creek, kept from downcutting by a hard resistant layer, flows along on top of this layer to tumble over the edge.

The trail curves to the right, following the creek upstream, where the grade eases a bit and you can see an older trail alignment below. Soon a large boulder on the ridge straight ahead marks a switchback to the left. (0.7 miles; 4,750 feet; 1.0 mile). A magnificent view greets you, with Mount Adams to the east and Mount St. Helens to the northwest. Stop to take a breather and admire the view, and look for phlox blooming at this sunny spot.

The grade eases momentarily, and then the ascent continues past two small meadows before crossing a seasonal stream. Soon you are overlooking a meadow and park area below the trail. You pass Cultus Lake, elevation 5,040 feet; a spur trail branches left to the lake. You cross the inlet creek on a causeway, and beyond you reach a junction (1.4 miles; 5,090 feet; 2.4 miles) where Lemei Trail 34 branches left. Continue right in predominantly red fir cover. The trail crests a low saddle and descends gently through a beautiful forest. You soon reach another junction (0.3 miles; 4,980 feet; 2.7 miles), where Lemei Lake Trail 179 branches left and the right-hand fork leads to Clear Lake in 300 yards.

Take the left-hand fork, which descends through heather and scattered conifers. You reach an unmarked junction just before a long meadow. The somewhat obscure right fork leads to Clear Lake. Continue straight ahead onto a long, flat meadow. Note the heavily eroded old trail beside your newer tread. The route crosses meadows sprinkled with small conifers and fringed with wildflowers. You leave the meadow in 0.5 miles and enter the forest paralleling the creek on your right.

You cross the inlet (0.6 miles; 4,830 feet; 3.3 miles) of Lemei Lake and turn right. The trail continues for a short distance alongside this lake, which has no outlet, then turns left to ascend onto a raised bench to the south. Now you meander through open parks where heather blooms in the spring and Native Americans picked ripe berries in the fall. When the berries are ripe,

Vertical Profile of Hike 21

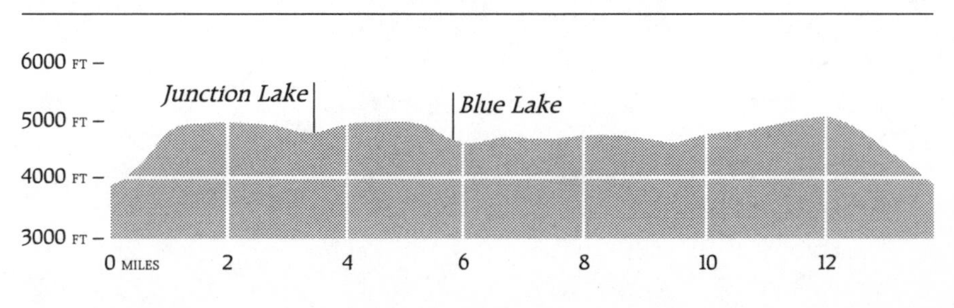

Pika

black bears like this area too. It is these open parks, sprinkled generously with patches of conifers, that provide a lot of the present-day aura of Indian Heaven. Continuing the delightful stroll through the heather and beargrass, you cross two seasonal streams (0.7 miles; 4,890 feet; 4.0 miles) as your trail undulates through these remarkable parks.

Before long, you reach a junction with the Pacific Crest Trail at the southwest end of Junction Lake.

[If you wish to shorten this hike, you may do so by not making this 3.9-mile round trip south along the PCT to Blue Lake.]

Turn left (south) onto the PCT at the junction. In a few yards, you cross the Junction Lake outlet stream on a plank bridge before reaching the junction with a trail leading to East Crater and an east-side roadhead.

The well-engineered, well-drained PCT uses causeways to minimize erosion, and on this tread you ascend gradually. Gentle undulations raise you to a point where you are treated to a view of Mount St. Helens to the northwest. Then you reach a high point (0.8 miles; 4,900 feet; 4.8 miles) and begin to descend.

Marching now along the edge of the plateau, which drops sharply to your left, you progress a short distance and then begin a steeper descent. In 0.6 miles, you can see a lake on your left a few hundred yards away through the trees. Farther still, a cascading stream flows from Lake Sahalee Tyee on the right, crosses the trail, and runs into an unnamed lake on your left. A short distance beyond, a faint trail branches right to another unnamed lake just yards from the trail.

Reaching Blue Lake, you can see that this pretty body of water is aptly named. At the northeast shore is the junction (1.1 miles; 4,660 feet; 5.9 miles) with Thomas Lake Trail 111, which branches right (west). Good camping can be found along the east shore of the lake on a small ridge. Some of the highly used camps are much too close to the water, but in this popular area they are used anyway. Within a few minutes' walk of Blue Lake are Lake Sahalee Tyee and Tombstone Lake, where additional campsites may be found.

A colony of pikas live in the talus jumble at the west end of Blue Lake. If you walk out into these rocks and sit still for a short period, you may see beady eyes staring at you from a few feet away, and the cute rodents may whistle or use their wide repertoire of vocalizations.

Blue Lake is the turnaround point of this hike, from which you return to Junction Lake the way you have come. Once you reach Junction Lake, you continue straight ahead (north) on the PCT, past the junction (2.8 miles; 4,730 feet; 8.7 miles) at which Lemei Lake Trail, over which you passed earlier, turns right.

On trail new to you now, you stride north along a pleasant route through lofty hemlock and red fir. Note that the moss on these mature trees begins some 10 feet above ground level, an indication of the depth of snow accumulation. Soon you reach a stream crossing, from which there is a good view of cascading falls 100 yards upstream. A few minutes later on your left, you pass a small meadow that is often filled with wildflowers.

Strolling still through forested glades, you soon reach another stream (0.8 miles; 4,650 feet; 9.5 miles) and cross. Here, too, there are cascading falls both upstream and downstream from the trail. Farther along you may be able to spot glacier fawn lilies blooming beside the trail. This lily blooms shortly after the snow leaves the ground in the spring. Soon you can see a crescent-shaped lakelet to the left and below, visible through the very tall trees in this area.

At a junction (0.3 miles; 4,750 feet; 9.8 miles), Elk Lake Trail 176 crosses the PCT; the left branch leads to Elk Lake and the right fork to Clear Lake. Continue straight ahead, past use trails that lead to Bear Lake, which lies on your left. The narrow peninsula that juts out from the near shore into this deep, pretty lake is too narrow for camping. Better campsites are on the southwest shore.

As your trail traverses above Bear Lake, observe the effects storm, age, and decay have had on the old-growth forest through which you are passing. Look for a small pond through the trees to your right. You soon come to Deer Lake (0.4 miles; 4,840 feet; 10.2 miles) on your left. Glacial

Mountain bluebird

moraines have dammed this water body. Just beyond, individual trees along the trail approach 5 feet in diameter.

Before long, you reach another junction (0.2 miles; 4,870 feet; 10.4 miles), as Indian Heaven Trail 33 branches right to Cultus Creek Campground.

[You can shorten this hike by turning right here onto Indian Heaven Trail 33 and proceeding 4 miles to the roadhead.]

Continue straight ahead on the PCT, which traverses around the southern shoulder of Bird Mountain. In less than a mile you can see a small, seasonal pond on the left, after which you cross an early-season runoff flow on a log-and-dirt structure. Ambling still in the trees, you reach a junction (0.7 miles; 4,990 feet; 11.1 miles) where Trail 29 to Placid Lake branches left. Again continue straight ahead on the PCT.

Within 0.3 miles you cross a saddle and enter a patch of young-growth hemlocks and firs, from 10 to 30 feet tall. There are no old-growth trees in this patch, possibly because insects or fire killed the trees at some point in the past. A few yards later you are back in healthy forest with larger trees again.

This section of the PCT is marked with the old-style Pacific Crest Trail System diamond, seen only rarely along the trail in Oregon and California but common in Washington. These older markers were made of enameled steel, and after a time they rust. Markers employing the new PCT emblem were later manufactured from painted aluminum. These do not rust, but the paint peels off easily. An even more recent solution is markers made of printed plastic. The print comes off these, too, however.

In 0.6 miles, a small, deep lakelet lies on your left, 100 feet below the trail. Soon you reach a four-way junction (0.9 miles; 5,120 feet; 12.0 miles) where the PCT continues straight ahead and Wood Lake Trail 185 branches left. Take the right branch, Cultus Creek Trail 108. You shortly cross a saddle with a rocky knob on your left and a beautiful view of Mount Adams if you move a few feet to the left of the trail into the open. The view from on top of the knob is even better than from trailside.

From the saddle, you begin a sharp descent that routes you along the top of a cliff. You make a half circle to the north, approach the edge of a cliff, and continue the descent to the south.

Soon you drop into a zone where Douglas fir and western white pine grow. Still heading downward, you reach the trail register box for inbound hikers, and a few yards farther, you cross the boundary out of Indian Heaven Wilderness. Before long, you are at the roadhead of Trail 108.

Turn right on the gravel road, keeping to the right, and within 200 yards you enter the roadhead parking area (1.8 miles; 3,990 feet; 13.8 miles) for Indian Heaven Trail 33.

22 ♦ KILLEN CREEK—MOUNT ADAMS WILDERNESS

Distance:	11.6 Miles
Low elevation:	4,720 Feet
High elevation:	6,084 Feet
Class:	Moderate
Hiking time:	8 Hours

Mount Adams lies at the latitude of Longview, Washington, and is 70 miles due east. This 12,276-foot volcano is the second highest mountain in Washington. Because Adams is composed of a series of cones along a north-south fault, its bulk makes it the second largest volcano in the United States. This mountain makes its magic felt—just stand close and look. The Pacific Crest Trail passes by within 3 horizontal miles of the summit.

The glacier-clad heights have had a colorful recent past. A Forest Service lookout was built in 1921 but was used for only four years, as cloud cover much of the time made it useless as a lookout. From 1929 to 1959, high-effort prospecting took place at the summit for a commercially viable sulfur mine; this mine was responsible, until the claim expired, for thousands of pack mule trips to the summit.

The Cascade region was uplifted and eroded down perhaps several times before the last uplift, which heaved up huge land blocks tilted at various angles. Affected was the region from Mount Baker in Washington to Lassen Peak in California. After these tectonics, 2 million years ago during the Pleistocene epoch, molten lava escaping through resultant fractures began to build Mount Adams's volcanic cone. Several outpourings along the fault account for the long, ridge-shaped profile of this mountain. Most of the cone as it appears today was accumulated between 30,000 and 10,000 years ago.

Up until about 10,000 years ago, the cold, frozen cap of the most recent ice age ground away at Mount Adams. Glaciers reached far down the surrounding valleys. Action of ice and embedded abrasives smoothed much of the angular jumble of lava, streamlining the mountain. As the glaciers

At Killen Creek, on the west slope of Mount Adams, the PCT passes through a wonderland of wildflower meadows, meandering streams, and forested knolls.

melted, many of the smoothed surfaces were buried deep beneath glacial till, rubble made up of silt, gravel, and rocks being carried along by the ice.

About 5,000 years ago, a huge avalanche of rock, weakened when sulfur from the crater combined with melted ice to create sulfuric acid, roared unbelievably from the summit carrying debris all the way down into the Trout Lake Valley. In 1921 and again in 1983, large avalanches broke free from the headwall left by the huge first fall. The 1921 avalanche covered almost 6,000 acres with debris.

While Native Americans had probably used the area surrounding Mount Adams since 6000 B.C., the first historic sighting of the mountain was by Lewis and Clark on October 19, 1805. Forty-nine years later, the summit was first climbed by white men, and only thirteen years went by before the first recorded climb by a woman. In 1942 the Mount Adams Wild Area was designated. Then, the Wilderness Act of 1964 designated 36,356 acres as the Mount Adams Wilderness.

Closed to the public briefly after the 1980 eruption of Mount St. Helens, the Mount Adams Wilderness was expanded in 1984 to its present size of 47,270 acres, all of it enthralling territory to the climber, hiker, and backpacker. Your experience among the varied ecosystems of the wilderness is enhanced by the ever-present mountain towering above.

There are several climbing routes up Mount Adams for the skilled climber. Many not so experienced attempt the South Climb route, which is not a technical climb. Still, surmounting any peak is a potentially dangerous activity. Weather changes, rockfalls, high wind, and icefield crossings are all situations in which caution is called for. The Forest Service urges all climbers to register before attempting the summit. Climbing and weather information can be obtained at the Mount Adams Ranger District office in Trout Lake or at the Randle Ranger Station.

The subalpine meadows crossed by the PCT in the wilderness rate among the finest along the entire 2,600-mile trail for wildflowers. Here west-slope species are found, often side by side with others from the drier east side. Some of the plants here are usually found in the Sierra. The result is interesting to the botanist and creates a riot of color in the meadows for the hiker.

In late summer, we noticed partridgefoot, pussy paws, beargrass, paint-brush, heather, blue gentian, penstemon, yellow monkey flower, cushion buckwheat, lupine, and false hellebore. Wildlife we spotted included mule deer, coyote, rough-legged hawk, raven, Clark's nutcracker, gray jay, junco, and robin.

DESCRIPTION

This hike begins at the Divide Camp trailhead and exits the trail portion of the hike at Killen Creek trailhead just 2.4 miles distant, along the gravel Forest Service road 2329. It is a loop hike if you walk the 2.4 miles along the road to the starting point. If you position transportation at the exit trailhead, the hike is a partial loop.

This hike is classified as moderate because of the ascent from the Divide Camp trailhead to the PCT, about 1,300 feet in elevation gain. The descent from the PCT to the west wilderness boundary at Killen Creek trailhead loses about 1,300 feet in elevation at a rate that will make the knees of the unconditioned hiker wobble. If you are accustomed to hiking, you can easily do this loop in one day. Camping in the Killen Creek area, however, is probably the epitome of subalpine experience, and this route is most enjoyable if done as an overnight hike. As such, if you take your time, the rating would come close to easy.

Because of the extreme beauty of the region, perhaps an almost perfect camping and hiking area, this wilderness can be crowded. Planning a trip during the week, when there are fewer hikers, will do much to enhance your wilderness experience at Mount Adams. If you can complete this hike in one day, you will help the area by not adding your camping impact to a place that is in danger of being loved to death.

Once the initial ascent is behind you and you are northbound on the PCT, it's fairyland time. Fingers of mountain hemlock divide subalpine meadows, each meadow with minibasins of sedges, grasses, and flamboyant wildflowers. The western slope of the Cascades radiates out from your position like a fan, dropping down into verdant drainages unfortunately marred by clear-cuts. Above are the stair-stepped, jagged ice surfaces of Adams Glacier, seemingly intent upon cutting the mountain in two.

MAP 22

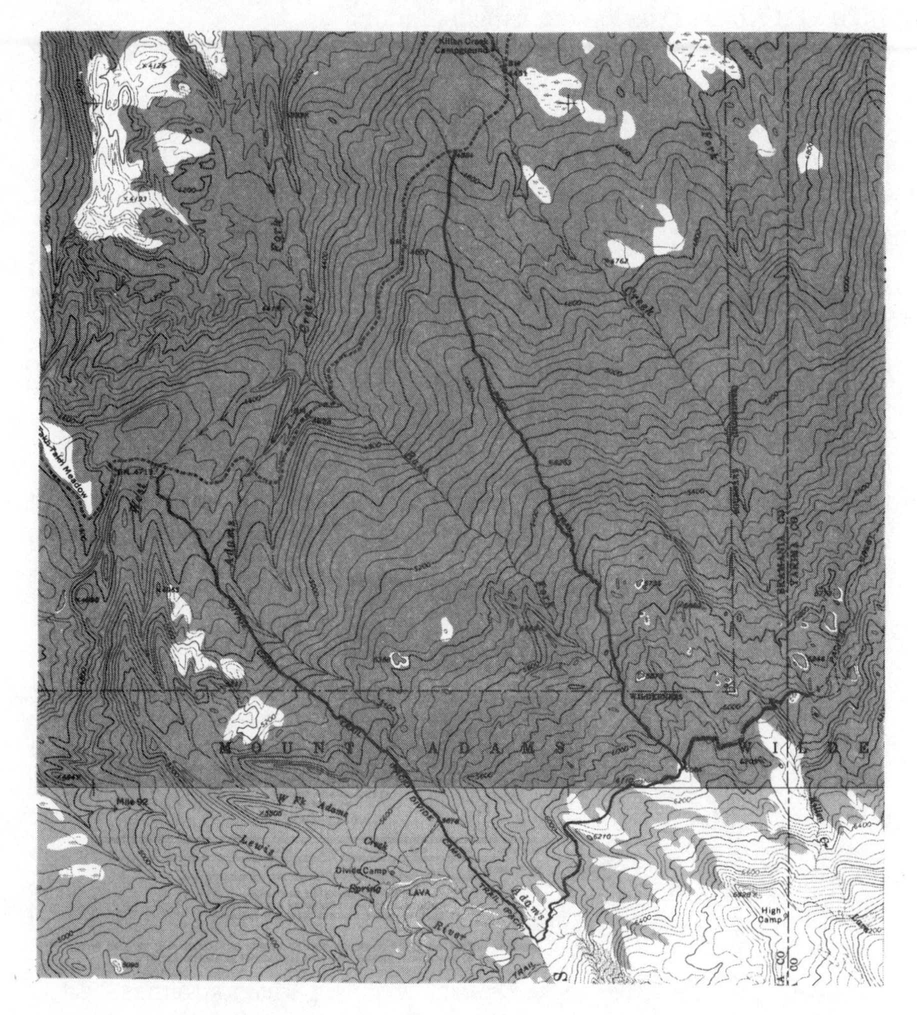

Early in this stretch you cross Adams Creek. At this writing drift logs have created a crossing very near the PCT. Adams Creek carries meltwater from Adams Glacier and, in the afternoon of a warm day or during snowmelt in the spring, can reach sizable proportions. This fact is evidenced by the broad flood channel; sudden high water has often eaten away streambanks and cut a new channel. The flow is at the low point in early morning.

This promenade along the PCT passes the junction with Killen Creek Trail, your exit route, and continues for almost a mile to the Killen Creek crossing, a 30-foot waterfall, and the camping area. You retrace this last section of just under a mile upon your return, an event that is still enjoyable because of the meadows of Killen Creek, the wildflowers, and the falls, and most of all, the atmosphere of the area.

You then regretfully return to Killen Creek Trail, a northwest turn on which delivers you onto a series of benches formed of avalanche debris. Dropping down this roller coaster into denser forest, you soon reach the Killen Creek trailhead, from which it is a 2.4-mile trudge southward along Forest Service road 2329 to Divide Camp trailhead.

In spite of the heavy snowpack, trails are usable by early July. Snowfall as early as October 1 can end the hiking season; the exact time varies from year to year. Contact the Mount Adams Ranger District in Trout Lake to learn the trail conditions.

Mosquitoes are present in the Mount Adams Wilderness and are numerous in the early season when there is a large amount of standing water. The nuisance diminishes steadily as meadows dry out, and by early September few mosquitoes remain.

The black bears in this area are shy, but around the more popular camps the potential for food loss is fair if precautions are not taken. Be sure to bear-bag your food.

Administrative agency: USFS

Gifford Pinchot National Forest
6926 East 4th Plain Blvd.
Vancouver, WA 98668
(206) 750-5000

Mount Adams Ranger District
Trout Lake, WA 98650
(509) 395-2501

USGS Map: 7.5′ series, Mount Adams West, Green Mountain, Washington

Declination: 21 degrees

DIRECTIONS TO TRAILHEAD

From Portland, Oregon, take Interstate 84 east 62 miles to Hood River. Turn north at Hood River and cross the Columbia River on the Hood River toll bridge to the north bank. Turn left (west) here on Washington Route 14. Proceed west 1 mile to the junction with Route 141, just east of the White Salmon River. Turn right (north) on Route 141 and proceed 21 miles north to the town of Trout Lake, Washington.

At the south edge of the Trout Lake community, turn right just before the service station at a sign reading "Randle" and "Mt. Adams Recreation Area." Proceed 2 miles to another fork and turn left on Forest Service road 23, signed "Randle." Proceed 27 miles on road 23 to the junction with Forest

Gray jay

Paintbrush

Service road 2329. Turn right on road 2329 and proceed 3.4 miles to trailhead 112, signed "Divide Camp." A short gravel spur leads to this trailhead, which is the entrance point for this hike.

While there is adequate space here to camp, there are no facilities. Just 2.4 miles north of Divide Camp, on road 2329, is the Killen Creek trailhead, the route's exit point.

TRAIL ROUTE DESCRIPTION

MAP 22

At the trailhead, elevation 4,720 feet, are located a bulletin board and trailhead register. Your trail crosses a cobbly flat and almost immediately enters the Mount Adams Wilderness. In forest that is mostly subalpine fir with a huckleberry understory, you ascend along a meandering route that leads you in 0.6 miles quite close to Adams Creek on your left. You can hear the downhill dash of this stream for some distance.

Tracks on the trail indicate that you're in prime elk habitat. As your ascent becomes more pronounced, forest understory diminishes noticeably. Soon you reach a spur trail (1.8 miles from last point; 5,320 feet above sea level; 1.8 total miles) that leads a few yards left to Adams Creek, your first good access to its gritty water. After a short, steep ascent, you are rewarded with an excellent view of Mount Adams and Adams Glacier, straight ahead through a natural avenue in the forest. The foot of the glacier is about 2 miles distant at this point, while the summit is some 4 miles southeast and 6,000 vertical feet above your present position.

You pass a snow course marker, placed so hydrologists can measure snowpack in winter. Crossarms are placed at 2-foot intervals on the vertical pole. Here also is the junction (0.4 miles; 5,680 feet; 2.2 miles) with the Divide Camp Trail, which turns right. Also in this subalpine meadow to your left is a marker of concrete blocks, set flush with the surface. Proceed straight (northeast) on the main trail.

Ascending through this subalpine meadow, you soon come across an old Forest Service sign delineating the eastern boundary of a grazing allotment, left from the days when grazing was allowed here. Beyond that, you pass another spur trail leading left to Adams Creek and soon reach the junction (0.7 miles; 6,040 feet; 2.9 miles) with the Pacific Crest Trail, which is running north-south. Your route turns left (north) onto the PCT.

Within 300 feet you reach a crossing with Adams Creek. The horse ford is downstream, while foot crossings can be accomplished on a series of logs a few yards upstream. Adams Creek carries the meltwater from Adams Glacier, the foot of which is about 1 mile upstream from your crossing. During heavy runoff or heavy melt periods, its flow can become heavy; some element of danger is involved at those times. The least flow is in the early morning, before daytime heat adds to the melt.

Across Adams Creek now, your trail traverses the loose, rocky, jumble of many flood channels created here by the wanderings of this creek in the past. After 0.3 miles, you leave the bouldery bottom behind and enter the shade of hemlock and subalpine fir clumps. Along this section, each little draw sports an inviting meadow and every ridge point offers shady clumps of trees.

You pass a 200-foot-long tarn on your left (1.1 miles; 6,110 feet; 4.0 miles) that may be dry during late season. Rambling along this beautiful traverse, you soon reach a junction (0.3 miles; 6,084 feet; 4.3 miles) where High Camp Trail 10 turns right and leads to climbing routes to the southeast. Fifty feet beyond this junction is another where Killen Creek Trail 113 turns left across a sandy flat. It is to this junction that you shall return. Now, however, continue straight ahead (north) on the PCT.

Mount Rainier is now visible to the northwest, while Mount St. Helens can be seen occasionally to the southwest. Descending via two switchbacks, you drop down to a flat meadow that has been visible below you, and all too soon you reach beautiful Killen Creek and the wooden bridge (0.9 miles; 5,940 feet; 5.2 miles) crossing it at the head of the falls.

Vertical Profile of Hike 22

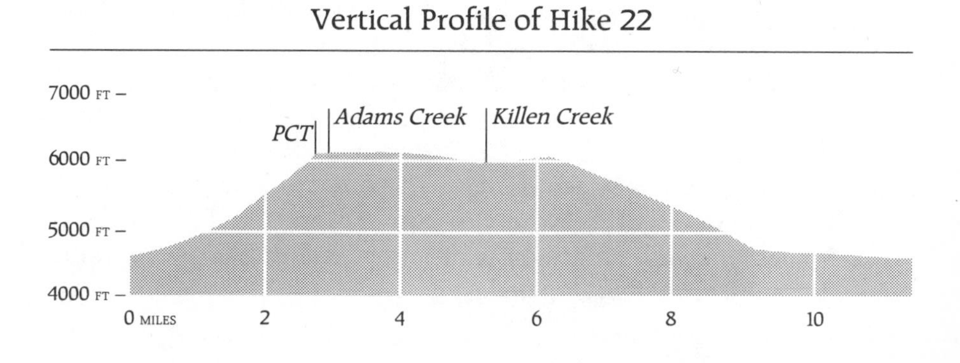

Campsites on the flat just below Killen Creek falls, one of the more popular overnight areas on the northern PCT, are almost always occupied on weekends. They are somewhat overused, but caution by hikers and stock users alike in recent years has helped to alleviate continuing damage. Visiting this area during the week rather than on the weekend will help to spread usage.

Views of Mount Adams from the meadow above the falls are incomparable, with the oxbow loops of Killen Creek wending through the wildflowers and sedges.

The PCT continues northward through Washington to Canada for more miles than most will want to experience, but at this point you turn about at Killen Creek and retrace your steps to the PCT–Killen Creek Trail 113 junction (0.9 miles; 6,084 feet; 6.1 miles). Turn right (northwest) here on Killen Creek Trail 113.

The trail crosses a sandy flat, which may become a watery tarn during periods of extreme runoff. Note that much of the sand on which you are treading is actually Mount St. Helens ash, carried here by winds during that mountain's eruption in 1980. Could there be any Mount Adams ash on the slopes of Mount St. Helens from some prehistoric eruption of our mountain?

At the brow of the first meadow, you descend to the level of the second meadow, and repeat this pattern with some frequency as you head southwestward with Mount Adams at your back. Some 0.8 miles along, you pass the barely noticeable ruins of an old log cabin on your right beside the trail. A few rotten logs and a bedspring bear testimony to what once was a shelter, probably for a sheep herder.

Crossing this meadow's drainage creek, you drop sharply down into a forested section and encounter water bars and log steps designed to minimize erosion. Hikers and horsemen have created parallel paths alongside this giant staircase, however, and the Forest Service is trying to discourage this practice by filling these paths with small logs and branches.

Leveling somewhat, your trail undulates and drops farther into a zone where ponderosa and western white pines join the forest mix. Soon your broad, dusty trail, which can become slippery mud if it is raining, joins with an abandoned roadbed that now becomes the trail. Your descent continues right to the Killen Creek trailhead (3.1 miles; 4,590 feet; 9.2 miles), where the parking lot is immediately to your right.

If you have been unable to arrange transportation from this trailhead, walk the few yards out to Forest Service road 2329 and turn left (south). In just 2.4 miles, you will reach the Divide Camp trailhead, your beginning point (2.4 miles; 4,720 feet; 11.6 miles).

23 ♦ PACKWOOD GLACIER—GOAT LAKE—GOAT ROCKS WILDERNESS

Distance:	17.3 Miles
Low elevation:	4,670 Feet
High elevation:	7,200 Feet
Class:	Moderate
Hiking time:	12 Hours

The Pacific Crest National Scenic Trail passes through Goat Rocks Wilderness, in Washington, on its 2,600-mile route to Canada from Mexico. This wilderness protects both sides of the crest some 20 miles southeast of Mount Rainier National Park. The geological origin of its varied landforms—cirques and vast basins, vertical headwalls, domelike peaks and sharp, pinnacle summits—is as described for the Cascades under other hikes in this book.

Of interest is the fact that the Goat Rocks themselves, now comprising Old Snowy Mountain and Ives Peak as well as their connecting ridge, are remnants of a single large volcano thought to have towered to more than 12,000 feet. Extinct since the early part of the Pleistocene some 2 million years ago, that towering cone has eroded to the present remnant ridge, which averages less than 8,000 feet today.

The area ranges from terrain at 3,000 feet covered with mixed-conifer forest to the 8,201-foot summit of Gilbert Peak and the alpine ridges around it. This imposing piece of real estate was first recognized on February 13, 1931, when 44,500 acres were designated as the Goat Rocks Primitive Area by the Forest Service. An increase in area to 72,440 acres was made in 1935, followed by expansion to 82,680 acres in 1940, along with the designation of the Goat Rocks Wild Area by the Forest Service.

The year of the Wilderness Act, 1964, saw this wild area become a wilderness. In 1984 Congress again increased its size. Today Goat Rocks consists of 105,600 wilderness acres. That this area should be preserved seems apparent, for walking along its precarious ridges and traversing breathtaking basins can be very uplifting.

The major northwest-southeast–trending ridge system of the wilderness is crossed near its center at Packwood Glacier by the PCT.

Northwest-flowing Packwood Glacier carves away at an outcropping of columnar basalt. An earlier south-flowing glacier in this area gouged the classic cirque now filled by Goat Lake, gem of the Goat Rocks Wilderness.

Crossing the snowfield at the upper end of Packwood Glacier on the 1978 trail relocation route places you at 7,000 feet, the highest elevation reached by the PCT in Washington.

Because of the expansive views, the close proximity of the alpine environment, and the presence of mountain goats, this wilderness is one of the most popular in the state. Few glaciers are so easily reached as is Packwood, while McCall Glacier grinds away on the east side of the Goat Rocks ridge dominated by Old Snowy. The end result is a lot of use, almost a loving to death of the more popular areas in the wilderness.

One way to enjoy more solitude on any hike into a popular area is to do your hiking in the middle of the week. Weekends are the more crowded times at destinations close to trailheads. You also will be more likely to find a private campsite if you plan to overnight somewhere along the trail between popular Snowgrass Flat and Goat Lake, rather than in those areas themselves. There are many suitable sites, the better of these well away from the PCT, honoring the recommended 200-foot setback from that trail for camping.

Goat Rocks Wilderness is notorious for bad weather; many hikers have spent an entire trip there without seeing much other than fast-moving clouds or drizzly rain. As in any high-altitude location, but especially in the northern Cascades, storms and snow showers can materialize any time of the year with scant notice. At such times the open character of these alpine slopes makes them unusually dangerous. For want of protection, people have become hypothermic and have lost their lives. Be sure you are properly equipped, understand wilderness survival, and most important, are willing to cancel or cut short your outing if bad weather materializes.

If summer weather is unstable, winter weather is predictably bad. Heavy snow blankets the wilderness, and high winds whistle across the ridges and passes. These winds are completely unobstructed, for the 180-degree arc to the west reveals only Mount Adams to the south, Mount St. Helens in the southwest, and Mount Rainier guarding the northwest quadrant. This expanse of open horizon makes this wilderness feel like it's at the top of the world.

The severe winters pose problems for wildlife. Elk herds migrate down and out to winter ranges, as do the deer. Other mammals, including the occasional black bear, hibernate. For the goats, though, it is another story. The same winds that ravage the peaks blow snow from open, south-facing slopes, exposing winter browse for the goats, which gather in such locations. All winter they survive there, their long coats and underwool keeping the driving wind from a fatal theft of their body heat.

Local wildlife we saw in midsummer included the elk, deer, mountain goat, hoary marmot, pika, chipmunk, ptarmigan, rough-legged hawk, peregrine falcon, red-tailed hawk, raven, gray jay, varied thrush, junco, and robin.

Wildflowers are abundant, actually carpeting some of the slopes. Species we found included pearly everlasting, vanilla leaf, avalanche lily, marsh marigold, asters, paintbrush, yarrow, cotton grass, mountain and Lewis monkeyflowers, azure gentian, anemones, larkspur, rock fringe fireweed, arrowleaf balsam root, and bear grass.

DESCRIPTION

This hike is a complete loop, plus a 1.6-mile segment where you retrace the PCT upon your return from Packwood Glacier.

Beginning in mostly lodgepole forest, the route climbs along a well-engineered trail to intersect the PCT just north of its emergence from a stunning traverse of Cispus Basin. On the PCT northbound across subalpine and alpine meadows, the gradient increases, a fact that is evident even though the grand wildflower display in this area much of the time is quite distracting.

Split Rock, lies to the right of the trail and provides a good excuse to postpone your ascent for a few minutes. This huge boulder, a volcanic

MAP 23

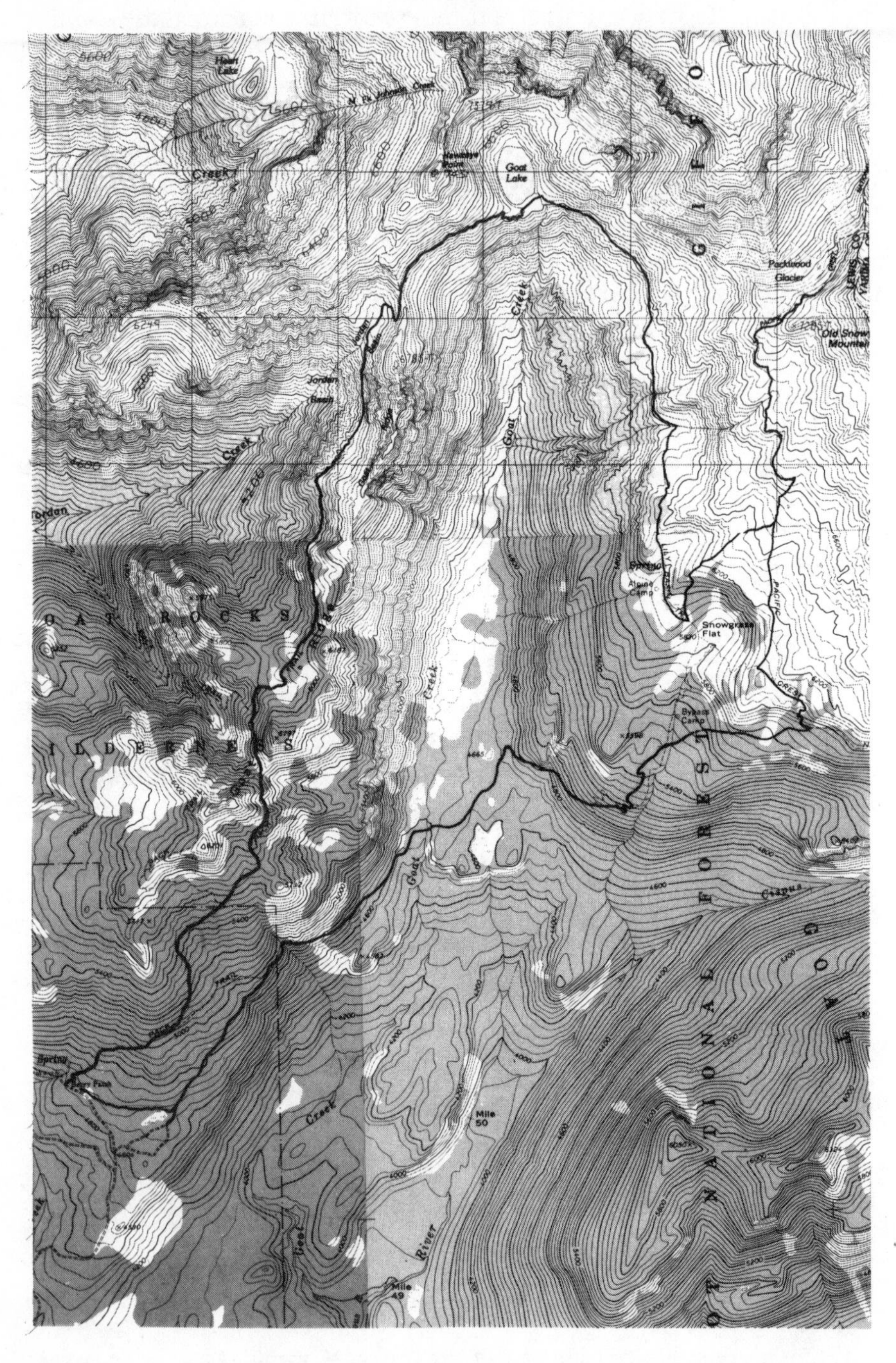
Goat Lake
Packwood Glacier
Old Snowy Mountain
Jordan Basin
Goat Creek
Snowgrass Flat
Alpine Camp
Bypass Camp
Mile 50
Mile 49
Cispus
River

remnant, was split apart long ago, and full-sized conifers prosper in the crack. If you look closely you will find matching surfaces on the two halves. Try to inspect the split rock without being distracted by the view of Mount Adams, looming closer than the horizon to the south.

Outcroppings of andesite lava beside the trail just before crossing a wash north of Split Rock show clear striations, the unmistakable mark of glacier passage. The wash itself may harbor snowbanks until the middle of summer.

A memorial, the Dana Mae Yelverton shelter, has suffered a collapsed roof. Much of the 12-foot-square structure is now in ruins. This tribute to a young woman who lost her life because of hypothermia on these slopes in 1963 was constructed by her church friends two years later. Unfortunately, the shelter has not been in place long enough to qualify for historic status, and the Forest Service plans to remove the collapsed structure rather than restore it. By the time you pass this spot, it is likely all you'll see is a bronze plaque.

Some snowbanks have perennial leases on their spots in Goat Rocks, so hiking this route is seldom a snowfree experience. You must negotiate or skirt at least one sloping snowbank, several hundred yards in extent, just before reaching Packwood Glacier.

The hiking season generally begins in earnest by mid-July, at which time most of your footsteps along the PCT will fall upon soil and rock. Snow can visit again, to remain for the winter, as early as late September. The most popular time for hiking in Goat Rocks is between late August and early September. Earlier or later than that will provide more solitude.

Administrative agency: USFS

Supervisor's Office
Gifford Pinchot National Forest
500 W. 12th St.
Vancouver, WA 98600
(206) 750-5000

Packwood Ranger District
P.O. Box 559
Packwood, WA 98361
(206) 494-5515

USGS map: 7.5′ series, Hamilton Buttes, Walupt Lake, Old Snowy Mountain, Packwood Lake, Washington

Declination: 21 degrees

Mosquitoes are a nuisance here during the period of snowmelt in the spring. Thereafter, their numbers diminish rather quickly. Wind, even of modest force, does much to keep mosquitoes burrowed deep into vegetation and away from hikers, and the slopes and ridges in Goat Rocks Wilderness usually enjoy a breeze.

While black bears are present in this wilderness, they are not considered a problem, especially at the higher elevations. Bear-bagging your food is a good idea, however, to prevent any occasional offender from becoming habituated. More of a problem here are squirrels, chipmunks, and mice, any of which can gnaw a hole and empty your pack of food in a single night. When hanging food, try to avoid pulling the bags up tightly against the limb. Rather, leave some space so the rodents will at least have to work for anything they pilfer.

DIRECTIONS TO TRAILHEAD

From Interstate 5, 14 miles south of Centralia, Washington, turn east on Route 12. Go 70 miles east to Johnson Creek Road (14 miles east of Randle and 3 miles west of Packwood), which is also signed "Walupt Lake." Turn south here onto gravel-surfaced Johnson Creek Road, and proceed 13.2 miles to the junction with Forest Service road 2150. Proceed 3 miles on road 2150 to the junction with road 040. Turn right on road 040, and within a short distance, take another right onto road 405, which is a loop. At the east end of this loop is Snowgrass trailhead, with a parking area but no facilities. Those wishing to camp here and requiring facilities may camp at nearby Chambers Lake.

TRAIL ROUTE DESCRIPTION

MAP 23

From the trailhead, where a bulletin board and a self-register box are located, 4,670 feet in elevation, take Snowgrass Trail 96A northward. In 200 feet you enter Goat Rocks Wilderness. The forest cover here consists principally of spruce, subalpine fir, and hemlock, with an understory of tall huckleberry. Within 0.2 miles, you reach a junction with horse trail 96, and your short-lived Trail 96A now becomes Snowgrass Trail 96.

After 1 mile, you have a good view of an elevated, subalpine ridge above, and shortly after that you cross a year-round tributary of Goat Creek (1.4 miles from last point; 4,640 feet above sea level; 1.4 total miles), your first reliable water source. Soon you cross another stream, ascend gently, and enter a rolling plateau that boasts large, old-growth trees. You cross Goat Creek (0.4 miles; 4,560 feet; 1.8 miles) on a wooden bridge, after which you turn north and continue ascending. Shortly your track turns eastward, as you cross a forested flat. You can see a stagnant pond 200 feet on your right.

You soon cross two creeks, just 40 yards apart. After 0.5 miles you approach a roaring tributary of the Cispus River but switchback left just before reaching it. Two switchbacks later, you again approach a stream, tumbling over moss-covered rocks. The ascent continues, leading you to a junction (2.1 miles; 5,520 feet; 3.9 miles) at which Snowgrass Trail 96 goes straight to join Trail 95. Turn right on Bypass Trail 97, which leads east to the Pacific Crest Trail.

Immediately you pass through subalpine meadows, and in just 0.3 miles, you cross the Cispus River tributary that you closely approached earlier. Foot logs here help keep your feet dry. North of the trail, 50 yards beyond the creek, are several large campsites in conifer groves. Your route now crosses a meadow, then makes a short, steep ascent without benefit of switchbacks onto the slope above.

Emerging from the forest, you cross a wet meadow, then cross two creeklets that begin under talus slides to your left. A series of camps occupies a wooded ridge at the far side of the meadow. Moving on, you reach a junction (1.0 miles; 5,890 feet; 4.9 miles) with the Pacific Crest Trail. The right branch leads to Cispus Pass. Turn left (north) here onto the PCT at the base of an andesite talus slide.

Swinging north now on a level traverse, your route soon turns east on an ascending course. Shortly you break out into a subalpine meadow that rolls upward to the northeast until it reaches the rocky jumble at the base of Goat Rocks, the jagged ridge so plainly visible from here. At the left (north) end of this ridge is 7,930-foot Old Snowy Mountain. Several glaciers, including McCall Glacier, lie on the north and east slopes of this peak.

Stunted subalpine firs are making questionable attempts at colonization of the meadow beside the trail, as are hemlocks. You cross a small spring stream, after which a spur trail leads left (west) to a camping area under a group of hemlocks. To the left of the trail, you can first hear and then see a roaring spring that gushes forth 5 feet wide and with others,

Vertical Profile of Hike 23

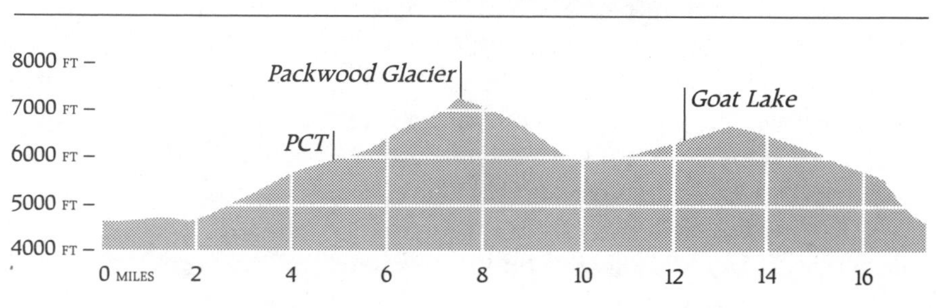

Mount Adams, many miles to the south, forms the backdrop for Split Rock, which broke apart centuries ago and is now a landmark along the PCT within Goat Rocks Wilderness.

forms the headwaters of the Cispus River tributary you have twice encountered.

Tramping upward onto a ridge, you reach the junction (1.0 miles; 6,270 feet; 5.9 miles) to which you shall return after visiting Packwood Glacier. At this junction, Snowgrass Trail 96 turns left, and you continue straight ahead (north) on the PCT. After a short climb, you reach Split Rock (0.2 miles; 6,400 feet; 6.1 miles), which lies on a small flat a few yards to the right of your trail. This house-size block of volcanic rock broke apart so long ago that large subalpine firs are now growing in the crevice between the two pieces.

Treading northward, you can see glacial striations in a resistant knob of andesite just to the right of the trail. To aid in finding the route when early-season snows prevail, posts have been set in rock piles in several places along here. You reach a rounded cairn laid up of thin pieces of shale on the point of a ridge just left of the trail. Beyond this, you reach the Dana May Yelverton shelter (1.1 miles; 6,980 feet; 7.2 miles), erected in the memory of a young woman who perished from hypothermia in this area. Unfortunately, snow loads have recently caused the collapse of the shelter, and it is unlikely to be repaired.

The view from this spot includes Mount Adams to the south, Mount St. Helens to the southwest, and Mount Rainier to the northwest. You can also look into Goat Lake, which occupies a textbook cirque 1.5 miles to the northwest at the north end of Goat Creek Canyon.

Tearing yourself away from this panorama can be difficult, but once you move on, your trail leads you across a perpetual snowfield. With Old

Snowy Mountain looming on the right, you reach the rim of the headwall of Packwood Glacier (0.3 miles; 7,200 feet; 7.5 miles) and look down into Upper Lake Creek Canyon. A wooden sign, sand-blasted by wind-driven snow, marks this spot. Immediately on the north, you can see the compressed snowbanks that form the upper end of the glacier. To the west, a knob of resistant columnar basalt is nonetheless being glaciated away. From below, down in the canyon, comes the roaring of Upper Lake Creek as Packwood Glacier ice melts.

At this point you turn around and retrace your steps southward on the PCT. You negotiate the snowfield, pass the shelter, swing by Split Rock, and arrive at the junction (1.6 miles; 6,270 feet; 9.1 miles) with Snowgrass Trail 96, on which you turn right (southwest), leaving the PCT.

Your route first leads southwest and then swings north as you traverse a level bench. Notice the gray sandlike material that has washed into low spots on the trail and open areas between plants. This is Mount St. Helens ash, carried here by wind in 1980 and now being concentrated in low areas as it is washed off all surfaces and gathered by runoff water.

Soon you cross a small stream and, just after it, camping areas on a ridge. An old trail in this area has been closed for rehabilitation; you go around on new alignment. Soon you arrive at a junction (0.8 miles; 5,835 feet; 9.9 miles) and leave Snowgrass Trail 96, which goes left. Ignore the trail leading straight ahead, and instead take the right-hand branch, Trail 86. Ignoring also the almost immediate right-branching spur that leads to a camping area, you continue along to the north, cross a small creeklet, and labor up a steep spot where numerous water bars have been installed.

Within 0.3 miles, you pass a small tarn and continue along a bench as you cross subalpine meadows. Descending slightly, your route leads into a beautiful, small basin, rimmed on the east side by talus slopes. Farther, you cross a stream (0.9 miles; 6,000 feet; 10.8 miles) near which there are campsites beneath clumps of hemlock. Leaving the basin, you now traverse up and around a talus jumble. This is really a moraine left by the most recent glacier to polish the pocket above you, through which a waterfall now descends.

You now come to a sign on a tree, identifying this as the Lily Basin Trail. From here you begin an ascent, cross a stream, and continue toward Goat Lake. After you cross several small springs, look for a clump of Alaska yellow cedars on your left. Soon, the long, U-shaped Goat Creek Canyon appears to your left. Just before you round the point, notice on your left a 15-foot-deep channel cut into the glaciated surface by Goat Creek.

You cross this outlet stream and reach Goat Lake (1.4 miles; 6,440 feet; 12.2 miles), where sandy beaches, much of which is Mount St. Helens ash,

Mountain goat

would beckon you to take a dip if the water was warmer. Goat Lake is often frozen over, however, until late in the season. Campsites are found south of the trail on several flat points among trees above the cliff.

Leaving the Goat Lake Cirque to the west, you switchback away from the lake and soon navigate a lengthy, ascending traverse along Goat Ridge. At a junction (0.9 miles; 6,600 feet; 13.1 miles), the Lily Basin Trail makes a sharp right up the hill to the north. Take Goat Ridge Trail 95 to the left, down the hill.

Descending sharply, you finally reach the flat bottom of this small basin, where a year-round stream flows. Campsites are located in the protection of hemlocks on an elevated knoll to the west. A few yards beyond, your trail follows the stream over the lip of this basin and begins another sharp descent. As the descent moderates, you begin a traverse along the ridge to your left. You pass a campsite and andesite slide, both to the left of the trail, and finally level after a short ascent.

Swooping down into the forest, your route passes a grassy, stagnant pond on the right that may be dry in late season. Short, steep switchbacks take you lower to a junction (2.4 miles; 5,800 feet; 15.5 miles) with Jordan Creek Trail 94, which is only lightly used and may be hard to find as it turns right (northwest) down the hill. Passing on, you ascend to a bench, move down, and then ascend again toward a saddle in the ridge through which you cross over to the south side.

With a view back to Goat Rocks now on your left, you descend again to a junction (1.0 miles; 5,510 feet; 16.5 miles) with Trail 95A, which turns right to encircle the ridge to the north. Strolling down your well-maintained track, you reach the Goat Ridge Trail 95 trailhead. In clear view of the parking lot, at the bulletin board, you turn left on level Trail 96, which parallels the gravel road just to your right. You pass a grassy lakelet just before reaching the junction (0.6 miles; 4,690 feet; 17.1 miles) with Snowgrass Trail 96A. Turn right here, and retrace your steps to the Snowgrass trailhead (0.2 miles; 4,670 feet; 17.3 miles).

24 ♦ PETE LAKE—ALPINE LAKES WILDERNESS

Distance:	22.0 Miles
Low elevation:	2,800 Feet
High elevation:	5,400 Feet
Class:	Difficult
Hiking time:	15 Hours

A mile north of Washington's Snoqualmie Pass, along the Pacific Crest Trail, is Alpine Lakes Wilderness, a large protectorate that extends northward to within 3 miles of Stephens Pass. At more than 393,000 acres, this wilderness contains just over a third of the nearly 1 million acres of rushing rivers, small lakes, high meadows, and deep forests below the high, glacier-clad mountains that grace this section of the Cascades.

Much was gained with the establishment of Alpine Lakes Wilderness in 1976, but there is yet more wilderness left in the area to save. A great controversy arose over the plans of developers, loggers, and miners to enter into and mar this wilderness. And further controversy has arisen from the desires of various conservation groups to preserve most of the pristine that is presently outside of the designated wilderness. Clear-cutting, that baneful activity of loggers in steep terrain (which seems to include most of Washington), presses in on every side.

To understand one of the forces acting upon this and other wilderness areas, it is necessary to go back to post–Civil War days, when Congress determined, in its wisdom, that granting alternating sections of land on either side of the proposed railroad rights-of-way would motivate construction. These lands could be sold to settlers and the proceeds used to build trackage.

Northern Pacific was granted one of the first, and largest, of these giveaways in 1864 on the condition that the railroad would be operational by 1875. In 1906 the railroad was finally completed over Snoqualmie Pass, on the designated right-of-way. This grant land amounts to some 600,000 acres in the Wenatchee and Snoqualmie National Forests, to say nothing of the other 43 million acres in the Dakotas, Montana, Idaho, and different areas in Washington.

When avalanches roar, all gives way before them, including this forest now reduced to a broken jumble. To reach this point, the avalanche had raced down one side of the canyon, crossed the bottom, and pushed 600 feet uphill on the opposite side.

Original grant lands near the western borders of Alpine Lakes Wilderness have been sold to Weyerhaeuser. In the 1940s, Northern Pacific sold lands to the northeast of the wilderness to other timber companies.

Resisting attempts at blocking, or consolidation of ownership, through land swap with the national forests, these private owners have instead used their ownerships to advantage in bidding on government timber. The presence of alternating sections of private land prevents consideration of vast areas as wilderness. Faced with the total situation, and supporting proliferation of logging roads, the national forests have gone about the business of selling timber. The establishment of the Alpine Lakes Wilderness culminated one of the most bitter conservation battles of the seventies.

This book is a trail guide, not a campaign platform, but perhaps the forgoing will help the hiker to understand the number and proximity of clear-cut scars bordering many wilderness areas, particularly in Washington.

The Cascades in the Apline Lakes Wilderness area are the eroded ruins of once-higher peaks; newer structures like Mount Baker to the north and Mount Rainier to the southwest have yet to be rounded by inexorable glaciers and other forces. Recent volcanism has not been a factor in this area.

The PCT relinquishes the crest divide when faced with Chickamin Peak and rugged, thrilling Lemah Mountain. Dropping into the watersheds of Lemah Creek, it enters the influence of the drier east side. Slopes tend to be quite steep, and the difference between alpine environments and deep forest at only 3,000 feet elevation is sometimes a matter of only 0.5 miles horizontal distance.

Several life zones are encountered along the route, and wildflowers are abundant here, with excellent variety. Very early in the season, we saw candystick, lupine, scarlet gilia, paintbrush, alpine lupine, pussy paws, pearly everlasting, heather, vanilla leaf, and alpine saxifrage. Wildlife spotted included the deer, hoary marmot, Douglas squirrel, chipmunk, junco, gray jay, raven, robin, red-breasted sapsucker, Cooper's hawk, and Stellar's jay.

If the west slopes of the Lemah Mountain area were intended to collect the most precipitation, the clouds were never notified. Deep snowfall occurs, probably because of the very close proximity to the true crest. While this is not an area where severe summer storms are common, you should always be prepared for showers and even snow flurries.

DESCRIPTION

This is a true loop hike, returning to the starting trailhead. The hike is classified as difficult because of elevation gains and losses. This loop is recommended as an overnight hike or even, if you can afford the luxury of spending more time, a hike to spread over three days.

On few other hikes does the transition from strolling along a peaceful, low-elevation river to striding across an alpine meadow occur in such a short distance. Or with such contrast.

From the start at Cooper Lake, the trail enters a mixed, old-growth conifer forest and meanders along a nearly level, wooded plain for miles until reaching Pete Lake. There, Lemah Mountain and its attendant glacier are visible—not quite overpowering, but just looming at the head of the drainage.

Then, diving again into dense riverbottom forest, the routing hides the view from sight. Not until the trail branches along a north tributary of Lemah Creek and begins a switchbacking ascent onto Escondido Ridge does the view return. This new perspective gives new scale; both glacier and mountain are much larger than they appeared from below.

At this switchback is a good demonstration of the power of snow avalanches. Originating on Lemah Mountain, avalanches have come down this chute for centuries. The most recent ones have touched new areas, wiping out acres of forest and carrying large trees far up the opposite slope like spears, top foremost. This jumble has caused the Forest Service quite a headache, and a portion of the trail has been rerouted to avoid clearing more than absolutely necessary of this giant pickup-sticks game.

While it is hard to discern while hiking it, the 2,200-foot ascent up to the level of Escondido Ridge actually moves you eastward. There is a gradual change to subalpine trees from lower varieties and sizes. At the end of the taxing ascent, the route levels out onto a subalpine shelf. Now in the world of cirques, tarns, heather, and hemlock, you move east and north and can savor views toward the Wenatchee Mountains, far to the east.

This area is controlled as far as camping is concerned, but a few designated camping areas are marked by signs. Weaving your way in and out of tarns and minibasins, you pass other tarns as well as their outlet stream, which tumbles down into Escondido Lake in the level valley floor below. Waptus Lake comes into view as you hike out along the spine of Escondido Ridge.

Then, turning your back on Escondido, you drop down to cross Quick Creek and ascend through elk-frequented forest to the top of Polallie Ridge. The route back to Cooper Lake is all downhill from here, making use of either the logging spur road built low along the northeast side of the drainage or trails.

The best season for this hike is late August through early September. Trails are usually passable at the higher elevations by July 1, however, and problem snows can be encountered around October 1. Check with the ranger district for trail conditions in the spring; in the fall it's anyone's guess when the first serious snow will come.

The abundance of surface water means prolific mosquitoes. The insects are particularly troublesome for a somewhat prolonged period because of the area's many small lakes and ponds. Carry repellent.

Administrative agency: USFS

Wenatchee National Forest	Cle Elum Ranger District
301 Yakima St.	West 2nd St.
Wenatchee, WA 98801	Cle Elum, WA 98922
(509) 662-4335	(509) 674-4411

USGS map: 7.5′ series, Polallie Ridge, Chikamin Peak, Mount Daniel, Washington

Declination: 19½ degrees

MAP 24

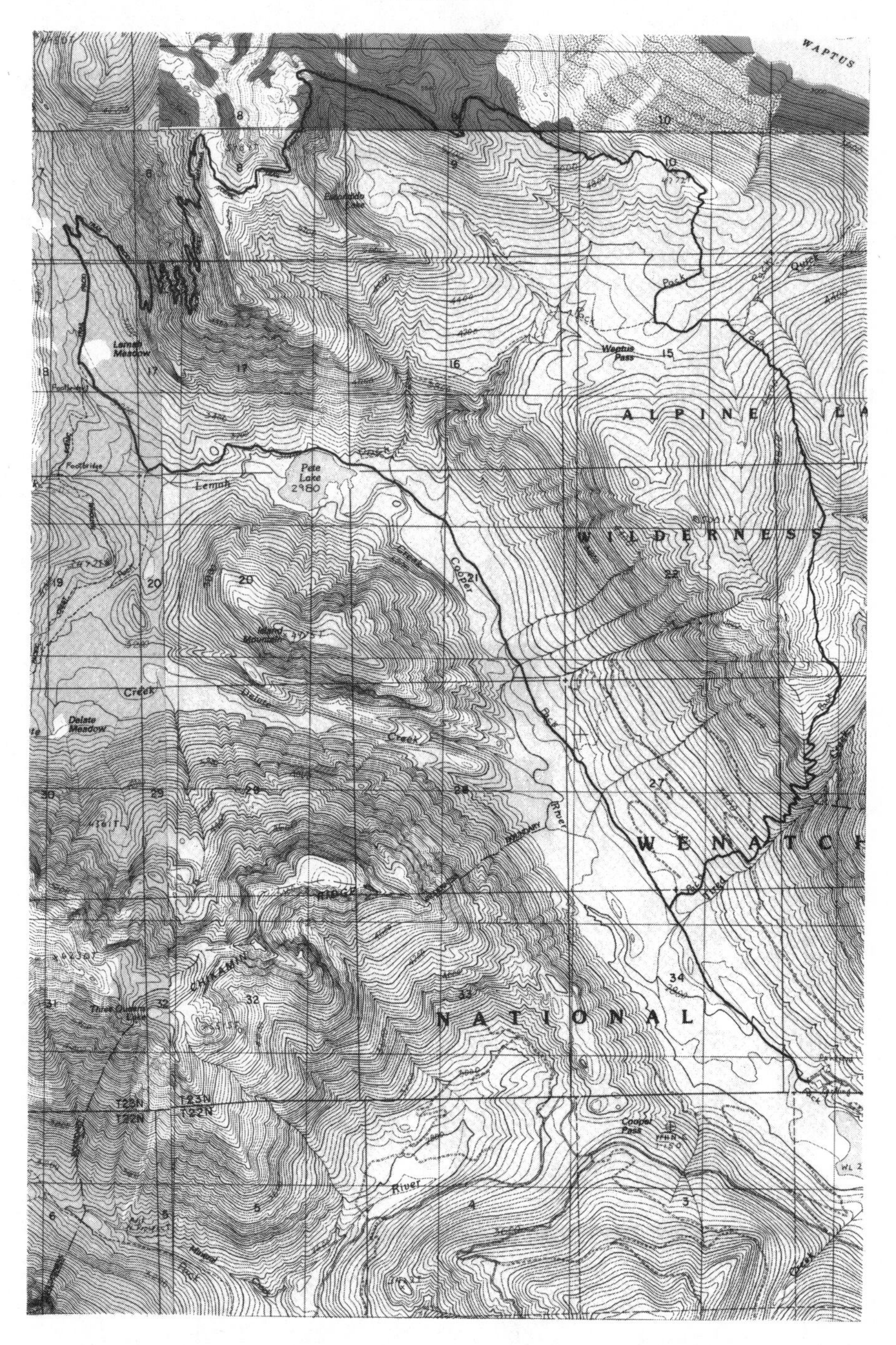
WAPTUS
Lemah Meadow
Waptus Pass
ALPINE
Pete Lake
2980
Lemah
WILDERNESS
Cooper
Creek
Delate Meadow
River
WENATCH
RIDGE
CHIKAMIN
NATIONAL
T23N
T22N
Cooper Pass

Black bears are not particularly sophisticated in Alpine Lakes Wilderness. Be sure to bear-bag your food to keep them that way.

DIRECTIONS TO TRAILHEAD

From Interstate 90, 30 miles east of Snoqualmie Summit, turn north at Cle Elum on State Route 903. Continue 5 miles to Roslyn, then 13.6 miles farther on Route 903 to a junction where Forest Service road 46 turns right onto a bridge crossing the Cle Elum River. Cross the river on road 46 and continue for 5 miles to the junction with Forest Service road 4616. Turn left on road 4616, ignoring two spurs that turn left to Cooper Lake, and in 0.7 miles turn left onto spur 113 to the Pete Lake trailhead. (Road 4616 is closed and gated at this junction.) Continue 0.7 miles on spur 113 to Owhi Camp and the parking area at the trailhead. There are a few campsites, tables, and a toilet here.

TRAIL ROUTE DESCRIPTION

You leave the hiker parking area on a broad trail, soon pass the junction where horse traffic joins, and climb onto a high bank above wide, beautiful Cooper River. The placid flow of this crystal-clear water sets the tone for the next several miles as you hike through a mixed-age, mixed-conifer forest. Soon you cross several watercourses that flow during runoff and then come upon a new trail alignment that branches right to bypass an old, eroded alignment that traversed a meadow. Your trail undulates, crosses more wet-season flows, and starts a gentle ascent before leveling again and continuing through the forest.

Look for kinnikinnick and lupine along this stretch, and notice the many trailside outcroppings that have been smoothly rounded by glacial action. A small pond lies on the left. Just past that, a prominent rounded boulder reposes on the right. Note the grooves carved in this rock as the ice flow ground by it while carrying imbedded stones.

You cross a stream (1.1 miles from last point; 2,825 feet above sea level; 1.1 total miles) just after passing a good campsite on your left. You need to cross via logs or rocks in early season. In 0.2 miles, you cross another small stream, then enjoy a level meander through tall old-growth trees. Corn lilies and ferns grow along the trail in this section. You cross yet another small stream and arrive at a junction (1.1 miles; 2,790 feet; 2.2 miles) where a bicycle trail branches right to road 235. Road 235 is also shown on some maps as road 4616 and parallels the river for approximately 2 miles, up the hill to your right (north). Continue straight ahead on Pete Lake Trail 1323.

As you enter the Alpine Lakes Wilderness (0.3 miles; 2,835 feet; 2.5 miles), note this ecologically rich riverbottom. You cross a small stream, then bypass another wet meadow on new alignment before crossing a creeklet and beginning an undulating, barely perceptible ascent. You cross yet another freshet and then what in early season is a sizable stream (1.1 miles; 2,855 feet; 3.6 miles), which usually can be crossed on nearby logs.

Soon you spot a rocky moraine on your left, part of the blockage that created Pete Lake. Just beyond this is a fallen log so large that the Forest Service rerouted the trail rather than attempting to cut through it. You next parallel the Cooper River on your left, overlooking inviting, deep pools. You pass a campsite on your left on the elevated bank, then reach a junction (0.5 miles; 2,920 feet; 4.1 miles). Here a use trail of branches left to the shore of Pete Lake just 100 or so yards distant. This large, level area among shady conifers is a popular camping spot, and the Forest Service has installed a toilet here. A sign reminds you not to tether or graze stock within 200 feet of the lake. Also at this point is a junction with Waptus Pass Trail 1329, which branches right. Continue straight ahead. You may note a wire or two seemingly sprouting from trees; these were once used to hang insulators for a Forest Service telephone line.

Climbing a few feet, you continue around Pete Lake. Use trails lead to overlook views of the lake on your left. Wild strawberry and paintbrush grace the trailside as you reach the end of the lake at a well-used horse-tethering area, from which your trail makes a left turn and parallels Lemah Creek running through an alder-choked bottom.

Your trail continues the pleasant meander along the creek, which is seldom seen because of the forest and alders. All too soon you reach a junction (1.6 miles; 2,970 feet; 5.7 miles) where Pete Lake Trail 1323 crosses Lemah Creek just below the confluence of its two tributaries. Horses can ford here during early season, but hikers should consider using a down-

Douglas squirrel

stream logjam. Luckily, your route is along Lemah Meadow Trail 1323B, which does not cross but turns right to continue upstream.

In 0.2 miles, the tread switches back and ascends for a minute before leveling again. Now you can see cliffs of volcanic material across Lemah Creek, where the slope often becomes vertical as the terrain changes dramatically. It is clear from the rising mountains around you that somewhere, soon, you are going to have to do some serious climbing. Your trail ascends gently for now, however, along a streamside routing, and while you often can hear the roaring current, your view is blocked by alders.

You soon reach a junction (0.8 miles; 3,170 feet; 6.5 miles) with the Pacific Crest Trail. Turning right, you continue upstream, shortly coming out on an open bank where you get a good view of the creek, here split into several channels. You drop down to cross a bracken-lined tributary on a wooden bridge and, in a few yards, another. Then your trail winds along overflow channels in the creekbottom and in a few minutes crosses a sizable double-channeled tributary. In early season, you can rock hop here or use convenient logs to cross.

You are treated to a view of open, forested glades beside the creek on your left and soon reach a jumble of downed trees (1.3 miles; 3,270 feet; 7.8 miles) through which the trail leads. Most of the logs are pointing the same direction, and you cannot miss the downed forest and bare slopes across the canyon. It is apparent that you are standing in an avalanche runout area. This was no ordinary avalanche, for here on the PCT, several hundred yards from the creekbottom and more than 100 feet higher, the avalanche mass was so formidable that it pushed down all the trees. Two-thirds of the way through this jumble, the Forest Service has rerouted the trail to the edge of the logjam. Here you begin the first of many switchbacks.

Shift into low gear here, for the next 2.3 miles is an unrelenting, though well-graded, climb. Along this south-facing slope are many different wildflowers, including crimson columbine and bleeding heart. You are treated to a cross-canyon view of the cirque from which the avalanche originated. Note Lemah Glacier living above and to the right and the cas-

Vertical Profile of Hike 24

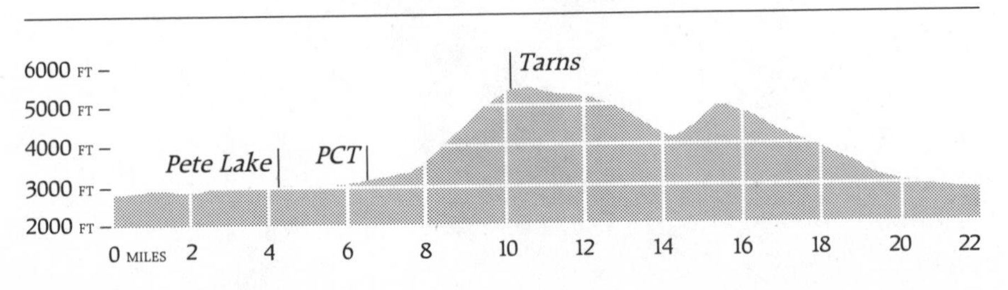

Elk

cading flow of meltwater descending from it. Other views open up of grassy meadows along the creek below, altogether a grand vista.

Exposed, sunny areas in this section host penstemon, paintbrush, phlox, wild strawberry, camas, larkspur, and kinnikinnick. Other flowers will be seen here depending on the season.

As you trudge up the last of the switchbacks, note that the larger trees of the riverbottom are gone and subalpine sizes are now present. You reach a cirque (2.3 miles; 5,480 feet; 10.1 miles) and soon can venture over to view the tarn that lies to the left of the trail. Because of the fragility of the subalpine environment, you should not camp anywhere in the next 2 miles. Turning to the right (east) now, your trail circumnavigates the eastern extension of this ridge, undulating only slightly along the shelf while providing long-distance views to the east and south.

Soon you have rounded one shoulder of the ridge and cross above a small meadow bowl (0.4 miles; 5,400 feet; 10.5 miles) below and to your right. Some years back, in order to minimize impact on the fragile meadows of this area, the Forest Service limited camping to the partially wooded ridge to the southeast of the small meadow.

Portions of the trail along this section have been blasted out of exposed rock in order to maintain the nearly level traverse you now enjoy. You round a broad ridge, then enter another series of cirques carved from the eastern face of Peak 6177. Several tarns lie to the left of the trail here, and shortly after you cross the inflow (0.5 miles; 5,305 feet; 11.0 miles) to the lowest tarn, you leave the protected no-camping area.

Your trail leads along an east-trending ridge, the downslope to your right. Note the many cedars in this area. In early season, yellow avalanche lilies grow in profusion along this stretch, which is heavily grazed by elk.

You leave the PCT at a junction (1.3 miles; 5,070 feet; 12.3 miles) where that long-distance trail branches sharply left around the spine of the narrow ridge, while you keep right on Waptus Burn Trail 1329C and continue along the ridge. In a short distance, your ridge trail begins to descend through gravelly sections among scattered red fir and hemlock separated by open patches of huckleberry and heather. Soon you pass two small lakelets on the right, elevation 4,620 feet. You descend farther past the ponds and are soon back on the ridgeline. You next reach a wooded flat, where wildflowers grow along a marshy area, and shortly come to a second area of level woods at 4,340 feet elevation.

At a junction (1.7 miles; 4,265 feet; 14.0 miles), Pete Lake Trail branches right.

[For a worthwhile side trip, take Pete Lake Trail for 0.7 miles to a junction with a spur trail that branches right 1.2 miles to Escondido Lake. Lying in a glacier-carved bowl, with meadow and forest along the shore, this is an idyllic spot and offers enjoyable camping.]

Continue straight ahead at the Pete Lake Trail junction. The trail descends through open forest on a broad ridge between two damp, grassy lowlands sprinkled with trees. You cross a spring stream on a deteriorated wooden bridge and then a second on planks in even worse condition. Soon you arrive at a junction (0.3 miles; 4,300 feet; 14.3 miles) where Waptus Lake Trail 1329 goes straight ahead. Turn right onto Tired Creek Trail 1309.

Descending a short distance, you reach a creek, which you can hop over, and begin a 1,100-foot ascent through mixed conifers along the edge of a ridge that leads southward between two small creeks. Note the many side trails, which were made by elk. Eventually you reach the summit (1.2 miles; 5,370 feet; 15.5 miles) and a trail junction, where Trail 1309 turns east and then south to Diamond Lake. Your Tired Creek Trail 1317, aptly named, branches right and drops down via generally well-graded switchbacks to reach road 235, shown on some maps as road 4616 (3.8 miles; 3,175 feet; 19.3 miles).

At the gravel road you have an option: You can walk downhill on the road (left) approximately 2 miles to spur 113, then turn right and in 0.7 miles arrive at the roadhead (2.7 miles total); or you can walk up the road 1 mile, then branch left on the marked trail, descend to the familiar Pete Lake Trail, turn left again, and walk 2.2 miles to the roadhead (3.2 miles total).

25 ♦ BLUE LAKE—GLACIER PEAK WILDERNESS

Distance:	30.4 Miles
Low elevation:	2,072 Feet
High elevation:	6,310 Feet
Class:	Difficult
Hiking time:	24 Hours

Located south of North Cascades National Park and east of Everett, Washington, Glacier Peak Wilderness lies both east and west of the Cascade Crest, surrounding 10,541-foot-high Glacier Peak. This dominant geologic feature of the area is secluded in the wilderness, easy to look at from a distance but remote when humans try to tread on its upper slopes. Named Da Kobad, meaning Great White Mother Mountain, by local tribes, Glacier Peak erupted last about 11,000 years ago, and ash from this peak has been identified as far as 300 miles to the east.

The wilderness is 464,219 acres in extent, reaching eastward to almost touch the shores of Lake Chelan. Glacier Peak is 6 miles horizontal distance inside the west border. The west slopes, where the Pacific Crest Trail snakes by, are influenced by maritime climate and receive abundant precipitation, most of which falls here as snow. The continental east side is much drier, as is the case along the entire Cascade range.

There are at least eighteen glaciers in the wilderness, no less than eleven of them sliding down the slopes of the aptly named Glacier Peak itself. The boisterous chocolate flow of the Suiattle River is spawned on the east and north slopes of the peak. The White Chuck River, a glacial-flour, milky stream, owes its life to meltwaters flowing west, while to the south the White River springs from two separate clusters of glaciers.

Perhaps it is true that there are no longer any unexplored regions in the conterminous forty-eight states, but in several portions of the most remote country in the northwest, there certainly are unexplored "spots"—small cirques or basins, wooded probably, difficult to penetrate and likely no more than a few acres in extent. Places like that exist and, just by the looks of it, there are probably such places in Glacier Peak Wilderness.

Glacier Peak caps the wilderness that bears its name; remote from even the nearest trailhead, this mountain has few visitors except serious hikers and climbers.

Completely untrammeled areas do exist in the wilderness, despite some 350 miles of trails, as well as cross-country travel and bushwhacking by the very rugged. This is because when several individual hikers start cross-country from a given spot to a given destination, they all will use more or less the same route. To do so is an instinctive trait. Many animals also are so directed, and that is why there are game trails.

Clumps of mountain hemlock and subalpine fir dot the expansive meadows and open ridges around the peak. These are the areas the PCT traverses—the areas so uplifting to the hiker who has been trudging through the forest with short-range views and no glimpses of the peaks. These are also the fragile areas, where trampling scars can take a decade or more to heal.

At lower elevations, because of the marine climate, old-growth conifers attain great sizes. Of special interest are the huge, old cedars found along the North Fork Sauk River as well as other places. This type of tree has supported a cedar shake and shingle industry in this area for decades. Few of these oldies remain outside wilderness and parks.

Wildlife here is plentiful and varied. Riverbottom areas proclaim their temperate rain forest status and abound with fungi and yellow banana slugs. The understory is thick and is made up of a variety of plants. As elevations increase, the understory thins in the red fir–lodgepole zone.

While making this hike in late summer, we saw these wildflowers: heather, anemone, lupine, false hellebore, asters, giant red paintbrush, sulfur paintbrush, pearly everlasting, horsemint, fireweed, Hall's desert parsley, and yarrow. Area wildlife spotted included the black bear, hoary marmot, porcupine, Douglas squirrel, chipmunk, golden eagle, red-tailed hawk, ptarmigan, flicker, gray jay, Clark's nutcracker, robin, and junco.

Gray wolves have been seen in Glacier Peak Wilderness in recent years. At least one breeding pair raised pups in the north portion of the

Cascades two separate times in the recent past. Wildlife biologists believe that these are wild wolves that have expanded their range south from British Columbia. Thus Washington joins Montana and Minnesota as states having natural populations of gray wolves. If you are fortunate enough to spot a wolf, please report your sighting to the Darrington Ranger District.

DESCRIPTION

This loop hike is recommended for no less than three hiking days. The classification is truly difficult; some of the trails are quite steep. If you are not in good condition, you will have some difficulty in reaching the excellent campsites at Blue Lake for the first night.

Beginning among giant cedars up to 7 feet in diameter, the route leads across the nearly level floodplain of the North Fork Sauk River. The departure from that plain is painful: You must negotiate a trail designed without much concern for gradient. This trail climbs out of the river canyon itself before aligning with a long ridge that terminates in Johnson Mountain, several miles to the east. While many sections of this segment are through forest, the latter part provides views that somewhat atone for the steep climb.

Campsites with water are scarce along this section; the best camping is at Blue Lake. From Blue Lake, the route is along the high trail, not passable for stock. Stock can detour south at this point and circumnavigate the south end of the ridge.

By the time the route joins the PCT, it has meandered and undulated for several miles through fantastic patches of blueberries and huckleberries. Most hikers enjoy this bounty, beginning around mid-August. So do the bears.

The PCT provides all the wonder and glamour that is expected of a status trail through a popular wilderness. Following along the crest, first to the east and later the west, the trail provides views of Glacier Peak as well as the White River Glacier cluster at the north edge of the White River drainage. The roaring of meltwater from these glaciers cascading down into the White reaches your ears, even when clouds obscure the spectacle.

Most of this segment is through meadows that are seldom lacking for wildflowers of some sort, even near the limits of the normal hiking season. In midsummer, the variety can be almost unbelievable. A possible second-night destination, with good camping nearby, is White Pass, practically surrounded by wildflowers.

Fickle is perhaps too mild a word to describe Glacier Peak weather. Ten feet or more of snow can remain on the PCT in early May, and some years the trails are not snowfree until mid-August. By early October, skiffs of snow have usually visited this high country, often to stay the winter. Drizzle, rain, or snow flurries can occur at any time of the year, so be wise and go prepared.

Mosquitoes here can make a trip miserable in early season under the right combinations of warm weather and calm air, so carry repellent.

The abundance of berry patches near the trail perhaps increases the chances of spotting a black bear here. If you're lucky and do see a bear, you'll note that the animal will leave as soon as it is aware of your presence. Bears are shy here and have not yet learned that backpackers carry food. Don't teach them; bear-bag your food.

At this latitude, there is a very remote possibility that you may encounter a grizzly bear. The grizzly is quite different from the black bear, in size, appearance, and reaction to humans. It is wise to contact the Darrington Ranger Station and ask if grizzlies have been seen in the north Cascade area that particular year. Learn to identify these bears; the Forest Service may have a pamphlet on bear identification.

Administrative agency: USFS

Mount Baker–Snoqualmie National Forest
Information Office
915 Second Ave.
Seattle, WA 98174
(206) 744-3200

Darrington Ranger District
Darrington, WA 98241
(206) 436-1155

USGS map: 7.5′ series, Glacier Peak West, Glacier Peak East, Poe Mountain, Bench Mark Mountain, Sloan Peak, Washington

Declination: 20 degrees

DIRECTIONS TO TRAILHEAD

Head north on Interstate 5 from Everett, Washington, for 15 miles to the State Route 530 exit. Turn east and proceed about 32 miles on Route 530 through Arlington to the town of Darrington.

Go to the stop sign at the far end of town and turn right (southeast) onto Forest Service road 20. Continue on road 20 past the end of the pavement, 16 miles to the junction with Forest Service road 49, signed "North Fork Sauk Trail." Turn left on road 49 and continue 6.8 miles. At this point a sign "North Fork Sauk Trail" directs you onto a gravel spur

MAP 25A

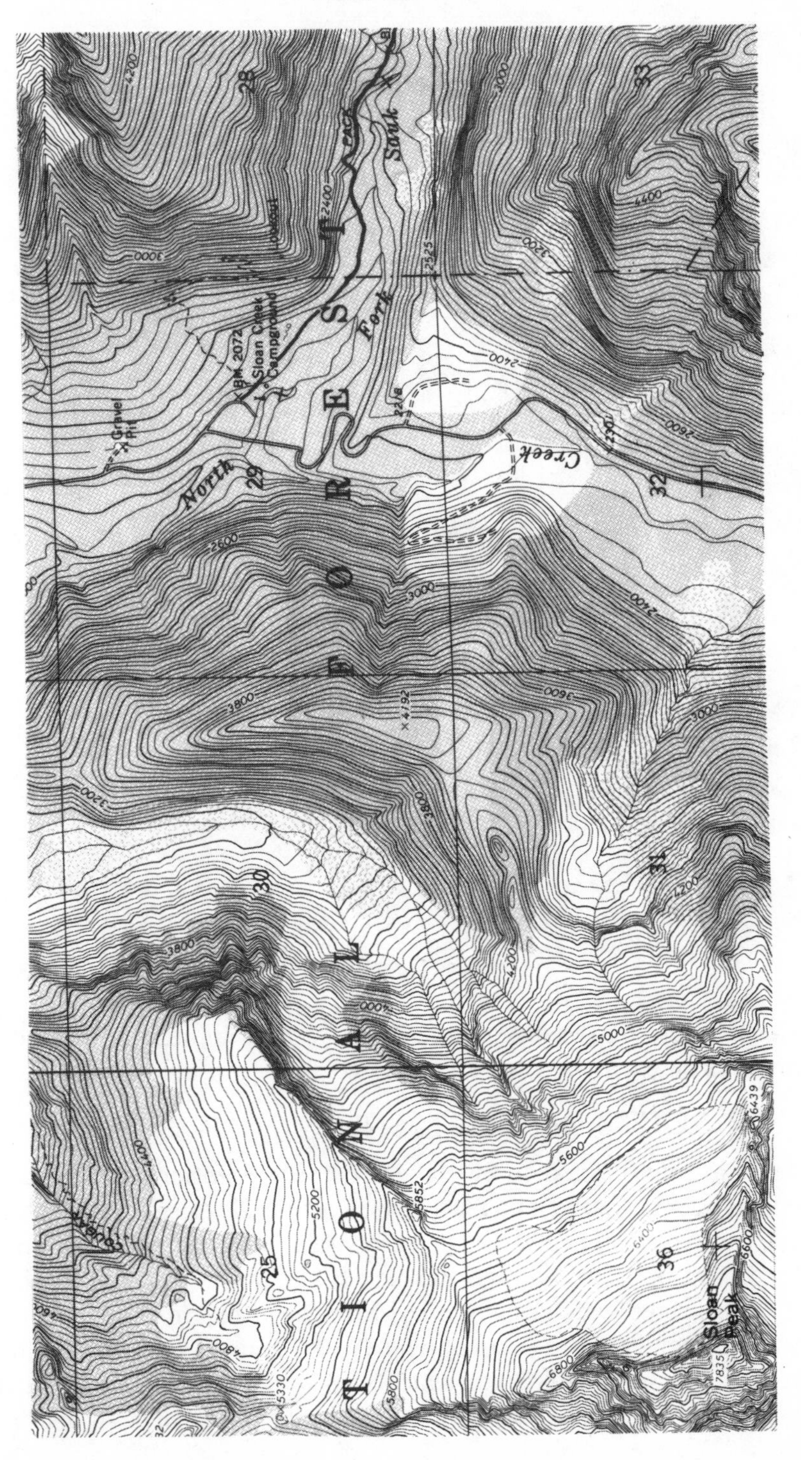
North
Fork
Sauk
Creek
Sloan Creek Campground
BM 2072
Gravel Pit
Lookout
Sloan Peak
7835
6439
5852
5330
4192
2525
28
29
30
31
32
33
36
25

MAP 25B

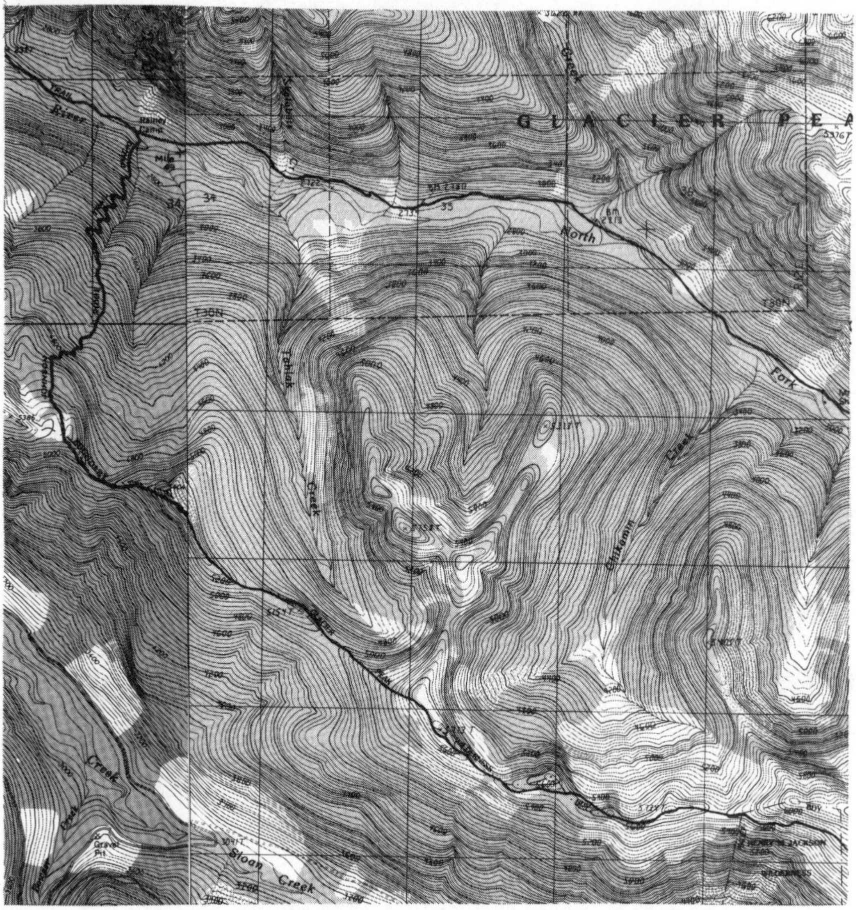

that turns left. Go 0.3 miles on this spur to the trailhead. There are four campsites here, a stock-loading ramp, two pit toilets, and two picnic tables.

TRAIL ROUTE DESCRIPTION

The trailhead is located on the left just before the entrance to the parking area, and here is found a bulletin board and a trail register for North Fork Sauk Trail 649. Within 200 feet, Red Mountain Trail 651 turns left. Continue straight on the main trail, which keeps to the level. Notice the beautiful, huge, old-growth western red cedars from 3 to 7 feet in diameter.

MAP 25B

You first leave the floodplain area in 0.5 miles but soon return to the flat along the North Sauk River, which is on your right. You cross a tributary creek, which can flow heavily during periods of rapid runoff. Your trail wends through more magnificent old-growth red fir and hemlock, depending upon occasional sections of corduroy to prevent stock damage in damp areas. Within another mile, you descend to the level of the river momentarily and soon come to a large campsite at a junction (2.0 miles from last point; 2,400 feet above sea level; 2.0 total miles).

Here the North Sauk Trail continues upriver, while Pilot Ridge Trail 652 turns right, past the campsite. Turn right and follow this trail to the river. Horses can ford here, but you should continue upstream 100 yards and cross the near flow to an island. Then move downstream 200 feet and cross the far flow, both on logs. Moving downstream a few yards, you intercept Pilot Ridge Trail 652 opposite the campsite and immediately turn left (south) up the hill.

You move up onto a bench for a moment's respite, then begin a very sharp ascent. This trail was built before specifications dictated maximum gradient, and the result is the slope up which you now labor without benefit of switchbacks. You cross a seep on a wooden causeway, continue upward, and cross a creek (1.3 miles; 3,620 feet; 3.3 miles), after which your ascent eases a bit and you traverse eastward. You top Pilot Ridge 0.4 miles beyond the creek and follow it southeastward. With your gradient now more or less at the mercy of the ridgetop, you move eastward, cross a spring flow, and soon are struggling up a 35 percent grade on a narrow hogsback.

Suddenly you break out into an opening to the west and are rewarded for your climb by a stunning view of Monte Cristo Peak and its attendant pinnacles and glaciers, which occupy 4 miles of ridgetop on the southwest side of the Sloan Creek drainage.

You traverse now through heather and blueberries, enjoying a breathtaking view of Glacier Peak to the northeast and Mount Rainier to the southwest. Now descending slightly off the ridge, your route undulates for a while, then drops to a low saddle (2.7 miles; 4,860 feet; 6.0 miles) before beginning more climbing. Soon you are laboring up more 30 percent grades, made tolerable only by the rewarding views to the south, east, and west.

After 0.6 more miles, you have reached an elevation of 5,450 feet and begin a long traverse along the steep south slope of a subalpine meadow. Passing the crest of a knob on your left, you descend to the more or less open ridgetop, which offers more views. On the intervening alpine ridge, miles away but in line with Glacier Peak, you can make out the long, ascending traverse of the Pacific Crest Trail.

Your trail describes easy traverses, alternating on either side of the ridge. Note that while the rocks you have been walking on so far have been sedimentary, now there is much mica schist in evidence as you descend sharply to a low, narrow saddle (2.2 miles; 5,405 feet; 8.2 miles).

MAP 25C

White Mountain
WENATCHEE
NATIONAL FOREST
White Pass
White River
Sauk
River
Reflection Pond
CHELAN CO
SNOHOMISH CO
GLACIER PEAK
WILDERNESS
Johnson Mtn
Blue Lake
Little Blue Lake
June Mountain
Meander Meadow
Kodak Peak
Dishpan Gap
Wards Pass

Blue Lake, sparkling like a precious stone, is imprisoned in subalpine solitude by the jagged headwalls of a classic cirque that opens only to the southwest.

Out in open subalpine meadows now, you can detect the unfortunate, almost universal erosion and trailing on the slopes from past commercial sheep grazing. This practice ceased on the west side in the 1960s, but the damage remains.

You contour southeast through wildflower meadows, where lots of blueberries also grow. Soon you see two small tarns below and to the right, in a broad cirque at the western base of Johnson Mountain. You round this cirque, then switchback over small recessional moraines left by one of the most recent glaciers to do its carving on Johnson Mountain. Old trail alignments confuse this segment for a few yards; then you round a ridge and reach a junction (1.8 miles; 5,880 feet; 10.0 miles) with Johnson Mountain Trail, which branches left to the summit. Continue straight ahead on the main trail.

Now descending west along the south edge of the cirque you just passed, you move downward for a short distance and then switch back toward the southeast. You are treated to a fleeting view of lower Blue Lake as you move along this descending traverse, make a 25-foot-long switchback to the right, and arrive at a junction (0.9 miles; 5,400 feet; 10.9 miles). Here Pilot Ridge Trail 652 turns right to pass by lower Blue Lake, June Mountain, and Bald Eagle Mountain. Turn left on Blue Lake High Route 652A. Note that this trail is impassable to stock.

Immediately you clamber up steep switchbacks and soon reach lovely Blue Lake (0.2 miles; 5,625 feet; 11.1 miles), an inspiring sight. The outlet creek leaves the lake via a shallow bay, in which the water goes

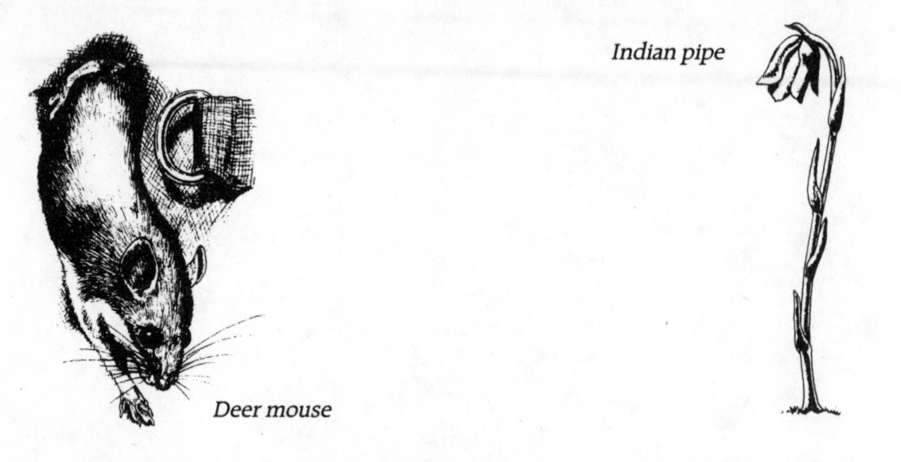
Indian pipe

Deer mouse

from limpid clear around the edges to a light green farther from shore. The deep water here is so blue your eyes will think they are being tricked. Set in a steep-walled cirque well away from the beaten track, Blue Lake is a tranquil spot. Numerous campsites are found on either side of the outlet creek.

You cross the outlet creek at right angles near the lake, walk 50 yards parallel to, but back from, the shoreline, and immediately start up steep switchbacks. You gain momentary relief as the route crosses a small, flat spot with a tarn, but then the trail begins to switchback again. Your route nears loose talus slopes and persistent, lasting snowfields, which can cover the trail in early season. If that is the case, it is much safer to go around the ridge on Pilot Ridge Trail.

None too soon you reach the ridge (0.6 miles; 6,310 feet; 11.7 miles) and here leave Glacier Peak Wilderness, as your trail leads down slippery switchbacks where you must watch your step. Continuing down a descending traverse along the slope, you move briskly eastward to a junction (0.6 miles; 5,750 feet; 12.3 miles) where Pilot Ridge Trail 652 rejoins your trail from the right. Continue along the left (east) fork.

Vertical Profile of Hike 25

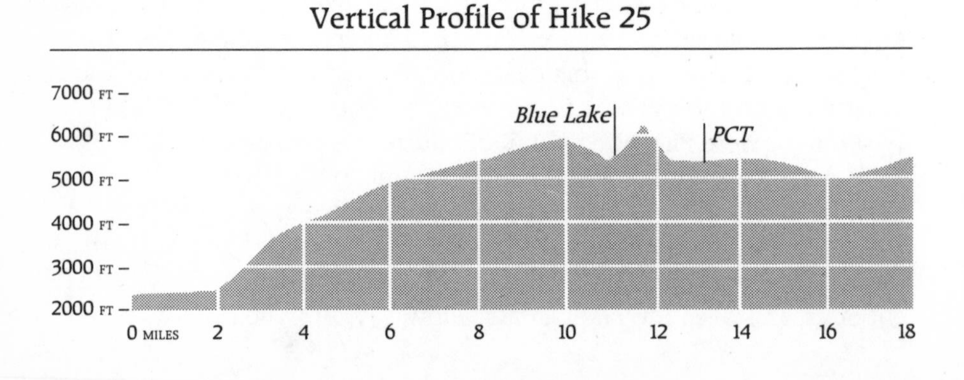

Striding along this scenic route, you soon come to another junction (0.8 miles; 5,600 feet; 13.1 miles), where Trail 1051 branches right to road 290. Directly ahead is the Pacific Crest Trail. Turn left (north) onto the PCT.

Winding your way along the PCT now, you soon reach another junction (0.9 miles; 5,500 feet; 14.0 miles), where a trail to the right proceeds eastward to Little Wenatchee Road. Keep to the left on the northbound PCT. Your easy path continues north via gentle traverses, now on the east side of the ridge, before dropping down toward the first pass. After 0.9 miles, you reenter Glacier Peak Wilderness.

Now a lengthy, curving ascent across a cirque faces you directly toward Glacier Peak, and shortly after that you reach Indian Pass and a junction (2.3 miles; 4,950 feet; 16.3 miles). Branching to the right is Indian Creek Trail 1502, leading to White River Road. Use trails going downhill to the left lead to camping areas. Continue straight ahead on the PCT.

After switchbacking through alternating forest and meadow, you soon enter a forest of hemlock and red fir as your ascent continues. Crossing a reliable stream (0.8 miles; 5,320 feet; 17.1 miles) that is a welcome water source, you soon pass a small, stagnant pond on your right. Your trail now levels, and you enjoy a westerly view before reaching a junction (0.9 miles; 5,380 feet; 18.0 miles) where a trail branches right to White River. There is room for a camp at the edge of the grassy meadow here, and water can usually be found in the ravine to the northwest. Continue northward on the PCT.

The trail climbs and crosses to the east of the north-trending ridge through a grassy saddle. Still ascending, the route leads in long switchbacks that traverse the south end of the ridge, moving you quickly to 50-foot-wide Reflection Pond (0.6 miles; 5,570 feet; 18.6 miles). This breezy spot, right on the crest, enjoys fantastic views. The campsites here are used frequently enough that the Forest Service has installed a toilet.

You cross to the east side of the ridge and begin a meandering ascent from which you can see White Glacier off to your right, as well as the

Vertical Profile of Hike 25

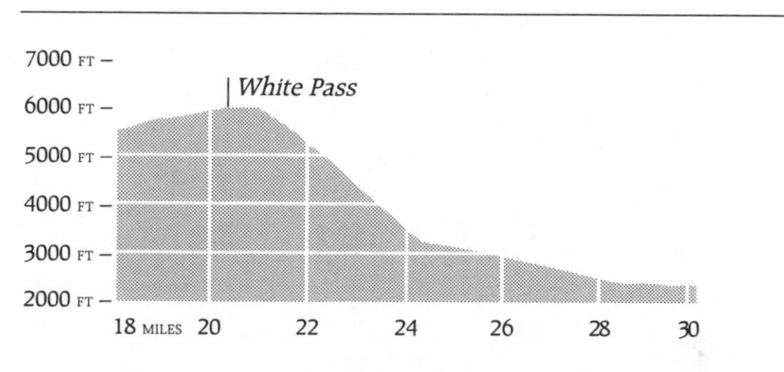

long series of cascades formed as its meltwater flows toward White River. Reaching the ridge, your trail undulates across the small knobs that lie between this point and White Pass. Once you reach White Pass (1.8 miles; 5,900 feet; 20.4 miles), note that camping is not allowed at the pass proper but is recommended in the basin to the southwest. A use trail leads to that area. Within a few strides, you reach the junction where a trail branches left to Foam Basin.

The PCT embarks now on a major traverse that ascends the southwest slope of White Mountain and ends at Red Pass. You soon reach a junction (0.5 miles; 5,915 feet; 20.9 miles), however, where you leave the PCT and turn left (west) onto North Fork Sauk River Trail, which begins a gentle downward traverse.

You pass occasional fingers of forest that are sending stunted outriders upward to test the timberline, which is not far above you. After 1 mile of descending, you reach switchbacks that promise to speed the drop. You now are in the center of a huge avalanche chute, which runs down from a more-than-adequate slope area above you. Notice the young hemlocks here that owe their existence to being resilient, while older trees, unable to bend with the avalanche, are snapped off and carried down the mountain. Within 0.5 miles you reach an area where some of these larger trees have been deposited. The trail itself, however, has been cleared of debris.

Douglas fir and western white pine appear in the scanty forest as you continue down the slope. After a seemingly endless descent, you enter forest (3.4 miles; 3,165 feet; 24.3 miles) with a long traverse to the west, break into the open momentarily, then reenter the forest. After another 0.3 miles, you reach a shelter constructed of split cedar. Old but reasonably intact, this could be a welcome find in heavy rain. Several good campsites are located here.

MAP 25B

Now your steep ascent is behind you, as you move downstream along the North Fork Sauk River. You reach a fine campsite quite close to the river, 0.6 miles beyond the shelter. Your trail undulates first near and then away from the flow. You are surrounded by huge, old-growth trees, mostly western red cedar. Soon you reach a sizable tributary stream (1.7 miles; 2,860 feet; 26.0 miles), which you can rock hop across. A flattened foot log with a wire cable handrail, provides a bridge at high water.

Two hundred yards below this stream is a fine, large campsite where the Forest Service has installed a toilet. Moving downstream again, you cross a number of small freshets in the next 2 miles. Before long, you reach a junction (2.4 miles; 2,355 feet; 28.4 miles) where Pilot Ridge Trail 652 branches left. This is the junction where you left North Fork Sauk River Trail at the beginning of your hike. You now retrace your steps downstream to the trailhead (2.0 miles; 2,355 feet; 30.4 miles).

MAP 25A

♦ Bibliography

BOTANY

Elmore, Francis H. *Shrubs and Trees of the Southwest Uplands.* Tucson, AZ: Southwest Parks and Monument Association, 1987.

Jaeger, Edmund C., and Arthur C. Smith. *Natural History of Southern California.* Berkeley, CA: University of California Press, 1966.

Little, Elbert L. *The Audubon Society Field Guide to North American Trees, Western Region.* New York: Alfred A. Knopf, 1988.

MacMahon, James A. *Deserts.* The Audubon Society Nature Guide. New York: Alfred A. Knopf, 1990.

Niehaus, Theodore F., and Charles L. Ripper. *Pacific States Wildflowers.* Boston: Houghton Mifflin, 1987.

Ross, Robert A., and Henrietta L. Chambers. *Wildflowers of the Western Cascades.* Portland, OR: Timber Press, 1988.

Spellenberg, Richard. *The Audubon Society Field Guide to North American Wildflowers, Western.* New York: Alfred A Knopf, 1988.

Storer, Tracy I., and Robert L. Usinger. *Sierra Nevada Natural History.* Berkeley, CA: University of California Press, 1963.

Weeden, Norman F. *A Sierra Nevada Flora.* Berkeley, CA: Wilderness Press, 1988.

Whitney, Stephen. *Western Forests.* The Audubon Society Nature Guide. New York: Alfred A. Knopf, 1985.

GEOLOGY

Alt, David D., and Donald Hyndman. *Roadside Geology of Northern California.* Missoula, MT: Mountain Press, 1975.

Alt, David D., and Donald Hyndman. *Roadside Geology of Oregon.* Missoula, MT: Mountain Press, 1991.

Baldwin, Ewart M. *Geology of Oregon.* 3rd ed. Dubuque, IA: Kendall/Hunt Publishing Co., 1981.

Hill, Mary. *Geology of the Sierra Nevada.* Berkeley, CA: University of California Press, 1975.

Pearl, Richard M. *How to Know the Minerals and Rocks.* New York: McGraw-Hill, 1957.

Pough, Frederick H. *A Field Guide to Rocks and Minerals.* 4th ed. Boston: Houghton Mifflin, 1976.

ZOOLOGY

Clark, William S., and Brian K. Wheeler. *Hawks.* Boston: Houghton Mifflin, 1987.

Ingles, Lloyd G. *Mammals of the Pacific States.* Stanford, CA: Stanford University Press, 1965.

Peterson, Roger Tory. *A Field Guide to Western Birds.* Boston: Houghton Mifflin, 1961.

Stebbins, Robert C. *Amphibians and Reptiles of California.* California Natural History Guide 31. Berkeley, CA: University of California Press, 1972.

Thompson, Mary, and Steven Thompson. *Huckleberry Country: Wild Food Plants of the Pacific Northwest.* Berkeley, CA: Wilderness Press, 1977.

Udvardy, Miklos D. F. *The Audubon Society Field Guide to North American Birds, Western Region.* New York: Alfred A. Knopf, 1977.

Whitaker, John O., Jr. *The Audubon Society Field Guide to North American Mammals.* New York: Alfred A. Knopf, 1988.

PCT HISTORY, NATURAL HISTORY

Farquar, Francis P. *History of the Sierra Nevada.* Berkeley, CA: University of California Press, 1965.

Gray, William R. *The Pacific Crest Trail.* Washington, DC: National Geographic Society, 1975.

Green, David. *A Pacific Crest Odessey.* Berkeley, CA: Wilderness Press, 1979.

Green, David. *Marble Mountain Wilderness.* Berkeley, CA: Wilderness Press, 1987.

King, Clarence. *Mountaineering in the Sierra Nevada.* Lincoln, NE: University of Nebraska Press, 1872 (1970).

Muir, John. *Mountaineering Essays.* Salt Lake City: Peregrine Smith Books, 1980.

Ross, Cindy. *Journey on the Crest.* Seattle: The Mountaineers, 1987.

Ryback, Eric. *The High Adventure of Eric Ryback.* San Francisco: Chronicle Books, 1971.

Wallace, David Rains. *The Klamath Knot.* San Francisco: Sierra Club Books, 1983.

BACKPACKING, MEDICAL

Hampton, Bruce, and David Cole. *Soft Paths.* Harrisburg, PA: Stackpole Books, 1988.

Wilkerson, James A., MD. *Mountaineering Medicine.* Seattle: The Mountaineers, 1990.

Wood, Robert S. *Pleasure Packing for the 80's.* Berkeley, CA: Ten Speed Press, 1980.

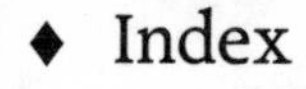

Index

Note: Hikes are indicated in **boldface**